THE REVELATION OF BAHÁ'U'LLÁH

Adrianople, 1863–68

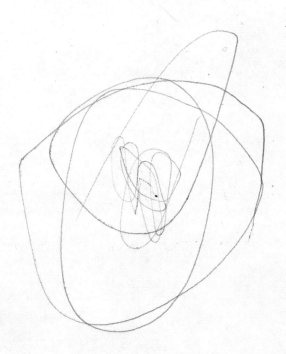

By the same author

TRUSTEES OF THE MERCIFUL
(Bahá'í Publishing Trust, London, 1972)

THE REVELATION OF BAHÁ'U'LLÁH,
Ba<u>gh</u>dád 1853–63

THE FIRST PAGE OF THE SÚRIY-I-AMR

In Bahá'u'lláh's own hand, revealed soon after the attempt on His life. His amanuensis read this Tablet aloud to Mírzá Yaḥyá to aquaint him formally with the mission of Bahá'u'lláh

THE REVELATION OF Bahá'u'lláh

Adrianople 1863 ~ 68

Adib Taherzadeh

GR

GEORGE RONALD
OXFORD

GEORGE RONALD, Publisher

46 High Street, Kidlington, Oxford OX5 2DN

ISBN 0 85398 070 5 (cased)
ISBN 0 85398 071 3 (paper)

Printed in Great Britain by
Richard Clay (The Chaucer Press), Ltd.,
Bungay, Suffolk

To those brilliant souls
the Bahá'í Pioneers and Teachers in every land
who have expended their lives and their substance
in the path of Bahá'u'lláh.

CONTENTS

ILLUSTRATIONS

NOTES AND ACKNOWLEDGEMENTS

The extracts from the Writings of the Báb and Bahá'u'lláh contained in this book are mainly from the matchless translations by Shoghi Effendi, the Guardian of the Bahá'í Faith, and their published sources are acknowledged in the references and bibliography. There are many other quotations from Persian manuscripts and publications, and these I have translated, unless otherwise indicated. Most quotations had to be edited prior to translation. The footnotes to these quotations, however, are mostly mine, and this is sometimes indicated explicitly where confusion may arise. Verses taken from the *Qur'án* are numbered in accordance with the Arabic text, although their numbering may differ from that given in English translations. Persian and Arabic names are transliterated in accordance with the system adopted for books on the Bahá'í Faith, but quotations are reproduced in their original form.

The early followers of Bahá'u'lláh seldom sought to be photographed. Occasionally group photographs were taken, from which it has been possible to obtain many of the individual photographs which I have included, in the belief that their historical interest outweighs the fact that some are faded and out of focus. It should be noted that Volume I includes photographs of a number of individuals who also feature in this volume. I am deeply indebted to the Audio-Visual Department of the Bahá'í World Centre for supplying most of these photographs, and also to the National Spiritual Assembly of the Bahá'ís of Írán, to Mr. Habib Manavi and to Mr. Ebrahim Khalili, who provided one each. The Radio Times Hulton Picture Library kindly supplied the view of Adrianople. I should like to thank Mr. Rouhullah Shakibai for his excellent reproduction of most of the photographs printed in this book.

I wish to acknowledge with sincere thanks the co-operation of the National Spiritual Assembly of the Bahá'ís of Írán, the Bahá'í Publishing Trust, London, and the Bahá'í Publishing Trust, Wilmette, Illinois, in permitting me to quote from their publications.

I desire to record my warm appreciation to Mrs. May Ballerio (née: Hofman) for her untiring efforts in helping me to speed up the preparation of the manuscript and for her skilful editing; also to Mr. Mark Hofman for the making of the index. My thanks go to Mrs. Rosemary O'Mara for proof reading and typing the manuscript from my original scribbled notes, many of which were illegible and often difficult to decipher, to Dr. Margaret Magill, to Mrs. Frances Beard and to Miss Eithna Early for additional typing assistance. I am also grateful to Mr. Rustom Sabit, Mrs. Sammi Smith and Mr. Paddy O'Mara for their careful reading of the proofs.

And finally, this volume, which has taken so long to produce because of the lack of time on my part, has been written during my free hours at home. I am indebted to my wife Lesley for her constant support and encouragement.

FOREWORD

This, the second volume of *The Revelation of Bahá'u'lláh*, follows the same pattern as the first one. The aim has been to describe the contents of some of the writings of Bahá'u'lláh revealed by Him in Constantinople and Adrianople. However, in order to present the background to the revelation of these writings, it has been found necessary to touch briefly upon the history of His life and that of His companions during His five-year sojourn in these two cities.

There is a distinctive tone in the Tablets of Bahá'u'lláh revealed in Adrianople in as much as they were revealed soon after the public unveiling of His station. In these He often portrays the treacherous behaviour of Mírzá Yaḥyá, the arch-breaker of the Covenant of the Báb, and, as the outpouring of His Revelation reaches its climax, He proclaims the advent of the Day of God to the generality of mankind and issues His summons to the kings and rulers of the world.

While for the most part the author has merely outlined the main points of a Tablet, he has in some cases dwelt at length on certain topics which constitute the basic spiritual verities of the Faith of Bahá'u'lláh and, at times, has deliberately taken excursions into other subjects which throw further light on the original theme, and which are thought to be of interest to the reader. A reading of the first volume is recommended prior to this one, to help provide continuity and further depth.

The study of the Tablets of Bahá'u'lláh is not similar to the study of a normal literary work, no matter how profound that might be. A Tablet is the repository of the Word of God, and to appreciate it one must acquire a pure heart and rid oneself of the veil of acquired knowledge. 'O My servants!' Bahá'u'lláh thus proclaims to the peoples of the world, 'My holy, My divinely ordained Revelation may be likened unto an ocean in whose depths are concealed innumerable pearls of great price, of surpassing lustre. It is the duty of every seeker to bestir himself and strive to attain the shores of this ocean, so that he may, in proportion to the eagerness of his search and the efforts he hath exerted, partake of such benefits as have been preordained in God's irrevocable and hidden Tablets.'

In writing this book the author has been able to do no more than skim the surface of this great Ocean.

1

Bahá'u'lláh in Constantinople

The five-year period that Bahá'u'lláh spent in Constantinople and Adrianople may be regarded as one of the most eventful and momentous times in His ministry. In this short period the sun of His Revelation mounted to its zenith and, in the plenitude of its splendour, shed its radiance upon the whole of mankind. This was also a most turbulent period in which He bore with much resignation and fortitude the pains, the betrayals and calamities heaped upon Him by His unfaithful brother Mírzá Yaḥyá who broke the Covenant of the Báb and rose up in rebellion against the One whom the world had wronged.

The arrival of Bahá'u'lláh in Constantinople, the capital city of the Ottoman empire, on 16 August 1863, marks a significant milestone in the unfoldment of His Mission. It was during Bahá'u'lláh's sojourn in the capital that the conciliatory attitude of the authorities changed to that of hostility as a direct consequence of the intrigues and misrepresentations of Ḥájí Mírzá Ḥusáyn Khán, the Mushíru'd-Dawlih, the Persian Ambassador. It was also during the same eventful period that the initial phase of the proclamation of the Message of Bahá'u'lláh to the kings and rulers of the world was ushered in by the revelation of a Tablet addressed to Sulṭán 'Abdu'l-'Azíz and his ministers sternly rebuking them for their actions against the new-born Faith of God and its Leader.

Probably very few among His loved ones had the vision at that time to foresee this banishment as only a further stage in His exile to the Holy Land where, according to prophecy, the Lord of Hosts, the Everlasting Father, was to manifest His glory to mankind. Some three thousand years before, Micah, the prophet of Israel, had foretold the appearance of the Lord in these words:

> In that day also he shall come even to thee from Assyria, and from the fortified cities, and from the fortress even to the river, and from sea to sea, and from mountain to mountain.[1]

How strikingly accurate was the fulfilment of this prophecy! Bahá'u'lláh came from Assyria; Constantinople and 'Akká are both fortified cities—the latter a fortress; He voyaged upon the Black Sea and the Mediterranean and journeyed from the mountains of Kurdistán to Mount Carmel.

Amos, another prophet of Israel, refers to Bahá'u'lláh in Constantinople when he says:

> For, lo, he that formeth the mountains, and createth the wind, and declareth unto man what is his thought, that maketh the morning darkness, and treadeth upon the high places of the earth, the Lord, the God of hosts, is his name.[2]

In one of His Tablets revealed in 'Akká Bahá'u'lláh states that this prophecy refers to Him, that it concerns the year eighty (1280 A.H.–A.D. 1863) and that the 'high places of the earth' are Constantinople and the Holy Land (Mount Carmel). Furthermore, alluding to Mírzá Yaḥyá whose title was Ṣubḥ-i-Azal (Morning of Eternity), He asserts that through His power the untrue morn was completely darkened.[3]

Bahá'u'lláh arrived in Constantinople in conspicuous majesty and was received by the authorities with great honour as He disembarked from the ship. He was driven with all the members of His family to the residence of Shamsí Big, an official who was present at the port and appointed by the Government to entertain its guests. His companions were given accommodation elsewhere in the city.

The house of Shamsí Big, a two-storey building in the vicinity of the Khirqiy-i-Sharíf mosque, proved to be too small a residence for Bahá'u'lláh and soon He was moved into the house of Vísí Páshá, a three-storey building more commodious than the first and situated near the mosque of Sulṭán Muḥammad. Neither of these houses exists today in its original form.

The house of Vísí Páshá, like most houses in those days, consisted of an inner and an outer apartment. Each consisted of three storeys. Bahá'u'lláh resided in the inner section on the first floor, and His family occupied the remainder. In the outer apartment, 'Abdu'l-Bahá lived on the first floor, the believers on the second, while the third floor was turned into a store and a kitchen.

Shamsí Big, on behalf of the Government, used to call every morning and attend to any matter pertaining to the needs and well-being of Bahá'u'lláh and His companions. In the courtyard a tent was pitched for two Christian servants whom the Government had sent to attend to shopping and various other duties.

Several eminent personalities including state ministers called on Bahá'u'lláh to pay their respects to Him. Among them was Kamál Páshá, a former Ṣadr-i-A'ẓam (Prime Minister), who was at that time one of the ministers of the Sulṭán. He knew several languages well and prided himself on this accomplishment. Bahá'u'lláh recounts one of His conversations with him in these words:

> One day, while in Constantinople, Kamál Páshá visited this Wronged One. Our conversation turned upon topics profitable unto man. He said that he had learned several languages. In reply We observed: 'You have wasted your life. It beseemeth you and the other officials of the Government to convene a gathering and choose one of the divers languages, and likewise one of the existing scripts, or else to create a new language and a new script to be taught children in schools throughout the world. They would, in this way, be acquiring only two languages, one their own native tongue, the other the language in which all the peoples of

> the world would converse. Were men to take fast hold on that which hath been mentioned, the whole earth would come to be regarded as one country, and the people would be relieved and freed from the necessity of acquiring and teaching different languages.' When in Our presence, he acquiesced, and even evinced great joy and complete satisfaction. We then told him to lay this matter before the officials and ministers of the Government, in order that it might be put into effect throughout the different countries. However, although he often returned to see Us after this, he never again referred to this subject, although that which had been suggested is conducive to the concord and the unity of the peoples of the world.[4]

Many of the high-ranking authorities who visited Bahá'u'lláh had expected Him to solicit their help in securing the support of the Government for Himself and His Cause, but they soon discovered that He was far removed from the expedient practices current among men. His standards were exalted above human statesmanship which is based upon compromise, and often upon deceit and selfish exploits. The authorities became conscious of His spiritual powers born of God and were deeply impressed by His uprightness and dignity. Some of these men had urged Bahá'u'lláh to send a plea to the Sublime Porte for a thorough and just investigation of His case so that any misgivings in the minds of the Sulṭán and his ministers might be dispelled.

Bahá'u'lláh is reported to have made this response:

> If the enlightened-minded leaders [of your nation] be wise and diligent, they will certainly make enquiry, and acquaint themselves with the true state of the case; if not, then [their] attainment of the truth is impracticable and impossible. Under these circumstances what need is there for importuning statesmen and supplicating ministers of the Court? We are free from every anxiety, and ready and prepared for the things predestined to us. 'Say, all is from God' is a sound and sufficient argument, and 'If God toucheth thee

with a hurt there is no dispeller thereof save Him' is a healing medicine.[5]

In one of His Tablets revealed soon after His arrival in Constantinople, Bahá'u'lláh expresses disappointment in the people He had met, saying that their welcome for Him was an act of formality and that He found them cold as ice and lifeless as dead trees.[6] In the *Súriy-i-Mulúk* (Súrih of the Kings), in a passage addressing the inhabitants of Constantinople, Bahá'-u'lláh states that He found their leaders as 'children gathered about and disporting themselves with clay'. And He further comments:

> We perceived no one sufficiently mature to acquire from Us the truths which God hath taught Us, nor ripe for Our wondrous words of wisdom. Our inner eye wept sore over them, and over their transgressions and their total disregard of the thing for which they were created. This is what We observed in that City, and which We have chosen to note down in Our Book, that it may serve as a warning unto them and unto the rest of mankind.[7]

The companions of Bahá'u'lláh, those faithful lovers of His glory who had travelled with Him to Constantinople, were given the privilege of attaining His presence from time to time. According to a list[8] which bears the seal of Bahá'u'lláh* and which was presumably prepared under His direction for the authorities in Baghdád, altogether fifty-four people including the members of His family were to accompany Him to Constantinople. Of these one child died, and at least two people, including Mírzá Yaḥyá, joined Him on the way.

The list comprises the following:

Mírzá Ḥusayn-'Alí [Bahá'u'lláh], 1; eldest son, 1; brothers, 2; female members of the household, 12;† children of all ages, 12

* For official purposes Bahá'u'lláh used His seal bearing the inscription 'Ḥusayn-'Alí'.

† Among them were the wives of His brothers including Mírzá Yaḥyá.

(less one who died); servants, 20;* others, with their own mules, [who would return], 7; horses, 6.

It is interesting to note that Bahá'u'lláh rode a red roan Arab stallion some of the way, but travelled mostly in a howdah† which was shared by His wife Ásíyih Khánum.‡ 'Abdu'l-Bahá supervised the entire convoy and organized and directed the activities of those to whom certain tasks were allocated. He often used to ride Bahá'u'lláh's horse in order to keep in contact with various members of the party. About an hour before entering a town, He would usually bring the horse to Bahá'u'lláh who would then ride into the town, while 'Abdu'l-Bahá took His place in the howdah; and the same arrangements were made when the caravan was leaving the town.

Lawḥ-i-Hawdaj

Bahá'u'lláh on many occasions had warned His companions of their fate and of the calamities which would befall them in future. Now He predicted dire afflictions in the *Lawḥ-i-Hawdaj* (Tablet of the Howdah) revealed in Arabic in the port of Sámsún on His way to Constantinople. At the request of His amanuensis, Mírzá Áqá Ján, He revealed this Tablet as He sighted the Black Sea from His howdah. As far as we know this was the first Tablet revealed by Bahá'u'lláh after He left Baghdád. In it He referred to the forthcoming voyage by sea and stated that it had been foreshadowed in the *Tablet of the Holy Mariner*. Thus he linked the Tablet of *Hawdaj* with the *Holy Mariner* and mentioned that the study of these two Tablets would enable the believers to understand the mysteries of the Cause of God and become strong in faith. The dire predictions already foreshadowed in the *Tablet of the Holy Mariner* would come to pass, He affirmed, and He further warned His companions of the 'grievous and tormenting

* Including His companions.

† See vol. I, p. 284, f.n.

‡ See vol. I, p. 15.

mischief' which would assail them from every direction, and would act as a divine touchstone through which the faith of every one would be severely tested and truth separated from falsehood.

Probably few among His companions realized that this 'grievous and tormenting mischief' would emanate from Bahá'u'lláh's own half-brother Mírzá Yaḥyá, precipitating a crisis of enormous proportions within the community, or that he would become the embodiment of man's rebelliousness, the centre of all the forces of darkness, who would arise to battle with the light of God's Supreme Manifestation.

By virtue of being close to the person of Bahá'u'lláh, the sincerity of His companions was tested to the utmost, for to associate with One who embodied within Himself the Spirit of God, and Who was the focal point of all His attributes and powers, required the highest degree of faith and detachment.* Any trace of self could destroy the soul of the believer. Another feature of this association was the way in which Bahá'u'lláh's awe-inspiring majesty affected those who came in contact with Him. The authority that emanated from Him, the radiance of His countenance and especially the magnetic power of His eyes, together with His all-encompassing love and compassion which surrounded all created things, exerted an influence which at once overwhelmed, vivified and comforted His disciples and transported them into the realms of the spirit.

Ḥájí Mírzá Ḥaydar-'Alí of Iṣfahán,† one of the most devoted disciples of Bahá'u'lláh and one who attained His presence in Adrianople and 'Akká on numerous occasions, has left some enlightening descriptions from his own observation. Referring to the effect which Bahá'u'lláh's presence had on the believers, he writes:

> To describe a spiritual experience is impossible. For example two or more people may attain the presence of

* See also vol. I, pp. 130–31.

† See Appendix III, also vol. I.

Bahá'u'lláh together. Each will regard His loving-kindness, compassion and bounty as directed to himself alone, and will be moved to declare 'He is my God'. Although all have attained the presence of the same blessed Person, Whose words are not addressed to one alone, yet His Words penetrate into the veins and arteries, into the hearts, minds and souls. Each one will be affected in a personal way and will experience inner spiritual feelings which he finds impossible to describe to others. All that can be said is that one may address his friend and say: 'I was intoxicated and in a state of ecstasy.' His friend, who may have experienced similar effects at some time, can only appreciate this feeling to the extent of his own susceptibility . . . I mean to say that whatever concerns one's inward feelings, spiritual perceptiveness, inner enlightenment, and all that pertains to the realms of divinity, is far removed from, and exalted above, nature, material things, place, time, form and substance. For example, no one can explain the state of maturity or the mental faculties of a mature person to a child who has not come of age, even though these relate to the world of nature. For the child has not yet acquired the capacity to understand. How much less is it possible, then, to explain a spiritual matter, an abstract condition, to an individual.

Should a person be enabled to acquire, through the bounty and assistance of God and His Manifestations, an inner spiritual feeling [as a result of attaining the presence of Bahá'u'lláh], letting it penetrate his soul, not in the form of a temporary flash or vain imagining, but as imbuing his very being, then such an attainment will pave the way for his progress in the realms of spirit, provided it does not become mixed with self-glorification and egotism . . .

The import of these words is that it is impossible to describe the effusions of the grace [of Bahá'u'lláh] experienced in His presence or to recount the effulgent glories of the Speaker on the Mount* . . .[9]

Concerning the power and the authority of Bahá'u'lláh, Ḥájí Mírzá Ḥaydar-'Alí writes:

* Bahá'u'lláh.

A certain man, who was a follower of Azal,* once requested the late Ḥájí Siyyid Javád-i-Karbilá'í . . .,† an early believer and one of the Mirrors of the Bábí Dispensation, to describe the countenance of the Báb . . . and its beauty. He said 'He was unsurpassed in beauty and sweetness; I saw in Him all the goodness and beauty ascribed to the person of Joseph.'

Since the questioner was an Azalí and a few other Azalís were also present, I felt that these men might deduce from the late Ḥájí Siyyid Javád's statement that he was also a follower of Azal. Therefore I asked him to tell us about the beauty of the One‡ in Whose holy presence the Kingdom of beauty prostrates itself and at whose threshold the most high realm of omnipotence and majesty raises a song of praise and glory. He replied, 'Know with absolute certainty that if anyone, whether friend or foe, claims that he was able to look directly into the blessed face of Bahá'u'lláh he is a liar. I tested this repeatedly and tried time and again to gaze upon His blessed countenance, but was unable to do so. Sometimes, when a person attains the presence of Bahá'u'lláh, he is so enamoured and carried away that in fact he becomes dumbfounded, awe-struck, oblivious of himself and forgetful of the world. And whenever he is not carried away, should he try to look into His blessed face with concentration, it would be like looking into the sun. In the same way that the eye is blinded by the effulgent rays of the sun, causing tears to flow, should one persist in gazing upon the countenance of the Blessed Beauty,§ tears will fill the eyes making it impossible to gain any impression of Him.'

I myself had this experience. During the seven months that I stayed in Adrianople, I was so carried away and dazzled [by His presence] that I was completely oblivious of myself and all creation. Fourteen or fifteen years later I arrived in the holy city of 'Akká, the luminous Spot round which

* Mírzá Yaḥyá.

† See *The Revelation of Bahá'u'lláh*, vol. I, pp. 221–4.

‡ Bahá'u'lláh.

§ Bahá'u'lláh.

circle in adoration the Concourse on High,* the Sinai of Revelation unto Moses. I attained the presence of Bahá'u'lláh for three months. During all this time I had wanted to know the colour of the blessed *táj*† He was wearing, and yet I forgot to think of it every time I was in His presence, until one day He adorned, perfumed and illumined the Garden of Riḍván‡ with His blessed footsteps. The realities of the promised gardens of Paradise, both hidden and manifest, lay prostrate at that Garden of Riḍván [Paradise]. He was having a midday meal in the room which pilgrims still visit and where a couch, chair, and some items used by Him are kept. Two or three people were standing inside and several outside the room. They were all enamoured of His peerless, imperishable and glorious Beauty. I saw the *táj* then . . . as I stood behind the friends and His companions . . . its colour was green . . .[10]

Another account which portrays the dazzling glory of the countenance of Bahá'u'lláh is to be found in the memoirs of Ḥájí Muḥammad-Ṭáhir-i-Málmírí,§ who went on pilgrimage to 'Akká about 1878. He remained there for nine months and was permitted by Bahá'u'lláh to attain His presence every other day. During these memorable meetings he longed to gaze fully into the face of Bahá'u'lláh, but every time he came into His holy presence, he found himself dazzled by His beauty and spellbound by His utterance; until one day he happened to look into the face of Bahá'u'lláh. This is a translation of his own words:

One day, I attained the presence of the Blessed Beauty. Graciously He bade me be seated. When I sat down, He

* The gathering of the holy souls in the next world.

† A tall felt head-dress worn by Bahá'u'lláh.

‡ Literally 'Garden of Paradise', the designation of a garden outside 'Akká which Bahá'u'lláh used to visit. It is not to be confused with the Garden of Riḍván outside Baghdád.

§ The father of the author; see *The Revelation of Bahá'u'lláh*, vol. I.

called Khádimu'lláh* and said, 'Bring tea for Áqá Ṭáhir'. Khádimu'lláh brought a cup of tea and handed it to me. As I took the cup into my hands, my eyes fell upon the face of the Blessed Beauty and I became unconscious. I could not take my eyes from the transcendent beauty of His countenance. He then said to me, 'Oh, look what you have done! You have spilt the tea and spoilt your *'abá*! † Protect this *'abá*, it is going to be your only clothing all the way to Persia. We also had only one shirt and underwear on Our journey to Sulaymáníyyih.'‡ From these words of the Blessed Beauty, I realized that I held only the saucer in my hand and had dropped the cup. The hot tea had poured over the *'abá* and penetrated my clothes, but I had not felt it at all. §[11]

Ḥájí Mírzá Ḥaydar-'Alí, to whom we have referred previously, has recounted a brief story in which he describes the reaction of some government officials in 'Akká when they saw Bahá'u'lláh for the first time. He writes in his book, the *Bihjatu'ṣ-Ṣudúr*:

> ... It was the festival of Riḍván, which was celebrated in the home of Jináb-i-Kalím.|| I was staying in the outer apartment of his house.¶ There were other apartments

* Literally 'the servant of God', a designation by which Bahá'u'lláh referred to Mírzá Áqá Ján, His amanuensis.

† A cloak worn by orientals.

‡ Ḥájí Muḥammad-Ṭáhir has written in detail the story of this *'abá*, and how on the way back home, all his belongings were stolen from him. The only things he was able to recover were this *'abá* and two envelopes. He wore the *'abá*, a thin silk material, over his shirt and shivered in the cold of winter, remembering the words of Bahá'u'lláh that it would be his only clothing on his way to Persia, and realizing how much Bahá'u'lláh had suffered from the cold of Sulaymáníyyih.

§ Passages quoted from Bahá'u'lláh in this account are not to be taken as containing His exact words. But they convey the import of what He said.

|| Mírzá Músá, the faithful brother of Bahá'u'lláh.

¶ Houses in those days consisted of two sections; the inner part was strictly for private residence, the outer section was reserved for visitors or guests. Meetings were held in the outer part.

occupied by non-Bahá'ís; one was the residence of a certain 'Big' or 'Pá_sh_á'* who had arrived in 'Akká as the head of customs and excise.

In the afternoon of the first day of Riḍván Bahá'u'lláh came out of the inner apartment to the place where the head of the customs and his officers were seated. As soon as He arrived, they arose spontaneously and, although it was not their way, they bowed. Lost in bewilderment and filled with wonder, they remained standing. Their hearts were enamoured of His peerless and beauteous countenance. Bahá'u'lláh went to them and spoke words of loving kindness. He then went back to the inner section. Bewildered and perplexed, the officer asked, 'Who was this distinguished personage? Is He the Holy Spirit or the King of Kings?' We answered, 'He is the father of 'Abbás Effendi'.†[12]

These accounts give some impression of the glory of Bahá'u'lláh and His awe-inspiring majesty, and perhaps explain why none of His disciples was able to write a pen-portrait of Him. The only pen-portrait we have was written by the orientalist, Edward Granville Browne, who was not a Bahá'í. This is how he describes his visit to the Mansion of Bahjí in 1890 and his meeting with Bahá'u'lláh:

> . . . my conductor paused for a moment while I removed my shoes. Then, with a quick movement of the hand, he withdrew, and, as I passed, replaced the curtain; and I found myself in a large apartment, along the upper end of which ran a low divan, while on the side opposite to the door were placed two or three chairs. Though I dimly suspected whither I was going and whom I was to behold (for no distinct intimation had been given to me), a second or two elapsed ere, with a throb of wonder and awe, I became definitely conscious that the room was not untenanted. In the corner where the divan met the wall sat a wondrous and venerable figure, crowned with a felt head-dress of the kind

* Titles for a high-ranking Turkish official.

† 'Abdu'l-Bahá.

called *táj* by dervishes (but of unusual height and make), round the base of which was wound a small white turban. The face of him on whom I gazed I can never forget, though I cannot describe it. Those piercing eyes seemed to read one's very soul; power and authority sat on that ample brow; while the deep lines on the forehead and face implied an age which the jet-black hair and beard flowing down in indistinguishable luxuriance almost to the waist seemed to belie. No need to ask in whose presence I stood, as I bowed myself before one who is the object of a devotion and love which kings might envy and emperors sigh for in vain!

A mild dignified voice bade me be seated, and then continued: 'Praise be to God that thou hast attained! . . . Thou hast come to see a prisoner and an exile . . . We desire but the good of the world and the happiness of the nations; yet they deem us a stirrer up of strife and sedition worthy of bondage and banishment . . . That all nations should become one in faith and all men as brothers; that the bonds of affection and unity between the sons of men should be strengthened; that diversity of religion should cease, and differences of race be annulled—what harm is there in this? . . . Yet so it shall be; these fruitless strifes, these ruinous wars shall pass away, and the 'Most Great Peace' shall come . . . Do not you in Europe need this also? Is not this that which Christ foretold? . . . Yet do we see your kings and rulers lavishing their treasures more freely on means for the destruction of the human race than on that which would conduce to the happiness of mankind . . . These strifes and this bloodshed and discord must cease, and all men be as one kindred and one family . . . Let not a man glory in this, that he loves his country; let him rather glory in this, that he loves his kind . . .'

Such, as far as I can recall them, were the words which, besides many others, I heard from Behá.* Let those who read them consider well with themselves whether such doctrines merit death and bonds, and whether the world is more likely to gain or lose by their diffusion.[13]

* Bahá'u'lláh. (A.T.)

Concerning those who accompanied Bahá'u'lláh to Constantinople, we know that a few among them were not pure in heart. Bahá'u'lláh had kept these men with Him so that their mischief could be checked. Only those who, through the grace of God, were able to submit themselves entirely to the will of God's Manifestation, who detached themselves from every desire, remained steadfast in His Cause and showed absolute faithfulness and humility, were worthy to be called His companions.

In future ages, when the station of Bahá'u'lláh will have been fully recognized, humanity will look back upon these souls, the embodiments of certitude and devotion, with feelings of praise and gratitude. For it was through their intense faith and love that they were enabled to receive the grace and bounties of God on behalf of all mankind. Had it not been for their loyalty and utter self-abnegation in the face of tests and calamities, the human race would have betrayed its God and postponed the establishment of the promised Kingdom upon this earth.

These disciples, many of whom laid down their lives in the path of Bahá'u'lláh, were the fruits of the Revelation of the Báb. It was He who created them especially for this Day. Indeed, the whole purpose of the Báb's Mission was to prepare His followers to become worthy to meet Bahá'u'lláh.

In one of His Writings[14] the Báb stated that the moment an individual could be found ready and able to understand the Revelation which would follow His, God would without an instant's delay manifest Himself and reveal His Cause. The Báb also gave the example of His own Revelation and affirmed that had Mullá Ḥusayn, the first to believe in Him, been ready to recognize Him even a few moments before he did, He would have announced His Mission that much earlier.

The person upon whom God had conferred the greatest capacity to understand the Revelation of Bahá'u'lláh was His eldest son 'Abdu'l-Bahá, Who at the age of nine instinctively knew the station of His Father. Soon after His arrival in

'Iráq, Bahá'u'lláh unfolded the Mission with which God had entrusted Him to 'Abdu'l-Bahá Who immediately acknowledged the truth of His Cause, prostrated Himself at His feet, and with great humility and earnestness begged the privilege of laying down His life in His Father's path.

Such momentous events do not come about casually. The hand of God was at work creating the means of manifesting His own Self to mankind. Not only was the Báb sent to pave the way for the coming of Bahá'u'lláh, but also 'Abdu'l-Bahá was created especially for the purpose of receiving the Revelation of Bahá'u'lláh on behalf of mankind. How significant it is that 'Abdu'l-Bahá, who was to become the instrument of such a sublime Revelation, was born the same night that the Báb communicated His Mission to Mullá Ḥusayn and set in motion the process of preparing His followers for the appearance of 'Him Whom God shall make manifest'.

Moreover, the history of the Bahá'í Faith demonstrates that the divine Power which raised up the incomparable figures of the Báb and 'Abdu'l-Bahá, and delineated their sacred missions, also vivified many other souls who recognized Bahá'u'lláh and embraced His Faith.

In every Dispensation those who recognized the Manifestation of God and followed Him became a new creation endowed with new spirit. This is the rebirth spoken of in the Holy Books. In one of His Tablets[15] best known for the beauty of its imagery, Bahá'u'lláh portrays a delightful panorama of divine mysteries. In allusive language He recounts some fascinating spiritual events in the worlds of God prior to the unveiling of Bahá'u'lláh's Revelation. It is impossible to describe these enchanting scenes, but their essence is that since there was no one capable of understanding this Revelation, God ordained the birth of a new creation. Bahá'u'lláh affirms that He unveiled His glory to mankind only after it appeared, and describes in glowing terms the exalted character of this new creation.

Having warned His companions of grievous tests which would descend upon them, Bahá'u'lláh in the *Lawḥ-i-Hawdaj* then addresses them in words of affection. He assures them of the bounties of God through which they may rid themselves of vain imaginings, purify their hearts from earthly desires and enter into the realms of nearness to God. He also reminds them that the Almighty has chosen them from among all humanity, has enabled them to recognize His Manifestation, bestowed upon them the unique distinction of being His companions, exalted their stations above all who dwelt on earth and has recorded their names in the 'Preserved Tablet'.*

The theme of the remainder of the Tablet is the greatness of the Revelation of Bahá'u'lláh. Addressing the whole of creation He bids mankind rejoice, for the Day of blissfulness has appeared, the day in which man has attained the presence of God.

The belief that one day man will attain the presence of his God is based on the Holy Scriptures of the past. In the *Qur'án* there are many references to this theme. In fact this is the clearest and most important promise given by the Prophet of Islám. The great Bahá'í scholar, Mírzá Abu'l-Faḍl, states that any man of insight who has a true knowledge of the *Qur'án* will bear witness that at least one-third of that Book deals with the advent of the great Day of God.

The following verses are only a few examples among many: 'As for those who believe not in the signs of God, or that they shall ever meet Him, these of my mercy shall despair, and for them doth a grievous chastisement await';[16] and 'let him then who hopeth to attain the presence of His Lord work a righteous work';[17] and again 'They who bear in mind that they shall attain unto the presence of their Lord, and that unto Him shall they return';[18] and yet again 'He ordereth all things. He maketh His signs clear, that ye may have firm faith in attaining the presence of your Lord.'[19]

* This term is a symbol for the knowledge of God Who 'knoweth all things and is known of none'.

Similar prophecies appear in great number in the New Testament also. For example: 'And there shall be no more curse: but the throne of God and of the Lamb shall be in it; and his servants shall serve him: and they shall see his face . . .';[20] and again 'And I heard a great voice out of heaven saying, Behold, the tabernacle of God is with men, and he will dwell with them, and they shall be his people, and God Himself shall be with them, and be their God. And God shall wipe away all tears from their eyes; and there shall be no more death, neither sorrow, nor crying, neither shall there be any more pain: for the former things are passed away.'[21]

The Old Testament is also full of the promise of the coming of the Lord God. Here are a few instances: 'It shall blossom abundantly, and rejoice even with joy and singing: the glory of Lebanon shall be given unto it, the excellency of Carmel and Sharon, they shall see the glory of the Lord, and the excellency of our God.'[22] 'Say to them that are of a fearful heart, Be strong, fear not: behold, your God will come with vengeance, even God with a recompence; he will come and save you.'[23] 'And the glory of the Lord shall be revealed, and all flesh shall see it together: for the mouth of the Lord hath spoken it.'[24] 'For, behold, the darkness shall cover the earth, and gross darkness the people; but the Lord shall arise upon thee, and his glory shall be seen upon thee.'[25]

In many of His Tablets Bahá'u'lláh has explained that God is beyond the comprehension of man and 'immensely exalted beyond every human attribute, such as corporeal existence, ascent and descent, egress and regress . . . He standeth exalted beyond and above all separation and union, all proximity and remoteness.'[26]

The view that God will come in person is completely against the nature of God. Such an event would reduce Him instantly from the realm of the infinite to that of the finite. But man can attain the presence of God by attaining the presence of His Manifestation.* In the Persian *Bayán* (6 : 7) the Báb has clearly

* See *The Revelation of Bahá'u'lláh*, vol. I, pp. 175–6, p. 185.

stated that any reference in the Holy Scriptures to the presence of God means the presence of 'Him Whom God shall make manifest'.

Ever since recorded history began the Prophets and Messengers of God have foretold an age of consummation for mankind. The visions of all the Prophets, the thoughts of many poets and seers have focused on the coming of the Lord,* and yet when He manifested Himself all the peoples of the world failed to recognize Him. Only a few beheld His glory and recognized His station. Therefore, how awe-inspiring is it to look back upon those days when less than three score men, women and children accompanied their Lord in person from Ba<u>gh</u>dád, crowded into a Turkish steamer at the port of Sámsún and sailed with Him to Constantinople, while men in general were unaware of such stupendous happenings. God passed them by and they remained in deep slumber.

Subḥánika-Yá-Hú

A beautiful tablet in Arabic and in Bahá'u'lláh's own hand was revealed in Constantinople on the eve of the 5th of Jamádíyu'l-Avval 1280 A.H. (19 October 1863), the anniversary of the Declaration of the Báb.† This Tablet, because of its opening verse, is known as *Lawḥ-i-Náqús* (Tablet of the Bell) and is also referred to as the *Subḥánika-Yá-Hú*. It was revealed following a request made through 'Abdu'l-Bahá by one of Bahá'u'lláh's companions, Áqá Muḥammad-'Alíy-i-Tambákú-Furú<u>sh</u>-i-Iṣfahání.‡ The revelation of this Tablet on such

* There are innumerable prophecies in Islám, Judaism and Christianity which indicate the date of this event as 1844, the year of the Báb's declaration.

† The Declaration of the Báb was on the evening of 5 Jamádíyu'l-Avval, 1260 A.H. (22 May 1844), but at present in the East, the anniversary of this festival is celebrated according to the lunar calendar.

‡ This is the same Muḥammad-'Alíy-i-Iṣfahání referred to in vol. I, p. 287. See also p. 370 below.

an auspicious occasion brought immense joy to the hearts of those who were celebrating that historic festival. Bahá'u'lláh opens this Tablet with these words:

> O Monk of the Incomparable One! Ring out the Bell, inasmuch as the Day of the Lord hath shone forth and the Beauty of the All-Glorious is established upon His holy and resplendent Throne.[27]

These few lines give us a glimpse of the majesty and sublimity of the Tablet. Like those revealed near the time of Bahá'u'lláh's declaration, this Tablet pulsates with an indescribable power that can emanate only from the Pen of the Supreme Manifestation of God. Here, the matchless utterances of Bahá'u'lláh, original and profound, are possessed of such beauty and rhythm as no pen can describe. Composed in a style that lends itself to collective chanting, this Tablet creates an atmosphere of ecstasy and joy when chanted by the believers.* Revealed soon after His departure from Baghdád, it announces in clear and majestic terms the rising of the Orb of His Revelation, asserts that He † who was hidden behind the veils of concealment is now made manifest, extols the potency and glory of His Cause, declares that the Day of God has come, summons the inhabitants of the highest Paradise to prepare themselves and acquire the capacity for attaining the presence of God,‡ bids his lovers rejoice and celebrate the coming of the Well-Beloved, and calls upon all created things to proclaim the glad-tidings of this Revelation to mankind. And finally, He prays for His companions: that they may become detached from everything besides Him, that their hearts may burn with the fire

* Not to be confused with congregational prayer, which (with the exception of the Prayer for the Dead) is forbidden by Bahá'u'lláh. Tablets in the original language are chanted by an individual. Occasionally, when there is a refrain in a Tablet, it has been customary for others to join in the refrain if it is suitable to do so.

† Bahá'u'lláh.

‡ See vol. I, p. 299, footnote.

of His love and become pure and without desire. He also prays that His companions, devoted to the promotion of His Cause, may become victorious over all who dwell on earth.

The history of the Faith amply demonstrates the fulfilment of this prayer. Through God's assistance, His disciples, though bitterly persecuted and lacking any earthly power, triumphed over the forces of darkness and won memorable victories for the Cause of their Lord. Two despotic monarchs, Náṣiri'd-Dín Sháh and Sulṭán 'Abdu'l-'Azíz were determined with unyielding hostility to uproot the foundation of the new-born Faith of God. The former, during whose reign the Báb was martyred and countless souls were massacred, tried his utmost to extinguish the light of the Faith and even to obliterate its very name from the pages of history, while the latter incarcerated its Author and imposed the harshest of restrictions upon Him and His companions. Yet today the Faith of Bahá'u'lláh is established in every part of the world and His followers, representing all colours, races and nations, are spreading His Cause with astonishing speed and earnestness. They have been, and are increasingly, bringing to the attention of a tormented humanity the fundamental verities of their Faith, its history, its teachings, its world-embracing institutions and its transforming power.

In past Dispensations, as in this Day, God has promoted His Faith through the work of men and women who were meek and humble. Of these people it is stated in the *Qur'án*: 'And We desire to show favour to those who were brought low in the land, and to make them spiritual leaders among men, and to make of them Our heirs.'[28]

Similarly these words are recorded in the Gospels: 'Blessed are the meek: for they shall inherit the earth.'[29]

By exalting His Cause through the aid of the lowliest among men, God has proved the ascendancy and power of His Manifestations. No one can accuse Them of having established religion through the influence of important people. For example, those few souls who first recognized and followed

Christ were not outstanding people. They were treated with contempt and were persecuted. Others who followed in their footsteps suffered the same fate and many of them died martyrs' deaths. Yet in spite of their seeming helplessness at the time, the Message of Christ was noised abroad and His Faith established. This is one of the proofs of the authenticity of His Mission.

Similarly, those who believed in Muḥammad in the early days were among the lowly and the outcast. This is why many people ridiculed the Prophet saying: 'We see in thee but a man like ourselves; and we see not any who have followed thee except our meanest ones of hasty judgement, nor see we any excellence in you above ourselves: Nay, we deem you liars.'[30] Muḥammad Himself was bitterly opposed and persecuted by the people of Mecca and eventually fled to Medina for safety. Yet, through the power of God, He and His disciples, though downtrodden and debased, triumphed over their adversaries and gave spiritual life to great multitudes.

The manner in which the Faith of Islám was established, however, is greatly criticized in the West. This is almost entirely due to distorted reports of fanatical Christians who, over the centuries, ignored the spiritual teachings and noble precepts of Islám, misinterpreted its doctrines, exaggerated its unfamiliar background and disseminated gross calumnies about its Author.

An interesting account of this is given by Ḥájí Muḥammad-Ṭáhir-i-Málmírí in his memoirs, quoting the gist of a long interview he had in Yazd with a certain Christian missionary who knew the Persian language well. The object of the interview was to prove the authenticity of the Message of Bahá'u'lláh. In the course of discussion the subject of Islám was broached. The following is a translation of a small portion of this dialogue:

> He [the Christian missionary] said to me 'How about Muḥammad?' I said 'I think in a sense the efficacy of

Muḥammad's word was greater than that of Christ.' 'How could that be?' was his prompt response. I replied, 'You know Christ was born and bred in the Holy Land which is an Eastern country. There He declared His Mission, spent years of His ministry and there He was finally crucified. Yet for well over six centuries His Faith did not make appreciable headway in any of the Eastern countries, while today every Muslim you may come across in the East regards Jesus as the Spirit of God and the Bible as the Word of God. The belief in Christ and the appreciation of His divine mission were brought to Eastern peoples through the influence of Muḥammad. Isn't that so?' 'That is right,' he said, 'but it was done by the sword.' I explained, 'During the thirteen years Muḥammad lived in Mecca after declaring Himself a prophet no sword was used, although throughout the whole time He was the object of ever-growing ridicule and oppression. These attacks grew so fierce at times that He used to take refuge in caves and dug-outs, and at last had to flee to Medina for safety. The skirmishes that Muḥammad took part in were entirely defensive in character. However, let us accept your assertions as correct. Let us assume that Muḥammad established His religion with the aid of the sword, whereas Christ diffused His Faith solely by the aid of the Holy Spirit. You know the sword is a deadly weapon; it takes life, it destroys, rends asunder. However, in the hand of Muḥammad it turned out to be a blessing in disguise. It brought spiritual life to some three hundred million souls; it united many warring factions and diverse communities into a permanent bond of unity and brotherhood; it raised the savage Arab tribes to the fairest heights of knowledge and culture. Now, be fair in your judgement, which task is more difficult and wonderful—to give life by means of a sword or by spiritual means? Which one is more skilful, the physician who heals his patients at once by giving them poison or the one who gradually brings relief by administering soothing drugs?'

'All right,' he said, 'but Muḥammad was a lustful polygamist whereas Christ did not even marry.' I replied 'If by saying Christ didn't marry you try to enhance His divine virtues I am afraid you are mistaken. Because Christ's physical body was the same as any other man's, and the fact that He did not marry was probably because He found no place to settle down, as during the short period of His Ministry He was moving about the country. Or if you want to attribute lack of sexual urge to Christ then such an implication would indicate physical deficiency rather than divine virtue, whereas the Messengers of God are perfect in body as in soul. In addition Christ has never said anything against matrimony. But suppose we take your premise, nevertheless no one can deny that Muḥammad was able to inculcate in His adherents the highest degree of chastity and moral rectitude, and to foster a wonderful measure of integrity and spiritual consciousness among a community so degenerate that in those days it had reached the lowest depths of savagery and ignorance. And today, well over 1300 years after Him, the evidence of His spiritual power, which still binds those multi-racial communities together, is quite discernible everywhere. Spirituality and sexual urge, like water and fire, are opposites. Muḥammad reconciled these two contrasting powers within His own self, whereas you say Christ was solely of pure spirit and conferred life as such. Now I leave this to your unbiased judgement to determine whether Muḥammad's nature was more spiritual or lustful. We must not, however, be misled by such material considerations. Christ taught: "Ye shall know the tree by its fruit." Then he said, "How about the truth of the mission of Bahá'u'lláh?"' . . . [31]

In most of the Tablets revealed in Constantinople and Adrianople, as in the *Lawḥ-i-Náqús*, Bahá'u'lláh urges His disciples to purge their hearts from worldly desires, and to cling fast to His Cause so that the words and evil whisperings of the unfaithful may not turn them from the path of Truth. When we study the events leading to the rebellion of Mírzá Yaḥyá in Adrianople we may realize the importance of such exhortations. As we shall see, several outstanding believers, some of whom were actually present in Constantinople when the *Lawḥ-i-Náqús* was revealed, were caught in the clutches of this crisis which later engulfed the community, and fell victims to its evil force.

But in spite of this, the exhortations of Bahá'u'lláh continued unabated. Indeed, one of the remarkable features of His life was His loving kindness to everyone who came in contact with Him. His divine and all-embracing mercy encompassed believers and unbelievers alike. Only when someone was about to harm the Cause of God did He expel him from His presence. To His followers He extended the hand of protection and guided them every step of the way. This is evident in all His Writings. His Tablets are replete with counsels, exhortations and guidance on spiritual, moral and social aspects of life. Even on personal matters Bahá'u'lláh always guided His disciples. To cite one example which concerns His journey to Constantinople: before His departure from Baghdád, Bahá'u'lláh advised His companions who were to travel with Him to grow their hair long in the same fashion as the Baktáshes* did. This measure was taken to give them prestige and some protection, as the Baktáshes were highly influential in Turkey. This statement must not be taken to mean that Bahá'u'lláh had approved the practice of men growing their hair long. The advice was given that they might conform to the conditions prevailing at the time and thus ensure their safety and well-being.

In Persia, too, there was some regard for the dervishes.† People did not harass them, nor did they interfere in their beliefs and practices. In those days, if a stranger arrived in a town the inhabitants were anxious to find out his identity and the real purpose of his visit. But not so in the case of the dervishes who often travelled from town to town. The public was accustomed to seeing dervishes come from distant lands, and often did not investigate them. In the early days of

* A Ṣúfí order very powerful at that time.

† Ṣúfís from various orders in Persia are categorically referred to as dervishes.

the Faith this situation helped some Bahá'í teachers in Persia who grew their hair long and dressed in the garb of the dervish. In this way they managed to move freely throughout the country without being harassed or persecuted.

There were also some genuine dervishes who had embraced the Faith during the ministries of the Báb and Bahá'u'lláh. Notable among them was Mírzá Qurbán-'Alí,* one of the Seven Martyrs of Ṭihrán. Naturally, these men continued to appear as dervishes. They carried their alms-boxes and followed the custom of singing the praises of the Lord in the bazaars and public places. These songs of praise, often recited from the works of famous poets, were among the most exciting performances of a dervish. Although Bahá'u'lláh had exhorted His followers to be wise and discreet when teaching His Cause and had advised them not to announce their faith in public, nevertheless some of the more audacious among these dervishes dared to sing the praises of Bahá'u'lláh in the streets and bazaars. Such unwise action inevitably brought untold suffering in its wake. At last Bahá'u'lláh sent a strong message to a few dervishes telling them to stop this practice and urging them to exercise wisdom.

Because of their habits of mendicancy and renunciation, a few of the dervishes who became Bahá'ís began to interpret the laws and ordinances of the Faith to suit themselves. In a Tablet Bahá'u'lláh denounces the attitudes and practices of these men who sought a sequestered life, and declares that they cared for nothing except eating and sleeping.[32]

Since Bahá'u'lláh addressed *The Seven Valleys* to a Ṣúfí, outlining the spiritual prerequisites for man to attain to his ultimate goal, and since He Himself went to Sulaymáníyyih in the garb of a dervish, some may be under the false impression that His teachings are in conformity with the practice of Ṣúfism. The study of His Cause will demonstrate that this is not so. That Bahá'u'lláh appeared as a dervish for two years in the mountains of Kurdistán was entirely due to the cir-

* See *The Dawn-Breakers*.

cumstances of His solitary retirement, and cannot be construed as an approval of the Ṣúfí way of life. The basic principle of Ṣúfism is that it is possible for man to have direct experience of God by seeking contact with the Source of being and reality, and thus attain absolute spiritual freedom wherein his intuitive senses may be allowed full scope. But the Faith of Bahá'u'lláh teaches that there can be no direct relationship between the Creator and the created, the Infinite and the finite, and that 'the door of the knowledge of the Ancient of Days being . . . closed in the face of all beings',[33] the only way that man can know God is through knowledge of His Manifestations. It is a major Bahá'í belief that man's spiritual advancement depends upon his obedience to, and practice of, the teachings of the Manifestations of God and not upon the promptings and dictates of his own life.

Another main difference between Ṣúfí and Bahá'í belief is that Bahá'u'lláh has prohibited asceticism and mendicancy. He has given His followers a different understanding of detachment and renunciation which is, in fact, opposite to the views held by Ṣúfís in general.

In one of His Tablets 'Abdu'l-Bahá states that *The Seven Valleys** gives us guidance in treading the path of detachment.[34] Its purpose is to teach the wayfarer how to love God. But in no way does it condone or justify the attitude adopted by many dervishes who claim to have renounced the world. Such men wander about like vagrants, are confused and lazy, live without work and are a burden to others. As already stated in an earlier volume, *The Seven Valleys* was revealed by Bahá'u'lláh in response to the questions of Shaykh Muḥyi'd-Dín, a man of learning who was well-versed in Ṣúfí philosophy. Bahá'u'lláh mentions in a Tablet[35] that *The Seven Valleys* was written before His Declaration in the idiom of the people concerned. In His divine wisdom, Bahá'u'lláh used the Ṣúfí terminology current at the time, so that the questioner might comprehend it. In this Tablet he also affirms that anyone, who in this day has

* See *The Revelation of Bahá'u'lláh*, vol. I, p. 96.

turned to Him and truly recognized His station, has indeed attained all the seven stages mentioned in that book.

Bahá'u'lláh has condemned asceticism, mendicancy and monasticism.[36] He states that there are people in certain islands who live among wild beasts, shut themselves away from humanity, abstain from eating and carry on an ascetic life. They consider themselves as leaders of men. Yet none of these acts is acceptable in the sight of God. In the same Tablet He describes His own observations while in Baghdád, where in a certain Ṣúfí quarter a man was inflicting severe blows upon himself until he fell unconscious to the ground. This foolish exercise, presumably carried out to attain mastery over self, was considered by his co-religionists as highly meritorious and a supernatural act. Bahá'u'lláh affirms that God is weary of these people.

In one of his works Mírzá Abu'l-Faḍl, the celebrated Bahá'í scholar, has carefully traced the decline in the fortunes of Islám, attributing it to the rise of Ṣúfism. After describing Islám's great contribution to mankind in fields of learning such as medicine, science, mathematics and astronomy he writes:

> . . . And all the countries and cities of Islám from east to west were illumined with the light of knowledge. But alas, before the newly planted trees of learning and education had yielded their fruit, the thorn of piety grew in the garden of this shining nation [Islám]. When the disease of Ṣúfism, which may be likened to paralysis and decay, afflicts the healthy organs of a nation, its joy, supremacy, advancement and influence will be completely obliterated. This disease has now been inflicted upon the nation of Islám. A great number of people in the name of ascetism and self-purification engaged in excessive prayer and meditation . . . Although in fairness it is admitted that some great men have appeared among these people and because of their genuine piety the hearts of some have been illumined with the splendours of the light of truth, yet, since the great majority were worshippers of their own selfish desires rather than God, and seekers after leadership instead of faith, they often invented

false devotions and introduced expressions alien to the principles of religion. Through their many deceitful acts they managed to turn towards themselves the hearts of kings and rulers. Consequently the vigour of the kings in disseminating science grew weak, and the diffusion of knowledge was replaced by adoration of the divines. The lights of learning began to dim slowly and the shadow of Ṣúfism spread instead.[37]

2

Mat͟hnavíy-i-Mubárak

One of the most beautiful works which Bahá'u'lláh revealed in Constantinople is the *Mat͟hnaví*. It is a masterpiece of Persian poetry, noted for the beauty and power of its composition, and acclaimed as one of the most soul-stirring among His poems. No pen can adequately describe the contents of this great work even in the original language. For every one of its three hundred lines is a book in itself with infinite depth and profound significances. Like a vast ocean which gushes out through a tiny outlet, Bahá'u'lláh reveals, with a potency that overwhelms the soul, a small measure of the glory and power of God and vouchsafes to mankind a glimmer of His divine Revelation. The knowledge He bestows upon the pure in heart, the mysteries He unravels for the sincere, the insight He confers upon the seeker, the wisdom He dispenses to the wise, and the counsels and exhortations He delivers to His loved ones, all these stand out in this divine poem as the ultimates to which man can hope to attain.

In this poem, and within the bounds of a finite world, Bahá'u'lláh has unveiled the mysteries of a vast and limitless Revelation, disclosed some of the realities of the world of man and indicated how he can achieve the summit of glory. Some of His exhortations in this work are in the same vein as those in *The Hidden Words*.

Bahá'u'lláh has identified Himself in the poem as the Day-Star of Truth which sheds its radiance upon all created things. Just as the physical sun is the primary cause of life on this planet, so the Supreme Manifestation of God is the source of spiritual life for all mankind. He releases spiritual energies into the human world which cause man to progress and grow.

In one of His Tablets,[1] Bahá'u'lláh states that the primary purpose of divine revelation is not merely the changing of laws in human society nor is it to impart knowledge; but rather, its purpose is to pour forth heavenly bounties so that at the time of divine revelation all created things may become the instruments of the grace of God and acquire fresh capacities.

When the *Mat͟hnaví* was revealed the news of the Declaration of Bahá'u'lláh and its significance had not been fully communicated to the Bábí Community. Therefore Bahá'u'lláh calls on Himself in this poem to rend asunder the veils and let the sun of His Revelation arise in full splendour. In another passage He calls on Himself to shed upon this dark world a measure of His light, to open the doors of the knowledge of God to humanity, and to waft over them the musk-laden breezes of His mercy so that the spiritually dead may be resurrected from their sepulchres of ignorance and heedlessness.

Alluding to the diffusion of the light of His Faith to the Western world, Bahá'u'lláh makes a remarkable statement. He urges the innermost spirit of God within Himself to unveil His glory so that the Sun may rise from the West. Elsewhere in His writings, Bahá'u'lláh has prophesied that although the Cause of God was born in the East, its influence would appear in the West.*

In the *Mat͟hnaví* Bahá'u'lláh describes His coming as the advent of the Day of God and the appearance of springtime. In many of His Tablets He has referred to this theme. Just as the physical spring gives new life to all creation in this world, so the Revelation of Bahá'u'lláh enables the hearts of men to be filled with His love and to manifest the noblest fruits of virtues and perfections. These heavenly qualities manifested by the believer do not originate entirely from himself. Without

* The rise and establishment of the Bahá'í Faith in the Western world has been remarkable. For further information see *God Passes By* and volumes of *The Bahá'í World.*

the light of the sun the eye is a useless instrument and the seed an impotent organism. Similarly if it were not for the appearance of the Manifestations of God no man could ever attain to nobility and righteousness. It is through the radiance of these Suns of Truth that humanity has been led progressively from darkness into light.

One of the themes of the *Mathnaví* is that man himself is a manifestation of God, that within him are deposited the powers and attributes of God, and that God's light is reflected in him; yet he is veiled from these bounties and spends the precious hours of his life unaware of the exalted forces latent within him. Bahá'u'lláh warns that not until man makes an effort to purify his heart can these qualities and attributes be manifested in him. In *The Hidden Words*, speaking with the voice of God, Bahá'u'lláh states:

> O Son of Being!
> Thou art My lamp and My light is in thee. Get thou from it thy radiance and seek none other than Me. For I have created thee rich and have bountifully shed My favour upon thee.[2]

Bahá'u'lláh teaches in the *Mathnaví* that man will not be able to receive the light of God in this day unless he acquires a new eye. Eyes which are fixed on the things of this world can never see the glory of His Revelation, and ears which are tuned to the voices of the ungodly cannot hear the melodies of the Kingdom. By 'new eyes' and 'new ears' He means spiritual eyes and spiritual ears. He states that since the eye of the spirit receives its light from God it is shameful to let it turn to a stranger, and re-affirms that the purpose of God in creating the inner eye was that man might behold the beauty of His Manifestation in this world. In *The Hidden Words* Bahá'u'lláh reveals:

> O Son of Dust!
> Blind thine eyes, that thou mayest behold My beauty; stop thine ears, that thou mayest hearken unto the sweet

melody of My voice; empty thyself of all learning, that thou mayest partake of My knowledge; and sanctify thyself from riches, that thou mayest obtain a lasting share from the ocean of My eternal wealth. Blind thine eyes, that is, to all save My beauty; stop thine ears to all save My word; empty thyself of all learning save the knowledge of Me; that with a clear vision, a pure heart and an attentive ear thou mayest enter the court of My holiness.[3]

In a Tablet[4] He affirms that should the eyes of an observer be as large as the universe and turn for one moment to someone other than Him, such a person is not worthy to enter His presence. We can appreciate this statement of Bahá'u'lláh if we ponder the case of a man who seeks illumination from a candle when the sun is shining at its zenith.

In another Tablet[5] Bahá'u'lláh explains that this is the Day of God, and nothing else is worthy of mention. He further states that this is the day of eyes, of ears and of hearts. He calls on His loved ones to try to acquire these three and reminds them that only a tiny impediment can prevent the eyes from seeing, the ears from hearing and hearts from understanding.

The veils which come between the inner eye of the soul and the Manifestation of God all originate from the world of man. A great many people in the world today are as yet unable to witness the glory of Bahá'u'lláh, the Supreme Manifestation of God, for they have wrapped their hearts in many veils. One of the cruellest veils is that of tradition. Men are born into a tradition and are inclined to remain as prisoners within it for life. History shows that whenever God has manifested Himself and brought new standards and teachings for mankind, such men have followed their fathers, religious leaders and countrymen in denouncing the new Manifestation of God. The best example is the coming of Christ when only a handful of people recognized Him, while the rest, who were slaves of tradition, rejected His Cause. One of the most important teachings of Bahá'u'lláh is that man should not imitate his fellow men in matters of faith, that he should carry out an unfettered search after truth and open his inner eyes to behold the glory of the new-born Faith of God in this day.

Another grievous veil which has prevented people from recognizing the Manifestation of God is that of knowledge. Men who possess knowledge often become proud, sometimes without realizing it, and close their eyes to the truth. This is one of those 'veils of glory'—spoken of in Islám and referred to by Bahá'u'lláh in many of His Writings, including the *Kitáb-i-Íqán*—whereby one of the lofty attributes of God becomes a barrier.* Though knowledge is a praiseworthy attribute for man to acquire and Bahá'u'lláh, like Muḥammad, has enjoined His followers to gain knowledge, yet it becomes a 'veil of glory' if through it man is rendered vain and egotistical.

In the early days of the Faith, a certain wealthy and knowledgeable person from Káshán set off with his family for pilgrimage to the cities of Najaf and Karbilá. Circumstances had forced him to engage a Bábí caravan-driver by the name of Háshim Khán to transport the party to its destination and back. The reason for his reluctance to travel in company with Háshim Khán, in spite of the fact that the latter was known to be the most trusted caravan-driver in the area, was that he was a Bábí. Háshim Khán was tall and strong. He had little education, yet his heart was touched by the light of God's infant Faith. As a result, he was endowed with the gift of understanding and was able to convince people in his simple way of the truth of the Cause he had espoused. He was commonly referred to as Háshim Bábí. The merchant and his family shunned Háshim throughout the journey. They did not wish to associate with one who in their estimation had embraced a heretical Faith. On such long journeys the party has to stop two or three times a day for rest and to feed the animals. On one occasion when they were resting, the merchant decided to speak to Háshim to try to guide him back to the fold. So he called him to come and join the others. Having thanked him

* See vol. I, pp. 43–4.

for his selfless service and care, he began to converse with Háshim and remarked, 'How is it that with all my knowledge, I have failed to appreciate the validity of the Message of the Báb while you, an almost illiterate person, claim to have recognized the truth of His Mission?'

Háshim took a handful of sand in his hand and said, 'People like me have no merit in society. They are like the sand in the desert which has no value, yet, when the sun rises in the morning this sand is the first to become illumined by its rays. A learned man, however, is like a precious jewel. It is kept in a box and locked up in a room, and when the sun rises it remains in darkness.' The merchant was moved by this answer. He continued to learn from Háshim all the way home, until the veils which obscured his vision were removed and the jewel of his heart was enlightened by the radiance of God's new-born Faith. This simple answer by Háshim is very profound indeed. While it exalts the station of knowledge, it demonstrates that when the Sun of Truth appears in the world, men of learning must make an effort to open their hearts and souls to its rays and to become illumined by them.

Other veils which prevent people from embracing the new Faith of God are prejudices of all kinds, materialism, wealth, power and many others which have surrounded human society today and plunged it into a state of utter darkness and deprivation.

Detachment

In the *Mathnaví* Bahá'u'lláh speaks about the potency of His Revelation and affirms that through it man can scale the loftiest heights of virtue and spirituality. He calls on His loved ones to endeavour to attain this station by turning to Him with pure hearts and with devotion, and then detaching themselves from earthly things. In many of His Tablets Bahá'u'lláh has stated that the greatest achievement for man is detachment from all things save God. The soul can acquire faith and progress towards God to the degree of its detachment from this world. But detachment is often misunderstood and is taken to mean renouncing the world. Many sects and groups of people are inclined to shut themselves away in monasteries or similar institutions, thinking that such a practice will enhance their spiritual status. The teachings of Bahá'u'lláh are emphatically against this. For instance, in His second Tablet to Napoleon III, Bahá'u'lláh addresses the monks in these words:

> O concourse of monks! Seclude not yourselves in churches and cloisters. Come forth by My leave, and occupy yourselves with that which will profit your souls and the souls of men. Thus biddeth you the King of the Day of Reckoning. Seclude yourselves in the stronghold of My love. This, verily, is a befitting seclusion, were ye of them that perceive it. He that shutteth himself up in a house is indeed as one dead. It behoveth man to show forth that which will profit all created things, and he that bringeth forth no fruit is fit for fire.[6]

Man may possess all the good things of the world, live in luxury and yet be detached from earthly things.* God has created this world and all it contains for man's use and enjoyment, provided he lives in accordance with the teachings of God.

Bahá'u'lláh in one of His Tablets[7] mentions that this world is filled with material bounties from God, that all good and beautiful things are manifestations of His attributes and that to possess them is not attachment. He warns, however, that the things of this world are all transitory and man should not fix his affection upon them, nor allow himself to be possessed by them. In the same Tablet Bahá'u'lláh explains the meaning of attachment to the world as being attachment to those who have denied Him and turned aside from His Cause. In another Tablet[8] Bahá'u'lláh states that there are three barriers between

* See vol. I, pp. 75–7.

God and man. He exhorts the believers to pass beyond them so that they may be enabled to attain His presence. The first one, which we have just discussed, is attachment to this mortal world. The second is attachment to the next world and all that is destined for man in the life hereafter. And the third is attachment to the 'Kingdom of Names'.

To understand the significance of the second barrier let us remember that the purpose of life is to know and worship God. One of the traditions of Islám states that in the beginning God was a hidden treasure; because He desired to be discovered and recognized, He created man. And man, through endeavour and spiritual instinct, has been successful in discovering God. Through the powers and attributes which God has bestowed upon him, as well as through the light which His Manifestations have shed on his path, he has been enabled to know his Creator* and worship Him. Bahá'u'lláh states in *The Hidden Words*:

> O Son of Man!
>
> I loved thy creation, hence I created thee. Wherefore, do thou love Me, that I may name thy name and fill thy soul with the spirit of life.[9]

And in a prayer which Bahá'u'lláh revealed for His followers to recite He writes: 'I bear witness, O my God, that Thou hast created me to know Thee and to worship Thee . . .' †[10]

This, therefore, is the purpose of creation. Man's deeds are praiseworthy in the sight of God when they are performed solely for His love and for no other reason. To this Bahá'u'lláh testifies in the *Kitáb-i-Aqdas*: 'Observe My commandments, for the love of My beauty.'[11] If man's motive for his actions

* Since it is not possible to know God in His essence, man attains to the knowledge of God when he knows His Manifestation. See vol. I, pp. 175–7.

† Worship of God is not only through prayer and devotion. Bahá'u'lláh has ordained that work performed in the spirit of service to mankind is also to be regarded as worship.

is that he may reap a reward for himself in the next world, then this is attachment. To be detached means to do everything for the sake of God and to seek no recompense.

What a contrast between this attitude and that prevailing in human society at the present time, where almost every action is designed to bring forth rewards for the individual. The attitude of expediency and self-interest has so conditioned the mind of man today that even in spiritual matters such as faith and belief in God, man often looks for something that will primarily satisfy his own needs. Many people today join one religion or another in the hope of receiving some spiritual help or other benefit such as peace of mind or salvation. This is not the right motive for following a religion. For the story of every religion is written with the language of love. A true lover has no ulterior motives or self-interest, but only a passionate love for his beloved. Man's first duty is to recognize and love the Manifestation of God and then to follow Him, for He alone in the whole of creation deserves to be glorified and exalted and is worthy of praise and worship.

Man, because of his animal nature, is a selfish being. The instinct for survival drives him to find food, clothing and other necessities of life. Then he seeks after security, wealth, power and similar possessions. All these, as well as his intellectual, emotional and spiritual pursuits, revolve around his own self, and are aimed to serve his well-being, prosperity and happiness. He is always in search of things to add to his possessions as long as he can derive some benefit from them.

When man encounters the Faith of God and recognizes its glory he tends to add it, in the usual way, to his other treasures. He puts his religion on a par with his other pursuits, and selfishly expects to benefit from it just as he benefits from his other possessions. He wants the Faith of God to serve him and bring him joy and satisfaction. This concept and practice is attachment to the world and against the law of creation. For God has not given His Revelation in order that it may satisfy the selfish interests of man. On the contrary, man is expected to arrange his life in such a way as to serve and revolve around the Revelation of God. If the individual follows the Cause of God unselfishly and with pure motive, his life will be so blessed that the powers and attributes of God will be revealed within his soul. Whereas if he seeks these attributes to gratify his own ego, such a motive will cause him to be deprived of the outpouring of God's grace and bounty.

In this day those who have fully recognized the station of Bahá'u'lláh, and are endowed with the gift of true understanding, have embraced His Faith not because they discovered that it would bring happiness to them, solve their personal problems, remove their afflictions and enrich their spiritual lives, but rather because they recognized that Bahá'u'lláh is the Manifestation of God for this age and were drawn to Him as iron is attracted to a magnet. Their eyes have been dazzled by the glory of His Revelation and their hearts seized by the potency of His Word. They know that the Cause He has revealed is exalted above all creation and that man has come into being primarily to serve it. This, and only this, should be the motive for following the Faith of God.

When the believer turns with true love to the Manifestation of God, he cannot help but leave aside his own interests and desires and seek only the good pleasure of His Lord. Yet in so doing, he will receive heavenly virtues and powers as a by-product of his love for and submission to the Manifestation of God. Indeed, it is true to say that the only people who experience real happiness and acquire divine virtues to the utmost are those who with no self-interest recognize and follow the Manifestation of God and are detached from the rewards of this life and the next.

Mírzá 'Azízu'lláh-i-Miṣbáḥ was one of the great scholars of the Faith. His life and learning have shed imperishable lustre on the annals of the Cause during the ministries of 'Abdu'l-Bahá and Shoghi Effendi. In his collection of gem-like meditations we find this short yet profound statement:

> He who seeks reward for his deeds will be given the Garden of Paradise; and he who seeks God is in no need of paradise.[12]

The third barrier which Bahá'u'lláh mentions is attachment to the 'Kingdom of Names'. In His Writings there are many references to this kingdom. For instance in a Tablet Bahá'u'lláh states:

> The Pen of the Most High is unceasingly calling; and yet, how few are those that have inclined their ear to its voice! The dwellers of the kingdom of names have busied themselves with the gay livery of the world, forgetful that every man that hath eyes to perceive and ears to hear cannot but readily recognize how evanescent are its colours.[13]

God in His own essence is exalted above attributes. However, in all His dominions and within each of His worlds, both spiritual and physical, He reveals the kingdom of His attributes. Every created thing manifests the names and attributes of God. In the spiritual world, these attributes are manifest with such intensity that man will never be able to comprehend them in this life. In the human world, however, these attributes appear within the 'Kingdom of Names' and man often becomes attached to these names.

In the *Lawḥ-i-Naṣír*,*[14] speaking with the voice of God, Bahá'u'lláh states that a name from among His names which He had created with one Word and into which He had breathed a new life, rose up against Him and opposed His authority. Because of attachment to this name, He testifies that some people of the *Bayán* rejected His Cause and deprived themselves of His glory. Here Bahá'u'lláh is alluding to the name 'Azal',† the title of Mírzá Yaḥyá. Indeed, this name, which is one of the attributes of God, became a barrier for many who blindly

* See pp. 245–47.

† 'Azal' (Eternity) is one of the attributes of God. This was a title conferred upon Mírzá Yaḥyá who was referred to as Ṣubḥ-i-Azal (Morn of Eternity).

followed him because of their attachment to an exalted title. Mírzá Yaḥyá himself was also misled by this name. He extolled its virtues and remained attached to it till the end of his life.

In many of His Tablets Bahá'u'lláh exhorts His followers not to become the bond-slaves of the Kingdom of Names. The well-known Islamic saying, 'The Names come down from heaven', has many significances. In this world every one of God's attributes is clad with a name, and every such name reveals the characteristics of its attribute. For instance, generosity is an attribute of God, and it manifests itself in human beings. However, a person who has this attribute often becomes proud of it and loves to be referred to as generous. When his generosity is acknowledged by other people, he becomes happy, and when it is ignored, unhappy. This is one form of attachment to the Kingdom of Names. Although this example concerns the name 'generosity', the same is true of all the names and attributes of God manifested within the individual. Usually, man ascribes these attributes to his own person rather than to God and employs them to exalt his own ego. For instance, a learned man uses the attribute of knowledge to become famous and feels gratified and uplifted when his name is publicized far and wide. Or there is the individual whose heart leaps with feelings of pride and satisfaction when he hears his name mentioned and finds himself admired. These are examples of attachment to the Kingdom of Names.

Human society at present exerts a pernicious influence upon the soul of man. Instead of allowing him to live a life of service and sacrifice, it teaches him to pride himself on his accomplishments. From early childhood he is trained to develop his ego and to seek to exalt himself above others. His ultimate aim is to achieve self-importance, success and power.

The Revelation of Bahá'u'lláh aims to reverse this process. The soul of man needs to be adorned with the virtues of humility and self-effacement so that it may become detached from the Kingdom of Names.

'Abdu'l-Bahá, the true Exemplar of the teachings of Bahá'u'-

lláh, demonstrated this form of detachment by His actions. Throughout His life, He never wished to exalt His name nor did He seek publicity for Himself. For instance, He had an immense dislike of being photographed. He said '. . . to have a picture of oneself is to emphasize the personality . . .'[15] During the first few days of His visit to London, He refused to be photographed. However, as a result of much pressure by the newspaper reporters, and persistent pleas by the friends to take His photograph, 'Abdu'l-Bahá acquiesced in order to make them happy.

The exalted titles which were conferred upon Him by Bahá'u'lláh were indicative of 'Abdu'l-Bahá's lofty station. Yet 'Abdu'l-Bahá never applied them to Himself. Instead, after the ascension of Bahá'u'lláh, He took the title of 'Abdu'l-Bahá (Servant of Bahá) and urged the believers to call Him only by this name. True servitude at the threshold of Bahá'u'lláh was all he prized. These are some of His words as He describes with utter self-effacement the reality of His station:

> My name is 'Abdu'l-Bahá. My qualification is 'Abdu'l-Bahá. My reality is 'Abdu'l-Bahá. My praise is 'Abdu'l-Bahá. Thraldom to the Blessed Perfection* is my glorious and refulgent diadem, and servitude to all the human race my perpetual religion . . . No name, no title, no mention, no commendation have I, nor will ever have, except 'Abdu'l-Bahá. This is my longing. This is my greatest yearning. This is my eternal life. This is my everlasting glory.[16]

One of the distinguishing features of Bahá'u'lláh's embryonic world order is that it does not harbour egotistical personalities. Bahá'u'lláh has conferred authority on its institutions, whether local, national or international. But the individuals who are privileged to serve on them are devoid of any authority. Unlike men who wield power in the world today and seek to acquire fame and popularity, members of Bahá'í institutions cannot but manifest humility and self-effacement if they are to

* Bahá'u'lláh.

remain faithful to Bahá'u'lláh. Those who do not succeed, through immaturity or lack of faith, in living up to these standards are indeed attached to the Kingdom of Names and are deprived of the bounties of God in this age.

To sever oneself from the Kingdom of Names may prove to be the most difficult task for a Bahá'í, and the struggle may indeed last a lifetime. If a man can only realize that his virtues are not intrinsically his own, but rather are manifestations of the attributes of God, then he is freed from the Kingdom of Names and becomes truly humble. Such a man will bestow divine perfections upon the world of humanity. This is the loftiest station that God has destined for man.

Some of the followers of Bahá'u'lláh attained this exalted station where they viewed their virtues as having emanated from the realms of God and not from themselves. One such person was Nabíl-i-Akbar,* who may be regarded as one of the most learned among the Apostles of Bahá'u'lláh. Ḥájí Mírzá Ḥaydar-'Alí has described a meeting at Qazvín where this great man was speaking to some of the believers. Here are some of his words concerning Nabíl-i-Akbar:

> I was so enchanted by the talks of this great Fáḍil † that I must have recounted his words in various gatherings on numerous occasions. One feature of his greatness was that no one could surpass his extraordinary power for expounding and elucidating matters. For instance, if he wished, he could prove that water was hot and dry and fire cold and wet, and no one was capable of arguing with him. Yet I have observed that even as the ocean of his utterance was surging and he was speaking with great vigour and conviction, he would, should someone point out a mistake he had made in his discourse, or should he himself become aware of it, immediately acknowledge his ignorance and confess his misjudgement.

* See vol. I, pp. 91–5.

† Literally 'an erudite man of great eminence'; an appellation by which Nabíl-i-Akbar was often known.

One of his profound and weighty observations was that man is naturally impotent, ignorant, weak, wretched and imperfect, whereas all strength, power, knowledge, wisdom, ascendancy, virtue and goodness are from God, praised be His glory. Therefore man should under all circumstances regard himself as imperfect, ignorant and a captive of self and passion. He should not feel depressed or hurt if people impute to him these characteristics which, after all, are inherent within him. On the contrary, he should be happy and thankful to them, while at the same time he should feel disappointed in himself, should take refuge in God and beg protection from his own base and appetitive nature.[17]

Men such as these were truly detached from the Kingdom of Names. No doubt it is concerning these men that Bahá'u'lláh writes:

> O Shaykh! This people have passed beyond the narrow straits of names, and pitched their tents upon the shores of the sea of renunciation. They would willingly lay down a myriad lives, rather than breathe the word desired by their enemies. They have clung to that which pleaseth God, and are wholly detached and freed from the things which pertain unto men. They have preferred to have their heads cut off rather than utter one unseemly word.[18]

These thoughts of Nabíl-i-Akbar are fully supported by the teachings of Bahá'u'lláh. Many Bahá'í prayers revealed by Him are replete with passages in which man confesses his weakness, ignorance and poverty and God's might, wisdom and sovereignty.

The Veil of Ego

There are passages in the *Mathnaví* in which Bahá'u'lláh exhorts man to burn away every veil that comes between him and God. Then and only then can he behold the beauty and grandeur of his Lord. One of these veils is the ego. Bahá'u'lláh calls on the individual to kindle a fire within his soul and burn away every trace of self so that the concept and the very word 'I' may totally disappear from his being. Indeed this is one of the most profound teachings of Bahá'u'lláh. When a person tries to exalt himself, to celebrate his own name and aspires to become famous he is, in fact, going right against the plan of creation. Such an individual hinders the flow of the bounties of God to himself. Although outwardly he may be considered a great success, in reality he has failed to fulfil the purpose for which he was created. When a man attains to real greatness, he then recognizes his helplessness, unworthiness and impotence. And when he becomes truly learned he genuinely discovers that he is ignorant. It is then that he can manifest the attributes of God within himself and impart them to others.

We find among the meditations of 'Azíz'u'lláh Miṣbáḥ the following utterances which truly exemplify his own life of detachment and self-effacement:

> To relinquish one's love for oneself and to destroy every trace of self, is a proof that one has comprehended the meaning of existence and the purpose of life.[19]
>
> The difference between true knowledge and formal learning is that the former creates lowliness and humility within the soul; the latter drives insatiably towards the search for glory and exaltation.[20]

Notable among those who had attained the station of true knowledge was Mírzá Abu'l-Faḍl, the great Bahá'í scholar and one of the Apostles of Bahá'u'lláh.* He is renowned for his vast knowledge, not only within the Bahá'í community but throughout the East. He was an acknowledged authority on many subjects including history and divine philosophy and was an outstanding master of Arabic and Persian literature. Once in academic circles in Egypt he was referred to as 'God of the pen, a pillar of history and the corner-stone of knowledge and virtue.'

* More information about him will be contained in vol. III of this series.

Dr. Ḥabíb Mu'ayyad, who knew him personally, has written a great deal in his memoirs concerning the greatness of this man. Here is one passage:

> Once people asked him [Mírzá Abu'l-Faḍl] how he had acquired this vast erudition and how he had become the recipient of this God-given knowledge. He became so displeased with his questioners that he angrily remarked 'Who is Abu'l-Faḍl!* What is Abu'l-Faḍl! I am only a drop from the vast ocean of Bahá'u'lláh's school. If you also enter the same school, you will become the master of Abu'l-Faḍl. If you don't believe me go to Gulpáygán,† see my relatives and then you will understand.'[21]

The following story gives us a glimpse of his greatness. In the early years of this century, 'Abdu'l-Bahá sent Mírzá Abu'l-Faḍl to the United States of America to teach and help the believers deepen in the Faith. After his return, he and a number of American pilgrims were seated in the presence of 'Abdu'l-Bahá in 'Akká. The pilgrims began to praise Mírzá Abu'l-Faḍl for the help he had given them, saying that he had taught many souls, defended the Cause most ably against its adversaries, and had helped to build a strong and dedicated Bahá'í community in America. As they continued to pour lavish praise upon him, Mírzá Abu'l-Faḍl became increasingly depressed and dejected, until he burst into tears and wept loudly. The believers were surprised and could not understand this, even thinking that they had not praised him enough!

Then 'Abdu'l-Bahá explained that by praising him they had bitterly hurt him, for he considered himself as utter nothingness in the Cause and believed with absolute sincerity that he was not worthy of any mention or praise.‡

Mírzá Abu'l-Faḍl has truly set an example for Bahá'ís to

* His name meant 'the father of learning'. (A.T.)

† The birthplace of Mírzá Abu'l-Faḍl where his relatives lived. (A.T.)

‡ This account by Harlan F. Ober was given to the writer by the Hand of the Cause of God Mr. John Robarts.

follow, in that throughout his Bahá'í life he never used the word 'I' to ascribe merit to himself.

Courage and Sacrifice

In the *Mathnaví* Bahá'u'lláh speaks about the greatness of His Cause, and in matchless language portrays the longing of the Prophets of the past to attain His presence and partake of the outpourings of His Revelation. In this poem He extols the lovers of His Beauty who unhesitatingly sacrifice their lives in the path of God, and exhorts them never to turn away from the field of martyrdom.

Those who truly recognized the station of Bahá'u'lláh accepted persecutions and sufferings for His love. They knew that after embracing the Faith of God their lives would be endangered. Indeed, when they left their homes to go out they could not be sure they would ever return. The enemy was poised at all times to strike at any one who was identified with the new-born Faith. So, those who followed the Báb and Bahá'u'lláh in the early days clearly understood that at any time they might have to lay down their lives in the path of God. This was their test of faith and the great majority of them remained steadfast till the end.

The following account depicting the scene of the martyrdom of one of the early believers, demonstrates this faith.

> Here is one who laid down his life in such a dramatic fashion that many among the multitude of spectators who had thronged the square to deride the victim and make merry at the sight of his execution were moved to tears. Even the hearts of those callous men who had been appointed to commit this heinous deed were deeply touched.
>
> The illustrious hero who appeared on this tragic scene was 'Alí-Akbar-i-Ḥakkák, a very attractive and handsome young man from Yazd, Persia. He was an engraver by profession and highly skilled in his art. He was married and had a four-year-old son by the name of Ḥabíbu'lláh. As soon as the

tragic news of the Nayríz upheaval reached Yazd, 'Alí-Akbar set out at once on a journey to visit the historic site where the peerless Vaḥíd together with his band of valiant crusaders had fought and fallen. On his return to Yazd he manifested such a spiritual joy and overwhelming zeal in the teaching work that soon he was denounced and branded as a 'Bábí' whereupon the despotic Governor had him arrested on a charge of heresy and reported the matter to Ṭihrán asking for instructions.

Nearly two months wore on and no word came from Ṭihrán. Therefore a fine was exacted from the captive and then he was released on bail on the understanding that as soon as the decree was received he should place himself immediately at the disposal of the Governor.

Unruffled by the dire fate which awaited him, 'Alí-Akbar resumed his occupation in a spirit of complete resignation until after a lapse of three months a message came from Ṭihrán to the effect that any person found to belong to the Bábí Faith should be put to death forthwith. This odious order invested the Governor with plenary powers to carry out his design. Therefore early in the morning of 15 July 1852 he sent his men to arrest 'Alí-Akbar at his home. Having done so they conducted him to the Governor's office in the barracks where the Governor interviewed him.

Though the people in Yazd were steeped in prejudice against the new Faith and apt to fly into a fierce fury at the sight of anyone who was identified as 'Bábí', they nevertheless admired 'Alí-Akbar for his rare qualities and charming manners. Moreover, his reputation as the best engraver had won him real affection by all who had come to know him. Even the Governor and the officials felt reluctant to have him executed. They did everything in their power to make him utter a mere word of lip-denial against the new Faith and thus save his own life. They employed many a word of persuasion, threat and promise but none could induce this valiant hero to recant nor did the pomp and might of a ruthless potentate influence this stout-hearted man of God to compromise his cherished faith in favour of this fleeting life and its earthly vanities. The Governor grew angry; he could not tolerate one who dared to challenge his authority and persist in his own ideas.

Furious with rage, the Governor summoned his Farrásh-báshí (chief steward) and ordered him to put this defiant Bábí to death at once by blowing him from the mouth of a cannon. The order was immediately passed on to the artillery unit who hauled their gun out of the barracks to the adjoining public square. Then the Farrásh-báshí accompanied by the executioner led the valiant victim to the square amidst a gathering multitude of spectators.

Eager to save 'Alí-Akbar from his fate, the Farrásh-báshí employed ingenious ways of intimidation and inducement in a futile effort to break down his spirit and make him abjure his allegiance to the new Faith.

The cannon from which he was to be blown was an old type muzzle-loader, and the Farrásh-báshí, knowing that it was as yet unloaded, hit upon the idea of staging a mock execution in the hope that the victim would succumb to the fright and terror that such an ordeal would usually provoke. Therefore, assuming a wild and serious look, he barked orders at the executioner to hurry up, tie down the victim tightly to the mouth of the gun and have him blown off without further delay. Thus 'Alí-Akbar was bound to the gun and left in this frightful position for quite a long while during which the gun crew kept running back and forth pretending to be adjusting their gun, as though they were just about to fire.

During the whole time the Farrásh-báshí was watching the victim closely, urging him to recant. However, he was amazed to see that instead of becoming terrified and shaken 'Alí-Akbar had maintained his calm and fortitude throughout. The Farrásh-báshí soon realized that intimidation had failed to bring about what he hoped for. He ran towards the gunner, stopped him from his false attempt at discharging the unloaded gun, and asked the executioner to set the victim free.

By that time (about 11 a.m.) the whole square was fully packed with a seething mass of spectators who looked stupefied and bewildered.

As soon as 'Alí-Akbar was unfastened the Farrásh-báshí came over to him expressing his sympathy in a kindly manner. He then conducted him to an adjacent public cistern away from the crowd where he offered him a seat near to himself on a little platform. He reasoned with 'Alí-Akbar most earnestly, urged and persuaded him again and again to denounce the Faith and save his own life, but the effort proved unsuccessful. There sat 'Alí-Akbar solid as a rock, immovable and uncompromising, resisting the full force of these dire tests. As these painful moments dragged on, the Farrásh-báshí began to perceive with bitter plainness that nothing whatever could induce this invincible youth to recant. Dismayed and disappointed, he led him back to the scene of death and ordered the gun crew to load their gun forthwith. Meanwhile a new idea occurred to him which might well prove effective in breaking down the victim's fortitude. He sent his men to fetch 'Alí-Akbar's poor wife and child to the scene—a very strong and challenging inducement indeed. After a few moments the unfortunate wife appeared in a state of panic holding the hand of their beloved child who looked sweet and attractive in his best suit.

She faced her husband and weeping bitterly implored, 'Come and have pity on this child!' 'What am I to do without you?' she sobbed. But 'Alí-Akbar did not answer; he turned his back on them. Again the wife and child came forward and stood in front of him. She flung herself at his feet, begging and imploring. But 'Alí-Akbar kept silent and once again turned away from them. Then the little child ran over to his father and grabbing the hem of his garment exclaimed 'Daddy, Daddy, why do you turn away from me? Don't you love me any more?'

These simple, these piercing words must have moved 'Alí-Akbar more than anything else. Perhaps he could not bear it, for he raised his head heavenward in such a gesture as to make an impassioned appeal. It seemed as if he were saying: 'Oh God! I entreat Thee to spare me from further temptations.'

The tragic episode had reached its climax. The occasion

had become so gripping, so heart-rending that many among the onlookers were stricken with grief and sympathy. Even the Farrásh-báshí's eyes were dimmed with tears.

The heroic self-renunciation and superhuman fortitude manifested by this gallant martyr shattered the last scrap of hope which the Farrásh-báshí entertained in making the victim abjure his faith. Browbeaten and dismayed, he decided to put an end to this sad spectacle by carrying out the Governor's order at once.

So the victim was presently bound up once again to the mouth of the cannon in front of his unfortunate wife and child. As soon as this had been done the site was cleared of all those who stood nearby, but the child refused to be pushed further away. He became restive and kept crying and pleading, 'Take me to my Daddy! Let me go near him!'

The dreadful end was now at hand. A tense feeling had seized upon the souls and a sense of dread and awe overwhelmed the whole mass of the people in the square.

At a sharp signal from the Farrásh-báshí the gunner ignited the explosive charge which was designed to send the victim sky-high, torn into bits in a split of a second. But to the profound amazement of all the gun didn't go off! Again and again the charge was ignited but the gun still wouldn't go off! Everybody looked stupefied and spellbound.

The Farrásh-báshí ran towards the victim and calling him by his name exclaimed, 'We don't want you to be killed; it seems that God does not wish it either. Now won't you have sympathy for your child?!' But he did not say a word, even when his horror-stricken wife and child rushed once again to his side. He stayed as calm and unconcerned as ever.

In the meantime the gunner was busy at the breech refilling the charge. The Farrásh-báshí paused a moment in earnest expectation. Perhaps he would now give way. Perhaps he would say a word of denial. Perhaps something would happen that could save his life.

However, to 'Alí-Akbar's mind a compromise was utterly unthinkable . . . The soul longed and craved to sacrifice his puny frame for the love of his Lord and to take his flight to the abode of the Beloved. Now the golden opportunity had offered itself . . . His prolonged and unexampled fortitude served increasingly to throw into relief the striking contrast between his own noble vision and the Farrásh-báshí's base pattern of thought.

Far from being grieved and shaken, how jubilant, how thrilled, how relaxed must have felt his soul when the Farrásh-báshí in his utter despair and bewilderment signalled once again to fire.

And this time in a flash of a second the body of 'Alí-Akbar, blasted into bits amidst a tremendous burst of fire and smoke, flew sky-high, then came down from heaven like a swarm of tiny meteors, accompanied by a shower of crimson droplets, to be scattered far and wide all over the square.

The Governor ordered that the fragments of his body should be left exposed until sunset, that they might be trampled upon by men and animals.

This tragic martyrdom came as a shattering blow to the entire body of the early believers, particularly to his unfortunate wife. Her grief knew no bounds as she continued to weep and wail, and to beat her head.[22]

In contrast to this heroism there were those who were so afraid of being identified with the Faith that they would literally run away from the followers of Bahá'u'lláh.

Ḥájí Muḥammad-Ṭáhir-i-Málmírí, in his detailed 'History of the Faith in the Province of Yazd'* has recounted this interesting story concerning a certain Siyyid Abu'l-Qásim-i-Bayḍá:

Áqá Siyyid Abu'l-Qásim was a merchant by profession and a gifted poet. His pen-name was Bayḍá [Shining]. He was a well-respected citizen who used to associate with merchants and dignitaries of the city. He was a staunch Muslim, very truthful and honest, and a grandson of Ḥájí Mullá Riḍá, a well-known Rawḍih-Khán (professional narrator of

* Not to be confused with the 'History of the Martyrs of Yazd' by the same author.

the tragedies of Karbilá where Imám Ḥusayn was martyred) who used to live in the district of Málamír and was a neighbour of this servant.* When Siyyid Abu'l-Qásim wanted to visit his grandfather he had to pass by the house of this servant. Because our house was known as the house of the Bábís, he was so frightened to approach it that he used to run with tremendous speed and pass it by as quickly as possible so as not to be affected by its evil influence. Eventually this man embraced the Faith, used to attend meetings in the house and often talked about his earlier days, saying, 'Every time I passed by this house my whole being would so tremble that during the whole day I felt disturbed and shaken.'[23]

A somewhat similar story is recounted by Ḥájí Mírzá Ḥaydar-'Alí when he was staying at a *khán*† with some believers in one of the towns of Persia. He describes how two people knocked on his door at night out of curiosity to find out about the beliefs of the Bahá'ís. After some hours of talking one of them accepted the Faith. This is the story as he writes it:

One of them embraced the Faith. The other one who was staying in the same *khán* took the *Kitáb-i-Íqán* to his room so that he might learn about the Cause. He told me the story himself in these words:

'In the evening I sat down and began to read. After a while I was overtaken by fear in case someone would walk in and find out that this was the book of the Bábís,‡ then my life and all my possessions would be gone with the wind. So I locked the door and continued to read the book. Then I thought that as it was early in the evening, if someone came and found that I had locked the room so early he would think that since you people were in the *khán*, the

* Ḥájí Muḥammad-Ṭáhir-i-Málmírí.

† Eastern inn with a large court-yard.

‡ For a long time the Bahá'ís have been referred to as Bábís by the Persians. Even now some still confuse the two.

reason for my locking the door was that I was reading the book of the Bábís. At this time I decided to go to bed and sleep. Then I began to think that if anyone discovered that I had gone to bed so early, he would become certain that the Bábís had left their book with me and therefore I had gone to bed early that I might arise later at night and read it peacefully. To be concise, at last I took the book into the stable and placed it in the manger. I returned to my room and began to meditate, wondering how I could read this book after all . . .'

At this point, he decided to read the *Qur'án* and pray. He continued:

'In a state of helplessness, humility and self-effacement I turned my heart to God, the Knower, the Merciful. I begged Him to show me the way to salvation and confer upon me the water of life. Suddenly it flashed across my mind that I was distressed, alarmed, and trembling with fear merely because I was trying to read or keep this book. How fearless and stout-hearted must have been its Author, from Whose heart, tongue and pen this book had come into being. To produce it was a miracle. How potent is His influence that He has filled the hearts of many people with such courage and strength as to welcome martyrdom.'[24]

Ḥájí Mírzá Ḥaydar-'Alí goes on to describe how this man embraced the Faith and acquired such courage that whenever he had time during his business hours he used to make copies of the *Kitáb-i-Íqán* in public and teach the people openly.

These incidents, common in those days, clearly illustrate that followers of the Báb and Bahá'u'lláh did not enter the Faith because of its novelty, or for any personal gain or sensational reason. This Cause was baptized in the fire of adversity and martyrdom and the heroic souls who embraced it had truly recognized its glory and were transformed into a new and wonderful creation.

In one of His Tablets[25] Bahá'u'lláh explains that the persecutions heaped on the believers, the opposition of the clergy and the perversity of the masses, all served to restrain unworthy souls from entering the Cause of God. In that same Tablet, He calls on His followers to appreciate the special bounties of this unique period in which only a few are chosen. For, when His Faith is fully established throughout the world, He states, men without merit will claim allegiance to it.

When Bahá'u'lláh was in Baghdád a certain Mírzá Muḥíṭ-i-Kirmání, a Shaykhí who had attained the presence of the Báb and whose attitude towards the Faith was that of concealed opposition, sent a message to Bahá'u'lláh through Prince Kayván Mírzá. He requested a confidential interview with Bahá'u'lláh late at night so that no one except the Prince would know about it. The reason given for this secrecy was that, should the meeting become public knowledge, the position of Mírzá Muḥíṭ in the Muslim community would be undermined. Bahá'u'lláh asked the Prince to share with him two lines of an ode He had composed while in Kurdistán, setting forth the conditions for those who wish to partake of His glory. These are the lines:

> If thine aim be to cherish thy life, approach not our court; but if sacrifice be thy heart's desire, come and let others come with thee. For such is the way of Faith, if in thy heart thou seekest reunion with Bahá; shouldst thou refuse to tread this path, why trouble us? Begone!

Bahá'u'lláh is reported to have said to the Prince, 'If he be willing, he will openly and unreservedly hasten to meet Me; if not I refuse to see him.'[26]

When Mírzá Muḥíṭ heard this, he did not find the courage to go and meet Bahá'u'lláh. A few days later he died.

Bahá'u'lláh touches upon several other subjects and reveals many mysteries in the *Mathnaví* which are beyond the scope of this work. Indeed this soul-stirring poem is a marvellous depository of divine wisdom, which it is impossible to exhaust.

3

The Exile to Adrianople

When we look at the circumstances which had led the Ottoman Government to remove Bahá'u'lláh from Baghdád, we recall the outright refusal of that Government to hand Bahá'u'lláh over to the Persian authorities and its reluctance to banish Him from Baghdád. When 'Abdu'l-Bahá was in the Garden of Riḍván prior to His departure for Constantinople, He wrote a letter to a relative in Persia in which He said that after bringing much pressure to bear upon the Ottoman Government, the Persian Ambassador Ḥájí Mírzá Ḥusayn Khán became so frustrated by the Sublime Porte that he cut his relationships with his friends in government circles, stayed at home for seven days and refused to see any of the Sulṭán's ministers. At last 'Álí Páshá,* a very close friend of his, found no alternative but to give in and order the removal of Bahá'u'lláh from Baghdád.

Now that Bahá'u'lláh was in Constantinople, the Persian Ambassador was making a desperate bid to misrepresent Him to the authorities and thereby secure their support for banishing Him further. The day after Bahá'u'lláh's arrival in Constantinople, the Ambassador sent Prince Shujá'u'd-Dawlih and Ḥájí Mírzá Ḥasan-i-Ṣafá, the two most prominent men in his circle, to call on Bahá'u'lláh on his behalf. He expected that Bahá'u'lláh would return the call and see him in person, but he soon found that this was not going to happen. In those days it was customary for prominent guests of the Government, soon after their arrival in the capital, to call upon the Shaykhu'l-Islám,†

* The Grand Vizir of the Sulṭán. See p. 413.

† The highest religious dignitary of the Islamic community.

the Prime Minister and other high-ranking officials. It was on the occasion of these visits that people solicited all kinds of favours, made deals and secured the support of the authorities for themselves. Bahá'u'lláh refused to do this and did not even return the visits of some of the Sulṭán's ministers who had already called on him to pay their respects.

Kamál Pá<u>sh</u>á and a few others went so far as to remind Him of this custom. Bahá'u'lláh responded by saying that He was aware of the practice but had no demands to make of anyone nor did He require favours from them; therefore there was no reason for Him to call. Bahá'u'lláh refers to this in the *Súriy-i-Mulúk* in these words:

> Call Thou to remembrance Thine arrival in the City (Constantinople), how the Ministers of the Sulṭán thought Thee to be unacquainted with their laws and regulations, and believed Thee to be one of the ignorant. Say: Yes, by My Lord! I am ignorant of all things except what God hath, through His bountiful favour, been pleased to teach Me. To this We assuredly testify, and unhesitatingly confess it.
>
> Say: If the laws and regulations to which ye cleave be of your own making, We will, in no wise, follow them. Thus have I been instructed by Him Who is the All-Wise, the All-Informed. Such hath been My way in the past, and such will it remain in the future, through the power of God and His might.[1]

This attitude of detachment played into the hands of the Persian Ambassador who decided to introduce Bahá'u'lláh to the Sublime Porte as one who was arrogant and proud, considering Himself subject to no law. The Ambassador did this mainly through the influence of Ḥájí Mírzá Ḥasan-i-Ṣafá. This was a man of learning who had travelled widely in Africa and Asia and had been living in Constantinople at the time that Ḥájí Mírzá Ḥusayn <u>Kh</u>án arrived there as Ambassador. He became an intimate friend of the Ambassador and was one of his closest confidants. Ḥájí Mírzá Ḥasan was also one of the leading figures among the Ṣúfís of Constantinople and was highly respected in government circles, as in those days there was much regard for the Ṣúfís in the country.

During Bahá'u'lláh's sojourn in Constantinople Ḥájí Mírzá Ḥasan visited Him more than once. He became aware of Bahá'u'lláh's innate knowledge and when in His presence showed much respect and humility; but outside he worked against Him. Knowing that his word carried much weight at the Sublime Porte, the Persian Ambassador used Ḥájí Mírzá Ḥasan as a tool to circulate unfounded reports among the authorities about Bahá'u'lláh's conduct and His aspirations. Indeed this man assisted the Ambassador ably in his campaign to discredit Bahá'u'lláh and misrepresent His Cause.

At last the machinations of Mírzá Ḥusayn Khán yielded their fruit. 'Álí Páshá, the Prime Minister, presented a report to the Sulṭán informing him of the Persian Government's request that Bahá'u'lláh be banished either to Boursa or Adrianople. He asked the Sulṭán's approval for banishment to Adrianople and suggested that an allowance of 5,000 qurúsh per month be given to Bahá'u'lláh for subsistence, adding that during His stay in Constantinople He had been a guest of the Government. He also enclosed the list* of all those who had accompanied Him from Baghdád to Constantinople.

Immediately upon receipt of this report the Sulṭán endorsed these measures and the edict was issued the following day. Shoghi Effendi has summarized the events leading to Bahá'u'lláh's further banishment in these words:

> No less a personage than the highly-respected brother-in-law of the Ṣadr-i-A'ẓam was commissioned to apprise the Captive of the edict pronounced against Him—an edict which evinced a virtual coalition of the Turkish and Persian imperial governments against a common adversary, and which in the end brought such tragic consequences upon the Sultanate, the Caliphate and the Qájár dynasty. Refused an

* See pp. 5–6.

audience by Bahá'u'lláh that envoy had to content himself with a presentation of his puerile observations and trivial arguments to 'Abdu'l-Bahá and Áqáy-i-Kalím, who were delegated to see him, and whom he informed that, after three days, he would return to receive the answer to the order he had been bidden to transmit.

That same day a Tablet, severely condemnatory in tone, was revealed by Bahá'u'lláh, was entrusted by Him, in a sealed envelope, on the following morning, to Shamsí Big, who was instructed to deliver it into the hands of 'Álí Páshá, and to say that it was sent down from God. 'I know not what that letter contained,' Shamsí Big subsequently informed Áqáy-i-Kalím, 'for no sooner had the Grand Vizir perused it than he turned the colour of a corpse, and remarked: "It is as if the King of Kings were issuing his behest to his humblest vassal king and regulating his conduct." So grievous was his condition that I backed out of his presence.' 'Whatever action,' Bahá'u'lláh, commenting on the effect that Tablet had produced, is reported to have stated, 'the ministers of the Sulṭán took against Us, after having become acquainted with its contents, cannot be regarded as unjustifiable. The acts they committed before its perusal, however, can have no justification.'

That Tablet, according to Nabíl, was of considerable length, opened with words directed to the sovereign himself, severely censured his ministers, exposed their immaturity and incompetence, and included passages in which the ministers themselves were addressed, in which they were boldly challenged, and sternly admonished not to pride themselves on their worldly possessions, nor foolishly seek the riches of which time would inexorably rob them.

Bahá'u'lláh was on the eve of His departure, which followed almost immediately upon the promulgation of the edict of His banishment, when in a last and memorable interview with the aforementioned Ḥájí Mírzá Ḥasan-i-Ṣafá, He sent the following message to the Persian Ambassador: 'What did it profit thee, and such as are like thee, to slay, year after year, so many of the oppressed, and to inflict upon them manifold afflictions, when they have increased a hundredfold, and ye find yourselves in complete bewilderment, knowing not how to relieve your minds of this oppressive thought . . . His Cause transcends any and every plan ye devise. Know this much: Were all the governments on earth to unite and take My life and the lives of all who bear this Name, this Divine Fire would never be quenched. His Cause will rather encompass all the kings of the earth, nay all that hath been created from water and clay . . . Whatever may befall Us, great shall be our gain, and manifest the loss wherewith they shall be afflicted.[2]

The night before His departure for Adrianople Bahá'u'lláh directed Nabíl-i-A'ẓam* and Mírzá Áqá surnamed Muníb † to travel to Persia in order to disseminate the news of Bahá'u'lláh among the Bábís, to teach them the Faith and help them to recognize His station. Others whom He dismissed from His presence that evening were Áqá Muḥammad-Báqir-i-Káshání, Khayyáṭ-Báshíy-i-Káshání, Áqá Ḥusayn-i-Naráqí, Mír Muḥammad-i-Mukárí,‡ and Áqá Siyyid Ḥusayn-i-Káshání. The last-named had a great sense of humour and at times he used to come into the presence of Bahá'u'lláh and make Him laugh with some amusing remark.

That evening witnessed a great commotion. The thought of separation from their Beloved plunged them into such grief that all the companions of Bahá'u'lláh were moved to tears. Knowing the vital need for someone in Constantinople to serve as a channel of communication for the believers in Persia and assist those who passed through the city, Bahá'u'lláh arranged for Áqá Muḥammad-'Alíy-i-Ṣabbágh of Yazd to remain there. This believer stayed for about two years in Constantinople until others were able to take over his work. He then proceeded to Adrianople where he joined the exiles and was once again close to his Lord.

On the day Bahá'u'lláh was to leave Constantinople, a

* See vol. I, pp. 202–6.
† ibid. pp. 283–7.
‡ See chapter 14.

devoted believer by the name of Mírzá Muṣṭafá arrived. He was a native of Naráq, and had embraced the Faith of the Báb in the early days. During Bahá'u'lláh's sojourn in 'Iráq he had visited that country, and attained His presence. He had remained there for some time, and beheld the glory of his Lord which was as yet unrevealed to the eyes of men. In Constantinople he had the opportunity to meet Him only once, when Bahá'u'lláh summoned him and directed him to return to Persia and engage in teaching His Cause. He went to Ádhirbáyján. The following are the words of 'Abdu'l-Bahá concerning this heroic soul:

> When Mírzá Muṣṭafá reached Ádhirbáyján, he began to spread the Faith. Day and night he remained in a state of prayer, and there in Tabríz he drank of a brimming cup. His fervour increased, his teaching raised a tumult. Then the eminent scholar, the renowned Shaykh Aḥmad-i-Khurásání, came to Ádhirbáyján and the two of them joined forces. The result was such overwhelming spiritual fire that they taught the Faith openly and publicly and the people of Tabríz rose up in wrath.
>
> The farráshes hunted them down, and caught Mírzá Muṣṭafá. But then the oppressors said, 'Mírzá Muṣṭafá had two long locks of hair. This cannot be the right man.' At once, Mírzá Muṣṭafá took off his hat and down fell the locks of hair. 'Behold!' he told them. 'I am the one.' They arrested him then. They tortured him and Shaykh Aḥmad until finally, in Tabríz, those two great men drained the cup of death and, martyred, hastened away to the Supreme Horizon.
>
> At the place where they were to be killed, Mírzá Muṣṭafá cried out: 'Kill me first, kill me before Shaykh Aḥmad, that I may not see them shed his blood!'[3]

It was customary at the time of execution for the victim to turn his face towards the Qiblih* of Islám. But Mírzá Muṣṭafá

* The point of adoration, the direction towards which the faithful turn at the time of devotion and prayers. For the followers of Muḥammad, this is the Ka'bah at Mecca. For Bahá'ís, it was the Person of Bahá'u'lláh during His lifetime, and since His passing it has been the Shrine of Bahá'u'lláh outside 'Akká.

turned towards Adrianople. He was reminded to face the Qiblih but he refused to do so. He said 'This is the true Qiblih,' and shouted 'Yá-Bahá'u'l-Abhá'.*

Another person who laid down his life in the path of God on that occasion was Mullá 'Alí-Naqíy-i-Ní<u>sh</u>ápúrí. These three believers were beheaded by the order of Sardár 'Azíz <u>Kh</u>án, the governor of Tabríz, in the same square in which the Báb had been martyred. This was in 1283 A.H. (A.D. 1866–67). Bahá'u'lláh revealed many Tablets for Mírzá Muṣṭafá and referred to his martyrdom in some of His Writings.† After the martyrdom of Mírzá Muṣṭafá, Bahá'u'lláh renamed his son after the father. This son and his mother were given the honour of serving in the household of Bahá'u'lláh in 'Akká. But after the ascension of Bahá'u'lláh, Mírzá Muṣṭafá broke His Covenant and rebelled against 'Abdu'l-Bahá.

In one of the coldest December months that Turkey had seen for years, Bahá'u'lláh and His family—including His two faithful brothers, Mírzá Músá, entitled Áqáy-i-Kalím, and Mírzá Muḥammad-Qulí, together with Mírzá Yaḥyá‡—set out on their journey to the city of Adrianople. The officer commissioned to take charge of the journey was 'Alí Big Yúz-Bá<u>sh</u>í. According to a statement by Mírzá Áqá Ján, it appears that Bahá'u'lláh was accompanied by twelve of His companions.[4] Among them was the notorious Siyyid Muḥammad-i-Iṣfahání whose evil spirit was increasingly casting its shadow upon the exiles. Through his satanic influence he brought much pain and anguish to their hearts and created severe tests and trials for them.

In the *Súriy-i-Mulúk*, addressing Sulṭán 'Abdu'l-'Azíz, Bahá'u'lláh speaks of His arrival in the city of Constantinople

* Literally 'O Thou the Glory of the Most Glorious', an invocation, the Greatest Name of God.

† For instance, see *Epistle to the Son of the Wolf*, pp. 72–3.

‡ On leaving Bag<u>h</u>dád, he had acquired a passport in the name of Mírzá 'Alí, a newly assumed name. During his sojourn in Adrianople and later in Cyprus, the authorities referred to him by this name.

in conspicuous glory and His departure 'with an abasement with which no abasement on earth can compare'.[5] He also describes the manner in which He and His loved ones were banished to Adrianople and the sufferings they were made to endure on their way to that city and on their arrival there. These are some of His words: 'Neither My family, nor those who accompanied Me, had the necessary raiment to protect them from the cold in that freezing weather.' 'The eyes of Our enemies wept over Us, and beyond them those of every discerning person.'[6]

The circumstances of Bahá'u'lláh's banishment were tragic as well as humiliating. The authorities did not give adequate time to Bahá'u'lláh and His party to prepare themselves for this long and hazardous journey. The weather was unusually cold, many rivers were frozen and the only way to obtain water on the journey was by lighting a fire and melting ice. The members of the party, which included women and children, were inadequately clad, yet some of them were made to ride in wagons normally used for carrying goods while others had to ride on animals. Of this journey Shoghi Effendi writes:

> Travelling through rain and storm, at times even making night marches, the weary travellers, after brief halts at Kúchik-Chakmachih, Búyúk-Chakmachih, Salvarí, Birkás, and Bábá-Ískí, arrived at their destination, on the first of Rajab 1280 A.H. (December 12, 1863), and were lodged in the Khán-i-'Arab, a two-storey caravanserai, near the house of 'Izzat-Áqá. Three days later, Bahá'u'lláh and His family were consigned to a house suitable only for summer habitation, in the Murádíyyih quarter, near Takyiy-i-Mawlaví, and were moved again, after a week, to another house, in the vicinity of a mosque in that same neighbourhood. About six months later they transferred to more commodious quarters, known as the house of Amru'lláh (House of God's command) situated on the northern side of the mosque of Sulṭán Salím.[7]

The two houses in Murádíyyih are now both completely demolished. An eye-witness has described the second house as a large mansion with eighteen rooms and a Turkish bath. Soon after their arrival the companions of Bahá'u'lláh found accommodation elsewhere and, as instructed by Him, engaged in trades and professions in the city.

It was not long after Bahá'u'lláh's arrival in Adrianople that its inhabitants became aware of His greatness and were deeply impressed by His genuine love and exalted character. Their leaders, including the Governor of the city and other high-ranking officials, as well as men of culture and learning, were drawn to Him and soon discovered that He was the source of all knowledge and the embodiment of virtues. Some of these people earnestly sought His presence, sat at His feet and received spiritual enlightenment from Him. Such were the marks of honour and esteem shown to Bahá'u'lláh that on occasions when He walked in the streets and bazaars the people spontaneously stood and bowed before Him. Their veneration for Him was profound and whole-hearted. Among the people He was referred to as 'Shaykh Effendi', a designation which carried with it great prestige at the time.

In Adrianople Bahá'u'lláh did not appear in public as much as He had done in Baghdád. Instead He allowed 'Abdu'l-Bahá to do this for Him. But He did occasionally visit the mosques of Murádíyyih and Sulṭán Salím where some of the learned and devout came in contact with Him, recognized His greatness and became His admirers. This is one of the remarkable features of the life of Bahá'u'lláh—that although the powerful machinery of a despotic and tyrannical government was directed against Him, bringing about untold personal suffering and persecutions, He yet evinced such glory and imparted such love that a great many people were magnetized by Him and were deeply affected by His peerless and exalted character. That a prisoner and an exile could exert such abiding influence upon men both high and low is one of the evidences of His Divine power and a sign of His authority as the Supreme Manifestation of God.

In spite of the hardships and rigours of yet another exile, the outpourings of the Revelation of Bahá'u'lláh continued unabated in Adrianople. In one of his writings dated 17th Jamádí 1281 A.H. (19 October 1864), Mírzá Áqá Ján has testified that from the days of 'Iráq up to that day, Tablets had been sent down successively and unceasingly from the heaven of the Will of God.[8] This process acquired still greater momentum in Adrianople. From the tone of these Tablets it became clear that the Revelation of Bahá'u'lláh had already entered a new phase and that He, who in previous years had only alluded to His station, was now openly summoning the believers to Himself as the Supreme Manifestation of God.

4

Súriy-i-Aṣḥáb

One of the early Tablets revealed in Adrianople is the *Súriy-i-Aṣḥáb* (Súrih of Companions). This Tablet played a significant role in the unveiling of the station of Bahá'u'lláh to the Bábís of Persia. It is a lengthy Tablet in Arabic and is addressed to Mírzá Áqáy-i-Muníb.* Bahá'u'lláh addresses the recipient of this Tablet as Ḥabíb (Friend) and in one instance He mentions Muníb by name. This appears to have led some scholars of the Faith to state that this Tablet was revealed for Mírzá Ḥabíb-i-Marág͟hi'í and that Muníb was also addressed in it. A careful study of the Tablet and other historical facts, however, make it clear beyond doubt that it was revealed for Mírzá Áqáy-i-Muníb whom He addressed as Ḥabíb. When Jináb-i-Muníb received this important Tablet, He arose with wisdom and courage to disclose the station of Bahá'u'lláh to those Bábís whom he considered faithful.

In order to appreciate the significance of the *Súriy-i-Aṣḥáb* and other early Tablets revealed in Adrianople, one must become more familiar with the state of the Bábí Community in Persia before and after the Declaration of Bahá'u'lláh. Knowledge of this background is helpful in acquiring a better insight into the writings of Bahá'u'lláh during this period.

Ever since the days of Bahá'u'lláh in Bag͟hdád, the great majority of believers in Persia had increasingly turned to Him as the focal point of the Bábí community. To Him they went for help and enlightenment and from Him received their guidance. His spiritual ascendancy and influence were so strikingly manifest that even the enemies of the Cause had felt their force.

* See vol. I, pp. 283–7 for further information about him.

For instance, as we have already learned, a congregation of the divines of Shí'ah Islám in 'Iráq demanded the performance of a miracle from Him, even though at that stage He had not claimed a station for Himself. It is clearly demonstrated that Bahá'u'lláh alone was the fountain-head of spiritual potency and the source of guidance for the Bábí community after the martyrdom of the Báb in 1850.

Many believers who had attained His presence in Baghdád had recognized His station while His glory was still wrapped within a 'myriad veils of light'.[1] Others had been forcefully struck by the manifold evidences of His supreme authority and innate knowledge. During the ten years of Bahá'u'lláh's sojourn in 'Iráq, these believers, on their return to their native lands, had described His greatness to their fellow believers and each according to his understanding extolled His virtues and powers. Added to these personal accounts of Bahá'u'lláh, numerous Tablets and Books streaming from His pen had enabled the majority of the believers to appreciate the unique and exalted position that He held within the community.

The State of the Bábí Community

But alas that human beings are not always sincere or faithful. There were those who were corrupt and egotistical and who longed for leadership. A few such men in various towns in Persia made mischief among the believers. They considered themselves followers of the Báb, but acted against His commandments and exhortations. Some of them had attained the presence of Bahá'u'lláh, only to become jealous of His rising prestige and authority. These men congregated around Mírzá Yaḥyá not because he had any outstanding qualities, nor because they particularly liked him, but rather because of their opposition to Bahá'u'lláh. For instance, Siyyid Muḥammad-i-Iṣfahání had no doubt concerning Mírzá Yaḥyá's weakness and superficial knowledge. Many times had he defeated Mírzá Yaḥyá in the course of an argument. The latter had always grown angry on these occasions. Once, before the days of Adrianople, he was so irritated by Siyyid Muḥammad's belittling of him that he took his complaint to Bahá'u'lláh Who called Siyyid Muḥammad, rebuked him for his behaviour and instructed him to leave Mírzá Yaḥyá alone.

To cite another example: once Shaykh Salmán, the devoted servant of Bahá'u'lláh and entitled by Him 'The Messenger of the Merciful',* asked Mírzá Yaḥyá to explain the meaning of a certain poem of Sa'dí. Mírzá Yaḥyá complied with this request and Shaykh Salmán received his reply. Upon reading the explanation, Siyyid Muḥammad-i-Iṣfahání reported to Bahá'u'lláh that the reply was inadequate and shallow and requested Him to stop Shaykh Salmán from taking such misleading statements to Persia. Furthermore, Siyyid Muḥammad, accompanied by Ḥájí Mírzá Aḥmad-i-Káshání,† went to the house of Áqáy-i-Kalím (Bahá'u'lláh's faithful brother) and there proved to Mírzá Yaḥyá that his explanations were erroneous. Yet from the early days in Baghdád, men such as these were spreading highly complimentary remarks about Mírzá Yaḥyá within the Bábí community in Persia. They circulated unfounded reports about his greatness and claimed that he was the successor to the Báb, that all the Writings of Bahá'u'lláh had emanated from Mírzá Yaḥyá, and that Bahá'u'lláh had usurped his position and forced him to hide himself away. Propaganda such as this always confuses the minds of simple-hearted people, especially when the great majority of them had never known Mírzá Yaḥyá. During the ten years of his sojourn in 'Iráq he had so effectively disguised himself that even a considerable number of believers who had lived there for years did not know him. For instance, when he joined Bahá'u'lláh's party at Mosul, he was able to introduce himself as a stranger, and some of Bahá'u'lláh's companions did not know his real identity. The fact that he was the nominee of the Báb was sufficient for the

* See vol. I, pp. 109–13.

† One of the unfaithful who became a follower of Mírzá Yaḥyá. See chapter 6.

rank and file of the believers to attach great importance to him.

However, most Bábís who had been able to meet Mírzá Yaḥyá were struck by his ignorance and cowardice. These men had no doubt about the station of Bahá'u'lláh and were convinced that Mírzá Yaḥyá was merely a figure-head appointed by the Báb for the purpose of diverting attention from Bahá'u'lláh. But those who had not attained the presence of Bahá'u'lláh were often confused by rumours and controversy among the Bábís concerning the position of Mírzá Yaḥyá.

Ḥájí Mírzá Ḥaydar-'Alí has left to posterity a vivid picture of the Bábí community in certain parts of Persia during the latter part of Bahá'u'lláh's sojourn in Baghdád, soon after the revelation of the *Kitáb-i-Íqán*. This account illustrates the turmoil and agitation created by Mírzá Yaḥyá's supporters and draws attention to their misrepresentations. These are his words as he recalls the early days of his conversion to the Bábí Faith:

> Although I was persecuted several times in Iṣfahán and suffered great hardships and ill-treatment, I was happy, on fire with the Faith, attracted and in love with the Writings and Tablets of the Báb, especially the Persian Bayán. I made two copies of this Book. The more I read it the more eager I became to read further. In those days everyone was convinced that the coming of 'Him Whom God shall make manifest' was at hand. I often used to say . . . that if the Dispensation of the Báb . . . were not followed immediately by the Dispensation of 'Him Whom God shall make manifest', then all the writings, tablets and testimonies of the Báb would remain unfulfilled and were useless. I did not have a heart-felt regard for Azal.* I used to remark, 'What is the difference between the hidden Azal and the Hidden Qá'im?† . . .' Furthermore, I regarded his writings to be truly nonsensical,

* Mírzá Yaḥyá. (A.T.)

† It is believed by the majority of Shí'ah Islám that the promised Qá'im is living, but hidden away from the sight of men. So was Mírzá Yaḥyá, who lived in disguise and whose whereabouts nobody knew.

except of course his quotations from the Writings of the Báb which were exalted words. However, I used to be condemned by my own conscience for these thoughts, as I had imagined my own understanding to be above that of other people. Then two holy Tablets from the Blessed Beauty* . . . arrived in honour of Zaynu'l Muqarrabín † and Áqá Muḥammad-'Alíy-i-Tambákú-Furúsh from Iṣfahán. These Tablets captivated me and I became enamoured of the utterances of Bahá'u'lláh.

Later . . . Ḥájí Siyyid Muḥammad, the uncle of the Báb . . . came for a visit to Iṣfahán and brought with him the *Kitáb-i-Íqán*, revealed in answer to his own questions. As a result of reading the *Kitáb-i-Íqán*, I became a thousand times more enchanted with the blessed utterances of the Ancient Beauty.‡ I used to mention quite openly that I regarded Bahá'u'lláh's magnanimity, His unique and incomparable reality, the power of His utterance, the sway of His pen and the persuasiveness of His proofs to be supernatural and the greatest and foremost miracle of all. But some people were not pleased with my views and would intimate to me that the *Kitáb-i-Íqán* had been written by Azal.

Even Mír Muḥammad-'Alíy-i-'Aṭṭár, one of the early believers, called on me and told me in confidence that 'since the Báb has always given the glad-tidings of the coming of "Him Whom God shall make manifest", has not laid down any conditions or specified any time for His advent, has enjoined upon all to accept and acknowledge Him as soon as He reveals Himself, has prohibited investigation, caution or delay [in accepting His Message], has condemned to hell-fire [those who do not recognize Him], has strictly forbidden the seeking of proofs from Him, and has regarded Himself as the servant and forerunner of "Him Whom God shall make manifest", all these have prompted Jináb-i-Bahá § to claim this position for Himself. He has imprisoned Azal and some times has whipped him so that he might answer His questions.

* Bahá'u'lláh. (A.T.)

† See vol. I, p. 25.

‡ Bahá'u'lláh. (A.T.)

§ Bahá'u'lláh. (A.T.)

These answers are recorded by Jináb-i-Bahá and published in His own name. Siyyid Muḥammad* has journeyed twice from Baghdád to Iṣfahán on behalf of Azal and has confidentially told the faithful about his loneliness and the wrongs he has suffered!'

My amazement at hearing this knew no bounds. I stated that it was impossible and I had never heard such nonsense and vain assertions. The words and passages in the *Kitáb-i-Íqán* were of a style easy to apprehend yet impossible to imitate. The words of Azal were neither weighty nor eloquent . . .

Soon I found that I had become well known and the city of Iṣfahán was becoming too small for me, and my friends were avoiding me.[2]

Eventually Ḥájí Mírzá Ḥaydar-'Alí decided to go on a retreat for a period of four months. He took four books with him, the *Qur'án*, the *Mathnaví*,† the *Bayán* and the *Kitáb-i-Íqán*, and went to live in a place away from everyone. He continues his story in these words:

At last I realized that to seclude oneself is a barbaric act and a waste of one's life. In order to acquire the good-pleasure of God and guide the people to Him, one must be self-sacrificing. I was watchful for the advent of the Supreme Manifestation of God, 'Him Whom God shall make manifest'. The hypocrisy, lies and machinations of Mír Muḥammad-'Alí and Siyyid Muḥammad were as clear as the sun to me. Therefore I decided to leave Iṣfahán.

Although I was most eager to attain the presence of the Day-Star of Revelation,‡ I was apprehensive lest my coming in contact with the two hypocrites Siyyid Muḥammad and Mullá Rajab-'Alí,§ who were in Karbilá and Baghdád, might somehow affect my soul and conscience. Therefore for a period of five or six years I travelled around Persia . . . With

* Siyyid Muḥammad-i-Iṣfahání. (A.T.)

† By Jalálí'd-Dín-i-Rúmí.

‡ Bahá'u'lláh. (A.T.)

§ A brother of the second wife of the Báb and a follower of Mírzá Yaḥyá.

great difficulties and hardships I visited many places sometimes on foot, sometimes riding, but I was in the utmost joy. I spoke everywhere about the Revelation of the Báb and gave the glad-tidings that the advent of 'Him Whom God shall make manifest' was at hand. In many towns I was persecuted, beaten and imprisoned . . .

In Shíráz I met Ḥájí Siyyid Muḥammad, the uncle of the Báb, and some other believers . . . They were filled with love for Him and were joyously awaiting the Revelation of 'Him Whom God shall make manifest'. There was no mention of Azal . . . The late Áqá Siyyid 'Abdu'r-Raḥím-i-Iṣfahání had made certain extracts from the *Bayán* and other books of the Báb through which he used to prove that Bahá'u'lláh, exalted be His glory, was the Promised One of the *Bayán*, that Azal was only a name without a reality, like a body without a soul. As a result of such pronouncements Áqá Siyyid 'Abdu'r-Raḥím was denounced by some. He used to give us the following account: 'After the martyrdom of the Báb when Azal had become famous, I travelled from Iṣfahán to Ṭihrán with the express purpose of meeting him. In the bazaar I met Bahá'u'lláh, the Day-Star of Revelation, the Speaker of Sinai . . . the mention of whose name has adorned the Books and Tablets of the Báb. I attained His presence at a time when His glory was hidden behind a myriad veils of light. He asked me if I had come to meet Azal? I answered in the affirmative. I had actually attained the presence of Bahá'u'lláh before this at Badasht. I had recognized His glory and greatness, His uniqueness and magnanimity by the manner in which Quddús and Ṭáhirih used to bow before Him. I also knew the deeds and actions of Azal; nevertheless since he was known as the nominee of the Báb I considered meeting with him as a means of nearness to God. I went, in the company of Bahá'u'lláh, to His house. He asked for tea to be served. Thereupon Azal brought the samovar and served the tea. He was standing in the presence of Bahá'u'lláh, from Whose tongue were flowing the rivers of wisdom and knowledge. After drinking tea, Bahá'u'lláh rose, and turning to Azal said, "He has come to see you", and then went into the inner court of the house. Azal sat down, I bowed and expressed my devotion to him, but he had nothing to say to me.'[3]

The controversy concerning Mírzá Yaḥyá's position lasted for the whole of the Baghdád and Constantinople periods, during which time no one openly challenged his position as the nominee of the Báb, and he always stayed near to Bahá'u'lláh for his own protection. It was after his rebellion against Bahá'u'lláh in Adrianople that any doubt which had hitherto confused the minds of some pure-hearted men was entirely eradicated.

The Declaration of Bahá'u'lláh in the Garden of Riḍván was made only to a few of His companions. The news of this historic event was not communicated to most Bábís until later. The *Súriy-i-Aṣḥáb* and other early Tablets disclosed the station of Bahá'u'lláh clearly and openly. Mírzá Áqáy-i-Muníb shared this important Tablet with many souls. Among them was Ḥájí Mírzá Ḥaydar-'Alí, who describes his feelings when he read this Tablet for the first time in these words:

> . . . I arrived in Ṭihrán at a time that Mírzá Áqáy-i-Munír* . . . was also in the city. The *Súriy-i-Aṣḥáb* had been revealed by the Pen of the Lord of Lords in his honour and was received by him. Since he was aware of my convictions and knew that my heart is turned towards the Ancient Beauty† . . . he called me and, in private, handed me the Tablet to read. With the perusal of each verse, I felt as if a world of exultation, of certitude and insight was created within me. After reading a few verses with great joy, I asked Mírzá Munír whether Siyyid Muḥammad had duped Azal, or Azal duped Siyyid Muḥammad, or whether the two of them had joined together in denying and opposing [Bahá'u'lláh] and had taken a course of obstinacy and hostility [against Him]. On hearing this Mírzá Munír was so delighted that he hugged me and said, 'Their enmity towards the Ancient

* Jináb-i-Muníb. (A.T.)
† Bahá'u'lláh.

Beauty is the cause of their unity. They deceive and mislead each other so that they may arise in enmity [against Him]'.

I was enraptured and set aglow by the *Súriy-i-Aṣḥáb*. It affected me so deeply that even now after the lapse of fifty years at an advanced age when torpidity, stiffness and cold have set in by nature, whenever I read this Tablet or remember my feelings on that day, I find myself filled with such joy that I pass into a state of intoxication and bewilderment.[4]

In the *Súriy-i-Aṣḥáb* Bahá'u'lláh addresses Mírzá Áqáy-i-Muníb with words of love and encouragement. He reminds him of the days when he journeyed with His Lord, when through his insight and devotion he had recognized the truth of His Cause. He bids Muníb thank the Almighty for having raised him from the depths of ignorance and bestowed upon him such favour and bounty. He calls on him, first to detach himself from all that is in heaven and on earth, and then to arise with supreme determination and steadfastness to awaken the people of the *Bayán*.

When we look at the state of the Bábí community at that time, we realize that Bahá'u'lláh had assigned a tremendous task to Muníb and other teachers, namely, the reorientation of that community and its transformation into a world community destined to embrace in the fullness of time the whole of mankind. The declaration of the station of Bahá'u'lláh as 'Him Whom God shall make manifest' in the gatherings of the friends was the most exciting and challenging event since the inception of the Faith two decades before. To counter the unwholesome elements in the Bábí community needed enormous courage, and to guide the pure in heart, great wisdom. Bahá'u'lláh had inspired His emissaries in Persia with these two characteristics.

The following is the testimony of Shaykh Káẓim-i-Samandar* who recounts the excitement and agitation among the believers

* He became an outstanding believer, and one of the Apostles of Bahá'u'lláh. We will refer to him in more detail in future volumes.

when they heard the *Súriy-i-Aṣḥáb* read out to them. He was one of those addressed by Bahá'u'lláh in this Tablet, and therefore Muníb sent him a copy which reached him in his native town of Qazvín.

> . . . He [Muníb] accompanied Bahá'u'lláh from Baghdád and at nights used to carry a lantern in front of Bahá'u'lláh's howdah. He went in His company as far as Constantinople. From there as instructed [by Bahá'u'lláh] he came to Persia. He used to teach the Faith very discreetly, until in Ṭihrán he received the *Súriy-i-Aṣḥáb* which was revealed in his name. By Bahá'u'lláh's permission he gradually removed the veil from the glorious countenance of the Cause. As a result, the trumpet was sounded and a new fervour and enthusiasm were created among the friends. Through earnest striving and by careful investigation each one was enabled to cross this delicate Ṣiráṭ.*
>
> When a copy of this Tablet (in which, among others, this insignificant servant is mentioned) reached the town of Qazvín, it precipitated a great upheaval and created a severe convulsion [among the community]. Several meetings for explanation and clarification were arranged. After discussions, talks, investigations and reference to the Holy Writings, each one of the community, somehow in some way, through the bounty of God was guided [to the Truth] and reached the stage of steadfastness.[5]

Through the creative influence of the *Súriy-i-Aṣḥáb* and other Tablets revealed in this period, and through the dedicated labours of some outstanding teachers of the Faith, the community throughout Persia was gradually cleansed from the ills which Mírzá Yaḥyá and his supporters had inflicted upon it.

* Literally 'road'. It is believed in Islám that on the Day of Judgement a very long bridge will be established and only those who are able to cross it will be saved. This bridge, according to tradition, is sharper than a sword, hotter than fire and thinner than a hair. All this signifies that when the Supreme Manifestation of God appears men will be severely tested and only those who pass the tests will attain to His glory. (A.T.)

It took much time and effort on the part of Bahá'u'lláh's valiant heroes until Mírzá Yaḥyá's satanic influence, his misrepresentations, falsehoods and calumnies, which had polluted the minds of the Bábí community for more than ten years, were eradicated. This process, begun in 1864, took two to three years, during which time the great majority of the Bábís in Persia joined the community of the Most Great Name.

Ḥájí Mírzá Ḥaydar-'Alí has made an interesting observation on the number of Bábís who entered the Cause of Bahá'u'lláh. He explains that Muḥammad and the Holy Imáms guided and nourished the nation of Islám for 260 lunar years* so that it might bring forth its fruit through the appearance of the Qá'im, the Promised One. After 1260 years the Báb, who was the fruit of Islám, appeared and yet only approximately one out of every hundred thousand Muslims entered His Faith and followed Him. In contrast to this the Báb guided the people of the *Bayán* for six years. He constantly gave the glad-tidings of the appearance of 'Him Whom God shall make manifest', prepared His followers for His coming, focused their attention on His greatness and glory, sowed the seed of His love in their hearts and watered it with the flow of His words. Consequently, when Bahá'u'lláh manifested His Cause, about ninety-nine per cent of the Bábí community recognized Him and embraced His Cause. Only one per cent through their selfish ambitions withheld themselves from His glory.

The mission of Muníb and other teachers whom Bahá'u'lláh sent to Persia during the early years of His sojourn in Adrianople was primarily to teach the members of the Bábí community. The *Súriy-i-Aṣḥáb* itself is also mainly directed towards the

* After the death of Muḥammad the Imáms were the spiritual governors of the Faith of Islám and elucidated its teachings. The last Imám died in the year 260 A.H. According to Bahá'í belief, a verse of the *Qur'án* anticipated that the promised Qá'im would appear a thousand years after this date, i.e. in 1260 A.H. (A.D. 1844). 'He governeth the Cause [of God] from heaven to earth; hereafter shall It return to Him for one day, whose length shall be a thousand years of those which you compute.' *Qur'án*, xxxii. 5.

Bábís, and Bahá'u'lláh has addressed several of them by name in this Tablet. In it He unveils the glory of His station and clearly proclaims Himself as the Supreme Manifestation of God whose advent the Báb had foretold. He identifies His person with the prophecy of the Báb concerning the year nine,* and states that through His Revelation the trumpet-blast † has been sounded. He calls on Muníb to proclaim these glad-tidings with courage and faith.

In this Tablet, Bahá'u'lláh explains to the people of the *Bayán* ‡ that He, in essence, is the same Reality as the Báb, and that the same Truth has been manifested again. He admonishes them for their blindness in not recognizing Him the second time, rebukes them for their failure to perceive the creativeness and potency of the Words revealed by Him, notwithstanding their claim that the Words of the Báb constituted the proof of the authenticity of His Message, and warns them that as long as they rejected His Revelation, they would be rejecting all the Revelations of the past including that of the Báb.

The utterances of Bahá'u'lláh reach their climax when He describes the greatness of His Revelation. The beauty and majesty of His words as He glorifies His own station are beyond description. Indeed the perusal of these passages in the original language is bound to ignite a fire in the heart of any sincere and pure-hearted soul, who will testify that no man, however great, can utter such words of consummate power and exalted character.

In peerless language Bahá'u'lláh proclaims that the Sun of His Revelation is shining in the midmost heart of creation, shedding its rays upon the whole world, but the blind are unable to appreciate it. He declares Himself as the sovereign

* 1852–3, the year of the birth of the Revelation of Bahá'u'lláh in the Síyáh-Chál of Ṭihrán. See vol. I, chapter 1.

† The sounding of two trumpet-blasts is prophesied in Islám as one of the signs of the Day of Judgement. The prophecy is interpreted as the advent of the Manifestations of the Báb and Bahá'u'lláh.

‡ Followers of the Báb.

Lord of all mankind and the Manifestation of God Himself, announces His establishment upon the throne of glory, affirms that no one is capable of undermining His sovereignty, states that the universe is but a handful of dust in His estimation, asserts that one word uttered by Him is sweeter than all that is revealed in the kingdoms of earth and heaven, and praises the true believers who attain His presence and witness the Revelation of His Words.

Since the full text of the *Súriy-i-Aṣḥáb* is not as yet translated into English it is not possible to put into words those exalted passages which Bahá'u'lláh has revealed, nor is it easy to convey their import in a befitting manner. Further, the unfamiliarity of Western readers with the terminology used by the Báb and Bahá'u'lláh makes this task more difficult still. The statements so far made are only poor attempts at describing some of the utterances of Bahá'u'lláh in this Tablet concerning the greatness of His Revelation.

The Station of Bahá'u'lláh

There are innumerable Tablets in which Bahá'u'lláh has proclaimed His station in similar terms. Some passages from these are translated into English by Shoghi Effendi, the Guardian of the Bahá'í Faith, and we may do well at this juncture to quote a few.

> He it is [Bahá'u'lláh] Who in the Old Testament hath been named Jehovah, Who in the Gospel hath been designated as the Spirit of Truth, and in the Qur'án acclaimed as the Great Announcement.

> But for Him no Divine Messenger would have been invested with the robe of prophethood, nor would any of the sacred scriptures have been revealed. To this bear witness all created things.

> The word which the one true God uttereth in this day,

though that word be the most familiar and commonplace of terms, is invested with supreme, with unique distinction.

The generality of mankind is still immature. Had it acquired sufficient capacity We would have bestowed upon it so great a measure of Our knowledge that all who dwell on earth and in heaven would have found themselves, by virtue of the grace streaming from Our pen, completely independent of all knowledge save the knowledge of God, and would have been securely established upon the throne of abiding tranquillity.

The Pen of Holiness, I solemnly affirm before God, hath writ upon My snow-white brow and in characters of effulgent glory these glowing, these musk-scented and holy words: 'Behold ye that dwell on earth, and ye denizens of heaven, bear witness, He in truth is your Well-Beloved. He it is Whose like the world of creation hath not seen, He Whose ravishing beauty hath delighted the eye of God, the Ordainer, the All-Powerful, the Incomparable!'

Naught is seen in My temple but the Temple of God, and in My beauty but His Beauty, and in My being but His Being, and in My self but His Self, and in My movement but His Movement, and in My acquiescence but His Acquiescence, and in My pen but His Pen, the Mighty, the All-Praised. There hath not been in My soul but the Truth, and in Myself naught could be seen but God.

The Holy Spirit Itself hath been generated through the agency of a single letter revealed by this Most Great Spirit, if ye be of them that comprehend . . .

Within the treasury of Our Wisdom there lies unrevealed a knowledge, one word of which, if we chose to divulge it to mankind, would cause every human being to recognize the Manifestation of God and to acknowledge His omniscience, would enable every one to discover the secrets of all the sciences, and to attain so high a station as to find himself wholly independent of all past and future learning. Other knowledges We do as well possess, not a single letter of which We can disclose, nor do We find humanity able to hear even the barest reference to their meaning. Thus have We informed you of the knowledge of God, the All-Knowing, the All-Wise.[6]

These statements of Bahá'u'lláh can be appreciated only by those who have recognized His station and are fully convinced that the Manifestation of God alone represents the Godhead in this World. He reveals God in every aspect and therefore stands far above the world of humanity. There is no comparison between the Creator and the created. Indeed, the world of being is as utter nothingness compared with the glory of the Manifestation of God. He and He alone can sing His own praise and extol His own virtues. Beyond Him, no one merits to be glorified. For the station of man is that of servitude and as such he is not worthy of mention when face to face with the Manifestation of the power and majesty of God. In the same way that the colours, the beauty and the life of all created things are dependent upon the rays of the sun, man's goodness and virtues all come to light as a result of the appearance of the Manifestation of God.

Although the Revelation of Bahá'u'lláh is immeasurably great and His station infinitely glorious, He should never be confused with God, the Invisible, the Inaccessible. Shoghi Effendi in explaining this theme writes:

The divinity attributed to so great a Being [Bahá'u'lláh] and the complete incarnation of the names and attributes of God in so exalted a Person should, under no circumstances, be misconceived or misinterpreted. The human temple that has been made the vehicle of so overpowering a Revelation must, if we be faithful to the tenets of our Faith, ever remain entirely distinguished from that 'innermost Spirit of Spirits' and 'eternal Essence of Essences'—that invisible yet rational God Who, however much we extol the divinity of His

Manifestations on earth, can in no wise incarnate His infinite, His unknowable, His incorruptible and all-embracing Reality in the concrete and limited frame of a mortal being. Indeed, the God Who could so incarnate His own reality would, in the light of the teachings of Bahá'u'lláh, cease immediately to be God. So crude and fantastic a theory of Divine incarnation is as removed from, and incompatible with, the essentials of Bahá'í belief as are the no less inadmissible pantheistic and anthropomorphic conceptions of God—both of which the utterances of Bahá'u'lláh emphatically repudiate and the fallacy of which they expose . . .

'From time immemorial,' Bahá'u'lláh, speaking of God, explains, 'He, the Divine Being, hath been veiled in the ineffable sanctity of His exalted Self, and will everlastingly continue to be wrapt in the impenetrable mystery of His unknowable Essence . . . Ten thousand Prophets, each a Moses, are thunderstruck upon the Sinai of their search at God's forbidding voice, "Thou shalt never behold Me!"; whilst a myriad Messengers, each as great as Jesus, stand dismayed upon their heavenly thrones by the interdiction "Mine Essence thou shalt never apprehend!" ' 'How bewildering to me, insignificant as I am,' Bahá'u'lláh in His communion with God affirms, 'is the attempt to fathom the sacred depths of Thy knowledge! How futile my efforts to visualize the magnitude of the power inherent in Thine handiwork—the revelation of Thy creative power!' 'When I contemplate, O My God, the relationship that bindeth me to Thee,' He, in yet another prayer revealed in His own handwriting, testifies, 'I am moved to proclaim to all created things "verily I am God!"; and when I consider my own self, lo, I find it coarser than clay!'[7]

In order to appreciate the claims of Bahá'u'lláh, it is essential to grasp the concept and recognize the functions of the 'Manifestation of God' who appears from age to age. But unfortunately we live in an age when godlessness has spread widely throughout the world and therefore this task becomes difficult. The leaders of religion have so distorted the essence of religion and dimmed its light that a growing number of people, mostly honest but disillusioned, are joining the ranks of the agnostics and atheists, while the great majority of those who claim to believe in God are not sure what their beliefs entail. The One, the Incomparable, the Omnipotent God, Whose praises have been extolled in all the Holy Books, is now either forgotten in the churches and in the minds of men or has become a subject of controversy, described in countless ways by those who still cling to their old and divided religions. The words 'God' and 'religion' have acquired strange connotations in this age, and this is due to the fact that the light of true religion has been obscured by the corrupt practices and misrepresentations of religious leaders. Mírzá 'Azízu'lláh-i-Miṣbáḥ,* one of the great scholars of the Faith, has written this profound and yet simple verse in his marvellous collection of poetry and meditations:

> If the bishops had not called vain imaginings religion, the philosophers would not have regarded religion as vain imaginings.[8]

In another instance he writes:

> There is one who worships God, yet is attached to an idol; there is another who, although he bows before an idol, is intoxicated with the wine of the Oneness of God.[9]

In many of His Tablets Bahá'u'lláh has warned that prior to the full establishment of His Cause the forces of irreligion and disbelief will spread in the world. In one instance He testifies:

> The vitality of men's belief in God is dying out in every land; nothing short of His wholesome medicine can ever restore it. The corrosion of ungodliness is eating into the vitals of human society; what else but the Elixir of His potent Revelation can cleanse and revive it?[10]

Not only is humanity turning towards waywardness and unbelief, but it is losing the language of religion altogether.

* See p. 38.

The central theme of religion revolves around the Manifestations of God,* the Founders of the world's great religions. One of the great stumbling-blocks in the way of their recognition, however, is that they appear as ordinary human beings devoid of learning and earthly power. Their apparent helplessness and abasement have led the majority of the people to deny Them. Only those with spiritual eyes have been able to witness the glory hidden behind Their human temples. This is the law of God through which good and evil are separated in this life. One of the governing principles of creation is that man will not be able to receive the bounties of God unless he acquires the capacity for them. The greatest bounty is the recognition of the Manifestation of God, and this is not given to man freely. He must earn it by cleansing the mirror of his heart so that the Sun of Truth may shine within it. The personal circumstances of the Manifestations of God, Who without any apparent greatness or superiority claim to be the vicegerents of God on earth, become the main cause of their rejection by the unbelievers.

In one of His Tablets Bahá'u'lláh states:

> He Who is the Day Spring of Truth is, no doubt, fully capable of rescuing from such remoteness wayward souls and of causing them to draw nigh unto His court and attain His Presence. 'If God had pleased He had surely made all men one people.' His purpose, however, is to enable the pure in spirit and the detached in heart to ascend, by virtue of their own innate powers, unto the shores of the Most Great Ocean, that thereby they who seek the Beauty of the All-Glorious may be distinguished and separated from the wayward and perverse. Thus hath it been ordained by the all-glorious and resplendent Pen . . .
>
> That the Manifestations of Divine justice, the Day Springs of heavenly grace, have when they appeared amongst men always been destitute of all earthly dominion and shorn of the means of worldly ascendancy, should be attributed to this same principle of separation and distinction which animateth

* See also vol. I: 'Manifestations of God'.

the Divine Purpose. Were the Eternal Essence to manifest all that is latent within Him, were He to shine in the plenitude of His glory, none would be found to question His power or repudiate His truth. Nay, all created things would be so dazzled and thunderstruck by the evidences of His light as to be reduced to utter nothingness. How, then, can the godly be differentiated under such circumstances from the froward?[11]

In another Tablet[12] He testifies that if the Manifestation of God so desires, He can through only one word conquer the world and possess the hearts of all its inhabitants. Should such a thing happen every man would acknowledge His truth, but there would be no merit in such an acknowledgement. Bahá'u'lláh states that God proves the hearts of His servants, so that good may be differentiated from evil. To bring this about, His Manifestations occasionally reveal the tokens of His glory and power and withhold them at other times. There are indications which point to the fact that on numerous occasions Bahá'u'lláh deliberately concealed from men, in order to test them, the signs of His all-encompassing knowledge and the tokens of His power. He drew a veil before His glory and therefore to many who were devoid of a penetrating insight He appeared to be unendowed with divine attributes.

The trials associated with the coming of the Manifestation of God are so great that even some who recognize Him and claim allegiance to His Cause find themselves unable to withstand these tests. Their faith and belief eventually wither and die. There are others who, through pride and ambition, aspire to achieve the same ascendancy as the Manifestation of God. Several people of note who came in contact with Bahá'u'lláh witnessed His greatness, but in their delusion sought to elevate themselves to His position. The basic reason for their blindness was that they gloried in their own accomplishments.

The Manifestation of God occupies a station far beyond the understanding of man. He dwells in a realm exalted above all created things. When He manifests Himself to man, He has no alternative but to communicate His Message in the language of man. But because he does this, He is looked upon as an ordinary human being, devoid of any divine powers.

In one of His Tablets[13] Bahá'u'lláh mentions that people are suffering from a disease which is very difficult to cure, namely, that those who have acquired a small measure of understanding and knowledge consider the Manifestation of God to be like themselves. They judge Him according to their own standards and therefore fail to appreciate His station. Bahá'u'lláh affirms that many are suffering from this disease today. He prays that God may remove the veil from their hearts so that they may recognize their own worth and be enabled to distinguish between the truth of His Cause and the affairs of men.

In the *Súriy-i-Aṣḥáb*, Bahá'u'lláh declares that nothing will benefit man in this day except love for Him. This love cannot be created in the hearts of men unless they purify themselves from attachment to all things. Then, and only then, He affirms, will the mirrors of their hearts reflect the image of His resplendent Beauty. Bahá'u'lláh confirms this in *The Hidden Words*:

> O Son of Spirit!
> My first counsel is this: Possess a pure, kindly and radiant heart, that thine may be a sovereignty ancient, imperishable and everlasting.[14]

Addressing the Bábí community He warns them in the *Súriy-i-Aṣḥáb* that this is not the day of questioning, for He who from eternity was hidden from the eyes of men is now come. He rebukes them for having failed to witness His glory and omnipotence. Alluding to the words of the Báb concerning the creative power conferred upon 'Him Whom God shall make manifest', Bahá'u'lláh asserts that all created things have come into being through a word of His mouth and in challenging language affirms that there is no soul among the whole of creation who has the power to stand before Him and utter one word in His presence. He testifies that every soul is humbled by the evidences of His sovereignty. He concludes with this moving challenge:

Within the throat of this Youth there lie prisoned accents which, if revealed to mankind to an extent smaller than a needle's eye, would suffice to cause every mountain to crumble, the leaves of the trees to be discoloured and their fruits to fall; would compel every head to bow down in worship and every face to turn in adoration towards this omnipotent Ruler Who, at sundry times and in diverse manners, appeareth as a devouring flame, as a billowing ocean, as a radiant light, as the tree which, rooted in the soil of holiness, lifteth its branches and spreadeth out its limbs as far as and beyond the throne of deathless glory.[15]

Similar statements are to be found in other Tablets. For instance, in the *Kitáb-i-Aqdas*, Bahá'u'lláh proclaims:

O ye leaders of religion! Who is the man amongst you that can rival Me in vision or insight? Where is he to be found that dareth to claim to be My equal in utterance or wisdom? No, by My Lord, the All-Merciful! All on the earth shall pass away; and this is the face of your Lord, the Almighty, the Well-Beloved.[16]

One of the unique features of the Revelation of Bahá'u'lláh is that for about ten years its Author chose not to disclose His station to the followers of the Báb, and yet during that period He revealed the verses of God unceasingly. Many were attracted to His person and those who had spiritual insight were able to recognize Him as 'Him Whom God shall make manifest', the Promised One of the *Bayán*. But He made no claim during that time, and counselled those who knew of His exalted station not to divulge it to others.

In the *Súriy-i-Aṣḥáb* Bahá'u'lláh explains the reason for this. He states that He unveiled His Cause gradually as a mercy to mankind. For had the light of so potent a Revelation been allowed to break upon the world suddenly, those who were spiritually weak would have been dazzled by its glory and would have perished by its impact.

In another instance in the same Tablet Bahá'u'lláh mentions

that should He disclose the full potency of His Word,* the earth would quake and the heavens be cleft asunder. However, by an act of concealment God has shown forbearance and mercy towards His servants. Indeed, as we survey the history of the Faith, we note that the Báb too unveiled His exalted station gradually to the eyes of men. He who was the 'King of Messengers', the Promised One of Islám and the 'Primal Point' from which was generated all created things, consented, in the early days of His Revelation, as a token of His loving-kindness to men, to be known merely as the Báb (Gate), believed by the Shí'ahs to be the intermediary between the Promised Qá'im and the people.† That claim was not as challenging as the subsequent revelation that He was the Qá'im Himself. As His followers acquired the capacity to bear the weight of His Message, He progressively revealed His station to them.

The Command to Avoid Sedition

In the *Súriy-i-Aṣḥáb* Bahá'u'lláh exhorts His companions to arise for the promotion of His Faith, and warns them that the sword will not bring victory to the Cause of God. The Cause will be exalted by pure deeds, detachment from all earthly things, and steadfastness in His love. In this connection Bahá'u'lláh gives His companions a directive: that if the army of the deniers should attack them, they should defeat it through the power of His Word and not resort to force.‡

* The significance and potency of the Word of God is more fully explained in vol. I.

† Although the claim of the Báb was that he was the 'Gate' to a greater revelation than His own, nevertheless the general public recognized the title of the Báb as indicating that He was the intermediary between the Qá'im and the people. In fact, some of His followers lost their faith or were shaken when they heard His claim to be the Qá'im Himself. See for instance the story of 'Aẓím, *The Dawn-Breakers*, pp. 227–8 (Brit.), p. 313 (U.S.).

‡ See also vol. I, pp. 278–9.

One of the most important injunctions of Bahá'u'lláh which appears in this and many other Tablets is to avoid stirring up sedition and mischief. This commandment is the basis of Bahá'í life and affects both the individual and society. It protects the soul from ungodliness and the community from corruption. In one of His Tablets[17] Bahá'u'lláh says that the believers should never take part in any affair from which the slightest odour of mischief or dissension may be detected. He exhorts them to flee from it as one would flee from a serpent.

In another Tablet He states:

> O ye that dwell on earth! The distinguishing feature that marketh the pre-eminent character of this Supreme Revelation consisteth in that We have, on the one hand, blotted out from the pages of God's holy Book whatsoever hath been the cause of strife, of malice and mischief amongst the children of men, and have, on the other, laid down the essential prerequisites of concord, of understanding, of complete and enduring unity. Well is it with them that keep My statutes.
>
> Time and again have We admonished Our beloved ones to avoid, nay to flee from, anything whatsoever from which the odour of mischief can be detected. The world is in great turmoil, and the minds of its people are in a state of utter confusion. We entreat the Almighty that He may graciously illuminate them with the glory of His Justice, and enable them to discover that which will be profitable unto them at all times and under all conditions. He, verily, is the All-Possessing, the Most High.[18]

As the gloom of strife and sedition deepens in the world today and mankind is helplessly drawn into its dark abyss, it becomes increasingly difficult to find any cause, whether religious, political or social, which can possibly be free from the 'odour of mischief'. On the other hand, the Cause of Bahá'u'lláh, which stands for unity and fellowship among the peoples of the world, intrinsically repels any attempt by individuals or groups to introduce into its unique system the pernicious influence of dissension, discord and wrangling. These are the words of Bahá'u'lláh in a Tablet addressed to Jamál-i-Burújirdí,* a proud and arrogant believer:

> Nothing whatever can, in this Day, inflict a greater harm upon this Cause than dissension and strife, contention, estrangement and apathy, among the loved ones of God. Flee them, through the power of God and His sovereign aid, and strive ye to knit together the hearts of men, in His Name, the Unifier, the All-Knowing, the All-Wise.[19]

Those who have embraced the Cause of Bahá'u'lláh, while associating with the followers of other religions in a spirit of love and friendship, will not take part in or lend support to any activity which tends to run counter to this basic principle of their Faith. A prime example is their non-participation by word or deed in political affairs. It may be true to say that no human institutions today are as corrupt as political ones. They are agencies through which man's worst characteristics find expression. For the motivating principle which governs politics today is self-interest; the tools it employs are, in most cases, intrigue, compromise and deceit; and the fruits it yields are mainly discord, strife and ruin. How could the followers of Bahá'u'lláh work within this framework? How could they take part in politics and remain loyal to those lofty principles enunciated by Bahá'u'lláh? The principles of universality and the oneness of the human race, of truthfulness and honesty, of uprightness and integrity, of love and fellowship are completely opposite to the way in which politics are conducted today.

Recognizing the destructive nature of the present-day order in human society, the bankruptcy of its political, religious and social institutions and their inability to bring unity to the human race, the Bahá'ís are engaged in erecting on a global scale the framework of a new world order based on the teachings of Bahá'u'lláh.†

* See pp. 118–19.

† For a comprehensive study of this subject, see the writings of Shoghi Effendi, especially *The World Order of Bahá'u'lláh* and *The Promised Day is Come*.

Describing the Bahá'í world community and its role in creating a new order for mankind, Shoghi Effendi, the Guardian of the Bahá'í Faith, writes:

> Conscious of their high calling, confident in the society-building power which their Faith possesses, they press forward, undeterred and undismayed, in their efforts to fashion and perfect the necessary instruments wherein the embryonic World Order of Bahá'u'lláh can mature and develop. It is this building process, slow and unobtrusive, to which the life of the world-wide Bahá'í Community is wholly consecrated, that constitutes the one hope of a stricken society. For this process is actuated by the generating influence of God's changeless Purpose, and is evolving within the framework of the Administrative Order of His Faith.
>
> In a world the structure of whose political and social institutions is impaired, whose vision is befogged, whose conscience is bewildered, whose religious systems have become anaemic and lost their virtue, this healing Agency, this leavening Power, this cementing Force, intensely alive and all-pervasive, has been taking shape, is crystallizing into institutions, is mobilizing its forces, and is preparing for the spiritual conquest and the complete redemption of mankind. Though the society which incarnates its ideals be small, and its direct and tangible benefits as yet inconsiderable, yet the potentialities with which it has been endowed, and through which it is destined to regenerate the individual and rebuild a broken world, are incalculable . . .
>
> Though loyal to their respective governments, though profoundly interested in anything that affects their security and welfare, though anxious to share in whatever promotes their best interests, the Faith with which the followers of Bahá'u'lláh stand identified is one which they firmly believe God has raised high above the storms, the divisions, and controversies of the political arena. Their Faith they conceive to be essentially non-political, supra-national in character, rigidly non-partisan, and entirely dissociated from nationalistic ambitions, pursuits, and purposes. Such a Faith knows no division of class or of party. It subordinates, without hesitation or

equivocation, every particularistic interest, be it personal, regional, or national, to the paramount interests of humanity, firmly convinced that in a world of inter-dependent peoples and nations the advantage of the part is best to be reached by the advantage of the whole, and that no abiding benefit can be conferred upon the component parts if the general interests of the entity itself are ignored or neglected . . .

Their Faith, Bahá'ís firmly believe, is moreover undenominational, non-sectarian, and wholly divorced from every ecclesiastical system, whatever its form, origin, or activities. No ecclesiastical organization, with its creeds, its traditions, its limitations, and exclusive outlook, can be said (as is the case with all existing political factions, parties, systems and programmes) to conform, in all its aspects, to the cardinal tenets of Bahá'í belief. To some of the principles and ideals animating political and ecclesiastical institutions every conscientious follower of the Faith of Bahá'u'lláh can, no doubt, readily subscribe. With none of these institutions, however, can he identify himself, nor can he unreservedly endorse the creeds, the principles and programmes on which they are based.

How can a Faith, it should moreover be borne in mind, whose divinely-ordained institutions have been established within the jurisdiction of no less than forty different countries,* the policies and interests of whose governments are continually clashing and growing more complex and confused every day—how can such a Faith, by allowing its adherents, whether individually or through its organized councils, to meddle in political activities, succeed in preserving the integrity of its teachings and in safeguarding the unity of its followers? How can it insure the vigorous, the uninterrupted and peaceful development of its expanding institutions? How can a Faith, whose ramifications have brought it into contact with mutually incompatible religious systems, sects and confessions, be in a position, if it permits its adherents to subscribe to obsolescent observances and doctrines, to claim the unconditional allegiance of those

* Written in 1936. In April 1977 there were Bahá'í institutions in at least 330 countries, islands and dependencies. (A.T.)

whom it is striving to incorporate into its divinely-appointed system? How can it avoid the constant friction, the misunderstandings and controversies which formal affiliation, as distinct from association, must inevitably engender?[20]

The Command to Teach

Throughout the *Súriy-i-Aṣḥáb*, Bahá'u'lláh urges Muníb to be steadfast, to put his trust in God and to be afraid of no one, even should all men draw their swords against him and assail him from every side. With the potency of His sublime words Bahá'u'lláh instils in him a spirit of might and power, directs him to teach His Cause fearlessly, but with wisdom and prudence, among the Bábís, commands him to tear away the veils which have prevented them from recognizing Him with such vigour that every other veil may be rent asunder from the faces of all created things, and assures him that God has bestowed divine protection upon him.

In many instances Bahá'u'lláh reminds Muníb to teach His Faith only to those who are sincere and to avoid the companionship of anyone who shows enmity towards Him. He counsels Muníb to share the *Súriy-i-Aṣḥáb* only with those Bábís whose faces are radiant with the love of God and not to reveal it to others.

From the early days of the Faith, Bahá'u'lláh has enjoined upon His followers to teach His Cause. His commandment, which is directed to every believer, is the basis of all Bahá'í activity and constitutes the bedrock upon which rests the spiritual well-being of the individual. Wishing to stress the paramount importance of teaching His Cause, Bahá'u'lláh, in a Tablet[21] addressed to Jamál-i-Burújirdí, states that should he be residing in the West and learn that a person in the East is anxious to attain the knowledge of God and the recognition of His Manifestation, then it is incumbent upon him, if he has the means, to travel to distant lands in order to bestow the water of life upon that enquirer. In another Tablet Bahá'u'lláh writes:

> Teach ye the Cause of God, O people of Bahá, for God hath prescribed unto every one the duty of proclaiming His Message, and regardeth it as the most meritorious of all deeds. Such a deed is acceptable only when he that teacheth the Cause is already a firm believer in God, the Supreme Protector, the Gracious, the Almighty. He hath, moreover, ordained that His Cause be taught through the power of men's utterance, and not through resort to violence. Thus hath His ordinance been sent down from the Kingdom of Him Who is the Most Exalted, the All-Wise. Beware lest ye contend with any one, nay, strive to make him aware of the truth with kindly manner and most convincing exhortation. If your hearer respond, he will have responded to his own behoof, and if not, turn ye away from him, and set your faces towards God's sacred Court, the seat of resplendent holiness.[22]

In the early days in Persia, the cradle of the Faith, teaching work went ahead with tremendous devotion and sacrifice. The believers worked together as a team. There were those who made contact with people, won their confidence, and after careful assessment of their motives and background introduced the Faith to them and brought them along to the gatherings of the friends. There were others who were knowledgeable and spoke at meetings, yet others who were excellent hosts and provided the right atmosphere for discussing the challenging claims of the Cause of God. All these friends worked together hand in hand. With absolute unity and devotion the believers consecrated their lives to teaching the Cause of Bahá'u'lláh until great numbers entered the Faith and many of them laid down their lives in His path.

It is true to say that during the seventy-seven years of the Heroic Age of the Faith (which included the ministries of the Báb, Bahá'u'lláh and 'Abdu'l-Bahá) the pure in heart among the Persian people were brought under the shadow of the Cause of Bahá'u'lláh. In this period the gem-like essence of that nation was attracted into the community of the Most Great Name.

In one of His Tablets Bahá'u'lláh affirms:

> By the righteousness of the one true God! If one speck of a jewel be lost and buried beneath a mountain of stones, and lie hidden beyond the seven seas, the Hand of Omnipotence would assuredly reveal it in this Day, pure and cleansed from dross.[23]

Indeed, the hand of divine power had within a short period raised up many heroes among the people of Persia, and made them the recipients of His grace and bounty.

Bahá'u'lláh has counselled His followers that the first step for a teacher is to teach his own self. In one of His Tablets He states:

> Whoso ariseth among you to teach the Cause of His Lord, let him, before all else, teach his own self, that his speech may attract the hearts of them that hear him. Unless he teacheth his own self, the words of his mouth will not influence the heart of the seeker. Take heed, O people, lest ye be of them that give good counsel to others but forget to follow it themselves. The words of such as these, and beyond the words the realities of all things, and beyond these realities the angels that are nigh unto God, bring against them the accusation of falsehood.
>
> Should such a man ever succeed in influencing any one, this success should be attributed not to him, but rather to the influence of the words of God, as decreed by Him Who is the Almighty, the All-Wise. In the sight of God he is regarded as a lamp that imparteth its light, and yet is all the while being consumed within itself.[24]

In His second Tablet to Napoleon III, Bahá'u'lláh addresses His followers and urges them in these words to teach the Cause:

> God hath prescribed unto every one the duty of teaching His Cause. Whoever ariseth to discharge this duty, must

> needs, ere he proclaimeth His Message, adorn himself with the ornament of an upright and praiseworthy character, so that his words may attract the hearts of such as are receptive to his call. Without it, he can never hope to influence his hearers.[25]

An important point which needs clarification is that the basic purpose of teaching is not merely to increase the membership of the Bahá'í community, although this happens as a result. The prime motive is that the individual may know Bahá'u'lláh and draw near to Him. In the whole creation there is nothing more important than the attraction of the soul to its God. In the physical world we observe the attraction which exists between the earth and every object which comes within its orbit. The earth tends to draw everything to itself and the final goal of every object is to reach and rest upon it. The same law of attraction binds the Creator to His creation. The soul is attracted to the worlds of God and if barriers which intervene between the two are lifted, the individual will reach his ultimate destiny. Teaching the Cause of God is the very act of removing these barriers. When the soul recognizes Bahá'u'lláh, it will reach its abode and there is nothing more meritorious in the sight of God than that His servants should be wholly drawn to Him.

The aim of the Bahá'í teacher is that the Message of God may be glorified and that the individual may be enabled to embrace His Cause, celebrate His praise, and draw nearer to Him. The act of teaching, more than anything else, evokes the good-pleasure of God. In one of His Tablets[26] Bahá'u'lláh states that there are two things pleasing to God: the tears shed in fear of Him and the blood of the martyr spilt in His path. But since Bahá'u'lláh has advised His followers not to volunteer to give their lives, He has replaced it with teaching His Cause.

In several Tablets Bahá'u'lláh has described the fear of God as the cause of nearness to Him. This statement may be difficult for some to appreciate. For why should a loving God be feared? Fear is engendered in man when he feels inadequate to deal with a situation, and confidence is generated when he finds himself completely in control. For example, a man who has been given a responsibility but has failed to fulfil his obligations will be filled with fear when he meets his superiors, because he knows that they will deal with him with justice. Man, in this life, fails to carry out the commandments of God. He commits sins and violates the laws of God. In such a case how can he feel at ease when he knows that one day he will be called on to account for his deeds? If man does not fear God, it is a sign either that he is without shortcomings or that he has no faith in the next life when he will have to answer for his wrong-doings. In *The Hidden Words* Bahá'u'lláh counsels His servants in these words:

> O Son of Being!
> Bring thyself to account each day ere thou art summoned to a reckoning; for death, unheralded, shall come upon thee and thou shalt be called to give account for thy deeds.[27]

The closer one draws to God, the more he becomes conscious of his wrong-doings and the more he will fear God. The following passages, gleaned from the Writings of Bahá'u'lláh, clearly indicate that the fear of God is the means by which man may acquire spiritual qualities and grow stronger in faith.

> The fear of God hath ever been a sure defence and a safe stronghold for all the peoples of the world. It is the chief cause of the protection of mankind, and the supreme instrument for its preservation. Indeed, there existeth in man a faculty which deterreth him from, and guardeth him against, whatever is unworthy and unseemly, and which is known as his sense of shame. This, however, is confined to but a few; all have not possessed, and do not possess, it. It is incumbent upon the kings and the spiritual leaders of the world to lay fast hold on religion, inasmuch as through it the fear of God is instilled in all else but Him.[28]

And again:

> Admonish men to fear God. By God! This fear is the chief commander of the army of Thy Lord. Its hosts are a praiseworthy character and goodly deeds. Through it have the cities of men's hearts been opened throughout the ages and centuries, and the standards of ascendancy and triumph raised above all other standards.[29]

In the *Words of Wisdom*, He states:

> The essence of wisdom is the fear of God, the dread of His scourge and the apprehension of His justice and decree.[30]

As already mentioned the other deed which is most acceptable in the sight of God is to lay down one's life in His path and die as a martyr.

One of the great mysteries of creation is the act of sacrifice. We will not be able to appreciate it fully in this world. Yet we can readily observe in nature that any created thing, if it is to be elevated to a higher kingdom, must give up its own existence and become part of a new and more exalted form of life. Man's greatest attainment on this earth is to serve the Cause of God. The eagerness and devotion with which he arises to serve the Cause invokes the good-pleasure of God, especially if the believer is ready to sacrifice his interests, time, possessions, and all that is dear to him, in order to render this service to His Lord. However, to be prepared to give one's life for the promotion of the Cause of God is man's ultimate sacrifice in this world and is the most meritorious in the sight of God. In *The Hidden Words* Bahá'u'lláh reveals:

> O Son of Man!
>
> Ponder and reflect. Is it thy wish to die upon thy bed, or to shed thy life-blood on the dust, a martyr in My path, and so become the manifestation of My command and the revealer of My light in the highest paradise? Judge thou aright, O servant!

> O Son of Man!
>
> By My beauty! To tinge thy hair with thy blood is greater in My sight than the creation of the universe and the light of both worlds. Strive then to attain this, O servant![31]

By replacing this greatest act of devotion with teaching the Cause, Bahá'u'lláh has discouraged his followers from seeking martyrdom. Instead He has commanded them to devote their entire lives to teaching His Cause to the whole human race.

In one of His Tablets[32] Bahá'u'lláh even explicitly states that in this dispensation it is preferable to teach with wisdom than to give one's life. Throughout His ministry Bahá'u'lláh exhorted His followers to teach the Cause of God with great wisdom. He did not approve of teaching the public indiscriminately. He repeatedly advised the believers in Persia, especially after the martyrdom of Badí',* that for their own safety and the protection of the Cause they should exercise more care and prudence in their approach to people and not excite or antagonize them. In one of His Tablets Bahá'u'lláh counsels His followers:

> In this Day, We can neither approve the conduct of the fearful that seeketh to dissemble his faith, nor sanction the behaviour of the avowed believer that clamorously asserteth his allegiance to this Cause. Both should observe the dictates of wisdom, and strive diligently to serve the best interests of the Faith.[33]

The great majority of Bahá'í teachers in Persia followed this advice. They taught the Faith to those who were earnest seekers, not to fanatics and trouble-makers. A few, who were unable to withhold themselves from mentioning the Faith in public, often brought untold suffering and even martyrdom upon themselves and the rest of the community. A notable example is Mullá Muḥammad-Riḍá of Muḥammad-Ábád,† who

* An illustrious youthful martyr of the Faith, whose exemplary sacrifice will be described in some detail in the next volume.

† For an account of his life, see vol. I, pp. 84–91.

spoke in public openly and with unbounded enthusiasm about the Faith. By so doing, however, he antagonized the fanatical populace who as a result created great trouble for the friends and inflicted many persecutions upon them. Bahá'u'lláh, in one of His Tablets,[34] affirms that Mullá Muḥammad-Riḍá had acted unwisely, but forgives him through His loving-kindness and mercy.

As we dwell on this important subject, let us remember that the commandment of Bahá'u'lláh to be wise in teaching and proclaiming His Cause was not intended only for the early believers who lived in the Heroic Age of the Faith. It is equally applicable to the present day and will remain as one of the essential prerequisites for bringing victory to the Cause of God throughout this Dispensation. Indeed, wisdom is one of the greatest gifts of God to man, and without it the individual will bring harm to himself and to the Cause.

But wisdom in teaching must not lead to apathy, compromise, or inactivity. The history of the Faith demonstrates that the early believers in Persia taught the Faith with zeal and enthusiasm, with courage and determination. They devoted their entire lives to seeking receptive souls and confirming them in the Faith. No earthly agency, no preoccupation ever deflected them from this exalted purpose. With that single-mindedness characteristic of the Heroic Age they spent hours of the day and night praying and devising plans to meet those whom they could attract to the Cause.

In most towns and villages in Persia the believers held meetings to which seekers of truth were admitted. However, these meetings were often held in the dead of night in someone's home. For the safety of the friends and the protection of the Faith the believers had to be very careful not to attract anyone's attention when entering or leaving a house. For the same reasons no enquirer would be admitted until they were assured of his sincerity. In spite of all this vigilance there were occasions when enemies of the Faith were able to deceive the believers and find their way to these meetings in the guise of seekers of truth. Such events always led to great trouble, for once the friends were identified, their lives could be in danger.

On the other hand, there were many occasions in which the believers, for various reasons, had to teach or defend their Faith in public. Depending on the circumstances, they often suffered great persecutions as a result.

The following account gleaned and translated from the memoirs of Ḥájí Muḥammad-Ṭáhir-i-Málmírí helps to illustrate the way in which the early believers grasped every opportunity to teach the Cause, and when the situation demanded it, demonstrated the validity of their faith in public fearlessly and with great eagerness. They faced the challenge with courage and resourcefulness even though they knew that their actions might lead to suffering and persecution.

Soon after his return from 'Akká where he attained the presence of Bahá'u'lláh, Ḥájí Muḥammad-Ṭáhir, as bidden, began his teaching work with unbounded enthusiasm and devotion in the district of Yazd. Bahá'u'lláh had personally taught him how to teach His Faith. Many people with whom he talked joined the ranks of the believers, but he never attributed this success to himself. He was absolutely convinced that the hand of Bahá'u'lláh was always at work. One of those with whom he came in contact was Mullá Muḥammad-i-Man<u>sh</u>ádí, a distinguished *mujtahid** and one of the leading figures among the divines of the district of Yazd. Being sincere and pure at heart, this great man recognized the truth of the Cause of God and later laid down his life in the path of Bahá'u'lláh. This is the story:

> In the winter, I paid a visit to Man<u>sh</u>ád † and stayed in the house of Raḍa'r-Rúḥ.‡ One day his brother, Áqá Mullá

* Doctor of Islamic law who has the authority to exercise independent initiative in enforcing the laws of Islám.

† A large village about forty miles from Yazd, well known for its Bahá'ís and Bahá'í martyrs. (A.T.)

‡ One of the outstanding martyrs of Man<u>sh</u>ád. Bahá'u'lláh said once, when Ḥájí Muḥammad-Ṭáhir was in His presence, that He liked Man<u>sh</u>ád because of Raḍa'r-Rúḥ. See vol. I, and p. 258 below.

Bábá'í, who was later martyred, talked about a certain Muslim divine [Mullá Muḥammad-i-Manshádí], saying that he was a good person. He asked my advice as to whether he should invite him, so that I could speak to him about the Faith. I thought there was no harm provided he did not create trouble. Mullá Bábá'í assured me that this man was not a trouble-maker . . . so I agreed that he should be invited.

Mullá Bábá'í informed me that Mullá Muḥammad was the most learned among the divines and that this opinion was shared by all the Muslim clergy in the city of Yazd, because most of the divines in the city usually spent two or three years studying at Najaf and Karbilá,* whereas Mullá Muḥammad had studied for twenty-one years at Najaf and had received the rank of *mujtahid* from three different leaders of the Shí'ah hierarchy. Since Mullá Muḥammad was a native of Manshád, he preferred to live in his home village rather than having his office in the city . . . He was an acknowledged authority on religious matters and the clergy in Yazd used to refer to him those problems about which they could not agree.

However, he came one evening. Although I was not a knowledgeable person, I did not feel in any way inadequate, since God, exalted be His glory, was assisting me. I spoke with Mullá Muḥammad for about four to five hours that evening. But he did not talk much. When leaving, he said that he would like to come the next evening and bring with him a certain Mullá 'Alí-Akbar. Mullá Bábá'í, however, felt it was not wise to invite Mullá 'Alí-Akbar since he might stir up trouble. But Mullá Muḥammad assured him that in his presence Mullá 'Alí-Akbar would not be able to do any harm.

So the next evening two of them came. Mullá 'Alí-Akbar was a brother-in-law of Mullá Muḥammad. He did not have great knowledge but was a meddler and an argumentative person who used to confuse the issues during conversation. That evening, he took part in discussions with me which lasted till midnight. In the course of discussion he continually tried to pervert the truth, but Mullá Muḥammad,

* Two holy cities of Shí'ah Islám where clergymen receive the rank of *mujtahid*. (A.T.)

who always realized this, would intervene and support my argument . . .

The next evening Mullá Muḥammad came alone, but he would neither agree nor disagree with my talks and explanations. When he was leaving I gave him the *Kitáb-i-Íqán* to read at home. When he arrived the next evening he said to me, 'I did not grasp much from your talks during this period, but after reading a part of this book, I was assured that God has manifested Himself, because these words are new and unique.' . . . So Mullá Muḥammad was confirmed in the Faith as a result of reading the *Kitáb-i-Íqán* . . .

The next day He ascended the pulpit and made the following statement: 'Up to now all of us have been used to consider that the Bábís are misled, but during the last few days I have come to realize, and I am now assured, that the Promised Qá'im has manifested Himself. Anyone who wishes to know this may investigate and find the truth for himself.'

Mullá 'Alí-Akbar who was sitting close to the pulpit shouted loudly 'Jináb-i-Mullá! What are you saying? Do you realize that after speaking in this manner you may not be allowed to come to the mosque again or to remain the Imám-Jum'ih?'*

Mullá Muḥammad answered 'I will not come to the mosque again.' And he never did.[35]

The news of Mullá Muḥammad's conversion to the Faith created a sensation in Man<u>sh</u>ád. Some were dismayed, some bewildered, and many were angered. The chiefs of the village who were Mullá Muḥammad's admirers and friends asked him to help them overcome their perplexity and confusion. In response to their request, he arranged a meeting to be held in the house of one of the chiefs and asked Ḥájí Muḥammad-Ṭáhir to go with him and speak to them about the Faith.

In his memoirs Ḥájí Muḥammad-Ṭáhir writes:

. . . Jináb-i-Mullá Muḥammad came and told me what had happened. He said that he had promised them [the chiefs of

* The leading divine of the Muslim community who leads prayers in the mosque.

the village] that tomorrow afternoon he and I would go to the home of Ḥájí Qurbán-'Alí . . . to speak about the Faith. I agreed to go, although I knew that such an action was unwise. But since he had promised to attend, I felt that I had to go, otherwise he might become somewhat shaken in his faith. In the meantime Mullá 'Alí-Akbar had become informed of this arrangement and had advised the chiefs that it was not wise for them to take part in discussions on their own. He told them that he intended to attend . . . and bring with him a number of clergymen.

The next day we went to the appointed place where we found about thirty-five people present. They included a number of 'ulamá* and dignitaries of Manshád, all of them opposed to the Faith . . . After a short while they suggested that we might begin discussion. I said to that gathering, 'You had better appoint one person from among yourselves to take part in the discussions and the rest just listen.' Unanimously they chose Mullá 'Alí-Akbar. I was absolutely sure that this meeting would bring about great trouble because a meeting such as this had never been held in Yazd or perhaps in any other place.[36]

Knowing that the spokesman for the divines was an argumentative person who distorted the truth and had no regard for logic or fairness, Ḥájí Muḥammad-Ṭáhir approached the subject in a manner that completely discomfited his opponent and confounded him throughout. He spoke for over four hours during which he recounted the history of past religions and demonstrated the truth of the Cause of Bahá'u'lláh through rational proofs as well as the *Qur'án* and traditions of Islám. Concerning that meeting Ḥájí Muḥammad-Ṭáhir writes:

That day God vouchsafed such confirmation and ascendancy that the Cause of God was proclaimed and its proof established for all. On that day Jináb-i-Mullá Muḥammad was transformed into a ball of fire. He was so enraptured that it is impossible for me to describe it . . .

That same evening, when the meeting was ended, a number

* Learned divines.

of divines . . . prepared a document, put their seals to it and sent it to Shaykh Muḥammad-Ḥasan-i-Sabzivárí* in Yazd. In this document they testified that Ḥájí Muḥammad-Ṭáhir had come to Manshád and converted Mullá Muḥammad who had openly proclaimed . . . the truth of the Faith of Bahá'u'lláh from the pulpit and had now withdrawn altogether from the mosque. They also stated that Ḥájí Muḥammad-Ṭáhir had been openly teaching the Bahá'í Faith in a public meeting at the home of Ḥájí Qurbán-'Alí. They expressed the view that the situation in Manshád was out of hand and asked for instructions.

Upon receiving this news Shaykh Muḥammad-Ḥasan wrote the death warrant of this servant, and took it along with the sealed document to Ḥájí Mu'addilu's-Salṭanih, the Governor of Yazd. Consequently two officials were sent to Manshád to arrest this servant. It was, however, providential that I had left for Mihríz † a day before the officials arrived. . . . On hearing the news, the believers in Manshád immediately dispatched a messenger . . . who reached Mihríz in time to warn me. Together with this friend we set off for the city [Yazd] . . . There I stayed for some time . . . out of sight . . . in the home of Ustád 'Alí-'Askar-i-Shál-Báf . . .‡[37]

During the time that he stayed in this house an event of great consequence took place. Concerning this he writes:

One day Ustád 'Alí-'Askar said to me 'There is a Zoroastrian youth by the name of Bahrám [later known as Mullá Bahrám] who comes to the door periodically to sell beetroot to us. He is a very nice young man. If it meets with your approval, I will bring him in to talk with you next time he calls here.' I said, 'Very well' . . . A few days later Jináb-i-

* The leading *mujtahid* of Yazd who was one of the greatest enemies of the Faith. He passed the death sentence on many believers who were martyred in that area. (A.T.)

† A village almost half-way between Yazd and Manshád. (A.T.)

‡ It was Bahá'u'lláh's instruction that Ḥájí Muḥammad-Ṭáhir should not allow himself to fall into the hands of the enemy, so that he might live to teach the Faith. (A.T.)

Mullá Bahrám came . . . and Ustád 'Alí-'Askar brought him to me.

Up to that time no one from among the Zoroastrians [in Yazd] had accepted the Faith. Indeed, the Bahá'ís could not even imagine that these people would embrace the Faith, because they were not involved in the early history and events associated with the Manifestations of God and were not included in any discussions concerning the Faith.* However, that day I spoke about the Faith to Mullá Bahrám.† He came the next day, and after a few days he acknowledged the truth of the Cause of Bahá'u'lláh. As a result, his blessed person attained such a state of joy and eagerness that it is difficult to describe. He became restless, and every time he visited us he showed much tenderness and often wept aloud. He then brought with him [a fellow Zoroastrian] Jináb-i-Áqá Rustam-i-Khursand, who also embraced the Faith after several meetings.[38]

Soon after his conversion to the Faith, Mullá Bahrám rose up with heroism and devotion to teach his fellow Zoroastrians. It was through his dedicated efforts that a great many from among his co-religionists joined the Faith. Later, 'Abdu'l-Bahá conferred upon him the title of Akhtar-i- Khávarí (Star of the East).

After three months of seclusion in the home of Ustád-'Alí-'Askar, Ḥájí Muḥammad-Ṭáhir left for the village of Mihríz. But somehow the enemies discovered his whereabouts and made another attempt to arrest him and have him executed. But the hand of Bahá'u'lláh protected him, and he left just in time. Eventually he had to leave the Province of Yazd until the situation had changed.

* There is a large Zoroastrian community in Yazd. In those days, apart from some trade and business links, they had almost no cultural or religious relationship with the Muslim community. Today a great number of Bahá'ís in Persia come from Zoroastrian background. The first Zoroastrian to believe in Bahá'u'lláh was Kay-Khusraw-i-Khudádád, although Suhráb-i-Púr-Kávús in Káshán recognized the truth of the Bábí Faith during the ministry of the Báb.

† It should be noted that Mullá Bahrám had previously met other Bahá'ís who had informed him about the Faith. (A.T.)

In the meantime, as a result of Mullá Muḥammad's conversion to the Faith and the proclamation of the Faith to the clergy, the situation at Manshád reached crisis point. Having failed to capture Ḥájí Muḥammad-Ṭáhir, the ecclesiastical hierarchy in Yazd, in desperation, arranged for the arrest of six Bahá'ís at Manshád. These six men were taken to the city and put in prison. From there, they were sent to Iṣfahán to appear before Prince Mas'úd Mírzá, the Ẓillu's-Sulṭán, the Governor of the Province. They were chained together and, escorted by armed officials, were made to walk, in the heat of summer, a distance of about 250 miles.

One of these men, a certain Áqá Siyyid Muḥammad-'Alíy-i-Gázur, had become ill while in prison. Yet Shaykh Muḥammad-Ḥasan-i-Sabzivárí, the notorious *mujtahid* of Yazd, ordered that this sick man was to lead the chained prisoners to Iṣfahán and carry on his shoulder the extra length of chain and the heavy iron spike* attached to it. On hearing this, Fáṭimih-Bagum, the only sister of Áqá Muḥammad-'Alí and a devoted Bahá'í, volunteered to accompany the prisoners on foot and carry the extra length of chain.

Although in those days women lived a sheltered life, seldom left the confines of their home and never took part in public affairs, Fáṭimih-Bagum, a maiden, twenty-seven years of age, was determined to walk with the prisoners. The friends tried very hard to dissuade her from going, pointing out the hazards of the journey by foot in the heat of the summer and under such difficult circumstances. But their pleas brought no result. She is reported to have told the believers: 'How can I allow them to take my brother . . . and five other beloved of God to Iṣfahán, while I stay here! I shall go with these six persons to Iṣfahán. If they decide to kill them, they must first take my life and then proceed to execute the rest . . . My life is not more precious than theirs.'

With a courage and steadfastness that amazed the officials and

* The spike would be used to fasten the chain to the ground when they were resting or sleeping at night.

onlookers, Fáṭimih-Bagum, walking barefoot and wearing her veil, led the party of prisoners to Iṣfahán, and carried the end of the chain and the spike on her shoulder all the way.

These men were sent to prison on arrival in Iṣfahán. Through the efforts of Fáṭimih-Bagum, who managed to plead their case to Prince Ẓillu's-Sulṭán, they were freed and sent back to Yazd. But the persecutions did not stop here. Some years later these valiant souls were martyred. Fáṭimih-Bagum herself was dragged out of her home and done to death in such humiliating circumstances as no pen can describe. The indignities to which her body was subjected after her martyrdom constitute one of the most shameful episodes in the history of the Faith.

As to Mullá Muḥammad, once the great *mujtahid* of Manshád, whose conversion to the Faith of Bahá'u'lláh had sparked off such cruelties, he renounced the leadership of the Muslim community after his recognition of the station of Bahá'u'lláh. Having no earthly possessions to support himself and his family, he found no alternative but to earn his living by working as a building labourer. He was a tower of strength to the Bahá'ís and served the Cause with great humility and self-effacement, until after some years he won the crown of martyrdom and laid down his life in the path of Bahá'u'lláh.

The same people who were once his admirers and servants, who used to bow before him as he appeared in their midst, who crowded in the mosque to hear him speak and lead them in prayer, were now intent upon taking his life, for he had embraced the Cause of God. During the Bahá'í massacre of 1903 in the city of Yazd and neighbouring villages Mullá Muḥammad was martyred. The crowds dragged his body through the village and delivered it to the flames.

This chain of events, leading one to another, amply demonstrates that teaching the Cause in the early days needed great courage and wisdom. It also shows that victories won for the Faith of God have often resulted in trials and persecutions which in turn have spurred the believers on to achieve greater victories for their Lord.

5

Tablet of Aḥmad (Arabic)

The *Lawḥ-i-Aḥmad* (Tablet of Aḥmad) is one of the best known Tablets of Bahá'u'lláh, translated into English and many other languages. It was revealed around 1282 A.H. (1865) in honour of Aḥmad, a native of Yazd. A cursory glance at the original Tablet makes it clear that Bahá'u'lláh wrote this before He was poisoned by Mírzá Yaḥyá.*

The life story of Aḥmad is very interesting. An account of his life is recorded in the annals of the Faith prepared by the Bahá'í community of 'I<u>sh</u>qábád. According to this account he lived to be one hundred and died in the year 1320 A.H. (1902). In his unpublished 'History of the Faith in the Province of Yazd', Ḥájí Muḥammad-Ṭáhir-i-Málmírí has also written a brief account of Aḥmad's life. In it he states that Aḥmad died at the age of one hundred and thirteen!

Probably one of the reasons for this discrepancy is that in an Islamic community, people often did not know the date of their birth. There was no such thing as public registration of births; some parents used to record the birth of their children privately, but the individual did not care about the date. He did not attach importance to his birthday, nor did he ever celebrate it. This attitude was due to the teachings of Islám which taught man to be self-effacing and not to glory in himself. The only person whose birthday merited celebration was the Prophet of God.

Aḥmad was born into a rich and influential family in Yazd. From his early days, when he was still in his teens, he felt a great attraction towards mysticism. At that age he often

* See chapter 7.

secluded himself in a room in order to commune with God. His greatest hope in life was to come face to face with the promised Qá'im (Promised One of Islám). He listened to any person who would show him the way, and often sat at the feet of ascetics and dervishes who claimed to possess the divine light within them.

However, his father and the family, who were orthodox Muslims, were perturbed by the way Aḥmad was inclined towards mendicancy and asceticism. They brought much pressure upon him to relinquish his ideas, but Aḥmad's indomitable spirit could not be fettered by orthodoxy. Knowing that the atmosphere of his homeland was not conducive to his spiritual development, Aḥmad took the unusual step of leaving his home. In those days it was a rare occasion for a young person to leave his native town, especially without the consent of his parents. But Aḥmad was driven by an irresistible force to find the essence of Truth and attain the presence of the Qá'im.

Pretending that he was going to the public bath, one morning Aḥmad took a bundle of clothes and disappeared. He travelled towards the south until he reached India where he hoped he might find a clue leading him to his Beloved. This was possibly around 1242 A.H. (1826), some twenty years before the Declaration of the Báb.

According to Ḥájí Muḥammad-Ṭáhir-i-Málmírí, Aḥmad was over twenty years of age when he left Yazd. He writes:

> I was with him [Aḥmad] for about four years during the latter part of his life when he lived in Munj-i-Bavánát [in the province of Fárs]. He was twenty years of age during the reign of Fatḥ-'Alí Sháh when Prince Khánlar Mírzá was the Governor of Yazd. He was then leading an ascetic life, spending his time in prayer and meditation. He was inclined to be a dervish, and left Yazd for India in the garb of a dervish. On his way, in Búshihr [Bushire] he came in contact with a baker, and he remained there for some time. He used to recount some stories about this baker, saying that he [the baker] had a great station in the spiritual realms, was aware

of the divine presence and was reputed to be undergoing spiritual experiences. However, Aḥmad left Búshihr for Bombay where he continued his ascetic life and was engaged in prayer and meditation.[1]

Aḥmad has said that throughout these journeys he came in contact with many mystics, Ṣúfís and other leaders of thought. But he became disappointed and disillusioned. In spite of imposing upon himself a rigorous self-discipline, and carrying out many prayerful exercises such as prostrating himself and repeating a certain verse of the *Qur'án* twelve thousand times, he did not find the object of his quest in India.

Dismayed and disheartened, he retraced his steps to Persia. He made his home in Káshán where he married and worked as a hand-weaver. The following is an extract from his spoken chronicle to some believers.

> Some time passed, and the news of the Báb from Shíráz reached many areas including Káshán. A strong urge was created in me to investigate this message. I made enquiries through every channel, until one day I met a traveller* in the caravanserai. When I enquired of him, he said 'If you are a seeker of truth proceed to Mashhad † where you may visit a certain Mullá 'Abdu'l-Kháliq-i-Yazdí who can help you in your investigations.'
>
> After hearing this, I set off on my journey early next day. I walked all the way to Ṭihrán and from there to Mashhad. However, upon arrival I became ill and had to convalesce for two months in that city. On recovering, I called at the home of Mullá 'Abdu'l-Kháliq and informed the servant that I wished to meet his master. I met the Mullá and acquainted him with my quest. On hearing this, he became very angry with me and threw me out. However, I called again the next day, cried aloud and implored him to guide me. When he saw I was earnest and steadfast in my search for truth, he then told me to meet him that night in the mosque of

* This traveller must have been a Bábí himself.

† The distance between Káshán and Mashhad (Meshed) is approximately 500 miles.

Gawhar-Shád where he would put me in touch with someone who could tell me the whole truth.*

I went to the mosque in the evening, but after attending the prayers and listening to him preach, I lost him because of the crowds. The next morning, I arrived at his house and explained what had happened. He instructed me to go to the mosque of Pír-Zan that evening and promised that he would send someone there to meet me and take me to the appointed place. Guided by the man who met me in the mosque, after walking some distance I passed through a corridor into the courtyard of a house and went upstairs into a room. I saw a venerable figure who occupied the seat of honour. Mullá 'Abdu'l-Kháliq, who was standing at the door, intimated to me that this great man was the one he wanted me to meet. This was no less a person than Mullá Ṣádiq-i-Khurásání.†

After attending a few meetings I was enabled to recognize and acknowledge the truth of the Message of the Báb. Afterwards, Mullá Ṣádiq instructed me to return to my wife and family in Káshán and resume my work. He also advised me not to teach the Faith unless I found a hearing ear.

Thereupon, I returned to Káshán and soon discovered that Ḥájí Mírzá Jání of Káshán was also a believer. The two of us were the only Bábís in that city.

When the Báb was conducted from Iṣfahán to Ṭihrán, Ḥájí Mírzá Jání paid the sum of two hundred túmáns ‡ to the officers [in charge of conducting the Báb to Ṭihrán] who allowed him to entertain the Báb in his house where He stayed for two nights.§ Ḥájí Mírzá Jání also invited me to go there and attain the presence of our beloved Lord.[2]

* In those days, the believers were very careful not to disclose their Faith indiscriminately to the public. They taught the Faith only to those who were truly sincere.

† One of the outstanding followers of the Báb and Bahá'u'lláh. For more information about him refer to *The Dawn-Breakers*, *Memorials of the Faithful* and *The Revelation of Bahá'u'lláh*, vol. I.

‡ This was considered a very large sum of money in those days.

§ The Báb actually stayed three nights in Káshán. Some historians have stated that one of the reasons that Ḥájí Mírzá Jání gave to the officers for entertaining the Báb in his house, was that the two of them were merchants and Ḥájí Mírzá Jání was anxious to clear up his accounts with Him.

Aḥmad then describes his meeting with the Báb and talks about His majesty, dignity and beauty as He conversed with a few of the divines of Ká<u>sh</u>án. Soon after this the number of believers in Ká<u>sh</u>án increased and persecutions started. Aḥmad continues his story:

One day, a number of ruffians attacked the believers and took all our possessions, they even broke all doors and windows. I hid myself in the wind tower* of the house and remained there for forty days. The friends brought me food and water in secret.

Since it became difficult to live in Ká<u>sh</u>án, I set off for Ba<u>gh</u>dád. It was about five years since Bahá'u'lláh had taken up residence in that city. On the way, I met a stranger who was also travelling. Both of us indicated that our destination was Karbilá.† Throughout the journey we conducted ourselves as Muslims and prayed according to Muslim rites. On our arrival in Ba<u>gh</u>dád, I walked in the direction of the house of Bahá'u'lláh. I found that my friend was also going in the same direction, and soon I discovered that he was also a Bábí! We had both dissimulated our faith.‡

After being admitted to the house of Bahá'u'lláh, I attained His presence. He turned to me and said 'What a man! He becomes a Bábí and then goes and hides in the wind tower!' § I remained in Ba<u>gh</u>dád for six years and worked as a

* Most old houses in central Persia had a huge ventilation shaft which looked like a tall tower. In the summer hot air would rise through it and cause a natural draught which helped cool part of the house. These were the wind towers which puzzled Marco Polo as he travelled through that part of the world.

† A holy city to which the followers of <u>Sh</u>í'ah Islám go on pilgrimage. Since Ba<u>gh</u>dád in those days was the focal point for the Bábís, people became suspicious, if someone set off for Ba<u>gh</u>dád, and often accused him of being a Bábí.

‡ Dissimulation of one's faith which is a form of lip-denial had been practised among <u>Sh</u>í'ah Muslims for centuries and was regarded as justifiable at times of peril. The Bábís often resorted to it also. It is, however, against the teachings of Bahá'u'lláh to dissimulate one's faith.

§ Not to be taken as the exact words of Bahá'u'lláh. However, they convey the sense of what He said. (A.T.)

hand-weaver. During this period my soul was bountifully nourished from His glorious presence and I had the great honour to live in the outer apartment of His blessed house.

One day, they brought the news of the death of Siyyid Ismá'íl of Zavárih.* Bahá'u'lláh said: 'No one has killed him. Behind many myriad veils of light, We showed him a glimmer of Our glory; he could not endure it and so he sacrificed himself.'† Some of us then went to the bank of the river and found the body of Siyyid Ismá'íl lying there. He had cut his own throat with a razor which was still held in his hand. We removed the body and buried it.

However, I was basking in the sunshine of Bahá'u'lláh's presence until the Sulṭán's decree for Bahá'u'lláh's departure to Constantinople was communicated. It was thirty-one days after Naw-Rúz that the Blessed Beauty went to the Garden of Najíb Pásh͟há. On that day the river overflowed and they had to open the lock gates to ease the situation. On the ninth day the flooding subsided and Bahá'u'lláh's family left the house in Bag͟hdád and went to the Garden. Immediately after their crossing, however, the river began to swell again and the lock gates had to be re-opened. On the twelfth day Bahá'u'lláh left for Constantinople. Some of the believers accompanied Him and some including this servant had to remain in Bag͟hdád. At the time of His departure, all of us were together in the Garden. Those who were to remain behind were standing on one side. His blessed Person came to us and spoke words of consolation to us. He said that it was better that we remain behind. He also said that He had allowed some to accompany Him, merely to prevent them from making mischief and creating trouble.

One of the friends recited the following poem of Sa'dí in a voice filled with emotion and deep sorrow:

> 'Let us shed tears as clouds pour down in the spring;
> Even the stones wail when lovers part.'

Bahá'u'lláh responded, 'These words were truly meant for today.'[3]†

* See vol. I, pp. 101–3.

† Not to be taken as the exact words of Bahá'u'lláh. However, they convey the sense of what He said. (A.T.)

These few stories of Bahá'u'lláh which Aḥmad has left to posterity, together with this brief account of his own life, constitute the major part of his spoken chronicle. In it he has not described in detail the tremendous impact which his attaining the presence of the Báb and Bahá'u'lláh had upon him. Nor has he spoken about those six glorious years that he lived in such close proximity to Bahá'u'lláh. But we know that there were very few among the companions of Bahá'u'lláh in Baghdád who acquired such faith and spiritual insight as Aḥmad did. He was vivified by the potency of the Revelation of Bahá'u'lláh, and had the capacity and worthiness to acquire from Him such great spiritual magnetism and radiance that they dominated his being throughout his long life.

Of him, Ḥájí Muḥammad-Ṭáhir-i-Málmírí writes:

> Aḥmad stayed in Baghdád for some years and attained the presence of Bahá'u'lláh there. He became the recipient of His bounties and favours. Once he told me that he had beheld the innermost Beauty of the Blessed Perfection.* He was speaking the truth, because he had a Tablet in the handwriting of Bahá'u'lláh which testified that Aḥmad had gazed upon His hidden Beauty.[4]

After Bahá'u'lláh's departure for Constantinople, Aḥmad remained in Baghdád and served the Faith in that city with great devotion. However, in his heart he was longing to attain the presence of His Lord again. After some time, he could no longer bear to stay away and so he set off for Adrianople. When he arrived in Constantinople, Bahá'u'lláh sent him a Tablet which is now universally known as the *Tablet of Aḥmad*. On reading this Tablet, Aḥmad knew what was expected of him. He surrendered his own will to Bahá'u'lláh's and instead of completing his journey to Adrianople and attaining the presence of His Lord, he returned to Persia with the sole purpose of teaching and propagating the Message of Bahá'u'lláh to the Bábí community.

* Bahá'u'lláh. (A.T.)

Following the example of Muníb and Nabíl-i-A'ẓam who were sent by Bahá'u'lláh to teach His Cause, Aḥmad travelled extensively throughout Persia and gave the glad-tidings of the coming of 'Him Whom God shall make manifest' to many of the Bábís. Through his dedicated efforts a great many recognized the station of Bahá'u'lláh and became His ardent followers. The Bábí community at that time was in such a state of deprivation and perversity that sometimes the Bábís showed hostility towards Bahá'í teachers. In his spoken chronicle Aḥmad has recounted one such incident in Khurásán. He says:

> I left Ṭihrán for Khurásán and spoke to many concerning the advent of 'Him Whom God shall make manifest'. I went to Furúgh* (Province of Khurásán) in the garb of a dervish, and spoke about 'Him Whom God shall make manifest' to Mullá Mírzá Muḥammad † and his brothers. In the course of our discussions they became aggressive and fiercely assaulted me. In the struggle which ensued they broke my tooth. When the fighting had stopped and emotions subsided, I resumed the discussion, saying that the Báb had specifically mentioned that 'Him Whom God shall make manifest' would appear by the name of Bahá. They promised to accept the claims of Bahá'u'lláh should I be able to verify my statement. I asked them to bring the Writings of the Báb to me. They made an opening in the wall and took out all the Writings which were hidden for fear of the enemy.‡ As soon as I opened one of them, we found a passage which indicated that 'He Whom God shall make manifest' would bear the

* Bahá'u'lláh has designated new names for certain towns and villages in the Province of Khurásán: Furúgh (Brightness) for Dúgh-Ábád; Madínatu'r-Riḍván (City of Paradise) for Níshápúr; Madínatu'l-Khaḍrá (the Verdant City) for Sabzivár; Fárán (Párán) for Tún; and Jadhbá (Ecstasy) for Ṭabas. Bahá'í writers use the new designations in their writings.

† A survivor of the struggle of Shaykh Ṭabarsí, he became an ardent follower of Bahá'u'lláh.

‡ To protect the Holy Writings as well as their own lives, the early believers often kept the Writings in containers which were hidden in the walls or under the ground.

name of Bahá. They happily embraced the Faith of Bahá'u'lláh and I left them and travelled to other towns.[5]

It is interesting to note that these brothers in Furúgh became outstanding Bahá'ís, especially Mírzá Maḥmúd-i-Furúghí, the son of Mullá Mírzá Muḥammad. He was an heroic soul, an embodiment of faith and courage, and the indefatigable defender of the Covenant of Bahá'u'lláh.

Concerning Aḥmad and his latter days, Ḥájí Muḥammad-Ṭáhir-i-Málmírí has written the following:

> For some time Aḥmad lived and worked in Káshán. The Tablet of Aḥmad (Arabic) was revealed in his honour and he used to carry with him the original Tablet which is in the handwriting of the Blessed Beauty. However, his wife died in Káshán and his daughter* was married to a man who held the post of Saqqá-Báshí [water supplier] to the court of Náṣiri'd-Dín Sháh in Ṭihrán. Soon after this he went to Shíráz and then to Nayríz where he married again and lived in that area for about twenty years. He also spent some time at Sarvistán (province of Fárs). He was a very simple man, pure and truthful. The reason for his coming to Munj was that he wanted to go to Ṭihrán. His daughter . . . had written repeatedly to Áqáy-i-Bashír-i-Iláhí,† requesting him to arrange for her aged father to go to Ṭihrán, as she longed to see him once again. However, Aḥmad was not much inclined to go. He was ninety-six years of age when he arrived at Munj, but was in the utmost health and vigour. He spent most of his time in reading the Holy Writings, especially his own Tablet which he chanted very often. He stayed for four years in Munj until the Afnán‡ arranged for him to travel to Ṭihrán in the care of his trusted servant. He stayed for some time in Ṭihrán and went for a visit to Qazvín.[6]

* Soon after Aḥmad became a Bábí he lost his only son who was survived by a young boy named Jamál, the grandson of Aḥmad. Later Aḥmad took Jamál under his care and protection and Jamál remained a steadfast Bahá'í all his life.

† A believer of wide repute in Shíráz.

‡ Mírzá Muḥammad-Báqir-i-Afnán.

The *Tablet of Aḥmad* is endowed with a special potency, and for this reason the believers often recite it at times of difficulty or trouble. Although a short Tablet, it contains all the verities of the Cause of Bahá'u'lláh and may be regarded as a charter setting out the requirements of faith and servitude for the individual.

In it Bahá'u'lláh refers to Himself as the 'Nightingale of Paradise', the 'Most Great Beauty' and the 'Tree of Life' and proclaims His august station to those who are pure in heart; He announces the advent of the Day of God and clearly indicates that he who attains His presence has entered the presence of God.

In the opening passages of this Tablet, Bahá'u'lláh announces the exalted nature of His Revelation. The terms He has used are such as to leave no doubt, for the followers of the Báb, that He was unmistakably declaring Himself to be 'Him Whom God shall make manifest', the Promised One of the *Bayán*. He also makes it clear that only those who are sincere and detached from everything may approach His court of holiness.

The fact that Bahá'u'lláh, in this and many other Tablets, emphasizes sincerity as a prerequisite for recognition of His station is in itself one of the proofs of the authenticity of His Message. In the presence of God there is no room for hypocrisy and deceit. In the same way that light dispels darkness, the power of truth rejects falsehood.

However, through His mercy God shows forbearance in order that the unfaithful may have the opportunity to mend their ways. For years Bahá'u'lláh tolerated the companionship of some insincere and perfidious men, with such magnanimity and grace that they all felt at ease in His presence. Ḥájí Mírzá Ḥaydar-'Alí, in his soul-stirring book of reminiscences, the *Bihjatu'ṣ-Ṣudúr* (The Delight of the Hearts), has recorded what Bahá'u'lláh said on this subject in 'Akká:

> . . . He [Bahá'u'lláh] then said 'If people had eyes to see, they would not confuse the signs of God with those of

others. By observing the unseemly conduct of some of those who circle around Me, they would be enabled to realize, to a greater extent, the glory, the majesty, the greatness, the power and the ascendancy of God, the All-Sufficient, the Sin-Coverer, the Forgiving, the Merciful, He Who is patient and forbearing. We hear lies, but We conceal them and remain silent. Then the people who lie think that We have believed their words and that they have managed to confuse the issue in Our presence.'*[7]

In a Tablet to a certain Muḥammad-'Alí, Bahá'u'lláh reveals the following:

I swear by the beauty of the Well-Beloved! This is the Mercy that hath encompassed the entire creation, the Day whereon the grace of God hath permeated and pervaded all things. The living waters of My mercy, O 'Alí, are fast pouring down, and Mine heart is melting with the heat of My tenderness and love. At no time have I been able to reconcile Myself to the afflictions befalling My loved ones, or to any trouble that could becloud the joy of their hearts.

Every time My name 'the All-Merciful' was told that one of My lovers hath breathed a word that runneth counter to My wish, it repaired, grief-stricken and disconsolate to its abode; and whenever My name 'the Concealer' discovered that one of My followers had inflicted any shame or humiliation on his neighbour, it, likewise, turned back chagrined and sorrowful to its retreats of glory, and there wept and mourned with a sore lamentation. And whenever My name 'the Ever-Forgiving' perceived that any one of My friends had committed any transgression, it cried out in its great distress, and, overcome with anguish, fell upon the dust, and was borne away by a company of the invisible angels to its habitation in the realms above.

* These are not the exact words of Bahá'u'lláh. They are the recollections from memory of Ḥájí Mírzá Ḥaydar-'Alí, as no one would be capable of taking notes in the presence of Bahá'u'lláh and in any case this would have been considered disrespectful in such a holy atmosphere, except when He revealed Tablets and his amanuensis took them down.

> By Myself, the True One, O 'Alí! The fire that hath inflamed the heart of Bahá is fiercer than the fire that gloweth in thine heart, and His lamentation louder than thy lamentation. Every time the sin committed by any one amongst them was breathed in the Court of His Presence, the Ancient Beauty would be so filled with shame as to wish He could hide the glory of His countenance from the eyes of all men, for He hath, at all times, fixed His gaze on their fidelity, and observed its essential requisites.[8]

In another Tablet[9] He explains that through His attribute 'The Concealer' He has concealed the faults and shortcomings of many deceitful men, who, as a result, have thought that the Manifestation of God was ignorant of their evil deeds. These men did not realize that through the knowledge of God Bahá'u'lláh was fully aware of their wrong-doings, but the sin-covering eye of God had not disclosed their iniquities. Only when they were about to harm the Cause of God did He expel them from His presence and cast them out from among the 'people of Bahá'. This is how, for example, Bahá'u'lláh treated Siyyid Muḥammad-i-Iṣfahání, or Ḥájí Mírzá Aḥmad-i-Ká<u>sh</u>ání* and several others who for years were associating with Him. Otherwise their insincerity was so obvious that even Bahá'u'lláh's faithful companions had noticed it. Eventually He dismissed these unfaithful souls and they threw in their lot with Mírzá Yaḥyá.

There were others who remained in the Faith for several decades, although from the beginning it became clear to many that they were corrupt and sinful men. Notorious among them were Jamál-i-Burújirdí, entitled by Bahá'u'lláh, Ismu'lláhu'l-Jamál (The Name of God, Jamál), and Siyyid Mihdíy-i-Dahají entitled Ismu'lláhu'l-Mihdí (The Name of God, Mihdí). For many years these ambitious and deceitful men were foremost among the teachers of the Faith and their fame spread throughout the community. However, their hypocrisy was known to those who were close to them. Bahá'u'lláh concealed their

* See chapter 6.

faults, revealed many Tablets for each of them, exhorted them to faithfulness and nobility and with forbearance and magnanimity overlooked their shortcomings. However, He admonished them for some of their actions which were harmful to the Faith.

For example, on one occasion, two outstanding believers, one of whom was later appointed by Bahá'u'lláh as one of the Hands of His Cause, were on their way to the province of Khurásán to meet the believers and teach the Cause. Jamál-i-Burújirdí became highly jealous of these two men. Secretly he warned the friends to keep away from them and introduced them with a vulgar term as two foreboders of evil. This action evoked the wrath of Bahá'u'lláh. The veil of concealment which for years had protected Jamál in the hope that he would repent, was now rent asunder. The sin-covering eye of God which through loving-kindness had watched over him for so long was withdrawn. In a wrathful Tablet Bahá'u'lláh condemned the actions of Jamál and severely rebuked him for his behaviour. Jamál, however, survived this great blow which for a time shattered his prestige and reputation among the friends. He was a master of hypocrisy and soon managed to regain his position as one of the renowned teachers of the Faith in the community.

After the ascension of Bahá'u'lláh, Jamál and Siyyid Mihdí both broke the Covenant and rebelled against 'Abdu'l-Bahá. They and their supporters tried very hard to bring divisions in the Faith, but were utterly confounded by the power of the Covenant, and soon perished.*

In the *Tablet of Aḥmad* Bahá'u'lláh pays a moving tribute to the Báb and affirms that He was the King of Messengers. This statement, which constitutes one of the basic beliefs of the followers of Bahá'u'lláh, had a special significance for Bahá'í teachers in those days. For their primary mission was to teach the Cause of Bahá'u'lláh to the members of the Bábí community.

* For more details of their lives see p. 264 ff. and p. 272 ff. respectively.

Those who have denied and opposed the Manifestations of God have always resorted to using the two weapons of the weak, namely persecution and the dissemination of false propaganda. Certainly some of the Bábís who had rejected the Cause of Bahá'u'lláh used this second weapon and spread false accusations that the Bahá'ís had no regard for the Báb. Such preposterous claims were designed to poison the minds of simple-hearted people. Bahá'u'lláh, in this Tablet and many others which were revealed in this period, extols the station of the Báb, refers to the *Bayán* as the Mother Book and enjoins on all to obey its laws and ordinances. However, most of these laws were later abrogated when Bahá'u'lláh formulated the laws and ordinances of His Faith in the *Kitáb-i-Aqdas* (The Most Holy Book) which became the Mother Book of this Dispensation.

One of the most illuminating passages in the *Tablet of Aḥmad* is the following:

> O people, if ye deny these verses, by what proof have ye believed in God? Produce it, O assemblage of false ones.
>
> Nay, by the One in Whose hand is my soul, they are not, and never shall be able to do this, even should they combine to assist one another.[10]

In this challenging statement Bahá'u'lláh reaffirms that one of the mightiest proofs of His divine station is His Word. In His Writings Bahá'u'lláh states that the first testimony which establishes the truth of the Manifestation of God is His own Self. Often it is said that the proof of the sun is the sun itself. These are the words of Bahá'u'lláh revealed in the *Lawḥ-i-Ashraf*:*

> Say: The first and foremost testimony establishing His truth is His own Self. Next to this testimony is His revelation. For whoso faileth to recognize either the one or the other He hath established the words He hath revealed as proof of His reality and truth. This is, verily, an evidence of His tender mercy unto men.[11]

* See chapter 10.

The disciples of Bahá'u'lláh who were endowed with pure hearts and had the inestimable privilege of attaining His presence were similar to those who have seen the sun with their own eyes. They witnessed the glory of His Revelation and were in no need of proofs. The arguments, controversies and doubts are always heard from those quarters which are placed in darkness.

In this day, however, in order to recognize the station of Bahá'u'lláh we must turn to His words. For the Word of the Manifestation is endowed with spiritual forces beyond the ken of men. No human being, however accomplished, not even the whole of the human race put together, could ever hope to create such spiritual potency as is released by the Word of God. Indeed, one of the differences between the Word of God and the word of man is that the former derives its power from the worlds of God, is creative and penetrates deep into the hearts of men; while the latter pertains to the world of creation. It is limited and basically impotent. The word of man has no lasting influence upon society unless it derives its potency from the teachings of God.

History has amply demonstrated the power of the Word of the Manifestations of God. Moses appeared poor and helpless in the eyes of Pharaoh, but His Word had such influence as to defeat the forces of tyranny and transform the children of Israel from a state of bondage into that of sovereignty. Christ was condemned for proclaiming a new Message. The civil and ecclesiastical authorities, hand in hand, crucified Him in order to destroy His Cause. His Word, however, potent and creative, penetrated into the western world, changed the hearts of millions, swept aside the standards of the Roman Empire and reared a new civilization in its place. Likewise Muḥammad, often misunderstood in the West, revealed the Word of God as recorded in the *Qur'án*. His teachings and words shaped the conduct of a multiracial nation for centuries and now after a thousand years the influence of His words and the signs of His sovereignty are discernible among the Muslim communities.

The utterances of the Báb and Bahá'u'lláh constitute the Word of God for this age. So tremendous has been the effect of Their words that thousands of men and women have gone to the field of martyrdom and given their lives in order to promulgate Their teachings.

The Old Testament, the New Testament, the *Qur'án*, the Bábí and Bahá'í Scriptures, all have been the source of guidance, inspiration and spiritual life for many millions. No other book, however exalted its theme—and there are millions of them—has had a comparable influence upon the minds and souls of men as these heavenly books.

A careful study of the Faith of Bahá'u'lláh will demonstrate that the efficacy and potency of His words are unprecedented in the annals of mankind. We can already witness the creative power of the words of Bahá'u'lláh within the present society. To cite one example, Bahá'u'lláh wrote only a few lines in the *Kitáb-i-Aqdas* enjoining upon His followers to establish, in every town, a House of Justice* (at present known as a Spiritual Assembly). This injunction, written just over a hundred years ago by a prisoner in 'Akká, exerted such an influence upon the hearts that thousands of men and women from all walks of life, of all colours and backgrounds, left their homes, scattered throughout the world, pioneered to the most inhospitable outposts of the globe, suffered many hardships and difficulties, sacrificed their substance and poured out their resources in order to establish these institutions. And they are continuing to carry out this commandment until every locality on this planet has its House of Justice. Such is the creative power of the Word of God uttered by Bahá'u'lláh! The same is true of every other commandment issued by the Supreme Pen.†

Addressing the unbelieving Arabs, the Voice of God proclaims in the *Qur'án*:

* Not to be confused with the Universal House of Justice, the supreme international body of the Faith.

† Bahá'u'lláh.

> And if ye be in doubt as to that which We have sent down to Our Servant,* then produce a Súrah like it, and summon your witnesses, beside God, if ye are men of truth.[12]

When this verse was revealed, a few learned men among the unbelievers composed some verses and publicized them saying that they were much more eloquent than the words of Muḥammad. But they did not realize that their verses could not influence a soul, whereas the *Qur'án* revolutionized the lives of millions throughout the world, and in its own time created a great civilization embracing many nations.

These words of Bahá'u'lláh in the *Tablet of Aḥmad* 'Produce it, O assemblage of false ones!' echo the words of the *Qur'án*, but with this greater challenge: 'Nay, by the One in Whose hand is my soul, they are not, and never shall be able to do this, even should they combine to assist one another.'[13]

Another proof of the Manifestations of God is the manner in which They influence society. This is a unique phenomenon which no man can ever hope to equal. Let us consider some of the ways and means by which a human being can become a leader and establish a following for himself. History shows many examples. For instance, a despotic ruler can rely on his power to subdue millions under his leadership. People will rally around him as long as he remains in power. Once he is gone, the whole system collapses, and his followers are dispersed. Similarly, a man of wealth and affluence who is willing to bestow his riches upon the people may emerge as a leader. As long as his support is forthcoming there will be many who will cluster around him. A person with social popularity and prestige may find himself becoming the centre of attraction for some admirers. A strong-willed man, by appealing to the lower nature of man, or exciting the people's sentiments, may succeed in bringing about an uprising or a revolution in which he himself becomes a focal point. Another category worth mentioning is the religious leader who leads by teaching his

* Muḥammad.

congregation what they already believe. Should he ever decide to teach them something new, and persist in doing this, he is almost bound to be dismissed from office.

In all these examples the leader must rely on some worldly agency in order to succeed in his plans to influence people. Such an agency could be earthly power, or wealth, or social or political prestige, or religious leadership or many more. The Manifestation of God, however, lacks all these material forces.

Let us take the example of Christ. When He appeared and manifested His Cause among the Jews, He did not have earthly power or wealth by which He could influence His followers. Because of the circumstances of His birth He did not have any social standing in the community. He was not promoting His Cause by appealing to the lower instinct of man. Nor was He a religious leader preaching the established religion of the time; on the contrary He was teaching a new faith. During the three years of His ministry He suffered persecution and in the end was crucified. Yet there was a mysterious power in His Cause which penetrated the hearts of many people who became His followers. And even after the lapse of almost two thousand years, millions still turn to Him in devotion and love. This demonstrates the power of the Holy Spirit and shows the contrast between human enterprise and divine Revelation.

Similarly, the Cause of Bahá'u'lláh is spreading and being established throughout the world solely through the power of God. However, being the Supreme Revelation of God, it is endowed with a potency greater than all the Revelations of the past.* Though its Author spent forty years of His ministry in exile and imprisonment under the most cruel circumstances, though the forces of two despotic potentates were leagued against Him, yet in the course of that ministry He never sought assistance for the promotion of His Faith from anybody, nor did he try to establish it through compromise, expedient measures or material means. With a meekness that is characteristic of all the Manifestations of God, He submitted Himself to

* See vol. I, pp. 64–7.

His enemies and bore with resignation and patience the wrongs they inflicted on Him. In spite of bitter opposition, however, the proclamation of His Message from His prison cell reached the ears of the most powerful rulers of the time. The light of His Faith projected itself, during His lifetime, to thirteen countries on the Asiatic and African continents. That light is now diffused over the entire surface of the earth. His teachings have become the Spirit of the Age and the institutions of His World Order, designed to bring about the oneness of the human race on this planet, are rising throughout the world.

All these achievements, foreshadowing the future triumph of the Cause of Bahá'u'lláh and its establishment in the fullness of time as the all-encompassing religion for mankind, have come about through the power of Bahá'u'lláh which is born of God, while the forces of this world work against Him.

Every religion has a period of validity during which it exerts a great influence upon humanity and brings about spiritual and material development, especially for those who have embraced it. The Word of the Founder of that religion influences the hearts of people and His teachings can be put into practice. But when a new Manifestation of God appears the former religion becomes ineffective. Its influence wanes and its creative power diminishes. Its message no longer moves the heart and its teachings cease to be practical. For God has imparted to the new Revelation the validity, inspiration and influence which will lead humanity to a further point in the course of its development. The following verse in the *Qur'án* clearly indicates that for every religion there is a time of birth and a time of death:

> Unto every nation* there is a prefixed term; therefore when their term is expired, they shall not have respite for an hour, neither shall they be anticipated.[14]

In this day, the power of God and His mighty Revelation animates the Cause of Bahá'u'lláh, endowing it with a world-

* The word 'nation' is a translation of the Arabic word 'ummat' which also means religious community.

vitalizing spirit which, unaided by any earthly agency, diffuses its light over the entire surface of this planet, and builds the foundations of a universal order for the advancement and spiritualization of the entire human race.

In the *Tablet of Aḥmad*, Bahá'u'lláh reveals:

> . . . verily, he who turns away from this Beauty* hath also turned away from the Messengers of the past and showeth pride towards God from all eternity to all eternity.[15]

This statement reaffirms one of the fundamental verities of the Faith of God, that divine Revelation is progressive, the latest Manifestation of God embodying within His Revelation the essence of all past Revelations. This is similar to a human being who contains within himself at every stage in his life those qualities and attributes which he had previously acquired.†

Through the potency and inspiration of His words Bahá'u'lláh instilled in Aḥmad a tremendous power of faith and detachment. He conferred upon him the capacity and strength to become as 'a flame of fire' to His enemies and 'a river of life eternal' to His loved ones. Water and fire have different characteristics. Water gives life, enabling things to grow; whereas fire, while burning away objects which are perishable, creates warmth and incandescence in solid materials. The love of Bahá'u'lláh, once implanted in the heart of the believer, needs to be nourished and watered. On the other hand, the evils of hate and animosity which have been imbedded in the hearts of the enemies must needs be consumed with the fire of the love of God, so that those who are sincere may acquire the radiance and warmth of faith. Aḥmad and other distinguished teachers of the Faith who travelled throughout the land performed this function. They enthused the believers, raised their spirits and vivified their souls with the life-giving waters of the Cause of

* Bahá'u'lláh.

† See vol. I, p. 65.

God. On the other hand, they appeared as a 'flame of fire' to the enemies of the Cause.

Bahá'u'lláh has made similar exhortations in other Writings. For example, in a Tablet[16] to Umm-i-'Aṭṭár (Mother of 'Aṭṭár), He counsels her not to associate with those who have denied His Cause and risen against Him. But if ever she met them, she should appear as the 'fire of God' so that they might feel the warmth of her love towards her Lord. In another Tablet,[17] he urges a certain believer to burn, with the fire of the Word of God, the hearts of those who have denied Him and turned aside from His Cause.

Statements such as these should not be taken literally. Bahá'u'lláh never taught His followers to act aggressively towards others. But there is an invisible power, a spiritual dynamism in the Cause of God which removes every obstacle in its path and shatters the forces of its enemies. Some of Bahá'u'lláh's disciples were endowed with this power. Their tongues were as swords tearing asunder those hearts which were filled with animosity towards the Blessed Beauty. Through the potency and fire of their utterance these heroic souls burned away the veils of prejudice and hatred and overwhelmed the forces of the unfaithful who had arisen to subvert the edifice of the Cause of God.

In a Tablet which was revealed for Ḥájí Mírzá Aḥmad of Ká<u>sh</u>án,* Bahá'u'lláh exhorts his servants in these words:

> Be ablaze as the fire, that ye may burn away the veils of heedlessness and set aglow, through the quickening energies of the love of God, the chilled and wayward heart. Be light and untrammelled as the breeze, that ye may obtain admittance into the precincts of My court, My inviolable Sanctuary.[18]

Faith in God and steadfastness in His path are relative terms. The strength of a weak person is considered weakness for a strong man. To the saint, the love and devotion of the insincere

* See chapter 6.

towards God is nothing but profanity. Therefore the measure of faith varies with the individual. Bahá'u'lláh in His Tablet has summoned Aḥmad to attain the highest degree of faith. His exhortations to him are designed to lead him and others to the summit of steadfastness and courage. It is difficult to visualize that God may require a higher degree of steadfastness and faith than that demanded by Bahá'u'lláh in these words:

> And be thou so steadfast in My love that thy heart shall not waver, even if the swords of the enemies rain blows upon thee and all the heavens and the earth arise against thee.[19]

These words of Bahá'u'lláh may well serve as a criterion by which the individual may determine whether he has said this Tablet with 'absolute sincerity'. The sign of sincerity is that the believer rises to such heights of faith and steadfastness that his heart does not waver even if he finds himself faced with martyrdom at the hand of the enemy. The fact that Bahá'u'lláh has established this exalted standard of faith is in itself a proof that many people will arise and achieve it. For the words of Bahá'u'lláh are creative, and the moment He uttered them, He instilled a new spirit of courage into the hearts of those who had truly recognized Him. Not only had Aḥmad become endowed with the power of faith, but many others reached the loftiest heights of certitude and heroism. These souls completely banished every trace of trepidation and doubt from their hearts, remained steadfast as a mountain in the Cause of God and fearlessly faced their executioners.

To cite one example, let us recount some of the events leading to the martyrdom of one of the outstanding followers of Bahá'u'lláh, Ḥájí 'Abdu'l-Majíd-i-Ní<u>sh</u>ápúrí, who became the embodiment of faith and detachment. He was the father of Áqá Buzurg entitled Badí', who at the age of seventeen attained the presence of Bahá'u'lláh in the barracks of 'Akká, delivered the Tablet of Bahá'u'lláh to Náṣiri'd-Dín <u>Sh</u>áh and was consequently put to death by his men.

Ḥájí 'Abdu'l-Majíd, addressed by Bahá'u'lláh as Abá Badí' (Father of Badí') embraced the Faith during the ministry of the Báb. He was among those early believers in the province of Khurásán taught by Mullá Ḥusayn-i-Bushrú'í.* He took part in the struggles at Shaykh Ṭabarsí† and was one of the survivors of that bloody upheaval.

On his way to that fortress, Abá Badí', who was a wealthy man, was also the first to obey the exhortation of Mullá Ḥusayn calling on his companions to discard their earthly possessions and leave behind everything except their swords and horses. He flung by the roadside a satchel full of turquoise which was worth a fortune. When the news of the Declaration of Bahá'u'lláh reached him, Abá Badí' joyously acknowledged His station and with great devotion spent his days in serving His Cause. In 1876, at an advanced age, longing to attain the presence of Bahá'u'lláh, he travelled to 'Akká where he basked in the sunshine of His glory. He has left to posterity the following spoken chronicle concerning one of his memorable interviews with Bahá'u'lláh:

> One day I had the honour to be in the presence of the Blessed Beauty when He was talking about Badí' who had attained His presence, carried His Blessed Tablet to Ṭihrán [for Náṣiri'd-Dín Sháh] and won the crown of martyrdom. As He was speaking, my tears were flowing profusely and my beard became wet. Bahá'u'lláh turned to me and said 'Abá Badí'! A person who has already spent three-quarters of his life should offer up the remainder in the path of God . . .' I asked 'Is it possible that my beard which is now soaked in my tears may one day be dyed crimson with my blood?' The Blessed Beauty replied 'God willing . . .'‡[20]

* The first person to believe in the Báb. For further information see *The Dawn-Breakers*.

† See *The Dawn-Breakers*.

‡ The words attributed to Bahá'u'lláh are not necessarily His exact words. These are the recollections of Abá Badí', but convey the sense of what He said.

Abá Badí' returned to his native land of Khurásán, his heart glowing with the fire of the love of Bahá'u'lláh and his soul radiant with the light of His glory. He used to attend the gatherings of the friends at Mashhad where he enthused and encouraged them to steadfastness in the Cause of God and also read to them passages from the *Kitáb-i-Aqdas*, the first copy of which he had brought to Khurásán. One of the subjects he often discussed was the then imminent fulfilment of the prophecy of Bahá'u'lláh concerning the downfall of Sulṭán 'Abdu'l-'Azíz mentioned in the Tablets of *Ra'ís* and *Fu'ád*.* He spent most of his time transcribing the Tablets of Bahá'u'lláh.

The enthusiasm with which Abá Badí' taught the Faith soon aroused the animosity of the enemies of the Cause. Foremost among them were his own brother and sister who reported his activities to a certain *mujtahid*, Shaykh Muḥammad Taqíy-i-Bujnúrdí. They informed him that their brother, a Bábí for many years, had been one of the disciples of Mullá Ḥusayn and had fought at Shaykh Ṭabarsí, and that his son had been put to death by order of the Sháh. They disclosed all his activities including his recent visit to Bahá'u'lláh and his open teaching of the Bahá'í Faith. The *mujtahid* was alarmed by these reports and despatched two of his men to question Abá Badí' who openly spoke to them about his beliefs and proclaimed the Message of Bahá'u'lláh to them. This open confession of faith meant that there was no difficulty then in issuing his death warrant. This was in 1877, one year after Abá Badí' had attained the presence of Bahá'u'lláh in 'Akká. He was then eighty-five years of age.

As the machinations of the clergy and the people were beginning to bear fruit, an implacable enemy of the Cause, Shaykh Muḥammad-Báqir of Iṣfahán, stigmatized by Bahá'u'lláh as 'Wolf',† arrived in Mashhad, and played a major part in this heinous crime. At first he ordered that Abá Badí' appear before him. When the latter did not pay any attention to his orders, he joined hands with the fore-mentioned Shaykh Muḥammad-

* These Tablets will be discussed in vol. III.

† See *Epistle to the Son of the Wolf*, Introduction.

Taqí and a certain <u>Sh</u>ay<u>kh</u> 'Abdu'r-Raḥím who was foremost among the divines of <u>Kh</u>urásán. These three *mujtahids* sent a petition to Prince Muḥammad-Taqí Mírzá, the Rukni'd-Daw-lih, a brother of the <u>Sh</u>áh and the Governor of <u>Kh</u>urásán, demanding the execution of Abá Badí'. The Prince was good-natured and very reluctant to harm the Bahá'ís, but could not resist the enormous pressures which were brought to bear by the clergy. He issued orders for the arrest of Abá Badí' who was taken into custody. But the Rukni'd-Dawlih, unwilling to harm the prisoner, did not pursue the matter any further. The divines became impatient with him and took their complaint to Náṣiri'd-Dín <u>Sh</u>áh. The King issued orders that the victim should be freed only if he denied allegiance to the new Faith.

After this, <u>Sh</u>ay<u>kh</u> Muḥammad-Báqir kept on pressing the Prince for execution. He went to the home of the Governor and discussed his evil plans with him. These involved tying Abá Badí' to an airborne balloon which had just been brought to Ma<u>shh</u>ad as a novelty, and letting him fall to his death. As discussions were proceeding, a tragedy struck the home of the Prince. His young daughter, to whom he was very attached, fell into a pool in the house and was drowned. The grief-stricken Prince left the meeting and <u>Sh</u>ay<u>kh</u> Báqir's plans had to be abandoned. The wife of the Prince was convinced that the tragic death of her daughter had come about as a punishment from God for inflicting imprisonment upon the aged Abá Badí'. She rebuked her husband very sternly and the only thing he could do was to order the transfer of Abá Badí' to other quarters whose officer in charge was friendly to the Bahá'ís.

<u>Sh</u>ay<u>kh</u> Muḥammad-Báqir, who could no longer tolerate the passive attitude and delaying tactics of the Prince, sent another complaint to the <u>Sh</u>áh. For the second time, the monarch instructed the Prince to release the prisoner if he recanted, otherwise to deal with him in accordance with the law of religion. The Prince, who was very anxious to save Abá Badí' from execution, sent two prominent men to talk to him and induce him to recant his faith. One was Mírzá Sa'íd <u>Kh</u>án, the

former Minister of Foreign Affairs;* the other was Prince Abu'l-Ḥasan Mírzá, the Shaykhu'r-Ra'ís,† who was a follower of Bahá'u'lláh. These two men pleaded with him on behalf of the Governor, that for his own protection he should make a statement that he bore no allegiance to the Cause. Only then would the Governor be able to defend his case and save his life. They explained to him that there was no other way, because the hands of the Governor were tied and he could do nothing else to avert this situation.

Abá Badí' stood firm and resolute. He could not barter his Faith for this transitory world. The love of Bahá'u'lláh had so magnetized him that there was no fear in his heart. He told them to convey to the Rukni'd-Dawlih that he could neither recant nor dissimulate his Faith, and that he would be prepared to give his life if necessary. The Governor did not give up. He persevered in his plan to induce Abá Badí' to recant. He is reported to have sent about twelve men at different times, all of whom were reckoned among the dignitaries of the Province of Khurásán, to persuade him to change his course of action. But they all failed. One of these men reported that instead of paying heed to the exhortations of the Rukni'd-Dawlih, Abá Badí' was engaged in teaching him the Faith of Bahá'u'lláh. Eventually the end came. The Prince had no choice but to carry out the wishes of the clergy and therefore issued orders for the execution of Abá Badí'.

One day before his martyrdom, Abá Badí' asked a certain believer, Khadíjih Khánum, who used to visit him every day in jail and was a link between him and the believers, not to come again, for he knew that the next day was to be his last in this world. He had a dream that they brought a horse on which to

* See vol. I, pp. 225–6.

† He was a poet of remarkable talent, a literary man of great eloquence, who because of his rank and personality was able to carry on his public function and at the same time associate with the Bahá'ís. He attained the presence of 'Abdu'l-Bahá in the Holy Land and has written many moving poems in glorification of Bahá'u'lláh and 'Abdu'l-Bahá.

take him away; he mounted the horse, but when he arrived at Maydán-i-Arg (a public square at Ma<u>sh</u>had) he fell from the horse. He told <u>Kh</u>adíjih <u>Kh</u>ánum that this public square would be the scene of his martyrdom.

The following day, the jailer secretly informed the believers that the fateful hour had arrived and the execution would take place that day. The friends, grief-stricken, gathered in the House of Bábíyyih* praying and waiting for news. In the meantime a number of government officials, the executioners and a large crowd of people had gathered outside the prison. After a few hours, the old but imposing figure of Abá Badí' emerged from the prison. His radiant face and white beard gave him a dignified bearing, while the heavy chain around his frail neck made him the very picture of meekness and resignation. He was conducted amid the jeers and insults of a hostile crowd to the court of the Governor. On the way he faced the spectators and, beaming with joy, recited these two lines of a celebrated Persian poem:

> To God's pleasure we are resigned;
> A chained lion feels no shame.
> To my neck the Beloved's cord is tied;
> He leads me whither His will ordains.

In the government house, he appeared before three people: the Governor, the fore-mentioned Mírzá Sa'íd <u>Kh</u>án and <u>Sh</u>ay<u>kh</u> Muḥammad-Báqir. The latter, addressing Abá Badí', said: 'We have no doubt about your being a Bahá'í, but if you are not, you must now execrate and denounce the Founders of this Faith.' Abá Badí' refused to do so. The <u>Sh</u>ay<u>kh</u> then asked him: 'What was wrong with Islám that you became a Bahá'í?' Abá Badí' spoke about the beliefs of the followers of Bahá'u'lláh and concluded his statement by saying that the reality and the essence of Islám was within this Faith. Next the Governor

* An historic house which was once the centre of great activities for the Bábís in Ma<u>sh</u>had. See *The Dawn-Breakers*.

pleaded with Abá Badí' to comply with the Shaykh's orders, but he again reiterated his refusal. The Shaykh insisted that unless he uttered words of execration against Bahá'u'lláh, he must be put to death. Mírzá Sa'íd Khán, who had previously interviewed Abá Badí' in the prison, was perturbed by the attitude of the Shaykh and stated that he found nothing in the prisoner's statements to indicate that he was an infidel and blasphemous, deserving of death. The Shaykh, angered by these remarks, merely pointed out to Mírzá Sa'íd Khán that he could not hope to secure the prisoner's freedom with these words, and thus deal a blow to the Faith of Islám. Addressing the Governor, the Shaykh then reiterated his verdict of death and the former ordered his men to carry it out.

Abá Badí' was led by the executioners to Maydán-i-Arg where great crowds had gathered to watch him die. One of the friends pushed his way through the people, until he came close to him. There he pleaded with him to recant at the last moment, saying it would save his life and would do no harm to his Faith. In reply Abá Badí' recited this Persian poem:

> Set thy trap for another bird;
> This is the phoenix and it nests high.

The Governor, who was very reluctant to shed the blood of a holy and innocent man, hoped that the fierce scene of execution might frighten Abá Badí' and induce him to recant. Just as the execution was about to take place a special envoy from the Governor arrived at the scene and for the last time pleaded with him in vain to save his own life. But Abá Badí' was the embodiment of steadfastness in the Cause of God. Neither the clamour of the people, their insults and persecutions, nor the dreadful sight of the executioner, who stood dagger in hand beside him, were able to deter him from the path of God. Most probably at the height of his ordeal his soul was communing with Bahá'u'lláh, longing to take its flight to the realms of the spirit. His thoughts must also have been focused on those memorable hours he had spent with His Lord in 'Akká, and the martyrdom of his beloved son at the age of seventeen, 'The Pride of the Martyrs of the Faith'.* Surrounded by thousands who were steeped in prejudice and hatred, hurling abuse and curses at him, this great hero, this old man of God glowed with the fire of faith and certitude. He stood serene and calm, unperturbed by the ferocity and brutality of his persecutors.

At last the officer in charge gave the signal and the executioner, dressed in red, stepped forward. He removed Abá Badí''s head-dress, shawl and cloak, brought him a bowl of water,† turned him to face the Qiblih ‡ of Islám and with a powerful stroke of the dagger ripped him open from waist to throat. His head, exposed for the public to see, was placed on a marble slab and his body dragged through the bazaars until it was abandoned at the city morgue. Many ruffians stayed near the corpse and prevented his family from approaching it. His inconsolable daughter (the sister of Badí'), with tears streaming from her face and holding her baby son in her arms, stood for hours at a distance along with her husband in order to visit the battered remains of her illustrious father. But the mob kept on hurling stones at them and she was forced to leave the scene in an agony too heart-rending to describe. The believers, who were watching these developments with great concern, worked out a plan to rescue the remains of Abá Badí'. Since his body was placed in the morgue in front of the mosque of the Sunnís, it was only natural for a Sunní to remove it. So one of the Bahá'ís, dressed in the garb of a Kurd and accompanied by two others, managed to take the body, carry it out of the city gate and bury it in the dead of night at a disused cemetery.

Thus ended the life of one who, till the end, stood firm and

* A title conferred on Badí' by Bahá'u'lláh.

† It is a ritual among the Shí'ah Muslims to offer a bowl of water to anyone who is to be put to death. This is because, at the time of his martyrdom, Imám Ḥusayn was thirsty. He had asked for water, but was denied it by the enemy.

‡ 'Point of Adoration' for the Muslims in Mecca, to which they turn in prayer.

immovable as a mountain in the Cause of his Lord, and with his own life-blood testified to its truth. He amply demonstrated the power of Bahá'u'lláh Who, through a single word, had created a new race of men, and instilled into them such faith that they became the embodiments of these words: 'And be thou so steadfast in My love that thy heart shall not waver, even if the swords of the enemies rain blows upon thee and all the heavens and the earth arise against thee.'

6

Lawḥ-i-Aḥmad (Persian)

Unlike the *Tablet of Aḥmad* in Arabic, this is a lengthy Tablet in Persian and was revealed for Ḥájí Mírzá Aḥmad of Káshán. He was a half-brother of Ḥájí Mírzá Jání and Ḥájí Muḥammad Ismá'íl,* the latter entitled Dhabíḥ (Sacrifice) and Anís (Companion) by Bahá'u'lláh. Ḥájí Mírzá Jání was the first to embrace the Faith of the Báb in Káshán. He had attained the presence of the Báb in Mecca and had become an ardent believer. When the Báb was on His way to Ṭihrán, Ḥájí Mírzá Jání, after having secured permission from the officials who were conducting the Báb to the Capital, entertained Him in his house for three days. Later he was martyred in Ṭihrán.†

As a result of association with this brother, Ḥájí Mírzá Aḥmad and his other half-brother, Ḥájí Muḥammad Ismá'íl both became Bábís.

Unlike his two brothers who stayed steadfast in the Cause of God, Ḥájí Mírzá Aḥmad showed unfaithfulness to Bahá'u'lláh and became a follower of Mírzá Yaḥyá. He first attained the presence of Bahá'u'lláh in Baghdád and later accompanied Him to Constantinople and Adrianople. He was one of those whom Bahá'u'lláh took with Him in order to check his mischief. In one of His Tablets[1] Bahá'u'lláh refers to Ḥájí Mírzá Aḥmad as one who attained the presence of His Lord and was honoured to associate with Him, yet failed to recognize His station. He heard the voice of God many a time but did not respond. The *Lawḥ-i-Aḥmad* (Tablet of Aḥmad) was revealed by Bahá'u'lláh in Adrianople, in order to guide him to the path of faith and

* See pp. 411–13 ff.

† See *The Dawn-Breakers*.

belief. This Tablet demonstrates the loving-kindness and forbearance of Bahá'u'lláh. For Ḥájí Mírzá Aḥmad was a man insincere in heart, vulgar in conduct and foul in language. The counsels of Bahá'u'lláh fell on deaf ears. Instead of mending his ways, he remained heedless, joined hands with Mírzá Yaḥyá and created much dissension and discord among the companions. At last, Bahá'u'lláh expelled him from His presence and ordered him to leave Adrianople for 'Iráq. While in 'Iráq, Aḥmad sought the company of some evil men, who eventually killed him mainly because of his vile language.

Almost two-thirds of this Tablet has been rendered into English by Shoghi Effendi, the Guardian of the Faith.* In it Bahá'u'lláh has poured out His loving counsels and exhortations upon the Bábís in general and Aḥmad in particular. In order to appreciate this Tablet we must remember that it was revealed in the early part of His sojourn in Adrianople and prior to Mírzá Yaḥyá's attempt to assassinate Him. It was a period in which some corrupt elements among the Bábís were raising their heads and sowing the seeds of sedition among the believers. They gathered around Mírzá Yaḥyá, boosted his ego and made of him an idol in their midst. Because of their deviation from the path of truth and their insincerity towards Bahá'u'lláh, the spirit of these men became truly satanic. The reason for this is that God has created man to 'love and worship Him'. But man violates the laws of God and commits many sins which are injurious to himself. However, God is merciful and through His grace forgives His servants. Indeed, if it were not for God's bounty no created thing could come into existence, nor could any human being ever progress in this or the next world. The study of the Holy Writings reveals that the mercy of God and His forgiveness which have encompassed all creation are withheld from those who recognize the Manifestation of God but knowingly and consciously arise to oppose Him. In fact, by doing this they try to assume the same station

* The passages are included in *Gleanings from the Writings of Bahá'u'lláh*, sections CLII and CLIII.

as the Manifestation of God and endeavour to place themselves on the same level. This action, which violates the Covenant of God, is unforgivable unless the individual, who has become spiritually dead, turns to God in genuine repentance. Christ refers to it as the 'sin against the Holy Ghost'. It invokes the wrath of God and obstructs the channels of grace from on high.

The few Bábís, including Ḥájí Mírzá Aḥmad, who gathered around Mírzá Yaḥyá for the sole purpose of opposing Bahá'u'lláh, were of this category. Their thoughts, their words and their deeds were devoid of truth. They spent their time in Adrianople creating dissension, poisoning the minds of the believers, and devising evil plans to uproot the Cause of God and bring division within its ranks.

The *Lawḥ-i-Aḥmad* was revealed by Bahá'u'lláh to bring these men back to their God. He begins the Tablet by urging Aḥmad to possess a pure heart. This is part of the opening paragraph:

> O banished and faithful friend! Quench the thirst of heedlessness with the sanctified waters of My grace, and chase the gloom of remoteness through the morning-light of My Divine presence. Suffer not the habitation wherein dwelleth My undying love for thee to be destroyed through the tyranny of covetous desires, and overcloud not the beauty of the heavenly Youth with the dust of self and passion. Clothe thyself with the essence of righteousness, and let thine heart be afraid of none except God. Obstruct not the luminous spring of thy soul with the thorns and brambles of vain and inordinate affections, and impede not the flow of the living waters that stream from the fountain of thine heart. Set all thy hope in God, and cleave tenaciously to His unfailing mercy.[2]

In this Tablet Bahá'u'lláh defines the real purpose for which God bestowed faculties on man:

> Thine eye is My trust, suffer not the dust of vain desires to becloud its lustre. Thine ear is a sign of My bounty, let not

the tumult of unseemly motives turn it away from My Word that encompasseth all creation. Thine heart is My treasury, allow not the treacherous hand of self to rob thee of the pearls which I have treasured therein. Thine hand is a symbol of My loving-kindness, hinder it not from holding fast unto My guarded and hidden Tablets . . .[3]

These exalted concepts give us a glimpse of the nobility and purity to which man, under the shadow of the Cause of Bahá'-u'lláh, will attain. The study of the Writings clearly indicates that the purpose underlying the Revelation of Bahá'u'lláh is to create a new race of men whose thoughts and deeds will reflect and manifest in this world the most lofty attributes and divine virtues. In this connection it is appropriate to quote an interesting account of Nabíl-i-A'ẓam concerning several statements which were made by Bahá'u'lláh to certain Persian princes in Baghdád on the subject of the future nobility of mankind. This is known as 'Panj Kanz' (Five Treasures). The following is a translation of a part of it:

. . . Once there were certain Persian princes in the presence of Bahá'u'lláh. He was engaged in conversation with them and with loving-kindness sought news of their country. In the course of this interview one of the princes made the following remark: 'How is it that You speak of spiritual matters to Your friends when they attain Your presence, while to us You talk only about the news of the town and the market?' He was trying to ask: 'How could such men who are devoid of learning and discernment be preferable to us?' In answer to him Bahá'u'lláh said:

'. . . I will tell you which people are worthy of listening to My utterances and attaining My presence. Suppose that a person is taken to a vast plain, on the right side of which are placed all the glories of this world, its pleasures and comfort, together with a sovereignty which would be everlasting and freed from every affliction and grief. On the left-hand side of this plain are preserved for eternity all the calamities, hardships, pains and immense sufferings. Then suppose that the

Holy Spirit appears before this person and addresses him in these words: "Shouldst thou choose to have all the eternal pleasures that are placed on the right side in preference to the calamities on the left, not the slightest thing would be reduced from thy station in the sight of God. And shouldst thou choose to be inflicted with innumerable sufferings that are placed on the left, not the slightest thing would be added to thy station in the estimation of God, the Almighty, the Unconstrained."

'If at that moment this person were moved to choose, with the utmost eagerness and enthusiasm, the left hand of abasement rather than the right hand of glory, then he would be worthy to attain My presence and hearken to My exalted words. In this connection the Tongue of Grandeur,* addressing the inquirers, says "If thine aim be to cherish thy life, approach not our court; but if sacrifice be thy heart's desire, come and let others come with thee. For such is the way of faith, if in thy heart thou seekest reunion with Bahá; Shouldst thou refuse to tread this path, why trouble us? Begone!" ' . . .†

To the same enquirer Bahá'u'lláh further said, 'My purpose in coming to this corrupt world where the tyrants and traitors, by their acts of cruelty and oppression, have closed the doors of peace and tranquillity to all mankind, is to establish, through the power of God and His might, the forces of justice, trust, security and faith. For instance [in the future] should a woman . . ., who is unsurpassed in her beauty and adorned with the most exquisite and priceless jewels, travel unveiled and alone, from the east of the world to the west thereof, passing through every land and journeying in all countries, there would be such a standard of justice, trustworthiness and faith on the one hand, and lack of treachery and degradation on the other, that no one would be found who would wish to rob her of her possessions or to cast a treacherous and lustful eye upon her beauteous chastity! . . .'

* Bahá'u'lláh.

† Two lines of the poem *Sáqí-Az-Ghayb-i-Baqá*, revealed by Bahá'u'lláh in Kurdistán and quoted in *The Dawn-Breakers*, p. 96 (Brit.), pp. 137–8 (U.S.).

Then Bahá'u'lláh affirmed, 'Through the power of God I shall transform the peoples of the world into this exalted state and shall open this most great door to the face of all humanity.'[4]

In this connection Bahá'u'lláh has revealed the following words concerning the people of Bahá:

> He is My true follower who, if he come to a valley of pure gold will pass straight through it aloof as a cloud, and will neither turn back, nor pause. Such a man is assuredly of Me. From his garment the Concourse on high can inhale the fragrance of sanctity . . . And if he met the fairest and most comely of women, he would not feel his heart seduced by the least shadow of desire for her beauty.[5]

Nabíl continues the story of Bahá'u'lláh's conversation with the princes:

> Concerning the sincerity of motive and purity of deeds, the Tongue of Grandeur* addressed them in these words:
>
> 'Suppose there is a very rich person whose wealth is enormous and beyond measure. And suppose that gradually and in the course of time he bestows so much of his wealth upon a poor person . . . that he himself is reduced to absolute poverty while the poor man has turned into a very rich man . . . Suppose in his poor and distressed state he reaches a situation in which he incurs some small debt. Being unable to pay it, he is brought to a public square in town where he is humiliated and punished. He is further informed that his release will not be considered until he pays his debt. At this point suppose he sees his friend (who once was poor and as a result of his generosity has become rich). Should the thought flash through his mind that he wishes that in return for all his generosity to him, this friend would now come forward and relieve him of this calamity, immediately all his deeds would become void, he would become deprived of the virtue of contentment and acquiescence, and would be shut away from the virtues of the human spirit.
>
> The same thing is true of the second man who has become

* Bahá'u'lláh.

rich (through the generosity of the captive). Should he think in his heart that he is obliged to pay this man's debts, free him from his ordeal, and enable him to live the rest of his life in comfort, because he had earlier shown immeasurable love and kindness towards him, then such a motive leading him to repay his friend's generosity (instead of giving for the sake of humanity) would cause him to be deprived of the chalice of sincerity and would drive him into the world of ignominy.

The only way acceptable to God would have been for the first man to have based his acts of generosity on humanitarian principles wholly for the sake of God. In the same way, the second rich man should have acted for the sake of God and as a duty to the world of humanity regardless of the events of the past or the future. Thus it is revealed: "We nourish your souls for the sake of God; we seek from you neither recompense nor thanks" ' . . .* [6]

In the *Lawḥ-i-Aḥmad* Bahá'u'lláh counsels humanity in these words:

O My servants! Deprive not yourselves of the unfading and resplendent Light that shineth within the Lamp of Divine glory. Let the flame of the love of God burn brightly within your radiant hearts. Feed it with the oil of Divine guidance, and protect it within the shelter of your constancy. Guard it within the globe of trust and detachment from all else but God, so that the evil whisperings of the ungodly may not extinguish its light. O My servants! My holy, My divinely ordained Revelation may be likened unto an ocean in whose depths are concealed innumerable pearls of great price, of surpassing lustre. It is the duty of every seeker to bestir himself and strive to attain the shores of this ocean, so that he may, in proportion to the eagerness of his search and the efforts he hath exerted, partake of such benefits as have been pre-ordained in God's irrevocable and hidden Tablets. If no one be willing to direct his steps towards its shores, if every one should fail to arise and find Him, can such a failure be said to have robbed this ocean of its power or to have

* *Qur'án*, lxxvi. 9.

lessened, to any degree, its treasures? How vain, how contemptible, are the imaginations which your hearts have devised, and are still devising! O My servants! The one true God is My witness! This most great, this fathomless and surging Ocean is near, astonishingly near, unto you. Behold it is closer to you than your life-vein! Swift as the twinkling of an eye ye can, if ye but wish it, reach and partake of this imperishable favour, this God-given grace, this incorruptible gift, this most potent and unspeakably glorious bounty.

O My servants! Could ye apprehend with what wonders of My munificence and bounty I have willed to entrust your souls, ye would, of a truth, rid yourselves of attachment to all created things, and would gain a true knowledge of your own selves—a knowledge which is the same as the comprehension of Mine own Being.[7]

This last statement is to be found in Islám also. In one of the traditions it is recorded, 'He who recognizes his own self has verily recognized God'. Mírzá Hádíy-i-Qazvíní, one of the Letters of the Living,* requested Bahá'u'lláh to explain among other things the meaning of this tradition for him. In a lengthy Tablet to Mírzá Hádí[8] Bahá'u'lláh explains that the soul of man, which He refers to as the rational faculty, is an emanation from the worlds of God. Every faculty in man, whether physical or spiritual, is a manifestation of the soul. For instance, each of the senses derives its power from the soul and every spiritual quality is due to it. Yet the sum total of all these faculties within a human being does not make the soul. So, we might ask, what is the soul? Bahá'u'lláh affirms that the soul is unknowable. Should one contemplate this theme till eternity, he will never be able to understand the nature of his soul, or fathom the mysteries enshrined in it. He then says:

Having recognized thy powerlessness to attain to an adequate understanding of that Reality† which abideth within thee, thou wilt readily admit the futility of such efforts as

* The first eighteen disciples of the Báb.

† The soul of man. (A.T.)

ḤÁJÍ MÍRZÁ ḤAYDAR-'ALÍ OF IṢFAHÁN

An outstanding follower of Bahá'u'lláh
and a defender of His Covenant
His memoirs are often quoted in this volume

USTÁD-MUḤAMMAD-'ALÍY-I-SALMÁNÍ

The barber, a devoted servant of Bahá'u'lláh and a well-known Bahá'í poet

may be attempted by thee, or by any of the created things, to fathom the mystery of the Living God, the Day Star of unfading glory, the Ancient of everlasting days.[9]

When man recognizes his impotence to know the nature of his own soul, and more so the nature of God, then he has attained the highest degree of knowledge and understanding. These are the words of Bahá'u'lláh:

> This confession of helplessness which mature contemplation must eventually impel every mind to make is in itself the acme of human understanding, and marketh the culmination of man's development.[10]

Bahá'u'lláh explains to Mírzá Hádí that in all the worlds of God this verse assumes many other meanings which are beyond the comprehension of man. Mírzá Hádí, who as mentioned was one of the Letters of the Living, failed at the end to remain loyal to the Cause of Bahá'u'lláh. He followed Mírzá Yaḥyá and deprived himself of the bounties of God. This tragic ending, for one who had the inestimable privilege of being one of the first eighteen disciples of the Báb, is a demonstration of how God tests His servants. The closer one gets to the Manifestation of God the more severe become the tests.*

There were a few others among the Letters of the Living who succumbed to the tests of God. One such was Mullá Ḥasan-i-Bajistání who attained the presence of Bahá'u'lláh in Baghdád. He expressed his doubts to Bahá'u'lláh concerning the Revelation of the Báb. One of his objections was that the Báb in His Writings extolled the virtues and praised the station of the Letters of the Living in glowing terms, and yet as a Letter of the Living himself, he knew that he was devoid of these qualities. Bahá'u'lláh answered that a farmer irrigates his field in order to water his crop. In this process, however, the weeds are also watered. He explained that the tributes paid by the Báb to the Letters of the Living, and the praises that He showered

* See vol. I, p. 130.

upon them, all referred to Mullá Ḥusayn, the first to believe in Him, and to a few others. The rest received these bounties as a matter of course.

The great majority of the Letters of the Living remained steadfast in the Cause of the Báb and no less than twelve of them laid down their lives in the path of their Lord. Most of the Letters of the Living died before the birth of Bahá'u'lláh's Revelation, but had the privilege of attaining His presence in Persia, when some were enabled to recognize His station.

Mullá Báqir-i-Tabrízí, who survived all the other Letters of the Living, was the only one who embraced the Cause of Bahá'u'lláh and remained loyal and devoted to Him. He accompanied Bahá'u'lláh to the Fort of Shaykh Ṭabarsí and was also present at the Conference of Badasht.* It was to him that the Báb had addressed these exalted words in praise of Bahá'u'lláh, 'Him Whom God shall make manifest':

> I have written down in My mention of Him † these gem-like words: 'No allusion of Mine can allude unto Him, neither anything mentioned in the Bayán' . . . 'Exalted and glorified is He above the power of any one to reveal Him except Himself, or the description of any of His creatures. I Myself am but the first servant to believe in Him and in His signs, and to partake of the sweet savours of His words from the first-fruits of the Paradise of His knowledge. Yea, by His glory! He is the Truth. There is none other God but Him. All have arisen at His bidding.'[11]

In answer to Mullá Báqir's question regarding 'Him Whom God shall make manifest', the Báb in a special Tablet promised him that he would attain His presence either in the beginning or towards the end of the year 'eight', 1268 A.H. (1852).

Soon after Bahá'u'lláh's release from the Síyáh-Chál of Ṭihrán, Mullá Báqir attained the presence of Bahá'u'lláh in Baghdád and, remembering the promise of the Báb, recognized

* For further information refer to *The Dawn-Breakers*.

† Him Whom God shall make manifest. (A.T.)

His station and became filled with the glory of His Revelation. He was an outstanding believer and teacher of the Cause. It was to him that the Báb, shortly before His martyrdom, entrusted a coffer containing all His important documents and Tablets, seals and agate rings, which was to be handed to Mullá 'Abdu'l-Karím-i-Qazvíní, surnamed Mírzá Aḥmad, who was instructed to deliver it to Bahá'u'lláh.

Soon after the declaration of the Message of Bahá'u'lláh, Mullá Báqir arose to teach His Cause with great determination and devotion among his fellow countrymen in the province of Á<u>dh</u>irbáyján. He wrote an epistle in which he refuted the claims and rejected the writings of Mírzá Yaḥyá. Longing to attain the presence of His Lord, he travelled twice to 'Akká, and on his last visit he obtained permission from Bahá'u'lláh to reside in Constantinople where he died around the year 1881.

In the *Lawḥ-i-Aḥmad* Bahá'u'lláh, rebuking those who had arisen to oppose Him, declares:

> O My servants! Let not your vain hopes and idle fancies sap the foundations of your belief in the All-Glorious God, inasmuch as such imaginings have been wholly unprofitable unto men, and failed to direct their steps unto the straight Path. Think ye, O My servants, that the Hand of My all-encompassing, My overshadowing, and transcendent sovereignty is chained up, that the flow of Mine ancient, My ceaseless, and all-pervasive mercy is checked, or that the clouds of My sublime and unsurpassed favours have ceased to rain their gifts upon men? Can ye imagine that the wondrous works that have proclaimed My divine and resistless power are withdrawn, or that the potency of My will and purpose hath been deterred from directing the destinies of mankind? If it be not so, wherefore, then, have ye striven to prevent the deathless Beauty of My sacred and gracious Countenance from being unveiled to men's eyes? Why have ye struggled to hinder the Manifestation of the Almighty and All-Glorious Being from shedding the radiance of His Revelation upon the earth? Were ye to be fair in your judgment, ye would readily

> recognize how the realities of all created things are inebriated with the joy of this new and wondrous Revelation, how all the atoms of the earth have been illuminated through the brightness of its glory. Vain and wretched is that which ye have imagined and still imagine![12]

Bahá'u'lláh further warns that in this Dispensation God will stay the hand of those who are working against His Cause. These are His ominous words:

> O heedless ones! Though the wonders of My mercy have encompassed all created things, both visible and invisible, and though the revelations of My grace and bounty have permeated every atom of the universe, yet the rod with which I can chastise the wicked is grievous, and the fierceness of Mine anger against them terrible.[13]

In one of His Tablets[14] Bahá'u'lláh mentions that if it were not for the bounty of God and the wisdom of His decree, the hand of divine power would have taken hold of those who had inflicted the slightest harm upon the believers, and this earth would not have harboured them for one moment. This is true of those who are weak and ignorant. However, Bahá'u'lláh states that in the case of those who have stood up with the utmost enmity to persecute the loved ones of God and have arisen with all their power to destroy His Cause, God, in this Dispensation, will assuredly strike them down.

The history of the Faith has amply demonstrated this phenomenon. All those who opposed the Faith and its central Figures—the Báb, Bahá'u'lláh and 'Abdu'l-Bahá—were made to suffer a condign punishment. Speaking of this retributory process, Shoghi Effendi, the Guardian of the Faith, writes:

> Kings, emperors, princes, whether of the East or of the West, had, as we look back upon the tumultuous record of an entire century, either ignored the summons of its Founders, or derided their Message, or decreed their exile and banishment, or barbarously persecuted their followers, or sedulously striven to discredit their teachings. They were visited

by the wrath of the Almighty, many losing their thrones, some witnessing the extinction of their dynasties, a few being assassinated or covered with shame, others finding themselves powerless to avert the cataclysmic dissolution of their kingdoms, still others being degraded to positions of subservience in their own realms. The Caliphate, its arch-enemy, had unsheathed the sword against its Author and thrice pronounced His banishment. It was humbled to dust, and, in its ignominious collapse, suffered the same fate as the Jewish hierarchy, the chief persecutor of Jesus Christ, had suffered at the hands of its Roman masters, in the first century of the Christian Era, almost two thousand years before. Members of various sacerdotal orders, Shí'ah, Sunní, Zoroastrian and Christian, had fiercely assailed the Faith, branded as heretic its supporters, and laboured unremittingly to disrupt its fabric and subvert its foundations. The most redoubtable and hostile among these orders were either overthrown or virtually dismembered, others rapidly declined in prestige and influence, all were made to sustain the impact of a secular power, aggressive and determined to curtail their privileges and assert its own authority. Apostates, rebels, betrayers, heretics, had exerted their utmost endeavours, privily or openly, to sap the loyalty of the followers of that Faith, to split their ranks or assault their institutions. These enemies were, one by one, some gradually, others with dramatic swiftness, confounded, dispersed, swept away and forgotten. Not a few among its leading figures, its earliest disciples, its foremost champions, the companions and fellow-exiles of its Founders, trusted amanuenses and secretaries of its Author and of the Centre of His Covenant, even some of those who were numbered among the kindred of the Manifestation Himself, not excluding the nominee of the Báb and the son of Bahá'u'lláh, named by Him in the Book of His Covenant, had allowed themselves to pass out from under its shadow, to bring shame upon it, through acts of indelible infamy, and to provoke crises of such dimensions as have never been experienced by any previous religion. All were precipitated, without exception, from the enviable positions they occupied, many of them lived to behold the frustration of their designs, others were plunged into degradation and misery, utterly impotent to impair the unity, or stay the march, of the Faith they had so shamelessly forsaken. Ministers, ambassadors and other state dignitaries had plotted assiduously to pervert its purpose, had instigated the successive banishments of its Founders, and maliciously striven to undermine its foundations. They had, through such plottings, unwittingly brought about their own downfall, forfeited the confidence of their sovereigns, drunk the cup of disgrace to its dregs, and irrevocably sealed their own doom.[15]

Bahá'u'lláh in the *Lawḥ-i-Aḥmad* reveals the role that man must play in creation. He states:

> O My servants! Be as resigned and submissive as the earth, that from the soil of your being there may blossom the fragrant, the holy and multicoloured hyacinths of My knowledge.[16]

In the same way that the earth must receive the rays of the sun and the showers of spring in order to produce its fruit, a human being must likewise turn to the Sun of Truth,* in this day to Bahá'u'lláh, so that he may fulfil the purpose for which he is created. This is a law of creation, for without this relationship, man remains a material being. Devoid of true spiritual life he produces a society in which prejudice, hatred and conflict become the pivot of his social life. And this is the plight of mankind today!

In this Tablet, Bahá'u'lláh repeatedly addresses Aḥmad and exhorts him to rectitude of conduct, purity of heart, and sincerity, urges him not to imitate the wayward, counsels him to illumine his eyes with the light of His Revelation and summons him to enter the straight path.

He states that the purpose underlying His Revelation has been to enable those who are pure-hearted and endowed with capacity to acquire faith and ascend to the realms of Glory. Otherwise, He affirms, His glory is exalted above, and independent of all understanding hearts. He gives the example of

* The Manifestation of God.

the sun. Should all the sighted peoples of the world testify to its light and those who are blind declare its darkness, neither of these testimonies could ever affect the sun. The praise or condemnation of the people relates to themselves, while the sun remains luminous and resplendent in the heavens and is independent of the views held by men. Of the greatness of His Revelation Bahá'u'lláh in this Tablet declares:

> O My servants! Through the might of God and His power, and out of the treasury of His knowledge and wisdom, I have brought forth and revealed unto you the pearls that lay concealed in the depths of His everlasting ocean. I have summoned the Maids of Heaven to emerge from behind the veil of concealment, and have clothed them with these words of Mine—words of consummate power and wisdom. I have, moreover, with the hand of divine power, unsealed the choice wine of My Revelation, and have wafted its holy, its hidden, and musk-laden fragrance upon all created things. Who else but yourselves is to be blamed if ye choose to remain unendowed with so great an outpouring of God's transcendent and all-encompassing grace, with so bright a revelation of His resplendent mercy? . . .
>
> O My servants! There shineth nothing else in Mine heart except the unfading light of the Morn of Divine guidance, and out of My mouth proceedeth naught but the essence of truth, which the Lord your God hath revealed. Follow not, therefore, your earthly desires, and violate not the Covenant of God, nor break your pledge to Him. With firm determination, with the whole affection of your heart, and with the full force of your words, turn ye unto Him, and walk not in the ways of the foolish. The world is but a show, vain and empty, a mere nothing, bearing the semblance of reality. Set not your affections upon it. Break not the bond that uniteth you with your Creator, and be not of those that have erred and strayed from His ways. Verily I say, the world is like the vapour in a desert, which the thirsty dreameth to be water and striveth after it with all his might, until when he cometh unto it, he findeth it to be mere illusion.[17]

7

The Forces of Evil Gather Momentum

As the news of the Declaration of Bahá'u'lláh as 'He Whom God shall make manifest' began to reach the ears of the Bábís in Persia, and a few Bahá'í teachers actively engaged in the propagation of His Cause and the dissemination of His newly-revealed Tablets, a crisis unprecedented in its scope and severity was brewing in Adrianople and soon assailed the companions of Bahá'u'lláh in that city. Originating from Mírzá Yaḥyá and engineered by Siyyid Muḥammad-i-Iṣfahání, it eventually engulfed the whole community, bringing in its wake untold sufferings to Bahá'u'lláh and creating a temporary breach in the ranks of the believers.

Soon after his arrival in Adrianople Mírzá Yaḥyá realized that his life was no longer in danger. He had feared persecution and death ever since the martyrdom of the Báb. It was this fear which had prompted him to hide himself away in Persia and 'Iráq for about thirteen years. During these years he lived in disguise and was often on the run going from one hiding-place to another, while maintaining contact with Bahá'u'lláh and arranging for his wives and family to live in His household. But now, in Adrianople, he knew the situation was different and there was no persecution. Bahá'u'lláh, soon after His arrival, had won the respect and admiration of the people of Adrianople including the Governor and other dignitaries. The co-operation and goodwill of the people became apparent when most of Bahá'u'lláh's companions, as directed by Him, engaged themselves in some work or profession and were integrated into the community.

Highly jealous of the rising prestige of Bahá'u'lláh and

aware of the declaration of His station as 'He Whom God shall make manifest', Mírzá Yaḥyá decided it was time to come into the open and wrest the leadership of the community from the hands of the One who had been his guide and refuge all his life, and who had, through His sin-covering eye, concealed many of his shameful deeds. Emboldened by Bahá'u'lláh's loving forgiveness, duped by Siyyid Muḥammad's enticing prospects and spurred on by his own ambitious lust for leadership, Mírzá Yaḥyá embarked upon a path which is exclusively reserved for the evil, namely, to attempt a person's life. This was his only way, for he knew that he had no power whatsoever to confront Bahá'u'lláh. It is a fact that whenever Mírzá Yaḥyá came into the presence of Bahá'u'lláh, he found himself speechless. The majesty and authority of the Supreme Manifestation of God was so overwhelming that he was unable to utter a word. Several people have testified to this including Mírzá Áqá Ján, who mentions that in the early days in Baghdád he discovered that Mírzá Yaḥyá was so insignificant in the presence of Bahá'u'lláh that he could not speak. This puzzled Mírzá Áqá Ján, until later he realized that Mírzá Yaḥyá was like anyone else in the presence of Bahá'u'lláh. However, Bahá'u'lláh had instructed His amanuensis not to disclose his observations to anyone.

It was not surprising for a man such as Mírzá Yaḥyá, who had already committed several crimes* including the issuing of orders for the assassination of some of the outstanding disciples of the Báb and His cousin, to make elaborate plans for the taking of Bahá'u'lláh's life. The first attempt, carried out by Mírzá Yaḥyá's own hands, was to poison Him. Shoghi Effendi has summarized this shameful episode in these words:

> Desperate designs to poison Bahá'u'lláh and His companions, and thereby reanimate his own defunct leadership, began, approximately a year after their arrival in Adrianople, to agitate his mind. Well aware of the erudition of his half-

* See vol. I, chapter 15.

brother, Áqáy-i-Kalím, in matters pertaining to medicine, he, under various pretexts, sought enlightenment from him regarding the effects of certain herbs and poisons, and then began, contrary to his wont, to invite Bahá'u'lláh to his home, where, one day, having smeared His tea-cup with a substance he had concocted, he succeeded in poisoning Him sufficiently to produce a serious illness which lasted no less than a month, and which was accompanied by severe pains and high fever, the aftermath of which left Bahá'u'lláh with a shaking hand till the end of His life. So grave was His condition that a foreign doctor, named Shíshmán, was called in to attend Him. The doctor was so appalled by His livid hue that he deemed His case hopeless, and, after having fallen at His feet, retired from His presence without prescribing a remedy. A few days later that doctor fell ill and died. Prior to his death Bahá'u'lláh had intimated that doctor Shíshmán had sacrificed his life for Him. To Mírzá Áqá Ján, sent by Bahá'u'lláh to visit him, the doctor had stated that God had answered his prayers, and that after his death a certain Dr. Chúpán, whom he knew to be reliable, should, whenever necessary, be called in his stead.

On another occasion this same Mírzá Yaḥyá had, according to the testimony of one of his wives, who had temporarily deserted him and revealed the details of the above-mentioned act, poisoned the well which provided water for the family and companions of Bahá'u'lláh, in consequence of which the exiles manifested strange symptoms of illness.[1]

In spite of this Bahá'u'lláh did not wish to disclose the wicked deeds of His brother to the public. He advised His companions not to spread the news. However, it was through Mírzá Yaḥyá's own actions later that the story had to be told. For soon after Bahá'u'lláh's recovery, Mírzá Yaḥyá openly and by insinuation shamefully claimed that it was Bahá'u'lláh who had tried to poison him! This outrageous and false accusation against One who was the well-spring of love and forgiveness served to unmask Mírzá Yaḥyá, and revealed his satanic nature to friends and strangers alike.

Some time passed and Mírzá Yaḥyá was still waiting for the opportunity to make another attempt on the life of Bahá'u'lláh. According to his plans the scene of attack this time was to be the public bath* which Bahá'u'lláh was sure to visit. With a certain subtlety he intimated to Ustád Muḥammad-'Alíy-i-Salmání,† the barber who was Bahá'u'lláh's bath attendant,‡ the merits of assassinating Bahá'u'lláh, and made it quite clear that it would be a service to the Faith of God if he would do this when attending Him in the bath. On hearing this suggestion Ustád Muḥammad-'Alí was so enraged that, as we shall see later, he felt a great urge to kill Mírzá Yaḥyá on the spot.

Ustád Muḥammad-'Alí was one of Bahá'u'lláh's disciples and had the honour to be His attendant in the bath since the Baghdád days; he continued this service in 'Akká. He was one of the servants of Bahá'u'lláh and a man of great courage and faith. He had recognized the station of Bahá'u'lláh with such depth and conviction that his whole being was dominated by a passionate love for Him, a love that knew no bounds and often carried him to the verge of rapture. Historians have stated that he was illiterate and claim that his autobiography was dictated by him. One thing, however, is clear: that even if he had barely learnt to read and write, he had no education whatsoever.

* In the days of Bahá'u'lláh it was necessary for most people in the Middle East to visit public baths as there were no bathing facilities in their houses. Public baths, which were set aside for men on certain days of the week, and for women on others, were mostly of the kind known as Turkish baths. People often visited them once a week and remained inside for many hours in order to wash and relax in the warm and steamy atmosphere. At the same time the gathering of people in one place created a social occasion where they exchanged news and discussed many topics. Often friends visited the bath together so that they could spend some hours with each other. Public baths provided customers with attendants who washed them and performed other services such as applying henna to the hair or shaving. Important people often had their own bath attendants.

† Not to be confused with the celebrated Shaykh Salmán.

‡ According to custom, a barber could often be a bath attendant also.

However, Bahá'u'lláh had bestowed upon him the knowledge of God. He became the recipient of such divine gifts that in spite of his illiteracy and humble origins, he was enabled to make a valuable contribution to Persian literature through his poems. In the history of the Faith we come across many distinguished Bahá'í poets, most of whom were men of learning and knowledge. Yet some claim that Ustád Muḥammad-'Alí's poems are endowed with a special power which makes them outstanding. Those who appreciate poetry have acknowledged the beauty, lucidity and profundity of his composition. The believers who recite his soul-stirring poems often become uplifted and inspired, transported from this mortal life into the world of realities. His words, deep and full of significances, move the soul and open before one's eyes vistas of love and adoration for Bahá'u'lláh.

Those who are as yet unaffected by the potency of the Revelation of Bahá'u'lláh may find it hard to believe that such a man, unlettered and unaccomplished, could ever rise to such heights as to make a notable contribution to human knowledge and literature. And when we study the life of Ustád Muḥammad-'Alí closely, and take into account his daily encounters with people, his manners and his language which at times were harsh and offensive, we realize that not only was he uneducated but he was also a somewhat unrefined person.

Nevertheless, when the heart is pure and the soul turns with sincerity and devotion to Bahá'u'lláh, it becomes the recipient of the knowledge of God referred to in Islám as 'a light which God casteth into the heart of whomsoever He willeth.'[2] Ustád Muḥammad-'Alí was an example of this; he may be described as a flame of the love of Bahá'u'lláh. His poems are likewise songs of love and rapture and we cannot find even one line in which he has deviated from this theme. The object of his adoration is none other than Bahá'u'lláh and this is made clear in his poems. He extols and glorifies Him in beautiful language and lays bare the fire of love which burns within his heart. Most of his poems were composed extemporaneously as he attended to Bahá'u'lláh's hair. When he came in contact with his Beloved he was carried into the realms of the spirit and became oblivious of all that was around him. It was in this state that these beautiful poems flowed forth in an uncontrollable fashion. Having no education, he would sometimes ask the meaning of some of the words he had used. For instance, Ḥájí Mírzá Buzurg-i-Afnán, a distinguished believer who for many years was the custodian of the house of the Báb in Shíráz, has recounted the following story:

> Salmání had a tiny barber's shop in 'Akká and in it had built a small platform with sun-baked bricks for his customers to sit upon. Many times I sat on that platform for hairdressing. He was illiterate and on occasions when he was busy dressing my hair he used to ask me the meaning of some of the words he did not know and which he had used in his poems.[3]

Ustád Muḥammad-'Alí was a native of Iṣfahán. His father sent him to a barber's shop when he was nine years old. At the age of fifteen he began to work on his own. Soon after, he came in contact with the Bábís in Iṣfahán and about three years after the martyrdom of the Báb, he embraced the Bábí Faith. Together with some others, Ustád Muḥammad-'Alí was persecuted in Iṣfahán for being a Bábí. Two of his co-religionists were martyred in the public square. They were Áqá Muḥammad-Javád and Mullá 'Alí, who danced his way to the field of martyrdom. These two devoted Bábís were conducted to the square and had to lie down until the executioner arrived and decapitated them. Then came the turn of Ustád Muḥammad-'Alí and a certain Ustád 'Abdu'l-Karím-i-Kharrát, a wood-turner.* However, the Governor ordered these men to be tortured and put in jail. Later their relatives paid a sum of money to the authorities as ransom and secured their freedom. After being released they both left Iṣfahán for Baghdád where

* He became a Covenant-breaker and has since been referred to as Kharáṭín (earth-worm).

they attained the presence of Bahá'u'lláh. Ustád Muḥammad-'Alí worked in Baghdád as a barber where he was given the honour of attending Bahá'u'lláh in the bath. He also attended Bahá'u'lláh's brothers, 'Abdu'l-Bahá, and other believers.

For the sake of honouring Bahá'u'lláh and the Cause of the Báb, the companions of Bahá'u'lláh in Baghdád and Adrianople had always shown consideration and regard for Mírzá Yaḥyá who, after all, was the nominee of the Báb and a brother of their Lord. This attitude, which was shown purely for the exaltation of the Cause of God, was misinterpreted by Mírzá Yaḥyá and led him to imagine that these men would be willing to carry out his orders regardless of their import. However, he soon discovered how gravely he had erred in his judgement by asking Ustád Muḥammad-'Alí, one of the most faithful servants of Bahá'u'lláh, to carry out his sinister design.

Ustád Muḥammad-'Alí in his memoirs has recounted in detail this shameful episode and the events leading to it. The following is a translation of some of his words:

> One day I went to the bath and awaited the arrival of the Blessed Beauty. Azal* arrived first. I attended to him and applied henna. He began to talk to me. For some time he was trying hard to make me his follower, but he was doing this in a secret way. He said to me: 'Last night I dreamt that someone had a sweeping brush in his hand and was sweeping the area around me.'† He gave me to understand that this person was the Blessed Beauty. From the tone of his conversation, I knew that he wanted me to do something for him, but he did not tell me anything and soon left the bath.
>
> Then the Blessed Beauty came in. There was a mirror on the wall, and as his image appeared in it, He recited this line of poetry, 'Thou art great, and the mirror too small to reflect Thy beauty.'

* Mírzá Yaḥyá.

† The connotation of these words in Persian is that Bahá'u'lláh was a humble servant of Mírzá Yaḥyá.

> I was deep in my thoughts concerning the words of Azal. I did not understand his purpose in implying that the Blessed Beauty was sweeping the floor around him. However, it was quite clear that he wanted me to carry out a special task for him. At the same time I noticed that Ḥájí Mírzá Aḥmad* was trying to convert me to follow Azal. During the course of several days he persisted in trying to win me over.[4]

Ustád Muḥammad-'Alí stood firm and immovable as a rock. He rejected Ḥájí Mírzá Aḥmad's arguments and at the end used such harsh and unspeakably offensive language that his opponent went to Bahá'u'lláh and complained. The following day, Mírzá Áqá Ján, as instructed by Bahá'u'lláh, gathered the believers together and in order to help them resolve their differences read out some Tablets including the *Lawḥ-i-Aḥmad* (Persian) which was addressed to the same Ḥájí Mírzá Aḥmad.

Ustád Muḥammad-'Alí continues in his memoirs:

> One day I was waiting at the bath for the arrival of Bahá'u'lláh. Azal came in first, washed himself and began to apply henna. I sat down to serve him and he began to talk to me. He said 'A certain Mírzá Na'ím, the former Governor of Nayríz, killed many believers and perpetrated many crimes against the Cause'. He then praised courage and bravery in glowing terms. He said that some were brave by nature and at the right time they would manifest that quality in their actions. He then continued the story of Mírzá Na'ím. 'From the persecuted family of the believers there remained a young boy aged ten or eleven. One day, when Mírzá Na'ím went into the bath, this boy went in with a knife. As he was coming out of the water, the boy stabbed him and ripped his belly open. Mírzá Na'ím screamed and his servants who were in the ante-room rushed in. They went for the boy, attacked and beat him. Then they went to see how their master was. The boy, although wounded,

* The recipient of the *Lawḥ-i-Aḥmad* (Persian).

rose up and stabbed him again.' Azal praised courage again and said 'How wonderful it is for a man to be brave. Now, see what they are doing to the Cause of God. Everybody harms it, everyone has arisen against me, even my Brother. I have no comfort whatsoever and am in a wretched state.' His tone and implications were that he, the successor of the Báb, was the wronged one, and his Brother (I take refuge in God!) was the usurper and aggressor. Then he once more praised courage and said that the Cause of God needed help. In all this talk, the tone of his remarks, the story of Mírzá Na'ím, the praise of courage and his encouragement to me, he was in fact telling me to kill Bahá'u'lláh.

The effect of all this upon me was so disturbing that in all my life I had never felt so shattered. It was as if the whole building was falling upon my head. I was frightened; without uttering a word I went out to the ante-room. My mind was in a state of the utmost agitation. I thought to myself that I would go inside and cut his head off regardless of consequences. Then I thought, to kill him is easy, but perhaps I would offend the Blessed Beauty. One thing which prevented me from carrying out my intention was the thought that if I killed him and then went into the presence of the Blessed Beauty, and He asked me why I had killed him, what answer could I give?

I returned to the bath and being extremely angry, I shouted at him 'Go and get lost, clear off!' He whimpered and trembled and asked me to pour water over him. I complied. Washed or unwashed he went out in a state of great trepidation, and I have never seen him since.

My state of mind, however, was such that nothing could calm me. As it happened, that day the Blessed Beauty did not come to the bath, but Áqá Mírzá Músáy-i-Kalím [Bahá'u'lláh's faithful brother] came. I told him that Azal had set me on fire with his sinister suggestion. Áqá Mírzá Músá said: 'He has been thinking of this for years, this man has always been thinking in this way. Do not pay any attention to him.' He counselled me to disregard the whole thing and went inside the bath.

However, when my work was finished in the bath, I went

to the Master* and reported to Him what Mírzá Yaḥyá had told me, and how I was filled with rage and wanted to kill him . . . the Master said, 'This is something that you alone know. Do not mention it to anyone, it is better that it remain hidden.' I then went to Mírzá Áqá Ján, reported the details of the incident and asked him to tell Bahá'u'lláh. He returned and said 'Bahá'u'lláh says to tell Ustád Muḥammad-'Alí not to mention this to anyone.'

That night I collected all the writings of Azal and went to the tea-room † of Bahá'u'lláh's house and burnt them all in the brazier. Before doing so, I showed them to seven or eight of the believers who were present. They all saw that they were the writings of Azal. They all protested to me and asked me the reason for doing this. I said, 'Until today I esteemed Azal highly, but now he is less than a dog in my sight'.‡ [5]

In the end Ustád Muḥammad-'Alí found himself unable to keep this matter to himself. Soon the news spread and created much fear and anguish in the hearts of the believers in Adrianople.

It was after this event that Bahá'u'lláh decided to announce formally to Mírzá Yaḥyá, as the nominee of the Báb, His claim to be the Fountain-head of Divine Revelation, 'Him Whom God shall make manifest'. Although Mírzá Yaḥyá was already informed of the declaration of Bahá'u'lláh and was aware of His claim through His Tablets, nevertheless, this announcement was of great significance, in so far as it left no excuse for Mírzá Yaḥyá to cloud the issue. Bahá'u'lláh had formally summoned him to pay allegiance to His Cause. Failure to do so would have meant the parting of the ways.

This announcement was made by Bahá'u'lláh through the revelation of a special Tablet known as *Súriy-i-Amr* (Súrih of

* 'Abdu'l-Bahá. (A.T.)

† In this room the believers often gathered, talked among themselves and drank their tea. (A.T.)

‡ In Persian, to call someone a dog sounds much more insulting than it does in English. (A.T.)

Command). In it He clearly stated His claims and conveyed the character of His Mission. He commissioned Mírzá Áqá Ján, His amanuensis, to take it personally to Mírzá Yaḥyá, read it aloud to him and demand a conclusive reply. Mírzá Yaḥyá asked for a time during which he could meditate his answer. This request was granted, and the following day he replied that he himself had become the recipient of divine Revelation, and it was incumbent upon all the peoples of the world to follow him and pay allegiance to his person.

Such a claim by one who was the embodiment of deceit and falsehood evoked the wrath of God, and was clearly regarded as a signal for the eventual split between Bahá'u'lláh and Mírzá Yaḥyá. We must bear in mind that the majority of the community in Adrianople was faithful to Bahá'u'lláh and wholly devoted to Him. The rest consisted of a few men who were evil or mischief-makers, and some weak and vacillating. They freely associated with each other and consequently tests and trials were immense at that period. Ever since their banishment to Adrianople the faithful companions of Bahá'u'lláh had been filled with anguish and sorrow as a result of the activities of Mírzá Yaḥyá and his supporters. With the revelation of the *Súriy-i-Amr* and Mírzá Yaḥyá's reactions, the contest between the forces of light and darkness came to a head. Embarking on an action reminiscent of His solitary retirement to the mountains of Kurdistán when the unfaithful were shamefully destroying the Cause of God, Bahá'u'lláh, who at this time was residing in the house of Amru'lláh, withdrew with His family to the nearby house of Riḍá Big which was rented by His order, and refused to associate with anybody. This was on 10 March 1866. The reason for this withdrawal, which fortunately was of short duration, was similar to that which had motivated Him to retire to Kurdistán a decade earlier: namely, to relieve the tension and alleviate the feelings of enmity which during the course of years had been engendered in the hearts of some by Mírzá Yaḥyá and were fanned into flame by his latest actions.

The withdrawal of Bahá'u'lláh on these two occasions produced a drastic effect on both the sincere and the unfaithful. It also afforded the exiles the freedom to choose between Him and Mírzá Yaḥyá. The true believers who were sustained by His unfailing grace found themselves suddenly cut off from the Source of Life. The Light went from their midst and their souls were plunged into a world of darkness and deprivation. Like plants which wither away and shrivel up when barred from the rays of the sun, the true disciples of Bahá'u'lláh, those lovers of His beauty, became dispirited and disconsolate. They would willingly have offered up their lives and all their possessions had they thought that such an action would bring about their reunion with their Beloved.

Aqáy-i-Kalím, the faithful brother and a staunch supporter of Bahá'u'lláh, who with 'Abdu'l-Bahá carried the weight of many responsibilities during the dark hours of tests and trials, especially during the absence of Bahá'u'lláh, has reported to Nabíl these words concerning Bahá'u'lláh's retirement in the house of Riḍá Big:

> That day witnessed a most great commotion. All the companions lamented in their separation from the Blessed Beauty.[6]

One of the companions of Bahá'u'lláh who was present at the time has left to posterity this account which portrays the feelings of His loved ones:

> Those days were marked by tumult and confusion. We were sore-perplexed, and greatly feared lest we be permanently deprived of the bounty of His presence.[7]

The enemies and the wavering souls who leaned towards Mírzá Yaḥyá, but who often attained the presence of Bahá'u'lláh, were discomfited in their activities as a result of His withdrawal. The guiding hand of Bahá'u'lláh which had so far sustained them, in spite of their unfaithfulness, and protected them with care and loving-kindness, was now withdrawn. They were thrown back on their own resources and were caught in the clutches of a strife which hastened their doom. As time passed, they sank deeper and deeper into the swamp of their own machinations and perished ingloriously.

When Bahá'u'lláh moved His residence from the house of Amru'lláh to the house of Riḍá Big, He ordered His brother Áqáy-i-Kalím to divide all the furniture, bedding and utensils and send half of them to the house of Mírzá Yaḥyá, and to see that he received his full share of the government allowance allocated to the exiles. He also directed that several items such as the rings of the Báb, His seals and some manuscripts be delivered to him. Mírzá Yaḥyá had longed to possess these relics which the Báb, before His martyrdom, had specifically sent to Bahá'u'lláh.

Upon His retirement to the house of Riḍá Big, Bahá'u'lláh took only one servant for Himself and His family. He instructed Áqáy-i-Kalím to take one of the companions to serve him and to appoint anyone of the companions whom Mírzá Yaḥyá might select as a servant to his household. Mírzá Yaḥyá asked for Darvísh Ṣidq-'Alí,* one of the most faithful disciples of Bahá'u'lláh. When informed of this, Bahá'u'lláh directed Áqáy-i-Kalím to tell the Darvísh to present himself to Mírzá Yaḥyá and serve him with the utmost truthfulness and sincerity, stating that no one among the unfaithful would be able to rob him of the love he cherished in his heart for the Blessed Beauty. He further urged the Darvísh to read the *Lawḥ-i-Laylatu'l-Quds* † (Tablet of the Holy Night) which had been revealed in his honour, and assured him that when he read it this time, he would be able to understand its hidden meanings.

No sooner did Áqáy-i-Kalím convey Bahá'u'lláh's message to Darvísh Ṣidq-'Alí, than he fell prostrate on the ground as a

* For a brief account of his life see *Memorials of the Faithful*, also *The Revelation of Bahá'u'lláh*, vol. I, p. 289, and below, pp. 329–30 ff.

† See p. 188.

gesture of humility and thankfulness to his Lord, and said that this message of Bahá'u'lláh and His loving-kindness were sufficient to sustain him, and that he would remain happy even if he had to endure afflictions for the rest of his life. While the Darvísh was in his service, Mírzá Yaḥyá offered him a sum of money which he refused, saying that Bahá'u'lláh looked after his needs and that he was serving Mírzá Yaḥyá solely in obedience to Bahá'u'lláh's command and not for money. Darvísh Ṣidq-'Alí, however, did not have to remain in the service of Mírzá Yaḥyá for very long. Through a succession of events he was relieved from this unpleasant task. Indeed, as we shall see, soon after Bahá'u'lláh's withdrawal to the house of Riḍá Big, all the followers of Bahá'u'lláh completely dissociated themselves from Mírzá Yaḥyá and were cleansed from the pollution of his satanic spirit.

The 'Most Great Separation'

The withdrawal of Bahá'u'lláh to the house of Riḍá Big and His refusal to meet any of the exiles created a situation in which some of the unfaithful openly turned against Him and transferred their allegiance to Mírzá Yaḥyá. Emboldened by the absence of Bahá'u'lláh, Siyyid Muḥammad-i-Iṣfahání, who until then used to attain His presence and associate with His loved ones, publicly threw in his lot with the arch-breaker of the Covenant of the Báb and, thinking that the arena was now cleared for him, openly rose up in opposition to Bahá'u'lláh and began a vigorous campaign to discredit Him among the people. A period of intense activity ensued in which Mírzá Yaḥyá and Siyyid Muḥammad played a major part. Assisted by their infamous allies and associates they loaded their letters with calumnies and false accusations against Bahá'u'lláh and disseminated them far and wide among the believers in Persia and 'Iráq.

These letters caused much confusion and dissension among some of the Bábí community in Persia. Certain individuals were misled by these slanderous statements and lost their faith altogether. A number of Bábís wrote to Bahá'u'lláh and begged for guidance and enlightenment. Several Tablets in this period were revealed in response to such questions. Other believers had already reached the stage of certitude in their faith. These souls were moved by the dissemination of these evil letters to take action, and they arose, together with others whom Bahá'u'lláh had specifically chosen, such as Nabíl, to champion the Cause of Bahá'u'lláh. They defended it most ably against those egotistical personalities in the Bábí community who were determined to bring division within the Cause of God.

It was Mírzá Yaḥyá himself who, by his actions, revealed to the Bábí community his disobedience to the Covenant which the Báb had so irrefutably established concerning 'Him Whom God shall make manifest', a disobedience long concealed by Bahá'u'lláh. The tests and trials which Bahá'u'lláh had foretold in His Tablets were now beginning to descend upon the believers. The news of the opposition of Mírzá Yaḥyá, the nominee of the Báb, created a great commotion among the Bábís, and served as a signal for the permanent rupture between him and his illustrious Brother.

It was during this period that Mírzá Yaḥyá entrusted one of his companions with some papers for distribution among the Bábís in Persia. On learning their contents, this man refused to comply with his orders and instead showed them to some faithful believers. These papers contained many statements misrepresenting Bahá'u'lláh and accusing Him of those very crimes which Mírzá Yaḥyá himself had already committed. They fell ultimately into the hands of Bahá'u'lláh's friends in Adrianople who were astonished by Yaḥyá's shameful behaviour when they saw them.*

Not satisfied with these perfidious deeds, Mírzá Yaḥyá decided to carry his rebellion to circles hitherto untouched by these matters. Thinking that Bahá'u'lláh would continue to

* Despite the contents of these letters, Bahá'u'lláh advised the messenger that he should carry out the instructions of Mírzá Yaḥyá and deliver them.

bear every false accusation and any amount of ill-treatment with resignation and forbearance, he sent a petition to Khurshíd Páshá, the Governor of Adrianople, and to the Governor's assistant 'Azíz Páshá. This communication, which the Governor shared with Bahá'u'lláh, was couched in obsequious language, contained false statements about Bahá'u'lláh and was aimed at discrediting Him in the eyes of the Governor, who was one of His most ardent admirers. One of Yaḥyá's false accusations was that he was not receiving his share of the allowance which the Government had allotted to Bahá'u'lláh and His fellow exiles. To support this claim he sent one of his wives to call on the Governor to complain that her husband's share of allowance was cut off by Bahá'u'lláh and that as a result he had become destitute and his children were on the verge of starvation.

As we have already stated, the fact was that Bahá'u'lláh had always supported Mírzá Yaḥyá and his family. And when He retired to the house of Riḍá Big, He had arranged for Yaḥyá to receive his full share of the government allowance.

Ḥájí Mírzá Ḥaydar-'Alí, who arrived in Adrianople a few months after these distasteful events and attained the presence of Bahá'u'lláh many times, has written concerning Mírzá Yaḥyá's petition to the authorities in these words:

> When Azal arose in hostility with his satanic spirit to oppose and challenge the Blessed Beauty, through calumnies and false accusations, he wrote a letter to the Governor of Adrianople. We* all saw this letter. It opened with these words: 'May my soul and body be a sacrifice for thee.' It went on to say: 'O thou 'Azíz,† we come to you in destitution, grant us some corn.' He continues falsely to accuse the Ancient Beauty of having cut off his livelihood.
>
> The opening sentence of his letter, the statement of his needs, and the complaints all demonstrate that God cannot be confused with man, and that there is no likeness between

* Referring to himself and other disciples of Bahá'u'lláh.

† 'Azíz Páshá, the Deputy Governor of Adrianople.

the two. We see the contrast, for instance, in these words of the Ancient Beauty as He addresses the late Sulṭán 'Abdu'l-'Azíz:* 'O thou Ra'ís [Chief], hearken to the voice of God, the Supreme Ruler, the Help in Peril, the Self-Subsisting. He verily calleth between earth and heaven and summoneth mankind to the scene of effulgent glory.'

In this blessed Tablet, He foreshadows that the Sulṭán would lose his throne and the country would pass out of his hands . . . To return to our subject: Bahá'u'lláh had, through an intermediary, proved to the Governor that these allegations [by Mírzá Yaḥyá] were false and, in a message, explained to him that these calumnies were designed to hurt and humiliate Him . . .[8]

The accusations of Mírzá Yaḥyá spread far and wide. Shoghi Effendi writes:

. . . He [Bahá'u'lláh] was soon after informed that this same brother [Mírzá Yaḥyá] had despatched one of his wives to the government house to complain that her husband had been cheated of his rights, and that her children were on the verge of starvation—an accusation that spread far and wide and, reaching Constantinople, became, to Bahá'u'lláh's profound distress, the subject of excited discussion and injurious comment in circles that had previously been greatly impressed by the high standard which His noble and dignified behaviour had set in that city.[9]

In a Tablet to Shaykh Salmán,† Bahá'u'lláh describes the agony of His heart for Mírzá Yaḥyá's shameful deeds. He recounts his calumnies concerning his share of the allowance, stating that it has always been divided between the exiles, and mentions that had it not been for the sake of those who accompanied Him, He Himself would never have accepted the government allowance in spite of all the hardships which such an action would have entailed. As we shall see later, when the campaign of calumnies was intensified, Bahá'u'lláh refused to

* This Tablet is actually addressed to 'Álí Páshá, the Grand Vizir.

† See chapter 13 and also vol. I, pp. 109–13.

draw this allowance and had to sell some of His belongings in order to provide for His livelihood.

One of the features of the life of Bahá'u'lláh was that although born of one of the wealthiest families in Persia and having lived many years in luxurious surroundings, He spent forty years of His Ministry in an austerity to which He had never been accustomed during the earlier days of His life. For two years he lived in the utmost poverty in the mountains of Kurdistán where many a day He subsisted on milk alone. In Baghdád He lived a simple life and had to endure many privations. 'There was a time in 'Iráq,' He affirms in a Tablet, 'when the Ancient Beauty . . . had no change of linen. The one shirt He possessed would be washed, dried and worn again.'[10] In Adrianople and 'Akká He submitted Himself to the privations and hardships which a ruthless enemy had imposed upon Him.

Although many believers through their devotion, and often by sacrificing their own needs, offered gifts to Bahá'u'lláh, He usually distributed such gifts among the poor and He Himself lived with the utmost simplicity. For example, Ḥusayn-i-Áshchí, a youth from Káshán who served Bahá'u'lláh as a cook in Adrianople and later in 'Akká, has left to posterity the following account of the days when He stayed in the house of Amru'lláh in Adrianople.

> This house [of Amru'lláh] was very large and magnificent. It had a large outer apartment where all the loved ones of Bahá'u'lláh used to gather. They were intoxicated with the wine of His Peerless Beauty . . . However, the means of livelihood were very inadequate and meagre. Most of the time there was no food which could be served to Bahá'u'lláh other than bread and cheese. Every day I used to save some meat and oil and store them in a special place until there was enough to cook. I would then invite Bahá'u'lláh to a meal on the lawn. We managed to save some money and buy two cows and one goat. The milk and yoghurt which were produced were served in the holy household . . .

In the winter there was a brazier* in each room. It was among my duties to light them. In order to economize I used to measure the amount of coal that I placed in each brazier. Someone had informed Bahá'u'lláh of this. He summoned me to His presence and said: 'I hear you count the pieces of coal which go into each brazier!' Bahá'u'lláh smiled and was very amused. He agreed that such economy was necessary in a large house.[11]

Because of the harmful actions of Mírzá Yaḥyá and Siyyid Muḥammad, Bahá'u'lláh was forced to end His withdrawal, which had lasted about two months, and come forward to protect the Cause of God from the onslaught of the unfaithful. It was at this time that Bahá'u'lláh expelled Siyyid Muḥammad from the gatherings of His followers and soon the 'Most Great Separation', which was a clear division between the followers of Bahá'u'lláh and those of Mírzá Yaḥyá, became public. The two-months' withdrawal of Bahá'u'lláh acted as a spiritual vacuum for the exiles in Adrianople. It created a great test and as a result each one of them showed the measure of his sincerity and faith. When the time of separation came, each person knew to which side he belonged. However, the great majority of the exiles remained steadfast in the Cause of Bahá'u'lláh. Only a few, who had gathered around Mírzá Yaḥyá, were expelled from the presence of Bahá'u'lláh. Several ambitious men and egotistical personalities in Persia also threw in their lot with Mírzá Yaḥyá. They strengthened his hand and, as we shall see later, he, instigated by Siyyid Muḥammad-i-Iṣfahání, intensified his evil activities and spread the seeds of dissension and strife among the authorities in the capital city of the Ottoman Empire.

* Portable fireplace made of cast iron in which charcoal is burnt.

8

The Promised One of the *Bayán*: Some Tablets

Lawḥ-i-Bahá

One of the Tablets revealed by Bahá'u'lláh during this period is the *Lawḥ-i-Bahá* (Tablet of Bahá). It was probably revealed just before Bahá'u'lláh took up residence in the house of Riḍá Big. For in it He refers to the anguish of His heart and states that He intends to withdraw from everybody in the community. This Tablet, which is in Arabic with parts translated by Himself into Persian, was revealed in honour of Khátún Ján, the eldest daughter of Ḥájí Asadu'lláh-i-Farhádí,* a native of Qazvín.

Khátún Ján was a devoted believer. Her father, Ḥájí Asadu'lláh, was one of the followers of Siyyid Káẓim-i-Rashtí. As Ṭáhirih was also one of the disciples of the Siyyid, there was a great friendship between Ṭáhirih and the daughters of Ḥájí Asadu'lláh. When the Báb revealed Himself, Ṭáhirih, who was then in Karbilá, acknowledged the truth of His Message and was named as one of the Letters of the Living. Soon after this news of the Báb's declaration reached Qazvín. Ḥájí Asadu'lláh and his family were among the early believers in that town. When Ṭáhirih returned to Qazvín, the bond of love and union between herself and the Farhádí family grew much stronger. Khátún Ján, in particular, became an ardent admirer of Ṭáhirih. She used to sit at her feet and was enthralled by Ṭáhirih's devotion and love for the Báb and Bahá'u'lláh.

Soon after Ṭáhirih's arrival in Qazvín, persecutions started

* See *The Dawn-Breakers.*

against the Bábís. Ḥájí Asadu'lláh, the father of Khátún Ján, was dragged from his sick-bed and at an advanced age was made to walk in chains, for a distance of no less than one hundred and seventy kilometres, in company with his fellow prisoners to a Ṭihrán prison. Concerning their fate Nabíl writes:

> No sooner were the captives delivered into the hands of the mischief-makers than they set about gratifying their feelings of implacable hatred towards them. On the first night after they had been handed over to their enemies, Ḥájí Asadu'lláh, the brother of Ḥájí Alláh-Vardí and paternal uncle of Muḥammad-Hádí and Muḥammad-Javád-i-Farhádí, a noted merchant of Qazvín who had acquired a reputation for piety and uprightness which stood as high as that of his illustrious brother, was mercilessly put to death. Knowing full well that in his own native town they would be unable to inflict upon him the punishment they desired, they determined to take his life whilst in Ṭihrán in a manner that would protect them from the suspicion of murder. At the hour of midnight, they perpetrated the shameful act, and the next morning announced that illness had been the cause of his death. His friends and acquaintances, mostly natives of Qazvín, none of whom had been able to detect the crime that had extinguished such a noble life, accorded him a burial that befitted his station.[1]

The tragic martyrdom of Ḥájí Asadu'lláh and others was the signal for further persecutions in Qazvín. The house of the Farhádís was plundered and all their belongings confiscated. Muḥammad-Hádíy-i-Farhádí, a nephew of Ḥájí Asadu'lláh and the husband of Khátún Ján, had to leave the city for his own safety and went to Ṭihrán.

In the meantime Ṭáhirih, by the order of an implacable enemy, was confined to the house of her father and constantly watched by certain women whose task it was to ensure that she did not leave her room except for performing her daily ablutions. As the situation became worse, the enemy planned to end the life of Ṭáhirih. Concerning this Nabíl writes:

The failure of the Sháh and of his government to inflict immediate punishment upon the malefactors encouraged them to seek further means for the gratification of their relentless hatred towards their opponents. They now directed their attention to Ṭáhirih herself, and resolved that she should suffer at their hands the same fate that had befallen her companions. While still in confinement, Ṭáhirih, as soon as she was informed of the designs of her enemies, addressed the following message to Mullá Muḥammad, who had succeeded to the position of his father and was now recognized as the Imám-Jum'ih of Qazvín: ' "Fain would they put out God's light with their mouths: but God only desireth to perfect His light, albeit the infidels abhor it" [*Qur'án* 9:33]. If my Cause be the Cause of Truth, if the Lord whom I worship be none other than the one true God, He will, ere nine days have elapsed, deliver me from the yoke of your tyranny. Should He fail to achieve my deliverance, you are free to act as you desire. You will have irrevocably established the falsity of my belief.' Mullá Muḥammad, recognizing his inability to accept so bold a challenge, chose to ignore entirely her message, and sought by every cunning device to accomplish his purpose.[2]

Mullá Muḥammad, mentioned by Nábil, was the chief enemy of the Bábís in Qazvín. It is interesting to note that he was the cousin and husband of Ṭáhirih. But soon after Ṭáhirih became a follower of Siyyid Káẓim, a rift came between them. Ṭáhirih left her husband and lived with her father. When she became a follower of the Báb, this rift became much greater. When she returned to Qazvín after having championed the Cause of the Báb, Mullá Muḥammad invited her to come and stay in his house. She sent this message to him:

> Say to my presumptuous and arrogant kinsman, 'If your desire had really been to be a faithful mate and companion to me, you would have hastened to meet me in Karbilá and would on foot have guided my howdah all the way to Qazvín. I would, while journeying with you, have aroused

you from your sleep of heedlessness and would have shown you the way of truth. But this was not to be. Three years have elapsed since our separation. Neither in this world nor in the next can I ever be associated with you. I have cast you out of my life for ever.'[3]

During the time that Ṭáhirih was confined in her home, the only person who managed to keep in touch with her was Khátún Ján. She went to her house almost every day, sometimes disguised as a beggar and sometimes as a washer-woman who would do her washing in the public waterway nearby. By this regular contact she performed an important function in bringing news to and from Ṭáhirih. She also managed to smuggle in food during the time that the enemies were bent upon taking the life of Ṭáhirih, and there was every possibility that they might attempt to poison her food. And finally she played a significant role, together with her husband Muḥammad-Hádí, in rescuing her beloved lady from imprisonment.

Almost coinciding with the fore-mentioned challenge which Ṭáhirih delivered to Mullá Muḥammad concerning her release, Bahá'u'lláh in Ṭihrán summoned to His presence Muḥammad-Hadíy-i-Farhádí, who had fled from Qazvín, and directed him to return there immediately and carry out the rescue operation which He had planned.* This is how Nabíl describes this episode:

Muḥammad-Hádí was charged to deliver a sealed letter to his wife, Khátún Ján, and instruct her to proceed, in the guise of a beggar, to the house where Ṭáhirih was confined; to deliver the letter into her hands; to wait awhile at the entrance of her house until she should join her, and then to hasten with her and commit her to his care. 'As soon as Ṭáhirih has joined you,' Bahá'u'lláh urged the emissary,

* Áqá Muḥammad-Hádí served Ṭáhirih in many other ways. For instance, he was among those who accompanied her to Badasht and there acted as a guard at the gate of the garden which was assigned to her by Bahá'u'lláh. For details of the conference of Badasht, see *The Dawn-Breakers*.

'start immediately for Ṭihrán. This very night, I shall despatch to the neighbourhood of the gate of Qazvín an attendant, with three horses, that you will take with you and station at a place that you will appoint outside the walls of Qazvín. You will conduct Ṭáhirih to that spot, will mount the horses, and will, by an unfrequented route, endeavour to reach at daybreak the outskirts of the capital. As soon as the gates are opened, you must enter the city and proceed immediately to My house. You should exercise the utmost caution lest her identity be disclosed. The Almighty will assuredly guide your steps and will surround you with His unfailing protection.'[4]

The manner in which Muḥammad-Hádí carried out the rescue operation with the help of Khátún Ján is described in detail by Shaykh Káẓim-i-Samandar:*

Ṭáhirih was confined in the house of her father. Mullá Muḥammad, her cousin and husband, was trying to poison her but had no access. None of the friends, with the exception of the eldest daughter of the late Ḥájí Asadu'lláh [Khátún Ján] who was truly devoted to her, was able to communicate with her. Khátún Ján contrived several plans and disguised herself in various forms. Posing as a washer-woman carrying her washing or appearing as a beggar, she managed to contact Ṭáhirih and take food to her. This was important since Ṭáhirih was taking precautions about the food which was given to her in the house, and consequently she was living under difficult circumstances.

Áqá Hádí,† . . . had fled to Ṭihrán. There he visited Vaḥíd whom he knew from earlier days. Vaḥíd took him to the Blessed Beauty and introduced him. Thereupon Bahá'u'-lláh wrote a letter to Ṭáhirih and directed Áqá Hádí to rescue her and bring her to Ṭihrán. Áqá Hádí returned to Qazvín in disguise. He managed with the help of his wife . . . who used her usual methods of contact, to hand the

* One of the Apostles of Bahá'u'lláh. More details of his life will be given in vol. III.

† Áqá Muḥammad-Hádíy-i-Farhádí, the husband of Khátún Ján. (A.T.)

letter to her. After reading the letter Ṭáhirih indicated that she would shortly come out of the house. She joined them about one hour later. Áqá Hádí and his wife immediately took Ṭáhirih to the house of their neighbour, a certain Áqá Ḥasan-i-Najjár [carpenter] who was a friend, a reliable confidant and one whom nobody suspected of harbouring her.

Shortly afterwards, her relatives discovered that Ṭáhirih was missing. They searched everywhere in vain and, when the news spread, the theological students and groups of ruffians crowded the streets and created a great upheaval again . . .

That night Áqá Hádí, with the help of a certain Áqá Qulí,* conducted Ṭáhirih out of the city through the gate of Sháhzádih Ḥusayn. They mounted the horses which were kept ready for them in the *abattoir* outside the city wall and . . . went to Ṭihrán. At first they arrived in the gardens of Imámzádih Ḥasan.† Áqá Qulí was to look after the horses while Ṭáhirih was resting, and Áqá Hádí had gone to the city to give the news of their whereabouts. In the meantime, a certain Karbilá'í Ḥasan, a merchant of Qazvín, had heard the news of Ṭáhirih's arrival and went there. Áqá Qulí, who did not know that this man was a friend, warned him not to come in, but the man came in with a smile. Áqá Qulí used force and twice smote him on the face. Ṭáhirih, who realized what had happened, ordered Áqá Qulí to stop. She called both of them to her, took some fruits from Karbilá'í Ḥasan and shared them with Áqá Qulí. When night fell, several horsemen arrived and with full honours escorted Ṭáhirih with her companions to the house of the Ancient Beauty [Bahá'u'lláh]. When the time for sleeping arrived, they showed Áqá Qulí to his bed. But because he was dressed in rags, he refused at first to sleep in such a luxurious bed. He pointed to his torn clothes and

* He was not a Bábí, but a faithful friend of Áqá Hádí and his confidant. He was a tradesman in the bazaar who understood the secret nature of the mission, and accepted to carry it out in spite of the dangers it entailed. (A.T.)

† On the outskirts of Ṭihrán. (A.T.)

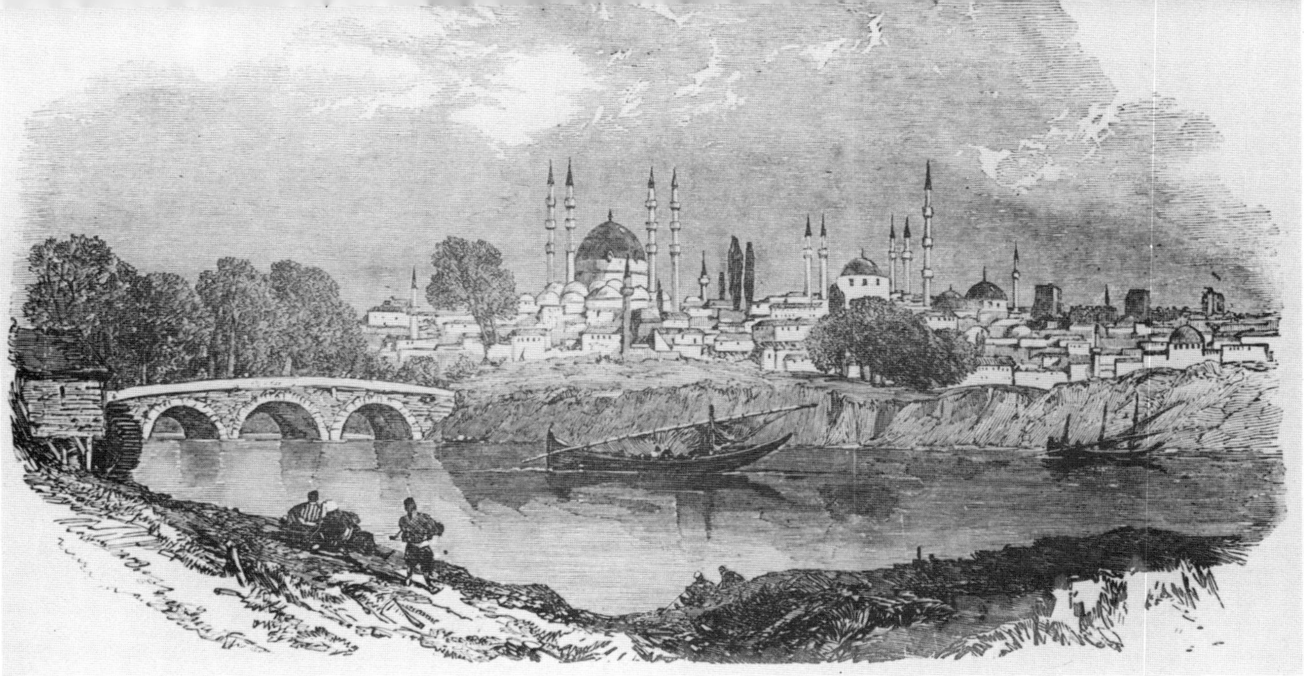

A VIEW OF ADRIANOPLE, 1853

RUINS OF THE HOUSE OF AMRU'LLÁH

One of Bahá'u'lláh's residences in Adrianople
A photograph taken in 1933

said to Ṭáhirih: 'I don't dare to get into this bed while dressed in this way.' But she persuaded him to sleep and assured him that God would soon provide him with a bed as luxurious as that.

The following day, Ṭáhirih, accompanied by Áqá Hádí, [leaving Áqá Qulí behind] went to a village outside Ṭihrán where a number of believers resided.* Bahá'u'lláh left home and soon returned with a porter who brought in a sack full of coins and emptied it on the floor.† He called for a saddle-bag to be brought in and asked Áqá Qulí to place the coins within it. But He instructed him to place the gold coins in one side of the bag and the silver in the other. Áqá Qulí, however, decided to put the gold in the bottom and the silver on the top! When Bahá'u'lláh saw this, He said 'Why did you do this? We told you to put the gold on one side and the silver on the other.' 'I did it,' replied Áqá Qulí, 'for the simple reason that if some coins should fall, either during the journey or when placing the saddle-bag on the horse or taking it off, they would be silver and not gold.' Bahá'u'lláh did not pursue the matter any further. He gave the bag and its key to Áqá Qulí who placed it on the horse's back and mounted. Bahá'u'lláh mounted His horse and, followed by Áqá Qulí, went to the village where Ṭáhirih was staying. Bahá'u'lláh and other guests spent the night there.

In the morning, Ṭáhirih awakened Áqá Qulí, told him to arise for the purpose of saying his prayers, and informed him that he was not fortunate enough to remain there and the time had come for him to return to his native Qazvín, otherwise, great troubles would arise thereto. Ṭáhirih was seated under the shadow of a tree writing letters. Áqá Qulí, having finished his prayers, came forward and stood beside

* This was possibly the village of Qú<u>ch</u>-Ḥiṣár owned by Bahá'u'lláh. (A.T.)

† In those days, money was only in the form of coins and there were no banking facilities. People used to carry the coins in bags. Wealthy people often had to carry their bags of money on horses. On all His journeys for the promotion of the Cause of God in Persia, Bahá'u'lláh was accompanied by the friends and servants and it was He who provided all the finance and entertained His guests. (A.T.)

Áqá Hádí in front of Ṭáhirih. At this time Bahá'u'lláh arrived, and Ṭáhirih finished writing. Bahá'u'lláh asked for the bag of money. He opened it and called Áqá Qulí to come forward. He then told him to hold out the hem of his garment, as He was about to pour some coins into it. As an act of courtesy and politeness Áqá Qulí hesitated to comply with Bahá'u'lláh's orders. Thereupon, his friend Áqá Hádí persuaded him to obey Bahá'u'lláh's instructions. So Áqá Qulí held out the hem of his garment and Bahá'u'lláh pushed His own hand nine times into the bag and emptied each handful onto his out-stretched cloak. As Bahá'u'lláh was pouring the coins out, Áqá Qulí for one brief moment wished in his heart that the coins were gold! Bahá'u'lláh instantly responded by saying: 'We give you enough to take you to Qazvín, the money for your wedding feast will reach you later. In any case it is your own fault, you put the gold in the bottom!'[5]

Áqá Qulí went home and delivered the letters of Ṭáhirih. If he had arrived any later there would have been great trouble, as his kinsmen had already become suspicous and were making enquiries about him from Khátún Ján. The faithfulness with which Áqá Qulí served Ṭáhirih pleased Bahá'u'lláh and, as He had promised him, soon after God bestowed upon him wealth and position. He became one of the influential men in Qazvín. Later, he went to live in Ṭihrán and till the end of his life he remained a friend of the Faith.

Khátún Ján, who had performed such heroic deeds during the life of Ṭáhirih, was plunged into grief and consternation when her beloved heroine was martyred. Some time after this she also lost her husband, Muḥammad-Hádí. But these calamaties did not quench the fire of faith which was burning within her breast. She continued to serve the Cause of God with fervour and enthusiasm. The seed of the love of Bahá'u'lláh had been sown in the heart of Khátún Ján by the hand of Ṭáhirih, who had recognized His station from the early days. Consequently Khátún Ján turned to Bahá'u'lláh with stainless faith and devotion throughout her life. Her sisters and some other members of the family also remained steadfast in His Cause. From the days of Baghdád, Khátún Ján used to receive Tablets from Bahá'u'lláh. This great bounty continued and when in Adrianople, at a time of greatest crisis, when He was so viciously attacked by the unfaithful, Bahá'u'lláh revealed the *Lawḥ-i-Bahá* in her honour, and poured out His heart to her.

In this Tablet He condemns the actions of the people of the *Bayán*, those who had arisen to take His life and inflicted upon Him so much suffering. He grieves that they had broken the Covenant of God, likens them to the followers of Islám who persecuted the Báb, stigmatizes them as the hosts of Satan, admonishes them for having ignored the commandments of God, and rebukes them for having caused the eyes of God to weep. He refers to Himself as Abraham in the hands of Nimrod, Christ in the midst of the Jews and Joseph betrayed by his brethren and thrown into a well.

It is in this Tablet that Bahá'u'lláh refers to His followers as the 'people of Bahá'. He calls on them to enter the 'Ark of God' which sails upon the 'Crimson Sea', an Ark which is exclusively intended for them. This is a reference to the words of the Báb revealed in the *Qayyúmu'l-Asmá'* in which He refers to the 'people of Bahá' as the 'companions of the Crimson-coloured Ark'. In the Writings, the 'Ark' is usually a designation for the Cause of God and the Covenant. The term 'people of Bahá' signifying the followers of Bahá'u'lláh as distinct from the 'people of the *Bayán*', the followers of the Báb, was first used in Adrianople when the 'Most Great Separation' took place. Those faithful to the Covenant of the Báb clearly identified themselves as Bahá'ís and those who broke His Covenant and followed Mírzá Yaḥyá were referred to as Bábís and sometimes Azalís. Consequent upon this, the greeting 'Alláh-u-Akbar' (God is the Most Great) which was used by the Bábís as a salutation among themselves was changed into 'Alláh-u-Abhá' (God is the Most Glorious).

Bahá'u'lláh affirms that every word revealed in the *Lawḥ-i-*

Bahá may be regarded by all mankind as ample testimony to the truth of His Cause. He further states that from the horizon of the Words revealed in that Tablet, innumerable suns of effulgent glory have appeared, suns which illumine the worlds of God and whose numbers are inscrutable to all except God. He exhorts the people of Bahá to turn the mirror of their hearts to their rays and become illumined by them.

Khátún Ján, for whom the *Lawḥ-i-Bahá* was revealed, longed to attain the presence of her Lord. At last her prayers were answered. Accompanied by her daughter and son-in-law, Ḥájí Ḥasan-i-Zargar, she travelled to 'Akká and for some time basked in the sunshine of His love and protection.

The home of Ḥájí Asadu'lláh, the father of Khátún Ján, is one of the historic sites in Qazvín. Before the appearance of the Báb it was the focal point of Shaykhí activity in that city. No less a person than Shaykh Aḥmad-i-Aḥsá'í* had stayed in that house. Later, it became the centre of Bábí and Bahá'í gatherings. Within its walls many eminent heroes of the Faith such as Ṭáhirih, Quddús, Vaḥíd and several others had been entertained. In one of its basement rooms, Áqá Muḥammad-Hádí had made swords for the defenders of the fortress of Shaykh Ṭabarsí,† swords which are rumoured to have been tested by Quddús and Vaḥíd when they passed through that town. Khátún Ján and her two sisters, who had inherited this house, donated it to the Cause. In a letter to Bahá'u'lláh they expressed the desire that it might be used as a Mashriqu'l-Adhkár.‡ Bahá'u'lláh accepted their gift and approved of their intention.

* The founder of the Shaykhí sect of Islám. See *The Dawn-Breakers*.

† The scene of many battles between three hundred and thirteen Bábís, the heroic defenders of the fortress, and the forces of the army—battles which were forced upon the Bábís and resulted in the defeat of a powerful army. Later most of its defenders were martyred. For more information, see *The Dawn-Breakers*.

‡ Literally 'the dawning-place of the mention of God', a Bahá'í House of Worship.

Lawḥ-i-Rúḥ

Among the Writings which appear to have been revealed by Bahá'u'lláh in the house of Riḍá Big during His two-months' withdrawal was the *Lawḥ-i-Rúḥ* (Tablet of the Spirit) in Arabic. Like many of His Tablets in this period, it has two major themes: one, the proclamation of His mission and the unveiling of His exalted station; the other, the opposition, the treachery and the wickedness of those Bábís who inclined towards Mírzá Yaḥyá and to whom Bahá'u'lláh has often referred as 'those who have joined partners with God'.

Denouncing the odious deeds perpetrated by these people, Bahá'u'lláh describes in tender language the anguish of His heart in that lonely house. He rebukes them for having inflicted upon God Himself such afflictions that He had to hide the glory of His countenance after it had been unveiled to men. Their evil actions had dishonoured His name among the people; He recalls, too, the humiliating incident when once He had to answer the door personally to the Governor of the City as there was no one available to serve Him; on that day the whole of creation wept at this abasement, while the hearts of those nigh unto God melted at this degradation.*

In the *Lawḥ-i-Rúḥ*, Bahá'u'lláh dwells further on the wickedness of Mírzá Yaḥyá and those who had gathered around him. Addressing a faithful believer named 'Alí, He refers to their plot to take His life in spite of the fact that His unceasing help and protection for over a decade had spread their fame widely. When they discovered their impotence to carry out their sinister designs, they pleaded innocence and began to spread

* We can appreciate this statement if we reflect on the humiliation to the institution of kingship, if a king had to usher in his visitors in person. Apart from the fact that Bahá'u'lláh was the Supreme Manifestation of God, and His loved ones and disciples were always ready to wait on Him with the utmost devotion, the customs of the time demanded that a man of eminence should have several servants in his household. It was inconceivable that a person of high position would ever take part in the actual running of his house.

false accusations against Him by attributing their own crimes to His person. Characterizing them as bond-slaves of the Kingdom of Names who pride themselves on their own positions, He prophesies that God will soon reduce them to utter nothingness until no trace will be left of them.

These words of Bahá'u'lláh have already been fulfilled. Whereas in the early days of the Faith, there were many who were misled by Mírzá Yaḥyá and raised the standard of rebellion against the Cause of God, in this day they have been reduced to insignificance.

In this Tablet Bahá'u'lláh foretells the triumph of His Cause when, ere long, God will raise up a new creation under its shadow. In another passage, He asserts that God will send down His hosts armed with power and might to assist the Manifestation of His own Self, and will cause the realities of the Prophets and Messengers to arise and serve His Cause.

Similar statements are found in other Tablets. In one of His Writings,[6] speaking of the greatness of His Revelation and the tests which accompany it, Bahá'u'lláh affirms that the realities of the Prophets and Manifestations of God were tested in this day. As we survey the history of the Cause, we come across certain truths which may stagger the imagination. The Báb, whose Revelation was described by Bahá'u'lláh as 'Mine Own Revelation', stated that the Letters of the Living* had the station of the Holy Imáms in the Islamic Dispensation.[7] In one of His Tablets[8] the Báb, enumerating the powers, the attributes and the exalted station of 'Him Whom God shall make manifest',† states that in the day of His Manifestation anyone whom He might appoint as a Prophet of God would be regarded as a Prophet from the beginning that has no beginning till the end that has no end. He further states that the will of God would never be realized except through the will of 'Him Whom God shall make manifest'.

These statements may well stagger the imagination. How-

* The first eighteen disciples of the Báb.

† Bahá'u'lláh.

ever, if we reflect upon the Cause of God we realize that Bahá'u'lláh has ushered in the Day of God, a Day that all the Prophets and Messengers of the past were longing to attain. His Revelation is the Revelation of God Himself, the Heavenly Father spoken of by Christ. Let us for a moment examine the station of Bahá'u'lláh in the light of the New Testament. Christ was manifested in the station of the Son. This does not mean that God, the Inaccessible, the All-Glorious, had a physical son. Such a literal interpretation would reduce God from the realm of the Infinite to that of the finite. In His essence He is exalted above all things, even His own attributes. Therefore, when Christ spoke about His station as the Son of God, He was establishing a relationship. He introduced Himself as the Son, and God as the Heavenly Father. A son who appears in public on behalf of his father must possess two major signs. He must have the authority of the father and manifest similar characteristics which he has inherited from him. In order to demonstrate the source of His authority, Christ chose to describe Himself as the Son of God and portrayed God as the Father. The terms 'Son' and 'Father' are both figurative in the New Testament.

Christ also made it clear that it was the Father who sent Him.

> For I have not spoken of myself; but the Father which sent me, he gave me a commandment, what I should say, and what I should speak.[9]

He also made it clear that He would return in the 'glory of the Father'.

> For the Son of man shall come in the glory of his Father with his angels . . .[10]

From those and many similar statements we can deduce that the same Heavenly Father who sent Christ will Himself be revealed.

Bahá'u'lláh, in many Tablets, has clearly proclaimed His station as that of the Father. Addressing the religious leaders of Christendom, He declares:

> O concourse of bishops! . . . He Who is the Everlasting Father calleth aloud between earth and heaven. Blessed the ear that hath heard, and the eye that hath seen, and the heart that hath turned unto Him Who is the Point of Adoration of all who are in the heavens and all who are on earth . . .[11]

And in another Tablet He announces this joyful tiding:

> He, verily, is come with His Kingdom, and all the atoms cry aloud: 'Lo! The Lord is come in His great majesty!' He Who is the Father is come, and the Son (Jesus), in the holy vale, crieth out: 'Here am I, here am I, O Lord, My God!' whilst Sinai circleth round the House, and the Burning Bush calleth aloud: 'The All-Bounteous is come mounted upon the clouds!'[12]

As we have already observed, the Reality of God is indivisible. In the world of creation, His Essence is manifested through His attributes. But in his own domain His Essence and attributes are one and the same. To describe Him by any attribute is tantamount to bringing Him down into the realm of limitations. These are the words of Bahá'u'lláh as He extols the Almighty in His inaccessible heights of glory.

> Too high art Thou for the praise of those who are nigh unto Thee to ascend unto the heaven of Thy nearness, or for the birds of the hearts of them who are devoted to Thee to attain to the door of Thy gate. I testify that Thou hast been sanctified above all attributes and holy above all names. No God is there but Thee, the Most Exalted, the All-Glorious.[13]

We know that God is the Source of all things and their Creator, but we can never know how He brings this about in the realm of His Essence. Even the Manifestations of God have no knowledge of this, for they have no access to His Reality. However, in this world there is a pattern for creation in so far as all things come into being through some means. For example, man comes to this world through the instrumentality of parents, although the power which causes his birth, and which proceeds from the realms of God, remains unknowable. If we presume that this power emanates from the Essence of God itself, then such an assertion, as already observed, is tantamount to limiting Him. Yet we know that all things must be generated from God Himself. This is the point where we realize that our minds can never fathom these realities. The way is completely barred for the finite to seek direct knowledge of the Infinite.

From the Writings of Bahá'u'lláh it appears that all the powers and attributes which God bestows upon creation emanate from the 'Kingdom of His Revelation'. Through the instrumentality of this kingdom, life, both physical and spiritual, is conferred upon all created things. It is from this kingdom that all the Revelations of God have originated and His Manifestations been sent down. Bahá'u'lláh explains in a Tablet[14] that although outwardly the Manifestation of God has many limitations, inwardly He dwells in the world of the Absolute, free from all limitations. This world of the Absolute, however, is different from the realm of God himself and, in relation to it, has its limitations.

The Lord of the 'Kingdom of Revelation' is Bahá'u'lláh, the Supreme Manifestation of God whose advent in the station of the Father has been promised in the Heavenly Books. This statement should not be misconstrued so as to contradict the basic principle of the oneness of the Manifestations of God. We have already referred to this theme in the former volume.* The Manifestations of God are the same in essence, but differ in the intensity of their Revelations. This is similar to an individual who retains the same identity, although he grows and develops his powers and capacities progressively.

* See vol. I, pp. 64–7.

In the *Lawḥ-i-Rúḥ* Bahá'u'lláh states that nothing can be found on earth or in heaven that will enrich mankind except to come under the shadow of His Cause. He further testifies that in this day, the value of one's faith in God depends on recognition of Bahá'u'lláh and enlightenment through His Revelation. To illustrate this, He uses the analogy of an unlit lantern, which does not serve its purpose and is of little value though it be made of the most exquisite crystal. If we reflect upon these words we may conclude that man's salvation in any age depends on his acceptance of the guidance given by God for that time in history.

Bahá'u'lláh has made similar statements in other Tablets. For example the opening paragraph of Bahá'u'lláh's most Holy Book declares in unequivocal language that the first duty of man to God is to recognize His Manifestation.

> The first duty prescribed by God for His servants is the recognition of Him Who is the Dayspring of His Revelation and the Fountain of His laws, Who representeth the Godhead in both the Kingdom of His Cause and the world of creation. Whoso achieveth this duty hath attained unto all good; and whoso is deprived thereof, hath gone astray, though he be the author of every righteous deed. It behoveth every one who reacheth this most sublime station, this summit of transcendent glory, to observe every ordinance of Him Who is the Desire of the world. These twin duties are inseparable. Neither is acceptable without the other. Thus hath it been decreed by Him Who is the Source of Divine inspiration.[15]

In one of the most beautiful passages of the *Lawḥ-i-Rúḥ* the voice of the Spirit from the Kingdom on high proclaims the exalted station of Bahá'u'lláh, and in moving language announces Him as the 'Beauty of the Adored One', the 'Trust of God' among the people, 'Soul of God Himself' manifested to His servants, 'God's Treasure' for all who are in heaven and on earth, the 'Word of God' for mankind, 'The Light of God' in the Kingdom of His Revelation, 'He Who enshrines within Himself such mysteries one word of which if revealed would rend the heavens asunder'. Designations such as these and many more are attributed to Bahá'u'lláh from the unseen realms of Glory. The voice of the Spirit continues to extol His station to such an extent that He tries to prevent it from revealing any further, but finds it to be endowed with the power of God and impossible to silence.

In the *Lawḥ-i-Rúḥ* is another fascinating scene in which the Pen of Bahá'u'lláh figuratively plays a major part. In this dialogue the Pen begins to lament while held between the fingers of Bahá'u'lláh and entreats His Lord to be allowed to disclose unto all created things one Word from the hidden mysteries of God so that the dwellers of the Kingdom might learn that of which no one has ever been informed. It appeals to the fingers of Bahá'u'lláh not to restrain it from vivifying the whole of creation with the living waters which from time immemorial have flowed within its inner being. It longs to be permitted to rend asunder the veils from the face of His Cause so that the ignorant may witness its glory. Seeing that Bahá'u'lláh is without a helper and afflicted with suffering, it seeks permission to lend Him assistance by using the power which the Almighty has bestowed upon it, a power which is generated by its mere movement and which is capable of subduing the whole of creation. It expresses amazement at Bahá'u'lláh's patience and forbearance in spite of His omnipotence and might, knowing that if He wished, He could, through the utterance of one Word, enable all mankind to arise for the service of His Cause. The Pen continues to plead in this vein with much earnestness and devotion, until the Tongue of Grandeur* exhorts it to restrain itself, not to divulge the mysteries of God's Revelation and to exercise patience under all circumstances.

In the *Lawḥ-i-Rúḥ*, Bahá'u'lláh counsels His loved ones to be united through the love of God, and to be as one soul in

* Bahá'u'lláh.

many bodies. He assures them that this act alone will defeat their enemies. He emphatically censures sedition, discord and division among the believers and warns that should they transgress they will harm the Cause of God.

Lawḥ-i-Laylatu'l-Quds

A Tablet which confirms this statement is the *Lawḥ-i-Laylatu'l-Quds** which was revealed in Adrianople in honour of Darvísh Ṣidq-'Alí and has as its theme the unity between the believers. Bahá'u'lláh in this Tablet exhorts His followers to be united in such wise that all traces of division and estrangement may vanish from among them. The following passages translated by Shoghi Effendi and included in *Gleanings from the Writings of Bahá'u'lláh* are extracted from the *Lawḥ-i-Laylatu'l-Quds*:

> The Most Great Name beareth Me witness! How sad if any man were, in this Day, to rest his heart on the transitory things of this world! Arise, and cling firmly to the Cause of God. Be most loving one to another. Burn away, wholly for the sake of the Well-Beloved, the veil of self with the flame of the undying Fire, and with faces, joyous and beaming with light, associate with your neighbour. Ye have well observed, in all its aspects, the behaviour of Him Who is the Word of Truth amidst you. Ye know full well how hard it is for this Youth to allow, though it be for one night, the heart of any one of the beloved of God to be saddened by Him.
>
> The Word of God hath set the heart of the world afire; how regrettable if ye fail to be enkindled with its flame! Please God, ye will regard this blessed night as the night of unity, will knit your souls together, and resolve to adorn yourselves with the ornament of a goodly and praise-

* When incarcerated in the barracks of 'Akká, one evening Bahá'u'lláh revealed a certain Tablet and referred to that evening as 'Laylatu'l-Quds' (Holy Night). But the *Lawḥ-i-Laylatu'l-Quds* revealed in Adrianople is not to be confused with that later Tablet.

worthy character. Let your principal concern be to rescue the fallen from the slough of impending extinction, and to help him embrace the ancient Faith of God. Your behaviour towards your neighbour should be such as to manifest clearly the signs of the one true God, for ye are the first among men to be re-created by His Spirit, the first to adore and bow the knee before Him, the first to circle round His throne of glory. I swear by Him Who hath caused Me to reveal whatever hath pleased Him! Ye are better known to the inmates of the Kingdom on high than ye are known to your own selves. Think ye these words to be vain and empty? Would that ye had the power to perceive the things your Lord, the All-Merciful, doth see — things that attest the excellence of your rank, that bear witness to the greatness of your worth, that proclaim the sublimity of your station! God grant that your desires and unmortified passions may not hinder you from that which hath been ordained for you.[16]

The thought of disunity had been so distressing to Bahá'u'lláh that in this Tablet He pours out His heart, saying that He would rather be afflicted with fresh calamities every day than see despondency and ill-feeling among the believers.

One of the outstanding counsels of Bahá'u'lláh in this Tablet concerns the manner in which two individuals should act towards each other. The spiritual principle upon which Bahá'u'lláh's advice is based constitutes one of the fundamental verities governing the creation of man. He states that nothing in this world can harm a man of insight. His integrity and exalted station will never be affected by whatever may befall him in this life. For when such a man shows love and humility towards another man for the sake of God, it is as if he has loved God and humbled himself before Him. This will cause the bounties and blessings of God to descend upon him and he will be rewarded for his deeds. If the other individual, however, reacts in the opposite way and treats his fellow man with contempt and pride, such an action will never affect the man whom he has despised, but will be regarded as showing hatred and arrogance towards God, and for this he will receive his punishment.

In one of His Tablets[17] Bahá'u'lláh states that in this Dispensation God has condemned those who create sedition and show malice towards people. Should a person be inclined to harm another, it is as if he has arisen against God to harm Him.

This teaching of Bahá'u'lláh throws a new light upon, and opens up an exciting approach to, human relationships. It confers upon the individual a great insight into the world of realities, enabling him to rid himself effectively of hatred, prejudice and many other vices often displayed by human beings in their association with one another. For example, a soul becomes offended when he is wrongly criticized and his actions denounced. In the normal course of events this can often lead to coolness, alienation, bitterness and even hatred between people. Unwarranted criticism and false accusations can place so much pressure upon the individual as to bring him to the point of utter destruction and complete breakdown. But when a person believes in the words of Bahá'u'lláh and sincerely follows this exalted teaching, his attitude towards his fellow man will completely change and he will become immune to this danger. For he knows that falsehood, enmity and malice can never affect him as long as he puts his trust in God, while the misdeeds of the offenders are directed towards God Who will punish them for their actions.

When a person reaches this stage of maturity and discernment, he will neither be discouraged by undue criticism, nor pleased with praise and glorification. It is always the ego which feels offended in the former case and gratified in the latter. The above-mentioned teaching of Bahá'u'lláh helps the individual to subdue his ego. The mere consciousness of the fact that one is acting against God in condemning and attacking his fellow man, is sufficient to deter him in the pursuit of such reprehensible behaviour. It also enables him to realize that as long as he turns to God, the forces of evil will never be able to harm him in any way.

The devout Mírzá 'Azízu'lláh-i-Miṣbáḥ, a man of great erudition to whom reference has been made in previous chapters, has written these thought-provoking words:

> Should they attribute blindness to a person who has seeing eyes, no harm can befall his sight, and should they acclaim the totally blind to be possessed of keen sight, such a compliment would be of no value to him. For, in reality, what is regarded as praiseworthy or condemnatory is the actual possession of sight or lack of it respectively, and not the affirmative or negative comments of people. From this it follows that the only sign of keen sight is when a person pays heed to neither the praise nor the condemnation of others.[18]

'Abdu'l-Bahá states[19] that if someone in the presence of Bahá'u'lláh mentioned that there was a slight disunity among the believers in any place, the Blessed Beauty would become so overwhelmed with grief that His face would display the signs of intense pain and displeasure. Many times Bahá'u'lláh affirmed to those who attained His presence, that if He knew that the Cause of God was becoming a source of division between two individuals, He would dispense with it.

The establishment of unity among the believers is the cornerstone of the teachings of Bahá'u'lláh. Without it the Faith and its institutions cannot function, neither can the individual or society make any progress spiritually or materially. Unity between the believers and, in the fullness of time, the unity of mankind, cannot be achieved by expedient measures, by man-made plans, or even by goodwill and understanding on the part of all humanity. By those and similar methods man may establish political unity, but not the unity envisaged by Bahá'u'lláh—a unity which surpasses all human limitations, which binds the hearts and souls of men in a spirit of true brotherhood and which derives its cohesive force from Bahá'u'lláh Himself.

Man is capable of achieving great feats in all fields of human activity. He can break the laws of nature, travel faster than sound and into space, can create, control and utilize sources of enormous energy. Nor is there any limit to what he can achieve in the future. But he has no power of his own to influence the hearts of men and enable two antagonistic individuals to love one another. If, by himself, he expends all the material resources at his disposal to unite two souls spiritually, he will fail. The uniting of the hearts of men is the function of the Manifestations of God. To this Bahá'u'lláh testifies in one of His Tablets:

> Out of the whole world He hath chosen for Himself the hearts of men—hearts which the hosts of revelation and of utterance can subdue. Thus hath it been ordained by the Fingers of Bahá, upon the Tablet of God's irrevocable decree, by the behest of Him Who is the Supreme Ordainer, the All-Knowing.[20]

In another Tablet He states:

> Unlock, O people, the gates of the hearts of men with the keys of the remembrance of Him Who is the Remembrance of God and the Source of wisdom amongst you. He hath chosen out of the whole world the hearts of His servants, and made them each a seat for the revelation of His glory. Wherefore, sanctify them from every defilement, that the things for which they were created may be engraven upon them. This indeed is a token of God's bountiful favour.[21]

When Manifestations of God appear, the hearts of Their followers, through the influence of the Word, become united in a bond of oneness. Though previously these souls were enemies, they become as lovers. They are transformed into a new creation and are given the power to influence others and change their hearts. This is the story of all religions. Moses, Christ and Muḥammad did this in Their days. Today, only the words of Bahá'u'lláh can change the hearts of men. The followers of Bahá'u'lláh, armed with the power of the creative

Word of God, have been able to unite the hearts of millions who were previously enemies. Jews, Christians, Muslims, Buddhists, and followers of other religions as well as pagans, agnostics and atheists in all continents of the globe, representatives of every race and almost every tribe, though speaking different languages and coming from different backgrounds, have, in this day, recognized the station of Bahá'u'lláh as the promised Father and become His followers. Through the influence of His Word, hatred and prejudice have vanished from their hearts and been replaced by spiritual unity and universal love for all mankind. This vast, ever-growing, harmoniously functioning world community of Bahá'u'lláh is something unique in the annals of mankind. It constitutes the pattern, and demonstrates the glory and the promise of the Bahá'í Commonwealth of the future. The unbiased observer who looks for proofs of the authenticity of the Message of Bahá'u'lláh may readily find that the power of unity which binds together the Bahá'í community of today is one of the most evident signs of its Founder's glory and divine origin.

9

Some Early Pilgrims

From the time that the news of Bahá'u'lláh's arrival in Adrianople reached the believers, many of them longed to travel to that city and attain His presence. At first only a few succeeded, but as time went on, and especially after the 'Most Great Separation' became effective, several believers from Persia came as pilgrims to the residence of the One who had unmistakably identified Himself as 'He Whom God shall make manifest'—the Revealer of God Himself and the Promised One of all ages. Some of these pilgrims were permitted by Bahá'u'lláh to remain in Adrianople while the majority were sent to Persia or the adjoining countries to spread His Cause among the people.

Ḥájí Mírzá Ḥaydar-'Alí

Notable among those who travelled to Adrianople and attained the presence of their Lord was Ḥájí Mírzá Ḥaydar-'Alí, one of the most illustrious of Bahá'u'lláh's disciples. Ḥájí Mírzá Ḥaydar-'Alí has written in his book, the *Bihjatu'ṣ-Ṣudúr* (Delight of the Hearts) some reminiscences of Bahá'u'lláh and of some events which he witnessed in Adrianople and later in 'Akká as well as in Persia and 'Iráq. He travelled to Adrianople in the year 1283 A.H. (1866–7) and was permitted by Bahá'u'lláh to remain there for about seven months. During this period he attained the presence of Bahá'u'lláh almost every day. As a result of this personal contact with Bahá'u'lláh, Ḥájí Mírzá Ḥaydar-'Alí was set on fire and was filled with a new spirit. He was an embodiment of detachment, humility and self-effacement. Having truly recognized the august station of Bahá'u'lláh, his whole being was dominated by a passionate love and adoration for Him.

Once a Muslim clergyman from Iṣfahán requested Ḥájí Mírzá Ḥaydar-'Alí to recount his impressions of Bahá'u'lláh. He did not, he said, wish to enter into discussion concerning proofs of the authenticity of His claims, but rather was interested in hearing about some of the things Ḥájí Mírzá Ḥaydar-'Alí had witnessed with his own eyes. Ḥájí Mírzá Ḥaydar-'Alí writes about his conversation with the clergyman:

> Much as I tried to explain to him [the clergyman] that contrary to all physical phenomena, which are possible of explanation, one cannot describe a spiritual experience, he was not able to understand. So I said, 'Before attaining His presence, I was hopeful of seeing many miracles—physical, intellectual and spiritual. Also I had stored up several questions in my mind and wished them answered. But when I beheld the light of His beauteous Countenance, I was transported into such a state that all the miracles I had hoped to see and all the physical and spiritual mysteries I had longed to understand, paled into insignificance. They all appeared to me as a mirage to which the thirsty hasten, not the pure water which quenches the thirst and gives life.' He [the clergyman] asked me, 'What did you see that enabled you to acquire such a state of mind and heart?' . . . I said, 'His blessed person appeared in the form of a human being, but His very movements, His manners, His way of sitting or standing, eating or drinking, even His sleep or wakefulness, were each a miracle to me. Because His perfections, His exalted character, His beauty, His glory, His most excellent titles and most august attributes revealed to me that He was peerless and without parallel. He was matchless with no one to join partners with Him, unique with no peer or equal, the One and Single without a deputy, the Ever-Abiding God, the Incomparable Being. He who "begetteth not, neither is He begotten and there is not anyone like unto Him" '.[1]
>
> He [the clergyman] said, 'But Bahá'u'lláh's father was one

of the outstanding ministers [of the Government], and His Son, 'Abbás Effendi,* is renowned throughout the world and is reputed to be the most perfect being on this earth.' I replied, 'Neither His father nor His Son were seated upon the Throne of the Speaker on Sinai,† they were not Founders of religion nor Revealers of the Book. Bahá'u'lláh alone is the Throne wherein abides the splendour of God's Revelation, the Mirror reflecting His light, He Who "begetteth not, neither is He begotten". Should you stand in front of a mirror and announce your identity, the mirror will do likewise, but in reality it is dissociating itself from you.' ‡ He [the clergyman] was very pleased with this answer and told me that it was a convincing and weighty reply which revealed many truths. He asked me to tell him more. I said, '. . . I saw a Person Who, from the human point of view, was like the rest of humanity. However, if one were to add the love, mercy and compassion of all the peoples of the world together, it would appear as a drop when compared with the ocean of His tender mercy and loving-kindness. I even seek God's forgiveness for making such a comparison. Similarly, if one brought together all the knowledge of sciences, crafts, philosophy, politics, natural history and divinity possessed by mankind, it would seem, in comparison with His knowledge and understanding, as an atom compared to the sun. If one weighed the might and power of kings, rulers, Prophets and Messengers against His omnipotence and sovereignty, His grandeur and glory, His majesty and dominion, they would be as insignificant as a touch of moisture compared with the waters of the sea . . . As I observed every one of His attributes, I discovered my inability to emulate Him, and realized that all the peoples of the world will never be able to attain to His perfections.' He [the clergyman] admitted that all these were miracles and constituted the signs and tokens of the power of God, exalted be His glory.[2]

* 'Abdu'l-Bahá. (A.T.)

† One of Bahá'u'lláh's designations. (A.T.)

‡ Ḥájí Mírzá Ḥaydar-'Alí is saying that 'Abdu'l-Bahá is a reflection of Bahá'u'lláh, that there is a vast difference between the two, and that the reflection is not the same as the reality of the One Who is reflected. (A.T.)

To some who have not recognized the station of Bahá'u'lláh, the above statements by Ḥájí Mírzá Ḥaydar-'Alí may seem exaggerated. The truth, however, is that if any just man were to describe his meeting with God, should this be possible, he would tell his story in the same vein and extol Him in the same fashion. To portray the powers and attributes of the Manifestation of God is beyond the capacity of man. For man can only communicate his feelings through the use of words, and words are inadequate tools for expressing spiritual phenomena or explaining divine qualities. It is for this reason that Ḥájí Mírzá Ḥaydar-'Alí, like many other Bahá'í writers who attained the presence of Bahá'u'lláh, has extolled the virtues and attributes of his Lord with absolute sincerity and to the best of his ability by using as many superlative adjectives as he could find. When reading his book one can appreciate his utter self-effacement and humility before Bahá'u'lláh, as well as his vision, his nobility, and purity of spirit.

He writes an interesting story of his own spiritual awakening and struggles:

> In the early days of the Faith in Iṣfahán, when I began to study the Tablets and Writings of the Báb, and listen to the explanations of the friends, I found the proofs of His Revelation convincing and conclusive and the testimonies supremely sound and perfect. So I was assured in myself that this Cause was the Cause of God and the Manifestation of His Grandeur, the dawning of the Day-Star of Truth promised to be revealed by the Almighty. But when I was alone with no one to talk to, I was often overtaken with doubts. The idle fancies of my past life, and the whisperings of the evil one were tempting me . . . God knows how much I wept and how many nights I stayed awake till morning. There were days when I forgot to eat because I was so immersed in my thoughts. I tried by every means to relieve myself of these doubts. Several times I became steadfast in the Cause and believed, but later I would waver and become perplexed and dismayed.
>
> Then one night I dreamt that a town-crier in . . . Iṣfahán

was announcing this message: 'O people, the Seal of the Prophets* is here in a certain house and has given permission for anyone who wishes to attain His presence to go there. Remember that a mere glance at His countenance is more meritorious than service in both worlds.' On hearing this, I hastened and entered the house. I had never seen such a building. I went upstairs and arrived in an area which had a roof over it and was surrounded by rooms and chambers. The Manifestation of the All-Glorious was pacing up and down and some people were standing motionless. I arrived and spontaneously prostrated myself at His feet. Graciously, He lifted me up with His own hands and, standing, said 'A person may claim that he has come here wholly for the sake of God, and has truly attained the presence of His Lord, when he is not held back by the onslaught of the peoples of the world, who with drawn swords attack him and intend to take his life because he has embraced the Cause of God. Otherwise, he cannot truthfully say that his motive was to seek God.'

On hearing these words, I woke up from my dream and found myself assured, joyous and thankful. All my doubts had completely disappeared. I learnt the mysteries of martyrdom, persecution and sufferings which were inflicted upon the believers in every Dispensation. I was amazed as I looked back upon the doubts I had entertained, my ignorance, low-mindedness, weakness of faith and shallowness of thought. I used to laugh at myself also, because in my wakeful hours, I had heard many similar statements and also read them in the Tablets and holy Books of the past, and was not assured by them. And now, through this dream, I had acquired faith and assurance . . .

However, time passed, and about fourteen years later I was in the 'Land of Mystery' † where I stayed for seven months. Every day, through His bounty, I used to attain the presence of Bahá'u'lláh once, twice and sometimes more. But during this period, I never thought of my dream. One evening about four or five hours after sunset I was sitting with Áqá Mírzá

* The Prophet Muḥammad. (A.T.)

† Adrianople. (A.T.)

Muḥammad-Qulí* and Áqá Muḥammad-Báqir-i-Qahvih-chí,† in the tea-room [a room set aside for Bahá'u'lláh's companions and visitors]. That day I had not attained the presence of Bahá'u'lláh and was most eager for an opportunity to do so. Although I could never bring myself to ask for permission, in my innermost heart I was entreating and invoking Him for this honour. But there was no hope, for it was far too late. Suddenly, the door opened and the Most Great Branch,‡ Who in those days was known as Sirru'lláh [the Mystery of God] entered and summoned me to follow Him. When I came out of the room, I saw the Ancient Beauty § pacing in the roofed area of the house. The stream of His utterance was flowing and a few souls were standing. I prostrated myself at His feet, whereupon He lifted me up with His blessed hands. He turned to me and said:

'A person may claim that he has arrived here wholly for the sake of God, and has truly attained the presence of His Lord, when he is not held back by the onslaught of the peoples of the world, who with drawn swords attack him and intend to take his life because he has embraced the Cause.' These were exactly the words I had heard fourteen years before, and I saw the same incomparable Beauty and the same building as in my dream. I stood by the wall, awe-struck and motionless. Gradually, I recovered and in a state of full consciousness attained His presence. My purpose in telling this story was not, God forbid, to attribute any miracles,¶ but rather to state the facts as they happened . . .

That evening there was talk of my leaving. Bahá'u'lláh sent a message to find out from me what my aims and intentions were. I entreated 'Abdu'l-Bahá and begged Him to intervene that my affairs might not be left in my own hands nor my wishes sought, but rather that Bahá'u'lláh might indicate His wishes and direct me to carry them out. I

* The youngest half-brother of Bahá'u'lláh and one who was faithful to Him; see vol. I, pp. 15–16. (A.T.)

† See pp. 329–30 ff. (A.T.)

‡ 'Abdu'l-Bahá. (A.T.)

§ Bahá'u'lláh. (A.T.)

¶ See vol. I, p. 291, f.n. (A.T.)

beseeched Him to send His confirmation and assistance so that I might be enabled to fulfil what was required of me. I further submitted that I was alone in this world, had no home or family and sought only the shelter of His Providence. Through mediation by 'Abdu'l-Bahá, this plea was accepted and I was told that Bahá'u'lláh would bestow upon me the honour and privilege of serving His Cause and would send down His confirmations and assistance to succour me.

So it was arranged that I should go to Constantinople and serve as a channel of communication for the believers who travelled to and from that city, as well as despatching letters and Tablets to various places . . . I arrived in Constantinople having taken with me books and Tablets in the handwriting of Áqáy-i-Kalím, 'Abdu'l-Bahá and others. I was accompanied by Mírzá Ḥusayn,* and we were both happy and successful in our service. Each week some Tablets would arrive for despatch to many parts and I used to read them. I also had the opportunity to meet the believers who arrived with the intention of making the pilgrimage to Adrianople. These had to remain a few days in Constantinople making preparations for the journey or seeking permission from Bahá'u'lláh for pilgrimage. They also stayed a few days on their way back.

I used to receive instructions from the late Áqá Muḥammad-'Alíy-i-Tambákú-Furúsh of Iṣfahán on matters which were connected with worldly affairs such as the purchasing of provisions and other goods, and from Áqáy-i-Kalím on spiritual matters. On one occasion, Áqá Muḥammad-'Alí ordered some tea. I purchased some and sent it off to him. Not being pleased with the tea he wrote me a very kind letter and lovingly pointed out that since I knew this tea would be served in the presence of Bahá'u'lláh and His family, I should have tried it first and been more careful in choosing a good brand.†

* Known as Mírzá Ḥusayn-i-Khurṭúmí of Shíráz, he accompanied Ḥájí Mírzá Ḥaydar-'Alí to Egypt. Both were taken prisoner, together with five others, and sent to the Sudan. This man later became a Covenant-breaker.

† One of the essential features of life, and one which gave much pleasure, especially at gatherings, was the serving of tea. Not only was the quality

This advice by an affable counsellor and sincere friend did not please me. My vanity and ignorance played their part here. I showed no regard for his courtesy, love and seniority and instead wrote him a reply which was wrong and unfair. The letter reached its destination. Soon after this, I received an exalted Tablet from the Ancient Beauty, the All-Bountiful, He Who conceals the faults of men and is the All-Merciful.* This Tablet was addressed to me, a sinful, arrogant, rebellious and conceited person. In it He assured me that I and my deeds were praiseworthy and blessed with His good-pleasure.

Upon reading this Tablet, I became aware of my errors and realized that I had made a grave mistake and committed a serious transgression. For in spite of my ignorance and the vanity of my youth, I had, through the study of the holy Tablets and my observations during the seven months that I had attained His presence, understood the way in which God works in this Most Great, this Most Ancient Revelation . . . and it is this, that in order to educate the sinners, edify the souls of the evil-doers, and teach them human virtues and the way of servitude Bahá'u'lláh chastises them with the scourge of loving-kindness and compassion, of tender mercy and grace. To them He manifests His attributes of the All-Merciful, the Concealer of the faults of men, the Forgiver of sins, and the All-Bounteous.

It was for this reason that I became distressed, sore-perplexed and dismayed. In a state of devotion and with tears I returned to God. I prayed, fervently entreating and invoking Him to accept my repentance. Again I turned to 'Abdu'l-Bahá, the Mystery of God, to mediate for me. As the rays of the Sun of His Name, 'the Concealer of sins', shone forth with greater intensity, as the waves of the Sea of His Mercy surged with greater fury and as the rains of His loving-

---

important, but also the preparation needed great attention and skill. Tea was served in small glass cups. In order to enjoy its aroma, nothing would be added to it except lump sugar which was broken off sugar cones. There were those who were expert tea-makers. In Adrianople it was Áqá Muḥammad-Báqir-i-Qahvih-chí who made tea for Bahá'u'lláh and His companions. (A.T.)

* Bahá'u'lláh. (A.T.)

kindness and compassion showered more profusely, I became seized with more fear and trembling. In brief, I was so overtaken with shame that I could not rest. I pleaded that the outpourings of Bahá'u'lláh's tender mercy and loving providence were well-nigh consuming me. I begged Him to direct me clearly to carry out that which was conducive to my serving the Cause and attaining His good-pleasure.

This time, Bahá'u'lláh instructed me to proceed to Egypt and there to teach the Cause with wisdom and utterance, with goodly deeds and lofty character. I knew that my sins were forgiven, I became confident and happy . . .[3]

Ḥájí Mírzá Ḥaydar-'Alí was arrested in Egypt. This happened as a result of his teaching unwisely and becoming known as a Bahá'í. He was sent to the Sudan as a prisoner and it was about nine years before he gained his freedom.*

Mírzá Muḥammad-'Alíy-i-Nahrí

Another distinguished believer who came on pilgrimage to Adrianople and attained the presence of Bahá'u'lláh was the devout Mírzá Muḥammad-'Alíy-i-Nahrí, who had had the privilege of meeting Him some years before in Baghdád. Mírzá Muḥammad-'Alí came from a prominent family in Iṣfahán blessed with material wealth and spiritual gifts. He and his brother Mírzá Hádí spent some years in Karbilá where they joined the Shaykhí sect and used to sit for hours at the feet of Siyyid Káẓim-i-Rashtí in order to receive spiritual enlightenment.†

It was in Karbilá that these brothers met the Báb for the first time. As they watched Him pray at the shrine of Imám Ḥusayn, they became deeply attracted to His person, and recognized in Him extraordinary powers. They became aware, too, of the profound reverence and high esteem in which He was held by

* For a brief account of his eventful life see Appendix III and vol. I, pp. 28–9.

† Concerning the Shaykhí sect and its leader Siyyid Káẓim, see *The Dawn-Breakers*.

Siyyid Kázim. No wonder that when the news reached them that a youth in S̲h̲íráz had declared Himself to be the Báb, they immediately recognized His identity.*

Obedient to the behest of the Báb, Mírzá Muḥammad-ʿAlí and his brother proceeded to Iṣfahán. On their way to that city they met Mullá Ḥusayn who acquainted them fully with the Cause. The zeal and enthusiasm of Mullá Ḥusayn, the staunchness of his faith and the ardour of his love for the Báb greatly inspired the two brothers and assisted them to recognize the truth of the new-born Faith of God. They attained the presence of the Báb in S̲h̲íráz at the time when He was under house arrest by order of the Governor of the province.† This meeting created a new spirit of dedication and certitude in Mírzá Muḥammad-ʿAlí and Mírzá Hádí and from that time on they ranked as foremost among the early disciples of the Báb.

From S̲h̲íráz, Mírzá Hádí went to Karbilá while Mírzá Muḥammad-ʿAlí returned to Iṣfahán. Soon after his arrival in that city, the latter learnt that his wife had died in Karbilá. He remarried and remained in Iṣfahán until the Báb arrived there on his way to Ṭihrán. Up to that time Mírzá Muḥammad-ʿAlí had no children. His first wife, who had died after a few years of marriage, had borne him no child. His second wife was also childless until an event of great significance took place.

Nabíl-i-Aʿẓam describes this joyous episode:

Ere the Báb had transferred His residence to the house of the Muʿtamid, Mírzá Ibráhím, father of the Sulṭánuʾs̲h-S̲h̲uhadá‡ and elder brother of Mírzá Muḥammad-ʿAlíy-i-Nahrí, to whom we have already referred, invited the Báb to his home one night. Mírzá Ibráhím was a friend of the Imám-Jumʿih, was intimately associated with him and controlled the management of all his affairs. The banquet which was

---

* Soon after His declaration the Báb instructed His disciples to spread the news but not to disclose His identity until a later date, when it would be announced.

† See *The Dawn-Breakers*.

‡ Mírzá Ḥasan, entitled by Baháʾuʾlláh the 'King of the Martyrs'. (A.T.)

spread for the Báb that night was one of unsurpassed magnificence. It was commonly observed that neither the officials nor the notables of the city had offered a feast of such magnitude and splendour. The Sulṭánu'sh-Shuhadá and his brother, the Maḥbúbu'sh-Shuhadá,* who were lads of nine and eleven respectively, served at that banquet and received special attention from the Báb. That night, during dinner, Mírzá Ibráhím turned to his Guest and said: 'My brother, Mírzá Muḥammad-'Alí, has no child. I beg You to intercede in his behalf and to grant his heart's desire.' The Báb took a portion of the food with which He had been served, placed it with His own hands on a platter, and handed it to His host, asking him to take it to Mírzá Muḥammad-'Alí and his wife. 'Let them both partake of this,' He said; 'their wish will be fulfilled.' By virtue of that portion which the Báb had chosen to bestow upon her, the wife of Mírzá Muḥammad-'Alí conceived and in due time gave birth to a girl, who eventually was joined in wedlock with the Most Great Branch,† a union that came to be regarded as the consummation of the hopes entertained by her parents.[4]

The new-born daughter was named Fáṭimih by her parents. Bahá'u'lláh, later on, conferred upon her the name of Munírih (Illumined). Her birth took place around the time that her father and her uncle Mírzá Hádí had gone to take part in the conference of Badasht.‡ It is interesting to note that at that conference the two brothers were among those who became extremely agitated when Ṭáhirih removed her veil. They reacted by leaving the scene of the conference and taking residence in the ruins of an old castle. Bahá'u'lláh sent for them, calmed their emotions and pointed out that it was unnecessary for them to desert their companions. When the conference of Badasht ended, the believers were attacked in the village of Níyálá. Mírzá Hádí died on the way home as a result of these persecu-

* Mírzá Ḥusayn, entitled the 'Beloved of the Martyrs'. A more detailed account of their lives will be given in future volumes. (A.T.)

† Reference to Munírih Khánum's marriage with 'Abdu'l-Bahá.

‡ See *The Dawn-Breakers* for details.

tions, and Mírzá Muḥammad-'Alí returned to Iṣfahán. Through the potency of his belief, he became a leading exponent of the Faith in that city. It was mainly through his help and guidance that those two of his nephews referred to by Nabíl and entitled the 'King of the Martyrs' and 'Beloved of the Martyrs' were confirmed in the Cause. They became the most illustrious among the martyrs of the Faith.

When Bahá'u'lláh was in Baghdád, Mírzá Muḥammad-'Alí conducted his two youthful nephews to that city where they attained His presence. They saw the Glory of God hidden behind many veils of concealment; their souls were magnetized by His love and transformed into a new creation. They truly detached themselves from this world and returned home in a spirit of joy and steadfastness.

Some years later Mírzá Muḥammad-'Alí travelled to Adrianople. Once again, he was privileged to attain the presence of His Lord and achieve his heart's desire. But he did not live long enough to witness the honour which was conferred upon his daughter Munírih Khánum in becoming the consort of 'Abdu'l-Bahá.

It was during the Adrianople period that certain events took place which paved the way for 'Abdu'l-Bahá's marriage in 'Akká some years later. The custom of the time, especially among the nobility, was to arrange the marriages of their sons and daughters when they were children. Most marriages were arranged inside the family and the couple had very little say in this choice. When 'Abdu'l-Bahá was a child in Ṭihrán, they chose for Him Shahr-bánú, a cousin, and betrothed her to Him. She was a daughter of Mírzá Muḥammad-Ḥasan, an older half-brother of Bahá'u'lláh.* When Bahá'u'lláh and His family were exiled to 'Iráq, Shahr-bánú remained in the district of Núr in Mázindarán, until in 1285 A.H. (1868) Bahá'u'lláh instructed His uncle Mullá Zaynu'l-'Ábidín† to conduct Shahr-bánú to

* See vol. I, p. 16.

† Bahá'u'lláh had four paternal uncles. Among those to whom He taught the Faith of the Báb in Núr were these uncles. Two of them rejected the

Ṭihrán and from there to arrange her journey to Adrianople.

No sooner had this news reached Sháh Sulṭán Khánum* (a half-sister of Bahá'u'lláh and a follower of Mírzá Yaḥyá), than she arose in enmity to prevent the marriage from taking place. She took Shahr-bánú to her home in Ṭihrán and practically forced her to marry instead Mírzá 'Alí-Khán-i-Núrí, the son of the Prime Minister. Bahá'u'lláh has referred to this in *Epistle to the Son of the Wolf*.† This marriage, so rudely imposed upon her, plunged Shahr-bánú into a state of perpetual grief and misery. Her youngest brother, Mírzá Niẓámu'l-Mulk, a faithful and devoted follower of Bahá'u'lláh, has recorded in his memoirs that after her marriage Shahr-bánú prayed fervently to God for her deliverance from her tragic plight. It seems that her prayers were answered, as shortly afterwards she became afflicted with tuberculosis and died.

As for Munírih Khánum, she spent her childhood and youth in Iṣfahán under the care and protection of her parents and illustrious cousins. Some time after the death of her father, the family, including the 'King of the Martyrs' and the 'Beloved of the Martyrs' decided that the time had come for her to be married. Therefore, arrangements were made for Munírih Khánum to be united in wedlock with Mírzá Káẓim, the youngest brother of the 'King of the Martyrs' and the 'Beloved of the Martyrs'.

When the wedding day arrived, a splendid feast was given and the festive atmosphere came to its climax when the couple were married. When the ceremony ended, however, a distressing incident turned everyone's joy into deep sorrow. The

---

Cause of God and actively rose up against it. These were Shaykh 'Azízu'-lláh and Ṣafí Qulí Big. The other two, Mullá Zaynu'l-'Ábidín and Karbilá'í Zamán, became ardent believers. The former accompanied Bahá'u'lláh to the fortress of Shaykh Ṭabarsí, and when Bahá'u'lláh was bastinadoed in Ámul, threw himself upon His feet and was beaten so much that he fainted. For details of the incident at Ámul, see *The Dawn-Breakers*.

* See vol. I, p. 50.

† *Epistle to the Son of the Wolf*, p. 170.

bridegroom, who up to then had been in perfect health, was suddenly struck down by a strange phenomenon as he approached the entrance of his home. He appeared to be stunned by an inexplicable force, and had to be helped to his feet. He became gravely ill and died soon afterwards.

After this tragic incident, Munírih Khánum turned her thoughts away from this world and spent her days in prayer and meditation. The circumstances of her marriage with 'Abdu'l-Bahá are very thrilling indeed. The following account, mainly in her own words, reveals the joy and excitement of such an exalted life:

> 'In compliance with the command of the Blessed Perfection (Bahá'u'lláh) Siyyid Mihdí Dhaji [Dahají] arrived in Persia, and later passed through Iṣfahán to promulgate the Cause of God. A great feast was prepared for him, and all the believers clustered around inquiring eagerly the news of the Holy Land, and all the details concerning the Blessed Family and an account of the imprisonment of the believers in the barracks of 'Akká. Among the inquirers was Shms os Zoha, [Shamsu'ḍ-Ḍuḥá] the wife of my uncle, and a member of the household of the King of the Martyrs. She asked of Siyyid Mihdí: "While you were in the Presence of Bahá'u'lláh, did you ever hear whether any girl had been spoken of or selected for the Master 'Abdu'l-Bahá?" He answered, "No, but one day the Blessed Perfection was walking in the men's apartment and speaking. Then He turned His face to me and said, 'Aga Siyyid Mihdí! I had a remarkable dream last night. I dreamt that the face of the beautiful girl who is living in Ṭihrán, whose hand in marriage we asked from Mírzá Ḥasan for the Greatest Branch, became dark and obscure. At the same moment, the face of another girl appeared on the scene whose countenance was luminous and whose heart enlightened. We have selected her to become the wife of the Greatest Branch.' Except for the above talk from the lips of the Blessed Perfection, I have heard nothing."
>
> 'When my aunt returned to the house and saw me, she declared by the One God that the very moment when Siyyid

Mihdí was relating to us the dream of Bahá'u'lláh, it had occurred to her mind that, without question, I was that girl, and ere long we would realize that she was right. I wept and answered: "Far be it, for I am not worthy of such a bounty. I beg of thee never let another word concerning the matter issue from thy lips; do not speak about it."'

Munírih Khánum continues the story of how she travelled to the Holy Land through successive instructions from Bahá'u'lláh to her relatives. En route to their destination they met many friends who tried to prevent them from going to the Holy Land, saying that in these days no one is permitted to go to 'Akká because some sad and unfortunate events had caused anew the incarceration of the friends, and the authorities did not permit any Bahá'í to enter the city of 'Akká. 'This news disturbed us a great deal, and we wondered what we should do, but Shaykh Salmán assured us that these conditions did not apply to us, and made us feel confident that we should enter the Holy Land with the utmost ease and tranquillity, even if all the believers were thrown into prison and under chains.' After many trials and difficulties on the way, they finally arrived in 'Akká.

'... members of the Blessed Family came to visit and welcome us. I returned with them, and for the first time stood in the Presence of the Blessed Perfection. The state of ecstasy and rapture that possessed me was beyond description. The first words of Bahá'u'lláh were these: "We have brought you into the Prison at such a time when the door of meeting is closed to all the believers. This is for no other reason than to prove to everyone the Power and Might of God." I continued to live in the house of Kalím for nearly five months. I visited Bahá'u'lláh many times and then returned to my abode. Whenever Kalím returned from his visit to the Blessed Perfection he would tell me of His infinite bounties, and bring a material gift from Him for me. One day he arrived with a great happiness in his face. He said: "I have brought a most wonderful gift for you. It is this—a new name has been given you and that name is Munírih (Illumined)."

'Then the night of union ... drew nigh. I was dressed in a

THE HOUSE OF RIḌÁ BIG

Where Bahá'u'lláh lived for a year. A recent photograph taken after the house was restored

RUINS OF THE HOUSE OF ‘IZZAT ÁQÁ

Bahá’u’lláh’s last residence in Adrianople
A photograph taken in 1933

white robe which had been prepared for me by the fingers of the Greatest Holy Leaf, and which was more precious than the silks and velvets of Paradise. About nine o'clock . . . I was permitted to stand in the Presence of Bahá'u'lláh. Attended by the Greatest Holy Leaf, I listened to the words of the Blessed Perfection . . . He said: "You are welcome! You are welcome! O thou My blessed leaf and maid-servant. We have chosen thee and accepted thee to be the companion of the Greatest Branch and to serve Him. This is from My Bounty, to which there is no equal; the treasures of the earth and heaven cannot be compared with it . . . Thou must be very thankful, for thou hast attained to this most great favor and bestowal . . . May you always be under the protection of God!" '[5]

Of her companionship with 'Abdu'l-Bahá, Munírih Khánum writes these words:

> If I were to write the details of the fifty years of my association with the Beloved of the world, of His love, His mercy and bounty, I would need fifty years more of time and opportunity in order to write it; yet, if the seas of the world were turned into ink and the leaves of the forest into paper, I would not render adequate justice to the subject.[6]

Mírzá 'Alíy-i-Sayyáḥ

The betrayal of the trust of the Báb by Mírzá Yaḥyá had plunged the Faith into a crisis of such magnitude that it shattered the unity and solidarity of the community and brought in its wake untold sufferings to Bahá'u'lláh and His loved ones. Without acquiring a full knowledge of all the machinations, plots and evil deeds of Mírzá Yaḥyá and his supporters, it is not possible to understand the extent of the harm which they inflicted upon Bahá'u'lláh and His Cause. A full account of their pernicious influence and foul deeds is beyond the scope of this work. Suffice it to say that the rebellion of Mírzá Yaḥyá caused so much pain and anguish for Bahá'u'lláh that the persecutions which were heaped upon Him by enemies from outside the Bahá'í community cannot compare with them.

Bahá'u'lláh remained in the house of Riḍá Big for about one year and then transferred His residence to the house of Amru'-lláh where He stayed about three months. In almost every Tablet revealed during this whole period, He refers to the unfaithfulness and perfidy of Mírzá Yaḥyá and the harm he had inflicted upon the Cause of God. One of the Tablets of this period is the *Lawḥ-i-Sayyáḥ*, revealed in honour of Mullá Ádí-Guzal, otherwise known as Mírzá 'Alíy-i-Sayyáḥ. The title 'Sayyáḥ' (Traveller) was given to him by the Báb. He was a native of Marágh̲ih, and had received his education as a mullá in that town. In the early days of the Faith he attained the presence of the Báb, recognized His station and was numbered among His followers. No sooner did he embrace the Cause of the Báb than he began to serve his Lord with great dedication and earnestness. When the Báb was imprisoned in the castles of Máh-kú and C̲h̲ihríq, Sayyáḥ served Him as a faithful messenger. He attained His presence many times in these fortresses and was one of His leading companions. From there he proceeded to various parts of Persia bearing the messages of the Báb to His followers and bringing their letters back to Him. On one occasion he carried some Tablets in the handwriting of the Báb together with an exquisite pen-case as a gift from the Báb to Quddús.

One of his unforgettable services to the Báb at a time when He was grief-stricken at the news of the martyrdom of many heroes in Mázindarán, was to visit, on His behalf, the spot where the martyrs of Ṭabarsí* had fallen. Concerning this Nabíl recounts:

> No sooner had He [the Báb] completed His eulogies of those who had immortalized their names in the defence of the fort, than He summoned, on the day of 'Ás̲h̲úrá,† Mullá

* See *The Dawn-Breakers*.

† The tenth of Muḥarram, the anniversary of the martyrdom of the Imám Ḥusayn, which fell in that year on 26 November 1849.

Ádí-Guzal, one of the believers of Marágh_ih, who for the last two months had been acting as His attendant instead of Siyyid Ḥasan, the brother of Siyyid Ḥusayn-i-'Azíz. He affectionately received him, bestowed upon him the name Sayyáḥ, entrusted to his care the visiting Tablets He had revealed in memory of the martyrs of Ṭabarsí, and bade him perform, on His behalf, a pilgrimage to that spot. 'Arise,' He urged him, 'and with complete detachment proceed, in the guise of a traveller, to Mázindarán, and there visit, on My behalf, the spot which enshrines the bodies of those immortals who, with their blood, have sealed their faith in My Cause. As you approach the precincts of that hallowed ground, put off your shoes and, bowing your head in reverence to their memory, invoke their names and prayerfully make the circuit of their shrine. Bring back to Me, as a remembrance of your visit, a handful of that holy earth which covers the remains of My beloved ones, Quddús and Mullá Ḥusayn. Strive to be back ere the day of Naw-Rúz, that you may celebrate with Me that festival, the only one I probably shall ever see again.'

Faithful to the instructions he had received, Sayyáḥ set out on his pilgrimage to Mázindarán. He reached his destination on the first day of Rabí'u'l-Avval in the year 1266 A.H. [15 January A.D. 1850] and by the ninth day of that same month [23 January A.D. 1850], the first anniversary of the martyrdom of Mullá Ḥusayn, he had performed his visit and acquitted himself of the mission with which he had been entrusted. From thence he proceeded to Ṭihrán.

I have heard Áqáy-i-Kalím, who received Sayyáḥ at the entrance of Bahá'u'lláh's home in Ṭihrán, relate the following: 'It was the depth of winter when Sayyáḥ, returning from his pilgrimage, came to visit Bahá'u'lláh. Despite the cold and snow of a rigorous winter, he appeared attired in the garb of a dervish, poorly clad, barefooted, and dishevelled. His heart was set afire with the flame that pilgrimage had kindled. No sooner had Siyyid Yaḥyáy-i-Dárábí, surnamed Vaḥíd, who was then a guest in the home of Bahá'u'lláh, been informed of the return of Sayyáḥ from the fort of Ṭabarsí, than he, oblivious of the pomp and circumstance to which a man of his position had been accustomed, rushed forward and flung himself at the feet of the pilgrim. Holding his legs, which had been covered with mud to the knees, in his arms, he kissed them devoutly. I was amazed that day at the many evidences of loving solicitude which Bahá'u'lláh evinced towards Vaḥíd. He showed him such favours as I had never seen Him extend to anyone. The manner of His conversation left no doubt in me that this same Vaḥíd would ere long distinguish himself by deeds no less remarkable than those which had immortalized the defenders of the fort of Ṭabarsí.'

Sayyáḥ tarried a few days in that home. He was, however, unable to perceive, as did Vaḥíd, the nature of that power which lay latent in his Host. Though himself the recipient of the utmost favour from Bahá'u'lláh, he failed to apprehend the significance of the blessings that were being showered upon him. I have heard him recount his experiences, during his sojourn in Famagusta: 'Bahá'u'lláh overwhelmed me with His kindness. As to Vaḥíd, notwithstanding the eminence of his position, he invariably gave me preference over himself whenever in the presence of his Host. On the day of my arrival from Mázindarán, he went so far as to kiss my feet. I was amazed at the reception accorded to me in that home. Though immersed in an ocean of bounty, I failed, in those days, to appreciate the position then occupied by Bahá'u'lláh, nor was I able to suspect, however dimly, the nature of the Mission He was destined to perform.' [7]

After the martyrdom of the Báb, Sayyáḥ tarried for a short while in Á<u>dh</u>irbáyján. He then proceeded to Karbilá where he resided for a considerable time. In the course of his interrogation in Constantinople in 1868,* he declared that he had lived in Karbilá for twelve years. He married the daughter of <u>Sh</u>ay<u>kh</u> Ḥasan-i-Zunúzí, an eminent disciple of the Báb and one to whom He had given the glad-tidings and the assurance of meeting the 'Promised Ḥusayn' † in Karbilá. Sayyáḥ himself was

* See pp. 328–9 ff.

† In <u>Sh</u>í'ah Islám, it is believed that after the advent of the Qá'im (the Promised One of Islám), Imám Ḥusayn will return. The name of Bahá'u'-

also promised by the Báb that he would attain the presence of 'Him Whom God shall make manifest'.

Sayyáḥ travelled to Adrianople in the early part of 1284 A.H. (1867). There he attained the presence of Bahá'u'lláh and told the believers, in one of their gatherings, how the promise made by the Báb concerning his meeting with 'Him Whom God shall make manifest' was fulfilled. He also wrote about this to Mírzá Yaḥyá. He was one of the most devoted followers of Bahá'u'lláh. When he had been in Adrianople three months,* Bahá'u'lláh sent him with Mishkín-Qalam † and Jamshíd-i-Gurjí to Constantinople on an important mission. The nature of this mission and their imprisonment in that city will be referred to later.

In the *Tablet of Sayyáḥ* Bahá'u'lláh unveils the glory of His station, states that He is the Ancient Beauty through Whose command the whole of creation has come into being, affirms that mankind turns to Him in adoration and clings to the hem of His bounty even though it is unable to recognize Him in His wondrous Revelation. He alludes to the followers of the *Bayán* who have denied and repudiated His Cause, refers to them as the people of sedition and the company of Satan, reminds them that for many years He had associated with them, but had hidden His glory from their eyes so that none might recognize Him; but they had risen up against Him in great enmity. It was then that He unveiled the beauty of His Countenance and shed the radiance of His Face upon all creation. He declares that the days of tests have come and that the balance has been established, a balance through which the deeds of all men will be

---

lláh was Ḥusayn-'Alí. It was in the summer of 1851 that Bahá'u'lláh encountered Shaykh Ḥasan in Karbilá and confided to him His station. See vol. I, pp. 207–8. It was from that time, before Bahá'u'lláh was imprisoned in the Síyáh-Chál, that Shaykh Ḥasan fully recognized the station of Bahá'u'lláh as 'Him Whom God shall make manifest'.

* When interrogated in Constantinople, Sayyáḥ stated that he stayed in Adrianople for three months.

† See vol. I, pp. 26–8.

weighed with justice. He proclaims to the peoples of the world that if they wish to hear the voice of God they should hearken to His wondrous melodies, and if they desire to behold the Face of God they should gaze into His beauteous Countenance. He warns them, however, that they shall not be able to do this unless they cleanse their hearts of all idle fancy and detach themselves from this world and all that is therein.*

It is in this Tablet that Bahá'u'lláh, by allusion, foretells His exile to the city of 'Akká, designating it as the 'vale of Nabíl'.† He describes in allegorical terms His arrival in that city in these words:

> Upon Our arrival, We were welcomed with banners of light, whereupon the Voice of the Spirit cried out saying: 'Soon will all that dwell on earth be enlisted under these banners.'[8]

There are passages in this Tablet which throw light on the severity of the tests which the believer encounters when he treads the path of faith. Alluding to the people of the *Bayán*, Bahá'u'lláh refers to some who were among the most holy of men, who worshipped God with great devotion, who were considered the most devout, who were endowed with the keenest insight; yet when the breezes of His Revelation were wafted over them, they were found to be shut out as by a veil from Him. This notwithstanding the fact that He associated with them for so long and manifested His glory to their eyes. He attributes the reason for this failure to pride and attachment to self and ego. He grieves that their acts of devotion and service had become the cause of pride and had deprived them of God's bounty.

The subject of detachment occurs in numerous Tablets. Perhaps it may be said that there are few, if any, among Bahá'u'lláh's exhortations which have been stressed so much as detachment from this world and from every selfish desire. We have already referred to this important theme in previous chap-

* See vol. I, pp. 187–9.

† The numerical value of the word Nabíl is equal to that of 'Akká.

ters. The perusal of the *Tablet of Sayyáḥ* makes it absolutely clear that Bahá'u'lláh's companions, because of their closeness to Him, could not remain faithful to the Cause of God unless they were able to cast out entirely the evil of self. Any trace of self-glorification, however insignificant, was fatal to them, and in His holy presence nothing but utter self-effacement could survive.

There were many among His disciples who were enabled to subdue their ego. By their words and deeds they demonstrated their utter nothingness when they came face to face with their Lord. These became the spiritual giants of this Dispensation, and through their faith they shed an imperishable lustre upon the Cause of God. It is concerning such men, during the days of Baghdád, that Nabíl writes:

> Many a night, no less than ten persons subsisted on no more than a pennyworth of dates. No one knew to whom actually belonged the shoes, the cloaks, or the robes that were to be found in their houses. Whoever went to the bazaar could claim that the shoes upon his feet were his own, and each one who entered the presence of Bahá'u'lláh could affirm that the cloak and robe he then wore belonged to him. Their own names they had forgotten, their hearts were emptied of aught else except adoration for their Beloved . . . O, for the joy of those days, and the gladness and wonder of those hours! [9]

That a few souls have been able to achieve such distinction, to soar into the realms of detachment, and to humble themselves before their Lord, augurs well for the human race which, in the fullness of time, is destined to follow in their footsteps. Today, the followers of Bahá'u'lláh cannot attain His presence in this life and therefore the tests which were particularly associated with His person do not seem to affect them. But the requirements of faith and the path to Bahá'u'lláh remain unchanged. It is necessary for the believer of today, as in the days of Bahá'u'lláh, to detach himself from all earthly things and to banish from his soul the traces of passion and desire, of ego and self-glorification, in order that he may truly appreciate the awe-inspiring station of Bahá'u'lláh and become a worthy servant of His Cause. If he fails to do this, although he may not be faced with the same perils that surrounded Bahá'u'lláh's companions, he is bound to feel a measure of doubt in his innermost heart concerning the Faith and may experience great conflicts in his mind. Although intellectually he may accept Bahá'u'lláh as a Manifestation of God and may be well versed in His Writings, he will not be able to have that absolute certitude which endows a human being with divine attributes and confers upon him perpetual contentment, serenity and happiness.

The acquiring of true faith is man's greatest accomplishment. Faith endows a human being with powers that no earthly agency can equal. By the power of their faith, the believers have overcome seemingly insurmountable obstacles and won memorable victories for the Cause of Bahá'u'lláh. In order to have faith, a man must banish from his heart every trace of vain imagination and idle fancy. Let us examine the road to the achievement of this exalted goal and explore the many pitfalls and obstacles which confront the soul in its quest.

There are two focal points of enormous power within a human being. One is the brain, the centre of intellect and thinking and the storehouse of his knowledge and learning. Through the agency of this faculty man can manifest the unique powers of the rational soul which distinguish him from the animal. The intellect is the greatest gift of God to man. But since man has free will, he may be led by his intellect either to faith and belief in God, or else to disbelief.

The other focal point is the heart which is the centre of warmth and love. The heart of man falls in love with the world and its own self. But it is also the habitation wherein God's attributes are revealed. Bahá'u'lláh states:

> O Son of Being!
> Thy heart is My home; sanctify it for My descent . . .[10]

It is within the heart of man that the spark of faith appears. But this can only happen when the heart becomes freed from attachment to the things of the world. Bahá'u'lláh declares in *The Hidden Words*:

O Son of Dust!

All that is in heaven and earth I have ordained for thee, except the human heart, which I have made the habitation of My beauty and glory; yet thou didst give My home and dwelling to another than Me; and whenever the manifestation of My holiness sought His own abode, a stranger found He there, and, homeless, hastened unto the sanctuary of the Beloved. Notwithstanding I have concealed thy secret and desired not thy shame.[11]

God has created man in such wise that the two focal points in his being, namely the mind and the heart, should complement each other. The mind without the heart illumined by faith does not acquire the capacity to investigate, or the language to understand, the truth of the Cause of God. Similar to the eye when deprived of light, it is unable to explore the world of the spirit. Instead, it develops its powers in the field of materialism and naturally rejects the concept of God and religion. Thus it becomes the most effective barrier to the individual's acquisition of faith. In such circumstances the heart becomes filled with love of the world and its own self, for it is a characteristic of the heart to love. If it is not allowed to love God, it will love itself and its worldly possessions. And this is one significance of the 'stranger' that Bahá'u'lláh refers to in *The Hidden Words*:

O My Friend in word!

Ponder awhile. Hast thou ever heard that friend and foe should abide in one heart? Cast out then the stranger, that the Friend may enter His home.[12]

To acquire faith man must cast out the 'stranger' from his heart. To the extent that he succeeds in doing this, he will acquire faith. Once the spark of faith is ignited within the heart it must be allowed to grow steadily into a flame, otherwise it could die because of attachment to this world. For instance, when an individual reaches a point where he recognizes Bahá'u'lláh as a Manifestation of God, his heart becomes the recipient of the light of God's Faith for this day. If the believer immerses himself from the start in the ocean of Bahá'u'lláh's Revelation, reads His writings daily not merely in order to add to his own knowledge but to receive the food of the spirit, seeks the companionship of the righteous, and arises to serve Him with sincerity and detachment, then he may steadily grow in faith and become a radiant and enthusiastic soul. He may obtain a deeper understanding of the writings and reach a point where both his mind and his heart work together in harmony. Such a believer will eventually find no conflict between the teachings of Bahá'u'lláh and his own thinking. He will discover many a wisdom hidden in the utterances of Bahá'u'lláh and will recognize the limitations and shortcomings of his own finite mind.

But if a believer, after having recognized Bahá'u'lláh, fails to follow this path, he may soon find himself in conflict with many aspects of the Faith of Bahá'u'lláh. His intellect may not be able to understand the wisdom behind many of His Teachings, he may indeed reject some of His precepts and eventually lose faith altogether. Some people struggle for years to overcome this problem, for they long to be confirmed in their faith. Often such an individual may be helped to acquire a true understanding of the Faith by those who truly believe in Bahá'u'lláh and are detached from this world.

But if everything else fails, the only remedy for the individual who still has a glimmer of faith in his heart, but who has doubts about the Cause, is to admit that he may be wrong in his assessment of the teachings of the Faith, to affirm that Bahá'u'lláh's knowledge is of God, and to surrender his feelings and thoughts completely to Him. Once he submits himself in this way and perseveres in doing so with sincerity and truthfulness, the channels of the grace of God open and his heart becomes the recipient of the light of true knowledge. He will discover, some time in his life, either by intuition or through prayer and meditation, the answer to all his problems and objections. Every trace of conflict will disappear from his mind. He will readily understand the reasons behind those very teachings which previously baffled his intellect, and will find many mysteries enshrined in the utterances of Bahá'u'lláh, mysteries of which he was completely unaware in earlier days.

The following words of Bahá'u'lláh in *The Hidden Words* demonstrate that not until man submits himself to God can he attain to the knowledge of His Revelation:

> O Son of Dust!
>
> Blind thine eyes, that thou mayest behold My beauty; stop thine ears, that thou mayest hearken unto the sweet melody of My voice; empty thyself of all learning, that thou mayest partake of My knowledge; and sanctify thyself from riches, that thou mayest obtain a lasting share from the ocean of My eternal wealth. Blind thine eyes, that is, to all save My beauty; stop thine ears to all save My word; empty thyself of all learning save the knowledge of Me; that with a clear vision, a pure heart and an attentive ear thou mayest enter the court of My holiness.[13]

The following story in the life of Mírzá Abu'l-Faḍl, the outstanding scholar of the Cause and its famous apologist, is one which demonstrates that reading the Word of God with the eye of intellect can lead a man astray. He himself has recounted the story that soon after he came in contact with the believers, they gave him the *Kitáb-i-Íqán* to read. He read it with an air of intellectual superiority and was not impressed by it. He even commented that if the *Kitáb-i-Íqán* was a proof of Bahá'u'lláh's claims, he himself could certainly write a better book.

At that time he was the head of a theological college in Ṭihrán. The following day a prominent woman arrived at the college and approached some students asking them to write an important letter for her.* The students referred her to Mírzá

* In those days people who were not educated often paid a small sum of money to a learned man to write letters for them. The essential requirements for writing good letters were good composition and fine penmanship.

Abu'l-Faḍl saying that he was an outstanding writer, a master of eloquence and a man unsurpassed in the art of composition. Mírzá Abu'l-Faḍl took up his pen to write, but found himself unable to compose the first sentence. He tried very hard but was unsuccessful. For several minutes he scribbled in the corner of the page and even drew lines on his own fingernail, until the woman realized that the learned scribe was unable to write. Losing her patience she arose to go and mockingly said to Mírzá Abu'l-Faḍl, 'If you have forgotten how to write a simple letter why don't you say so instead of keeping me here while you scrawl?'

Mírzá Abu'l-Faḍl says that he was overcome with feelings of shame as a result of this incident, and then suddenly remembered his own comments the night before about his being able to write a better book than the *Kitáb-i-Íqán*. He had a pure heart and knew that this incident was nothing but a clear answer to his arrogant attitude towards that holy Book.

However, it took Mírzá Abu'l-Faḍl several years to be convinced of the truth of the Cause of Bahá'u'lláh. He reached a stage where he accepted the Faith intellectually, but for years his heart was not convinced. The only thing which caused him to recognize the truth of the Cause of God after having struggled for so long was to submit himself and surrender his intellectual gifts to God. One evening he went into his chamber, and prayed with yearning as tears flowed from his eyes, beseeching God to open the channels of his heart. At the hour of dawn he suddenly found himself possessed of such faith that he felt he could lay down his life in the path of Bahá'u'lláh.* The same person who once had said he could write a better book than the *Kitáb-i-Íqán*, read this book many times with the eye of faith and found it to be an ocean of knowledge, limitless in scope. Every time he read it he found new pearls of wisdom within it and discovered new mysteries which he had not come across before.

* An account of the life of Mírzá Abu'l-Faḍl will appear in the next volume.

Faith comes to a man through submission to God. The surrendering of the self with all its accomplishments renders the soul free of attachment to this mortal world. It drives the 'stranger' away from the heart and enables him to receive the 'Friend' within its sanctuary. Bahá'u'lláh states:

> O Son of Man!
> Humble thyself before Me, that I may graciously visit thee . . .[14]

In another passage He reveals:

> O Son of Man!
> If thou lovest Me, turn away from thyself; and if thou seekest My pleasure, regard not thine own; that thou mayest die in Me and I may eternally live in thee.[15]

10

Illustrious Martyrs

Áqá Najaf-'Alíy-i-Zanjání

A devoted believer who came to Adrianople in the early years of Bahá'u'lláh's sojourn there was Áqá Najaf-'Alíy-i-Zanjání. He was an admirer of Mullá Muḥammad-'Alíy-i-Ḥujjat, and had been one of his companions during the struggle of Zanján.* After the horrid massacre there in 1851, forty-four of the survivors, including Áqá Najaf-'Alí, were despatched to Ṭihrán. All of them were put to death except for Áqá Najaf-'Alí whose life was saved by the kindness of a certain officer in the army. Later, he went to Baghdád and was permitted by Bahá'u'lláh to remain in 'Iráq. He was one of the devoted companions of Bahá'u'lláh who recognized His station during the days of Baghdád.

'Abdu'l-Bahá mentions[1] that all the way from Baghdád to the port of Sámsún, Najaf-'Alí would assist Mírzá Muḥammad-Qulí (Bahá'u'lláh's youngest brother) to erect the tent of Bahá'u'lláh in the various towns and villages in which the caravan stopped to rest. On one occasion they had some difficulty. The governor of the town, who was present, showed so much reverence for Bahá'u'lláh that he insisted on pitching the tent with his own hands.

In the year 1283 A.H. (1866–7), Najaf-'Alí was in Adrianople. Bahá'u'lláh sent him to Persia and gave him some Tablets to carry. Upon his arrival in Ṭihrán, he was arrested and taken to prison on the charge of being a follower of Bahá'u'lláh. They tortured him in order that he might disclose the identity of

* See *The Dawn-Breakers*.

those for whom he was carrying the Tablets. But Áqá Najaf-'Alí did not reveal any name. When the time for his execution arrived his body was already covered with deadly wounds as a result of these tortures. Bahá'u'lláh has referred to his martyrdom in these words:

> They arrested his honour Najaf-'Alí, who hastened, with rapture and great longing, unto the field of martyrdom, uttering these words: 'We have kept both Bahá and the khún-bahá (bloodmoney)!' With these words he yielded up his spirit.[2]

Shoghi Effendi has also written this brief yet moving portrayal of the martyrdom of Áqá Najaf-'Alí:

> Among the sufferers may be singled out the intrepid Najaf-'Alíy-i-Zanjání, a survivor of the struggle of Zanján, and immortalized in the *Epistle to the Son of the Wolf*, who, bequeathing the gold in his possession to his executioner, was heard to shout aloud 'Yá Rabbíya'l-Abhá'* before he was beheaded.[3]

Siyyid Ashraf and Abá-Baṣír

Another illustrious soul from Zanján who attained the presence of Bahá'u'lláh in Adrianople and later drank the cup of martyrdom in his native city was a youth by the name of Siyyid Ashraf.† His father, Áqá Mír Jalíl, a man of courage and considerable influence in the city, had been one of the companions of Ḥujjat in the struggle of Zanján, and was martyred. His mother 'Anbar Khánum, known in the Writings as Umm-i-Ashraf (Mother of Ashraf) is reckoned as one of the immortal heroines of the Faith.

* Literally 'O Thou my Lord, the Most Glorious', an invocation. (A.T.)

† Not to be mistaken for Áqá Mírzá Ashraf-i-Ábádi'í who was martyred in Iṣfahán, and concerning whom Bahá'u'lláh writes these words in the *Epistle to the Son of the Wolf*, p. 72: 'Before them one named Káẓim . . . and after them, his honour Ashraf, all quaffed the draught of martyrdom . . .'

Siyyid Ashraf was born during the siege of Zanján in the fortress of 'Alí-Mardán Khán.* Neither the hardships and sufferings of that cruel and mournful struggle nor the martyrdom of her beloved husband succeeded in breaking down the fortitude of Umm-i-Ashraf. On the contrary, they served to steel her faith and reinforce her physical endurance. In spite of many privations and trials she reared that infant and two young daughters with great affection and care.

When the Message of Bahá'u'lláh reached Zanján, Umm-i-Ashraf and her children embraced His Faith, recognized His station and turned to Him with the utmost devotion. As a youth, to meet his Lord face to face, Siyyid Ashraf travelled to Adrianople and attained his heart's desire. There he basked in the sunshine of Bahá'u'lláh's bounties, became filled with a new spirit and returned home with a renewed zeal and enthusiasm. The fire of the love of Bahá'u'lláh which was burning within his heart prompted him to make yet another pilgrimage to the abode of his Beloved. This time, accompanied by Ḥájí Ímán, one of the survivors of the Zanján upheaval, he took one of his sisters with him to Adrianople. Bahá'u'lláh showered His favours upon them, and after a short stay directed them to return to Zanján.

The circumstances of their dismissal from the presence of Bahá'u'lláh are described by a granddaughter of Umm-i-Ashraf. When Siyyid Ashraf and his sister left Zanján, there was a good deal of speculation about their whereabouts, especially among Ashraf's paternal uncles who were not Bahá'ís. They were anxious to prevent Ashraf and his sister from becoming involved in the Faith, so they put a great deal of pressure on their mother. They blamed her for having been the driving force behind her husband's activities in the Faith, activities which had resulted in his martyrdom, and now for being the major factor in her children's involvement in the Faith. About four months after the party had left Zanján, three of the uncles came on one occasion to rebuke Umm-i-Ashraf for sending her chil-

* For further details of the Zanján upheaval see *The Dawn-Breakers*.

dren away to attain the presence of Bahá'u'lláh. They became very aggressive and at one point even suggested immoral intentions on the part of her daughter. Umm-i-Ashraf could no longer bear their malice and evil suggestions. She left the room crying bitterly, raised her hands in supplication to Bahá'u'lláh and prayerfully beseeched Him to send her children home.

Later, Siyyid Ashraf, by checking the date with his mother, was able to verify that it was the morning after this night that Bahá'u'lláh summoned him, his sister and Ḥájí Ímán to His presence. He told them that the night before Umm-i-Ashraf had prayed to Him to send them back. Therefore they were to leave at once. That morning He particularly showered His praise and bounties upon Umm-i-Ashraf. Ashraf is reported to have said to Bahá'u'lláh, 'Adam ate the forbidden fruit and was cast out of heaven, in our case it is our mother who has done this to us!'

On their way home it was very clear to many that Ashraf had been transformed into a new creation. He could not help but display such radiance of spirit that, as attested by Ḥájí Ímán, all those who travelled with the caravan were deeply moved. Along the way he used to chant, in a beautiful voice, some poems and Tablets of Bahá'u'lláh he knew by heart. Whenever he wanted to chant, he used to unwind his green turban, the sign of his lineage, and place it around his shoulder. On these occasions he radiated such love, and he conveyed such power and beauty through his voice that the caravan drivers would often leave their duties and walk beside him instead, slowing down the speed of the caravan. Once Ḥájí Ímán asked one of them to go away, and attend to his work, so that the pace could be speeded up. 'How can I go,' he replied. 'Can't you hear the exhilarating voice of the descendant of the Prophet. He is undoubtedly a holy man. I have never seen such a radiant face before.'

According to the advice of Bahá'u'lláh, the sister of Ashraf was joined in wedlock to Ḥájí Ímán on her return home. Throughout his long life, Ḥájí Ímán became the target of many persecutions and spent some years in prison in Ṭihrán. At one time he shared with Mírzá 'Alí-Muḥammad-i-Varqá* and his son Rúḥu'lláh, both of whom were martyred, the weight of chains and fetters in the prison of Ṭihrán. But Ḥájí Ímán's life was providentially spared. He lived many years after, and served the Cause with great dedication. He travelled to 'Akká in 1330 A.H. (1913) where he attained the presence of 'Abdu'l-Bahá. He spent the remainder of his life in 'Ishqábád, and passed away in that city.

As to Siyyid Ashraf, he was directed by Bahá'u'lláh to teach His Cause to the sincere among the people of the *Bayán*. He began this work with unbounded zeal and enthusiasm. He built a room in the grounds of his estate outside the city and made it a centre of Bahá'í activities, praying, reading the Writings and meeting the believers. Having come in contact with the Source of divine power, and being transformed into a spiritual giant, Siyyid Ashraf radiated the love of Bahá'u'lláh to the friends, and enabled many of them to recognize Him as the Promised One of the *Bayán*.

A group of Bábís came to talk to Ashraf soon after his arrival from Adrianople. They were misguided by Mírzá Yaḥyá. One of them asked Ashraf about the station of Mírzá Yaḥyá. He simply replied that Bahá'u'lláh was the Sun of Truth resplendent and radiant in His glory, but Mírzá Yaḥyá acted as a thick dark cloud in front of it. These words caused the insincere and the unfaithful among the believers in Zanján to be separated from the true followers of Bahá'u'lláh in that city.

In his teaching work, Siyyid Ashraf was ably supported by Abá-Baṣír, whose name is for ever linked with the former. The original name of Abá-Baṣír was Áqá Naqd-'Alí. His father, a certain Ḥájí Muḥammad-Ḥusayn, was martyred in the struggle of Zanján. Áqá Naqd-'Alí was born blind but possessed such insight and understanding that Bahá'u'lláh gave him the title of

* Varqá was a distinguished poet and one of the Apostles of Bahá'u'lláh. We shall refer to his life in future volumes. Varqá married the daughter of Ḥájí Ímán. Varqá's children, however, were by a different marriage.

Baṣír (Seeing). He was one of the most steadfast followers of Bahá'u'lláh in Zanján. When it became clear to some members of his family that he had embraced the Cause of Bahá'u'lláh and was actively teaching it, they drove him out of his home. It was after this incident that Abá-Baṣír went to live with Siyyid Ashraf. The spiritual ties which united these two souls were further strengthened when Abá-Baṣír married the sister of Ḥájí Ímán, Ashraf's brother-in-law, and settled in that household permanently. Abá-Baṣír, in spite of his blindness, was a man of great capacity. He had memorized many verses of the *Qur'án* and the traditions, and had such a deep understanding of their meanings that many students of theology used to seek enlightenment from him.

The activities of Ashraf, Abá-Baṣír, and a few others, in promoting the Cause of Bahá'u'lláh, aroused the fears and antagonism of an enemy who vividly remembered the bloody struggle of Zanján only two decades before, when thousands of men and women had fought and died for their Faith with courage and heroism. The fire of hatred and fanaticism, which for some time had remained dormant, was now beginning to blaze, engulfing in its fury the most active and dedicated adherents of a revived and re-animated Faith. The divines issued the death warrant of Abá-Baṣír and Ashraf and handed it to the Governor of Zanján for implementation. As a result, orders were given that unless they recanted they must be put to death. Accordingly these two were arrested, and Abá-Baṣír was conducted to a meeting of the divines where he was asked to recant his Faith. Instead, he openly spoke about the Cause of Bahá'u'lláh and proved its divine origin most eloquently. This audacious confrontation only served to evoke the wrath of the clergy who unhesitatingly demanded his execution.

The executioner conducted Abá-Baṣír to the public square in front of the government house and beheaded him as he knelt in prayer, watched by thousands of men and women who had gathered to see him die. In the meantime, as these heart-rending afflictions were going on, Siyyid Ashraf was being cruelly persecuted in the prison. Yet there were some people, including Siyyid 'Abdu'l-Vásí', the Imám-Jum'ih of the city and a relative of his, who were anxious to save him from his fate, for he was dear to many because of his marvellous qualities and good conduct. They tried very hard to persuade him to recant and, when they failed to achieve their object, they sent for his mother to come and make him recant.

The divines clamoured for Ashraf's death. He was beaten so hard that blood flowed from under his nails, and was taken to the same public square where the body of Abá-Baṣír lay on the ground, exposed to the eyes of the onlookers. As soon as he beheld the decapitated body of his companion, he ran towards it and held it in his arms. His mother, Umm-i-Ashraf, arrived when he was covered in blood. It is reported by one member of the Ashraf family that she went forward, threw her arms around her son, kissed him on the cheeks, wiped away the sweat and blood from his face, took his bloodstained skull-cap as a souvenir and urged him again not to barter his precious faith for the fleeting days of a mortal life. ' "I will disown you as my son," cried the mother, when brought face to face with him, "if you incline your heart to such evil whisperings and allow them to turn you away from the Truth." '[4]

Although his mother exhorted him to remain faithful to the Cause of God, Ashraf, who had attained the presence of Bahá'u'lláh twice, was by himself a tower of strength. He had reached the stage of certitude in his faith and could not entertain the thought of compromise.

As his friends were putting pressure upon him to recant, the fore-mentioned Imám-Jum'ih is reported to have taken Ashraf into his arms, whispered a few words into his ears, and then, as he stood on a high platform, falsely proclaimed to the teeming multitude that Ashraf had recanted his Faith and should no longer be considered a Bahá'í. When he heard this false declaration, Ashraf, who was standing beside him, raised his hands and in a loud voice denied the allegation and announced that he had never recanted, nor would he ever do so. He remained steadfast in his love for Bahá'u'lláh until the executioner moved forward and ruthlessly dealt him a deadly blow. He was beheaded as he held the body of Abá-Baṣír in his arms.

Of As͟hraf and his mother, Nabíl writes:

> Faithful to his mother's admonitions, As͟hraf met his death with intrepid calm. Though herself a witness to the cruelties inflicted on her son, she made no lamentation, neither did she shed a tear. This marvellous mother showed a courage and fortitude that amazed the perpetrators of that shameless deed. 'I have now in mind,' she exclaimed, as she cast a parting glance at the corpse of her son, 'the vow I made on the day of your birth, while besieged in the fort of 'Alí-Mardán K͟hán. I rejoice that you, the only son whom God gave me, have enabled me to redeem that pledge.'[5]

Bahá'u'lláh has revealed a Tablet of Visitation jointly for As͟hraf, Abá-Baṣír and Áqá Mírzá Muḥammad-'Alíy-i-Ṭabíb, who also laid down his life in the path of Bahá'u'lláh in the city of Zanján. He has also extolled the station of As͟hraf and his mother in other Tablets. In one, He has revealed these exalted words concerning Umm-i-As͟hraf and her son:

> Call thou to mind the behaviour of As͟hraf's mother, whose son laid down his life in the Land of Zá (Zanján). He, most certainly, is in the seat of truth, in the presence of One Who is the Most Powerful, the Almighty.
>
> When the infidels, so unjustly, decided to put him to death, they sent and fetched his mother, that perchance she might admonish him, and induce him to recant his faith, and follow in the footsteps of them that have repudiated the truth of God, the Lord of all worlds.
>
> No sooner did she behold the face of her son, than she spoke to him such words as caused the hearts of the lovers of God, and beyond them those of the Concourse on high, to cry out and be sore pained with grief. Truly, thy Lord knoweth what My tongue speaketh. He Himself beareth witness to My words.

> And when addressing him she said: 'My son, mine own son! Fail not to offer up thyself in the path of thy Lord. Beware that thou betray not thy faith in Him before Whose face have bowed down in adoration all who are in the heavens and all who are on the earth. Go thou straight on, O my son, and persevere in the path of the Lord, thy God. Haste thee to attain the presence of Him Who is the Well-Beloved of all worlds.'
>
> On her be My blessings, and My mercy, and My praise, and My glory. I Myself shall atone for the loss of her son—a son who now dwelleth within the tabernacle of My majesty and glory, and whose face beameth with a light that envelopeth with its radiance the Maids of Heaven in their celestial chambers, and beyond them the inmates of My Paradise, and the denizens of the Cities of Holiness. Were any eye to gaze on his face, he would exclaim: 'Lo, this is no other than a noble angel!'[6]

In the *Epistle to the Son of the Wolf*, Bahá'u'lláh refers to A<u>sh</u>raf and his mother in these words:

> Ponder upon the conduct of Abá-Baṣír and Siyyid A<u>sh</u>raf-i-Zanjání. They sent for the mother of A<u>sh</u>raf to dissuade her son from his purpose. But she spurred him on until he suffered a most glorious martyrdom.[7]

Lawḥ-i-A<u>sh</u>raf

When Siyyid A<u>sh</u>raf was in Adrianople, Bahá'u'lláh revealed a Tablet in Arabic for him which is known as the *Lawḥ-i-A<u>sh</u>raf* (Tablet of A<u>sh</u>raf). A part of this Tablet has been translated into English by Shoghi Effendi and included in *Gleanings from the Writings of Bahá'u'lláh.** From its contents it appears that this Tablet was revealed some time after Mírzá Yaḥyá's attempt on the life of Bahá'u'lláh. In it He urges A<u>sh</u>raf to offer thanks to God for having enabled him to attain to His presence and behold His glory. He bids him take the Tablet of God back to

* Section LII.

his home and share it with those who have embraced His Cause. He directs him to inform the believers of His sufferings at the hands of the unfaithful and to impart to them the glad-tidings of His Revelation. He exhorts the faithful to arise and assist His Cause, counsels them to be as bountiful as the rain to those who believe in God and warns them not to be influenced by the misrepresentations of Mírzá Yaḥyá's followers, those who had opposed God, denied His proofs and mustered such audacity as to stand before His Face and make attempts on His Life.

In the *Tablet of Ashraf* Bahá'u'lláh admonishes the followers of the *Bayán* in these words:

> . . . The blind in heart, however, among the people of the Bayán—and to this God is My witness—are impotent, no matter how long the Sun may shine upon them, either to perceive the radiance of its glory, or to appreciate the warmth of its rays.
>
> Say: O people of the Bayán! We have chosen you out of the world to know and to recognize Our Self. We have caused you to draw nigh unto the right side of Paradise—the Spot out of which the undying Fire crieth in manifold accents: 'There is none other God besides Me, the All-Powerful, the Most High!' Take heed lest ye allow yourselves to be shut out as by a veil from this Day Star that shineth above the day-spring of the Will of your Lord, the All-Merciful, and whose light hath encompassed both the small and the great. Purge your sight, that ye may perceive its glory with your own eyes, and depend not on the sight of any one except yourself, for God hath never burdened any soul beyond its power. Thus hath it been sent down unto the Prophets and Messengers of old, and been recorded in all the Scriptures.[8]

Bahá'u'lláh in this Tablet summons Ashraf to hearken to the voice of Him Who is the Ancient of Days. He proclaims that the Blessed Beauty, in this day, has shed the radiance of the Greatest Name upon all other names and attributes. He exhorts him to adorn himself with goodly deeds and become steadfast in His love, so that he may abide under the shadow of His exalted Name.

The *Tablet of Ashraf* contains a significant statement concerning the power of prayer when freed from desire. He declares that the outpouring of grace in this day is so great, that should an individual raise his hands in supplication to God and ask for the treasures of earth and heaven, his wish will be granted even before he lowers his hands, provided that he is freed from attachment to all created things. Indeed, the key for attaining this glory lies in the word 'detachment'. From the study of the Writings it becomes clear that not until man reaches a state of absolute servitude wherein he dies to his own self, and has no desire except what God desires, can he ever ascend to such a lofty station.

The purest form of prayer is one which is freed from desire. Such a prayer will cause the bounties of God to descend upon the soul. Nevertheless, human beings have many needs in this life and when in difficulty, pain or grief, they turn to God for assistance. The Báb and Bahá'u'lláh have both revealed special prayers for various occasions to be said when one is in need. If a man must have a desire—and it is quite natural for him to do so—his prayer should be that in the end he may attain the good-pleasure of his Lord. For any other desire, even service to the Cause, meritorious though it is, will not necessarily result in his salvation. There have been some who rendered notable service to the Cause and yet spiritually their lives ended in tragedy. We may recall the words of Bahá'u'lláh:

> How often hath a sinner, at the hour of death, attained to the essence of faith, and quaffing the immortal draught, hath taken his flight unto the celestial Concourse. And how often hath a devout believer, at the hour of his soul's ascension, been so changed as to fall into the nethermost fire.[9]

However, the most befitting form of prayer is that of praising God. Through it the channels of grace are opened up and He bestows His powers and blessing upon the individual. Turning to God in prayer for the sole purpose of glorifying His Name and extolling His Attributes is the most natural move that man can make towards his Creator. It is like a plant which turns towards the sun. Although the sun pours out its energies regardless, yet, by its very nature, the tree cannot help but stretch its boughs and branches in the direction of the sun. For it to remain insensible to the life-giving rays of the sun is a sign that it is dead. To use another analogy, we see in nature that a babe cries for food and his mother feeds him. But if he does not hunger for food, he is not healthy even though the mother may feed him by force. This two-way relationship is the basis for growth. Similarly, God bestows His boundless favours and grace upon His creation, but man must by his own volition turn to Him in adoration and praise in order to receive them. If he fails to do this, he becomes deprived and spiritually starved. In *The Hidden Words* Bahá'u'lláh confirms this when He says:

> O Son of Being!
> Love Me, that I may love thee. If thou lovest Me not, My love can in no wise reach thee. Know this, O servant.[10]

The sign of true spiritual life in man is to yearn after God and long to adore and glorify Him. The Báb and Bahá'u'lláh have shown us the way by revealing most of their prayers in praise of God. These prayers evoke in the soul feelings of utter self-effacement and absolute poverty, while the power of God and His glory become the motivating influence in guiding and sustaining it throughout its life.

The power which can be generated in the heart of the believer, when he is freed from all desire and turns to God with songs of praise and glorification, is beyond the comprehension of man. Suffice it to say that many heroes of the Faith have derived their courage and steadfastness from this source. At this juncture it is befitting to quote one of the prayers of Bahá'u'lláh in glorification of the Almighty:

Lauded and glorified art Thou, O Lord, my God! How can I make mention of Thee, assured as I am that no tongue, however deep its wisdom, can befittingly magnify Thy name, nor can the bird of the human heart, however great its longing, ever hope to ascend into the heaven of Thy majesty and knowledge.

If I describe Thee, O my God, as Him Who is the All-Perceiving, I find myself compelled to admit that They Who are the highest Embodiments of perception have been created by virtue of Thy behest. And if I extol Thee as Him Who is the All-Wise, I, likewise, am forced to recognise that the Well Springs of wisdom have themselves been generated through the operation of Thy Will. And if I proclaim Thee as the Incomparable One, I soon discover that they Who are the inmost essence of oneness have been sent down by Thee and are but the evidences of Thine handiwork. And if I acclaim Thee as the Knower of all things, I must confess that they Who are the Quintessence of knowledge are but the creation and instruments of Thy Purpose.

Exalted, immeasurably exalted, art Thou above the strivings of mortal man to unravel Thy mystery, to describe Thy glory, or even to hint at the nature of Thine Essence. For whatever such strivings may accomplish, they never can hope to transcend the limitations imposed upon Thy creatures, inasmuch as these efforts are actuated by Thy decree, and are begotten of Thine invention. The loftiest sentiments which the holiest of saints can express in praise of Thee, and the deepest wisdom which the most learned of men can utter in their attempts to comprehend Thy nature, all revolve around that Centre Which is wholly subjected to Thy sovereignty, Which adoreth Thy Beauty, and is propelled through the movement of Thy Pen.

Nay, forbid it, O my God, that I should have uttered such words as must of necessity imply the existence of any direct relationship between the Pen of Thy Revelation and the essence of all created things. Far, far are They Who are related to Thee above the conception of such relationship! All comparisons and likenesses fail to do justice to the Tree of Thy Revelation, and every way is barred to the comprehension of the Manifestation of Thy Self and the Day Spring of Thy Beauty.

Far, far from Thy glory be what mortal man can affirm of Thee, or attribute unto Thee, or the praise with which he can glorify Thee! Whatever duty Thou hast prescribed unto Thy servants of extolling to the utmost Thy majesty and glory is but a token of Thy grace unto them, that they may be enabled to ascend unto the station conferred upon their own inmost being, the station of the knowledge of their own selves.

No one else besides Thee hath, at any time, been able to fathom Thy mystery, or befittingly to extol Thy greatness. Unsearchable and high above the praise of men wilt Thou remain for ever. There is none other God but Thee, the Inaccessible, the Omnipotent, the Omniscient, the Holy of Holies.[11]

11

Some Significant Tablets

Súriy-i-Damm

This Tablet (in Arabic) is addressed to Nabíl-i-A'ẓam and contains many celebrated passages concerning the greatness of His Revelation, as well as counsels and exhortations to Nabíl. Apparently it was revealed at a time when Nabíl, as instructed by Bahá'u'lláh, had returned to Persia after attaining His presence in Adrianople.

In this Tablet Bahá'u'lláh directs Nabíl to travel throughout the land, meet the sincere souls among the community, and rend asunder the grievous veils that have hindered them from recognizing the Countenance of Glory. As we have already stated, the mission of Nabíl and other disciples of Bahá'u'lláh at this period was primarily to teach His Cause to the members of the Bábí community. But He warns him not to associate with, and even to flee from, those who show enmity towards Him. This is mainly a reference to the Bábís who were unfaithful to the Cause and were drawn to Mírzá Yaḥyá.

This exhortation to shun those who arise to oppose the Centre of the Cause from within the community is unique in the field of religion. It is aimed at protecting the faithful from the pernicious influence of the egotist, the vainglorious and the insincere who strive to divide the Faith of God and bring schism within its ranks. In past Dispensations no provisions were made to protect the Faith from division. In many cases the followers interpreted the words of their Prophets to suit themselves and consequently many sects appeared within each religion. In this Dispensation Bahá'u'lláh has made strict provision to prevent this from happening. To no one, except the appointed Centre of His Covenant, 'Abdu'l-Bahá, has He given the right to interpret His Writings with authority,* and He has made it clear that if two people argue among themselves concerning their understanding of a subject in the Faith, both are wrong. These are among the provisions which are incorporated in the institution of the Covenant and which safeguard the unity of the Bahá'í community.

The Báb made a Covenant with His followers concerning 'Him Whom God shall make manifest'. Mírzá Yaḥyá and his supporters broke this Covenant, and instead of showing loyalty and submission to Bahá'u'lláh they rebelled against Him and strove with all their power to destroy the Cause of God. Unlike the Manifestations of the past, Bahá'u'lláh did not allow these poisonous elements to remain within the body of the Cause and contaminate it. He cast them out from the community and forbade His followers to associate with them.†

Bahá'u'lláh made a Covenant with His followers, that after His ascension they should all turn to 'Abdu'l-Bahá. Those who broke this Covenant and rose up against its Centre still regarded themselves as Bahá'ís. But 'Abdu'l-Bahá, following the example set by Bahá'u'lláh, expelled these unwholesome elements from the community, cleansed the Cause from their pollution, and instructed the believers to shun them for their own protection.

In a Tablet[1] 'Abdu'l-Bahá states that some people attain faith and certitude and arise to serve and teach the Cause of God, but later become confused and disenchanted. The reason for this is that they have disobeyed His commandments and have associated with the ungodly. Bahá'u'lláh has clearly exhorted His followers to avoid the company of the evil ones. In *The Hidden Words* He enjoins:

* 'Abdu'l-Bahá in his turn appointed Shoghi Effendi as Guardian of the Faith, and conferred upon him the same exclusive right of interpretation.
† See vol. I, pp. 129–37, 240–2.

O Son of Dust!

Beware! Walk not with the ungodly and seek not fellowship with him, for such companionship turneth the radiance of the heart into infernal fire.[2]

In one of His Tablets 'Abdu'l-Bahá declares:

> In short, the point is this: 'Abdu'l-Bahá is extremely kind, but when the disease is leprosy, what am I to do? Just as in bodily diseases we must prevent intermingling and infection and put into effect sanitary laws—because the infectious physical diseases uproot the foundation of humanity; likewise one must protect and safeguard the blessed souls from the breaths and fatal spiritual diseases; otherwise violation, like the plague, will become a contagion and all will perish.[3]

During the ministry of Shoghi Effendi similar events took place. But those who raised their heads to create schism in the Faith were cast out and, like their predecessors, perished and died. This principle of cleansing the community from the pernicious influence of the breakers of the Covenant, thereby protecting the unity of the Cause of God, has been of the utmost importance in the past and will continue to be so in the future.

In the *Súriy-i-Damm* Bahá'u'lláh counsels Nabíl to adorn himself with His characteristics, to waft the musk-laden breeze of holiness upon the believers and to bear with resignation and fortitude the sufferings and persecutions which may be inflicted upon him. He exhorts him to be resigned and submissive when sorely oppressed, reminds him that resignation and submission are among His own attributes and states that of all deeds there is nothing more meritorious in the estimation of God than the sighs of one wronged and oppressed who endures suffering with patience and fortitude. He urges Nabíl to seek the companionship of the loved ones of God wherever he goes, to appear among the people with dignity and serenity, to teach the Cause of His Lord in accordance with the capacity of those who hear him, and to rely upon God for His assistance and confirmations.

In this Tablet Bahá'u'lláh dwells upon the nature of His exalted Revelation as well as the sufferings and persecutions which were heaped upon Him by a perverse generation. The following passages translated by Shoghi Effendi are gleaned from the *Súriy-i-Damm*:

Praise be to Thee, O Lord My God, for the wondrous revelations of Thy inscrutable decree and the manifold woes and trials Thou hast destined for Myself. At one time Thou didst deliver Me into the hands of Nimrod; at another Thou hast allowed Pharaoh's rod to persecute Me. Thou, alone, canst estimate, through Thine all-encompassing knowledge and the operation of Thy Will, the incalculable afflictions I have suffered at their hands. Again Thou didst cast Me into the prison-cell of the ungodly, for no reason except that I was moved to whisper into the ears of the well-favoured denizens of Thy Kingdom an intimation of the vision with which Thou hadst, through Thy knowledge, inspired Me, and revealed to Me its meaning through the potency of Thy might. And again Thou didst decree that I be beheaded by the sword of the infidel. Again I was crucified for having unveiled to men's eyes the hidden gems of Thy glorious unity, for having revealed to them the wondrous signs of Thy sovereign and everlasting power. How bitter the humiliations heaped upon Me, in a subsequent age, on the plain of Karbilá! How lonely did I feel amidst Thy people! To what a state of helplessness I was reduced in that land! Unsatisfied with such indignities, My persecutors decapitated Me, and, carrying aloft My head from land to land paraded it before the gaze of the unbelieving multitude, and deposited it on the seats of the perverse and faithless. In a later age, I was suspended, and My breast was made a target to the darts of the malicious cruelty of My foes. My limbs were riddled with bullets, and My body was torn asunder. Finally, behold how, in this Day, My treacherous enemies have leagued themselves against Me, and are continually plotting to instil the venom of hate and malice into the souls of Thy servants. With all their might they are scheming to accomplish their purpose . . . Grievous as is My plight, O God, My Well-Beloved, I render thanks unto Thee, and My Spirit is grateful for whatsoever hath befallen me in the path of Thy good-pleasure. I am well pleased with that which Thou didst ordain for Me, and welcome, however calamitous, the pains and sorrows I am made to suffer.[4]

Nabíl faithfully carried out the instructions of Bahá'u'lláh. He travelled throughout Persia and confirmed a great many souls who embraced His Cause.

Súrihs of Ḥajj

During this period Bahá'u'lláh revealed the *Súriy-i-Ḥajj* (Súrih of Pilgrimage) for visiting the house of the Báb, sent the Tablet to Nabíl, and directed him to go to S͟hínáz.

In this Tablet Bahá'u'lláh prescribes the rites which have to be performed when pilgrims visit the house of the Báb. He instructed Nabíl to perform them on His behalf. When Nabíl carried out these lengthy rites, which begin outside the city and continue all the way to the house and inside, he attracted a great deal of attention and passers-by concluded that he had lost his mind!

Having carried out the instructions of Bahá'u'lláh in S͟hínáz, Nabíl received another Tablet, the *Súriy-i-Ḥajj* (Súrih of Pilgrimage) for the house of Bahá'u'lláh in Bag͟hdád, and was directed to proceed to that city and perform the rites of pilgrimage for that house also on His behalf. With great devotion and enthusiasm, and in spite of a curious public, he succeeded again in carrying out the rites ordained by Bahá'u'lláh in this Tablet.

These holy observances were later affirmed in the *Kitáb-i-Aqdas* and will be implemented in the future when the Cause of Bahá'u'lláh is fully established and circumstances radically changed.*

* See vol. I, pp. 211–12.

MÍRZÁ MUḤAMMAD ʻALÍY-I-NAHRÍ

A devout early believer
His daughter Munírih Khánum became the wife of ʻAbdu'l-Bahá

MÍRZÁ 'ALÍY-I-SAYYÁḤ

An attendant of the Báb, he visited Shaykh Ṭabarsí on His behalf
He became a devoted follower of Bahá'u'lláh and was among the Bahá'ís exiled to Cyprus

The Story of the Nightingale and the Crow

Around the time that the followers of Mírzá Yaḥyá were cast out of the community of the Most Great Name, Bahá'u'lláh revealed a beautiful Tablet in Persian, written in terms of imagery. It describes the true relationship between Bahá'u'lláh and Mírzá Yaḥyá. In this Tablet Bahá'u'lláh portrays Himself as a mystic Rose appearing in the Garden of Paradise.[5] The Rose, the object of adoration of the nightingale, calls out to its lovers to come and be united with the deathless beauty of the Beloved.

A few birds resembling nightingales come near the Rose but are not enchanted by its perfume and charm. There is a dialogue between the two which is beautiful and soul-stirring. The birds maintain that they are familiar with other roses and they argue that this One is not a true Rose, as it grows in a different garden. The Rose appeals to them in loving language and reminds them that there is only one Rose; once it appeared in Egypt, at another time in Jerusalem and Galilee, at a later period it manifested itself in Arabia, then in Shíráz and now it has unveiled its Beauty in Adrianople. It rebukes them for having focused their affection on their surroundings rather than on the True Friend and claims that they are the embodiments of evil and have only disguised themselves as nightingales.

Then the Rose tells them a story: It likens the birds to the Owl* who once argued that the song of the Crow was much more melodious than that of the Nightingale. Challenging this statement, the Nightingale demanded some evidence, and invited the Owl to investigate the truth by hearing the melody of each bird, so that the sweet music of the Bird of Heaven might be distinguished from the croaking of the Crow. But the Owl refused and said 'Once from inside a rose-garden the enchanting voice of a bird reached my ears, and when I enquired its origin, I was informed that the voice was that of the Crow. Simultaneously, a crow flew out of the garden and it became clear to me who the singer was.'

* The owl in Persian and Arabic literature is a symbol of doom and ruin.

'But that was My voice,' said the Nightingale to the Owl, 'and to prove it I can warble similar if not more beautiful melodies now.' 'I am not interested to hear Thy songs,' the Owl made reply, 'for I saw the Crow and have been assured by others that the melody from inside the garden was his. If the tune of this heavenly music was Thine, how is it that thou wert hidden from the eyes of men and Thy fame did not reach them?' 'Because of My beauty,' replied the Nightingale, 'I have been despised by My enemies. They were resolved to put an end to My life, and for this reason My melodies were noised abroad in the name of the Crow. But those with unsullied hearts and sanctified ears have been able to distinguish the voice of the true Nightingale from that of the Crow.'*

The story of the Owl ends here, and the Rose continues its dialogue with the birds disguised as nightingales. It tells them that they too are of the same nature as the Owl, in that they prefer their own vain imaginings to the multitude of proofs and testimonies which have been demonstrated by the rose-like beauty of the Friend. It calls upon them to recognize the Rose by its charm and perfume and not through their own standards. As these exhortations reach their climax, a beautiful nightingale † with a melodious voice enters the garden and, enchanted with the beauty of the Rose, begins to circumambulate it. 'Although outwardly you look like nightingales,' it addresses

* This story of the Nightingale and the Crow clearly refers to Bahá'u'lláh and Mírzá Yaḥyá respectively. In order to protect Bahá'u'lláh from the assaults of an implacable enemy, the Báb appointed Mírzá Yaḥyá as the leader of the Bábí community so that he might divert public attention from Bahá'u'lláh and at the same time provide a means whereby Bahá'u'lláh could unobtrusively direct the affairs of the Bábí community until such a time as His station was revealed to the eyes of men; (see *A Traveller's Narrative*, p. 62; p. 247 below and vol. I, pp. 53–4). For quite some time Bahá'u'lláh used to dictate various directions to Mírzá Yaḥyá, who would faithfully convey them to the community in his own name. His unfaithfulness to Bahá'u'lláh began when he came under the spell of the notorious Siyyid Muḥammad-i-Iṣfahání in 'Iráq.

† This signifies a faithful lover of Bahá'u'lláh, who has truly recognized Him.

the birds in a tone of rebuke, 'as a result of association with the Crow, you have learnt its ways and have acquired its characteristics.' Pointing to the Rose it then declares: 'This divine Rose is the object of the adoration of the nightingales of paradise, and this rose-garden is their abode. It is not a habitation for mortal birds. Take your leave and begone.'*

Having spoken in this language of imagery, Bahá'u'lláh exhorts His followers to gird up their loins in the service of their Lord and to protect the Cause of God from the onslaught of the unfaithful. He counsels them to adorn themselves with pure deeds and praiseworthy character, and assures them that only by living a virtuous life can they bring victory to the Cause and protect it from the assaults of the enemy.

In innumerable Tablets Bahá'u'lláh has urged the believers to rectitude of conduct, truthfulness, faith, holiness and noble deeds. In one of them He summons His loved ones to arise and assist Him by living a saintly life. These are His exhortations:

> One righteous act is endowed with a potency that can so elevate the dust as to cause it to pass beyond the heaven of heavens. It can tear every bond asunder, and hath the power to restore the force that hath spent itself and vanished . . .
>
> Be pure, O people of God, be pure; be righteous, be righteous . . . Say: O people of God! That which can ensure the victory of Him Who is the Eternal Truth, His hosts and helpers on earth, have been set down in the sacred Books and Scriptures, and are as clear and manifest as the sun. These hosts are such righteous deeds, such conduct and character, as are acceptable in His sight. Whoso ariseth, in this Day, to aid Our Cause, and summoneth to his assistance the hosts of a praiseworthy character and upright conduct, the influence flowing from such an action will, most certainly, be diffused throughout the whole world.[6]

In this Tablet Bahá'u'lláh warns His followers to be on their guard lest through their misdeeds they bring dishonour to the

* This is a reference to the followers of Mírzá Yaḥyá who were cast out of the community.

Faith. He states that any sinful action committed by them will inflict a grievous blow upon Him and will serve to promote the interests of the enemies of the Cause of God.

The study of the Writings clearly demonstrates that of all the sufferings inflicted upon Bahá'u'lláh, by far the greatest and the most grievous came from two quarters: one, those who betrayed Him, broke the Covenant of the Báb, and followed Mírzá Yaḥyá; the other, some of His own followers who by their corrupt deeds damaged the reputation of the Faith in the eyes of men, and caused Him much anguish and pain.

In one of His Tablets He pours out His heart in these words:

> I sorrow not for the burden of My imprisonment. Neither do I grieve over My abasement, or the tribulation I suffer at the hands of Mine enemies. By My life! They are My glory, a glory wherewith God hath adorned His own Self. Would that ye knew it!
>
> The shame I was made to bear hath uncovered the glory with which the whole of creation had been invested, and through the cruelties I have endured, the Day Star of Justice hath manifested itself, and shed its splendour upon men.
>
> My sorrows are for those who have involved themselves in their corrupt passions, and claim to be associated with the Faith of God, the Gracious, the All-Praised.
>
> It behoveth the people of Bahá to die to the world and all that is therein, to be so detached from all earthly things that the inmates of Paradise may inhale from their garment the sweet smelling savour of sanctity, that all the peoples of the earth may recognize in their faces the brightness of the All-Merciful, and that through them may be spread abroad the signs and tokens of God, the Almighty, the All-Wise. They that have tarnished the fair name of the Cause of God, by following the things of the flesh—these are in palpable error![7]

and again:

> My captivity can bring on Me no shame. Nay, by My life, it conferreth on Me glory. That which can make Me ashamed

is the conduct of such of My followers as profess to love Me, yet in fact follow the Evil One. They, indeed, are of the lost.[8]

Lawḥ-i-Naṣír

The *Lawḥ-i-Naṣír* was revealed in honour of Ḥájí Muḥammad-Naṣír, a native of Qazvín. This relatively long Tablet is, for the most part, in Persian, and a small part of it was translated into English by Shoghi Effendi and included in *Gleanings from the Writings of Bahá'u'lláh*.*

Ḥájí Naṣír was a well-known merchant and held in high esteem by his fellow citizens until he embraced the Bábí Faith. From that time onwards, he suffered persecutions and was bitterly opposed by the people. He recognized the divine origin of the Message of the Báb through Mullá Jalíl-i-Urúmí, one of the Letters of the Living.† It is reported that when Ḥájí Naṣír had acknowledged the authenticity of the claims of the Báb, Mullá Jalíl warned him that a mere acknowledgement was not sufficient in this day, that he could not call himself a Bábí unless he were prepared to lay down his life willingly in the path of God, should the enemy rise up against him. He bade him go home and search his heart to see whether he had sufficient faith to remain steadfast in the face of tortures and martyrdom. If he did, he was a Bábí, and otherwise not. Ḥájí Naṣír responded to the words of Mullá Jalíl by spending the whole night in prayer and meditation. At the hour of dawn, he felt possessed of such faith and detachment as to be ready to sacrifice his life in the path of his Beloved. Overnight, he became endowed with a new zeal and radiance which sustained him throughout his eventful life.

Soon the persecutions started; the first onslaught began when Ḥájí Naṣír became the target of attacks by a blood-thirsty mob in Qazvín. They plundered all his possessions and he was temporarily forced to leave his native city. When the situation

* Sections LIII and LXXV.

† For more information see *The Dawn-Breakers*.

calmed down he returned home. From there, in obedience to the call of the Báb, he proceeded to Khurásán. He was privileged to attend the conference of Badasht where, some historians have stated, he acted as a guard at the entrance of the garden which was reserved for Bahá'u'lláh's residence. From Badasht he proceeded to Mázindarán and was one of the defenders of the fortress of Shaykh Ṭabarsí.* As history records, hundreds of his fellow disciples were massacred in that upheaval, but the hand of divine power spared Ḥájí Naṣír's life and enabled him to render further services to the Cause of God.

He returned to Qazvín and engaged in his work once again, but soon another upheaval engulfed the believers. The attempt on the life of Náṣiri'd-Dín Sháh in 1852 † unleashed a wave of persecution against the Bábís. Ḥájí Naṣír was arrested in Qazvín and put in prison. But after some time he was released. Another imprisonment he suffered was in Ṭihrán, where he was chained and fettered. When released from his ordeal, he found that all his possessions were gone. It was through the help and co-operation of Shaykh Káẓim-i-Samandar ‡ that, in spite of much harassment by the enemy, Ḥájí Naṣír continued to earn a living, but he had to move his residence to the city of Rasht.

The crowning glory of his life was to attain the presence of Bahá'u'lláh in 'Akká. On this pilgrimage he was accompanied by the above-named Shaykh Káẓim. Bahá'u'lláh showered His bounties upon him and assured him of His loving-kindness. He spent the latter part of his life in the city of Rasht and was engaged in teaching the Cause of God by day and night. The enemies once again cast him into prison. This time, because of old age, he could not endure the rigours of prison life and his soul, after so many years of toil and suffering, took its flight to the abode of the Beloved. He died a martyr's death in the prison of Rasht in the year 1300 A.H. (1888).

* For details see *The Dawn-Breakers*.

† See *The Dawn-Breakers*.

‡ One of the Apostles of Bahá'u'lláh. We shall refer to him in more detail in vol. III.

When the news of Ḥájí Naṣír's death reached the enemies of the Cause, many of them, including children, attacked his corpse and pelted it with stones. As soon as his remains were brought home a number of ruffians forced their way in and attempted to dismember it. It is impossible to describe the feelings of horror and consternation which befell his family and loved ones as they stood helplessly watching the cruel atrocities perpetrated by the mob of heartless fanatics. They had Ḥájí Naṣír's nose cut off and his eyes gouged out before they were stopped by the neighbours who, in a humiliating manner, threw his body into a disused brick furnace in that vicinity and covered it with stones.

Bahá'u'lláh has paid glowing tribute to Ḥájí Naṣír for his steadfastness in the Cause of God and has revealed a Tablet of Visitation for him. In the *Epistle to the Son of the Wolf* He remembers him in these words:

> Among them was his honour, Ḥájí Naṣír, who, unquestionably, was a brilliant light that shone forth above the horizon of resignation. After he had suffered martyrdom, they plucked out his eyes and cut off his nose, and inflicted on him such indignities that strangers wept and lamented, and secretly raised funds to support his wife and children.[9]

The revelation of the *Lawḥ-i-Naṣír* in Adrianople was in response to Ḥájí Naṣír's request for clarification of the position of Mírzá Yaḥyá. He had been trying for some time to unravel this mysterious situation and to discover the station of Bahá'u'lláh. When the news of the rebellion of Mírzá Yaḥyá in Adrianople reached him, he wrote to Bahá'u'lláh and begged him for enlightenment. It is in this Tablet that Bahá'u'lláh throws light on the appointment, by the Báb, of Mírzá Yaḥyá as the leader of the Bábí community and mentions that only two people were informed of the real circumstances of his appointment.* He condemns his treacherous deeds, his attempt to take Bahá'-

* Mírzá Músá (Áqáy-i-Kalím) and Mullá 'Abdu'l-Karím-i-Qazvíní.

u'lláh's life, and his shameful accusations attributing his own crimes to Him.

A considerable portion of this Tablet is addressed to the people of the *Bayán*. Bahá'u'lláh reminds them of the innumerable prophecies and exhortations of the Báb concerning the exalted station of the One who was to come after Him. He proclaims to them in unequivocal language the glad-tidings of His Revelation, passionately counsels them to purge their hearts from vain and corrupt issues, summons them with the utmost loving-kindness to embrace His Cause, and grieves that so many of them had arisen in opposition to Him.

The following passage from the *Lawḥ-i-Naṣír*, included in *Gleanings from the Writings of Bahá'u'lláh*, is addressed to the people of the *Bayán*.

> Tear asunder, in My Name, the veils that have grievously blinded your vision, and, through the power born of your belief in the unity of God, scatter the idols of vain imitation. Enter, then, the holy paradise of the good-pleasure of the All-Merciful. Sanctify your souls from whatsoever is not of God, and taste ye the sweetness of rest within the pale of His vast and mighty Revelation, and beneath the shadow of His supreme and infallible authority. Suffer not yourselves to be wrapt in the dense veils of your selfish desires, inasmuch as I have perfected in every one of you My creation, so that the excellence of My handiwork may be fully revealed unto men. It follows, therefore, that every man hath been, and will continue to be, able of himself to appreciate the Beauty of God, the Glorified. Had he not been endowed with such a capacity, how could he be called to account for his failure? If, in the Day when all the peoples of the earth will be gathered together, any man should, whilst standing in the presence of God, be asked: 'Wherefore hast thou disbelieved in My Beauty and turned away from My Self,' and if such a man should reply and say: 'Inasmuch as all men have erred, and none hath been found willing to turn his face to the Truth, I too, following their example, have grievously failed to recognize the Beauty of the Eternal,' such a plea will,

assuredly, be rejected. For the faith of no man can be conditioned by any one except himself.[10]

In this Tablet Bahá'u'lláh affirms that the bounties of God have been vouchsafed to every human being, but only those who have the capacity and whose hearts are pure can receive them. He gives the example of the seed which will produce goodly trees if planted in fertile soil, whereas in barren land it will not develop. He urges Naṣír to become the recipient of the grace of God in this day, and asserts that if all the peoples of the world were to deprive themselves of its glory, it would have no effect upon the outpouring of the bounties of God.

Referring to Himself as the 'Celestial Youth', Bahá'u'lláh reveals these soul-stirring verses in the *Lawḥ-i-Naṣír* and extols the station of those who have recognized Him:

> O Naṣír, O My Servant! God, the Eternal Truth, beareth Me witness. The Celestial Youth hath, in this Day, raised above the heads of men the glorious Chalice of Immortality, and is standing expectant upon His seat, wondering what eye will recognize His glory, and what arm will, unhesitatingly, be stretched forth to seize the Cup from His snow-white Hand and drain it. Only a few have as yet quaffed from this peerless, this soft-flowing grace of the Ancient King. These occupy the loftiest mansions of Paradise, and are firmly established upon the seats of authority. By the righteousness of God! Neither the mirrors of His glory, nor the revealers of His names, nor any created thing, that hath been or will ever be, can ever excel them, if ye be of them that comprehend this truth.
>
> O Naṣír! The excellence of this Day is immensely exalted above the comprehension of men, however extensive their knowledge, however profound their understanding. How much more must it transcend the imaginations of them that have strayed from its light, and been shut out from its glory! Shouldst thou rend asunder the grievous veil that blindeth thy vision, thou wouldst behold such a bounty as naught, from the beginning that hath no beginning till the end that hath no end, can either resemble or equal.[11]

There is a verse in the *Qur'án* which states: 'We will surely show them our signs in the world and within themselves.'[12] This refers to the influence which the Manifestation of God exerts upon the whole creation. By His advent He releases to the world a measure of spiritual potency. He also manifests the tokens of His grace within the hearts of men. Bahá'u'lláh in the *Lawḥ-i-Naṣír* affirms that both these 'signs' have been manifested in this day. He states that the signs of His power and ascendancy have encompassed the world, and the whole creation has been endowed with a new capacity. They have even affected the hearts of men, and yet the peoples are blind to them.

When Bahá'u'lláh made these statements to Naṣír, the evidences of His influence in the world of humanity were not as clear as they are today. Any unbiased observer may witness that the energies released by His Revelation have set in motion a regenerative process which is now affecting the whole fabric of human society. On the one hand the compelling power born of His Revelation has illumined the hearts of millions who have recognized His station, followed His Teachings, and become the recipients of His Cause and the champion-builders of His World Order. The rest of mankind, on the other hand, as yet untouched by the light of His Faith, is deeply affected by the spirit of the age which is generated and sustained by each and every one of the teachings of Bahá'u'lláh. These people are caught up in the whirlwind of its resistless force. Helpless and confused, they recognize their inability to hold on to their age-old and antiquated orders, which have been their only haven and refuge for centuries. They make every effort to find a way to revive the old so that it may co-exist with the new. But as time goes on they are gradually realizing the futility of such attempts. Some try to adapt their time-honoured institutions to the new spirit of the age, but with every compromise they progressively weaken their cause. Others have given up hope, become disillusioned and passive, and even dropped out of society altogether.

The process of integration and consolidation which marks

the growth of the Bahá'í community is accelerating with every passing day, and derives its animating force directly from the Revelation of Bahá'u'lláh. No force in the universe can, before the appearance of the next Manifestation of God,* stop the onward march of the Faith or alter the course which God has chosen for the unfoldment and establishment of its Divine institutions. On the contrary, as history has clearly demonstrated, every incident, whether constructive or destructive, has been the cause of the advancement of the Faith of Bahá'u'lláh and will continue to be in the future. The selfless activities of its avowed adherents, as well as the opposition and persecutions of an unbelieving world will, hand in hand, further the interests of the Faith to the point where it will embrace the whole of mankind.

The process of disintegration, on the other hand, caused by man's indifference or opposition to the Cause of Bahá'u'lláh, is ruthlessly pulling down the old order. The spirit of the age released by Bahá'u'lláh may be likened to forces which press hard upon humanity and drive it towards universality and the oneness of mankind. When people, whether consciously or unconsciously, oppose these forces, they create tensions within their societies. Like a tidal wave as it gathers momentum, the magnitude of the forces released by Bahá'u'lláh is increasing day by day and consequently there will come a time when these tensions reach breaking-point.

Almost every war or distressing event which has happened on this planet during the last hundred years has been caused by man's opposition to the forces of universality and unity which have been influencing the world since the coming of Bahá'u'lláh. Racial, religious, national and other prejudices run counter to the teachings of Bahá'u'lláh. Any people, therefore, whose actions are motivated by prejudice, hatred, selfishness, greed and above all opposition to the principle of the oneness of mankind, will cause unrest, tension and bloodshed in the world and, sooner or later, seal their own doom.

* See vol. I, pp. 279–80.

Having looked briefly at the appearance of this 'sign' of Bahá'u'lláh's Revelation in the world, referred to in the forementioned verse of the *Qur'án* and in the *Lawḥ-i-Naṣír*, let us examine the other 'sign' indicated in that same verse, namely the manifestation of the tokens of God within the individual. Ever since the Declaration of Bahá'u'lláh in the Garden of Riḍván, His Revelation has endowed every soul with a new capacity and breathed a new spirit into every frame,* as His words testify:

> Verily, We have caused every soul to expire by virtue of Our irresistible and all-subduing sovereignty. We have, then, called into being a new creation, as a token of Our grace unto men. I am, verily, the All-Bountiful, the Ancient of Days.[13]

And the Báb has prophesied:

> The year-old germ that holdeth within itself the potentialities of the Revelation that is to come is endowed with a potency superior to the combined forces of the whole of the *Bayán*.[14]

Today, human beings everywhere, regardless of race, colour or nationality, have the capacity to attain to the knowledge of God and acquire spiritual qualities; and they have demonstrated that they can learn and become equally proficient in arts, cultures and sciences whether they come from the East or the West. This was not possible in the past when the majority of the peoples of the world were backward, when slavery was rife and vast numbers were under the domination of the few. But the universality of the Message of Bahá'u'lláh and the forces of new life released by Him within the individual, have given birth to a new race of men who have acquired a new vision and the will to think independently and act with purpose.

Because of his failure to recognize Bahá'u'lláh, man's new capacity, instead of leading him to the path of truth, has created enormous conflict and confusion within his mind. To appreciate this point, we must look back to the time just before the

* See vol. I, pp. 277–8 and 280.

coming of Bahá'u'lláh. Then, human beings throughout the world were reasonably satisfied with their lives. There was not as much contention and strife among people. The majority accepted their traditional religious beliefs, and there were not so many agnostics and atheists as there are now, neither were there so many religious sects. But with the coming of Bahá'u'lláh, the situation changed radically.

To illustrate this, let us use the analogy of light and darkness. If a number of people were to live in a darkened room, there would be no reason for them to argue about things they could not see. But should the room be lit, everyone would be able to see for himself. It would be then that differences could arise concerning the shape and order of things in their midst.

Before the Faith of Bahá'u'lláh was born, mankind was in a state of darkness. People held their beliefs as a matter of course and seldom involved themselves independently in controversial issues. It was mainly the rulers and religious leaders who held the reins and guided the masses to whatever they felt was appropriate. But when the Sun of Truth appeared, the minds of men were illumined. They acquired a new vision and began to think for themselves. People started to question the validity and truth of their Faiths and within a short period of time great differences occurred. Religions were divided, many sects came into being and multiplied with the passage of time. Great numbers left their religions altogether and swelled the ranks of agnostics and atheists. Millions of people rose up to demand their rights. Revolutions took place in several parts of the world and new doctrines and ideologies were promulgated. Arts and sciences suddenly burst into a new era of unprecedented technological advance, establishing a marvellous system of communication throughout the world.*

All these developments within the last hundred and fifty years have not come about accidentally. They are due to the infusion of a new capacity into every soul. Bahá'u'lláh, in one of His Tablets, proclaims:

* See vol. I, p. 217.

> Through the movement of Our Pen of glory We have, at the bidding of the omnipotent Ordainer, breathed a new life into every human frame, and instilled into every word a fresh potency. All created things proclaim the evidences of this world-wide regeneration.[15]

In addition to the two fore-mentioned 'signs', Bahá'u'lláh declares that the very profusion of the Words sent down to Him by God constitutes yet another sign establishing the truth of His Revelation for this day. Concerning this profusion, Bahá'u'lláh informs Naṣír that

> Such are the outpourings . . . from the clouds of Divine Bounty that within the space of an hour the equivalent of a thousand verses hath been revealed.[16]

As we have already mentioned, many of the disciples present when Bahá'u'lláh revealed the verses of God were awestruck by the outward evidences of His great power and glory.* In the *Lawḥ-i-Naṣír* Bahá'u'lláh refers to this and affirms that had it not been for man's spiritual weakness, He would have granted permission for all to be present at the time of Revelation, so that they might witness its outpouring and behold the transcendent majesty of the One who is the Revealer of the Word of God.

In this Tablet Bahá'u'lláh unveils the exalted station of the true believers and describes the wretchedness of the deniers. He states that every human being in this day potentially contains within himself all the powers and attributes that are to be found in the physical creation. The counterpart of the heavens, the mountain, the valley, the tree, the fruit, the river and the sea may be found to exist in every soul. They appear as divine virtues in the believers, and as satanic vices in the deniers. For example, in the faithful are manifested the heavens of under-

* For more information concerning the manner of Revelation, the potency of the Word and the vastness of the Holy Writings, refer to vol. I, chapter 3.

standing, the trees of oneness, the leaves of certitude, the fruits of the love of God, the seas of knowledge and the rivers of wisdom. Whereas in the deniers one finds the heaven of faithlessness, the earth of hatred, the trees of rebellion, the branches of pride and the leaves of lust and wickedness.

But the believers are of two kinds. Some are unaware of this bounty. They have deprived themselves of His grace through unworthy deeds and are shut out as by a veil from beholding its great glory. Others who have been endowed with insight through the Mercy of God, are able, with both their inner and outer eyes, to witness within themselves the signs of His power and the wonders of His handiwork. This is a state in which the individual becomes independent of all things but God, and will possess infinite powers over all things. Indeed he will encompass in his soul all that has been created in this universe. Bahá'u'lláh states that should such a soul, conscious of these powers within him, arise with determination to serve the Cause of God, he would establish his ascendancy over all humanity, even if all its forces were to be arrayed against him.

The history of the Faith is replete with stories of the heroism and courage of men and women who attained this lofty station. The immortal names of Mullá Ḥusayn, Quddús, Ṭáhirih, Vaḥíd, Ḥujjat and Badí' are a few examples among many. These souls had acquired such ascendancy and influence in the realms of God that their words became creative. When faced with the onslaught of the enemy they demonstrated a strength and power that can only be described as superhuman.

Mullá Ḥusayn, the first to believe in the Báb, has left the following testimony concerning his complete transformation on the night of His declaration:

> This Revelation, so suddenly and impetuously thrust upon me, came as a thunderbolt which, for a time, seemed to have benumbed my faculties. I was blinded by its dazzling splendour and overwhelmed by its crushing force. Excitement, joy, awe, and wonder stirred the depths of my soul. Predominant among these emotions was a sense of gladness and

strength which seemed to have transfigured me. How feeble and impotent, how dejected and timid, I had felt previously! Then I could neither write nor walk, so tremulous were my hands and feet. Now, however, the knowledge of His Revelation had galvanised my being. I felt possessed of such courage and power that were the world, all its peoples and potentates, to rise against me, I would, alone and undaunted, withstand their onslaught. The universe seemed but a handful of dust in my grasp. I seemed to be the Voice of Gabriel personified, calling unto all mankind: 'Awake, for lo! the morning Light has broken. Arise, for His Cause is made manifest. The portal of His grace is open wide; enter therein, O peoples of the world! For He who is your promised One is come!'[17]

Ever after that memorable evening Mullá Ḥusayn became endowed with superhuman courage and fortitude. Every incident connected with his life of service to the new-born Faith of God demonstrates this. The same is true of many other disciples of the Báb and Bahá'u'lláh.

For example, the following incident in the life of Vaḥíd* stands out as an example of his powers born of God and is reminiscent of many such heroic deeds. In the year 1850 in Yazd, at the instigation of Navváb-i-Raḍaví, one of the powerful dignitaries of the city, a great many people arose to attack Vaḥíd. This is how Nabíl-i-A'ẓam recounts the story:

Meanwhile the Navváb had succeeded in raising a general upheaval in which the mass of the inhabitants took part. They were preparing to attack the house of Vaḥíd when he summoned Siyyid 'Abdu'l-'Aẓím-i-Khu'í, surnamed the Siyyid-i-Khál-Dár, who had participated for a few days in the defence of the fort of Ṭabarsí and whose dignity of bearing attracted widespread attention, and bade him mount his own steed and address publicly, through the streets and bazaars, an appeal on his behalf to the entire populace, and urge them to embrace the Cause of the Ṣáḥibu'z-Zamán. 'Let them know,' he added, 'that I disclaim any intention of waging holy warfare

* See *The Dawn-Breakers* and vol. I, Appendix III.

against them. Let them be warned, however, that if they persist in besieging my house and continue their attacks upon me, in utter defiance of my position and lineage, I shall be constrained, as a measure of self-defence, to resist and disperse their forces. If they choose to reject my counsel and yield to the whisperings of the crafty Navváb, I will order seven of my companions to repulse their forces shamefully and to crush their hopes.'

The Siyyid-i-Khál-Dár leaped upon the steed and, escorted by four of his chosen brethren, rode out through the market and pealed out, in accents of compelling majesty, the warning he had been commissioned to proclaim. Not content with the message with which he had been entrusted, he ventured to add, in his own inimitable manner, a few words by which he sought to heighten the effect which the proclamation had produced. 'Beware,' he thundered, 'if you despise our plea. My lifted voice, I warn you, will prove sufficient to cause the very walls of your fort to tremble, and the strength of my arm will be capable of breaking down the resistance of its gates!'

His stentorian voice rang out like a trumpet, and diffused consternation in the hearts of those who heard it. With one voice, the affrighted population declared their intention to lay down their swords and cease to molest Vaḥíd, whose lineage they said they would henceforth recognize and respect.[18]

Shortly after this, in another incident, great numbers surrounded the house of Vaḥíd intending to attack him and his companions who had recently embraced the new Faith of God. Concerning this Nabíl writes:

The enemy followed him [a certain believer by the name of Muḥammad-'Abdu'lláh] to that house, fully determined to seize and slay him. The clamour of the people that had massed around his house compelled Vaḥíd to order Mullá Muḥammad-Riḍáy-i-Manshádí, one of the most enlightened 'ulamás of Manshád, who had discarded his turban and offered himself as his doorkeeper, to sally forth and, with the aid of six companions, whom he would choose, to scatter their forces. 'Let each one of you raise his voice,' he commanded them 'and repeat seven times the words "Alláh-u-Akbar",* and on your seventh invocation spring forward at one and the same moment into the midst of your assailants.'

Mullá Muḥammad-Riḍá, whom Bahá'u'lláh had named Raḍa'r-Rúḥ,† sprang to his feet and, with his companions, straightway proceeded to fulfil the instructions he had received. Those who accompanied him, though frail of form and inexperienced in the art of swordsmanship, were fired with a faith that made them the terror of their adversaries. Seven of the most redoubtable among the enemy perished that day, which was the twenty-seventh of the month of Jamádíyu'th-Th͟ání [10 May A.D. 1850]. 'No sooner had we routed the enemy,' Mullá Muḥammad-Riḍá related, 'and returned to the house of Vaḥíd, than we found Muḥammad-'Abdu'lláh lying wounded before us.'[19]

It is interesting to note that the Bábís throughout their short and eventful history resorted to force in defending themselves against the enemy.‡ In these defensive battles, they often sent out a few men to attack the great armies which surrounded them, and in almost every case inflicted humiliating defeats upon their adversaries.

At the time that the enemies of Bahá'u'lláh in 'Iráq were plotting to take His life and destroy the Cause of God, a number of the divines in that country were contemplating waging holy war against the Bábís.§ One day, a number of friends were standing in the presence of Bahá'u'lláh as He paced the reception quarters of His house. Among them were two

* 'God is the Most Great'.

† See vol. I and p. 99 above. (A.T.)

‡ Bahá'u'lláh has forbidden His followers to follow this practice which was current among the Bábís. Although Bahá'u'lláh has counselled His followers not to resort to force in the face of persecution, this does not mean that they should stand idly by and make no defence of themselves when personally attacked. For further details see vol. I, pp. 278–9.

§ See vol. I, p. 144.

seditious men who were closely allied with these divines, but pretended to be friends of the Faith. Bahá'u'lláh was talking to the believers and is reported to have said: 'The divines have called upon some crusaders to come from Najaf and Karbilá to wage holy war against us.' Then turning to the two mischief-makers, He stated, 'I swear by the Almighty God, that I need not send more than two of My people to put them to rout and pursue them as far as Káẓimayn.'* [20]

These few examples demonstrate the power which true faith in God can engender in the believers. This power which animated the disciples of the Báb and Bahá'u'lláh is the same as that to which Christ refers:

> . . . For verily I say unto you, if ye have faith as a grain of mustard seed, ye shall say unto this mountain, Remove hence to yonder place; and it shall remove; and nothing shall be impossible unto you.[21]

Bahá'u'lláh promises in a Tablet[22] that if a believer becomes steadfast in the love of his Lord and detaches himself from this world, God will enable him to influence the realities of all created things in such wise that through the power of the Almighty he can do anything he desires. When a person achieves this stage of maturity, he will utter no word except for the sake of God, will not move except towards Him and will not see anything but His Beauty. Such a person will never be afraid of anyone even if all humanity should rise up against him.

Lawḥ-i-Khalíl

The news of Bahá'u'lláh's Declaration on the one hand and Mírzá Yaḥyá's rebellion on the other, as already stated, caused confusion and doubt in the minds of some believers in Persia. Among those who wrote to Bahá'u'lláh for clarification and enlightenment was Ḥájí Muḥammad-Ibráhím-i-Qazvíní, whom

* Káẓimíyyah, near Baghdád.

Bahá'u'lláh addressed as 'Khalíl'.* This believer was further confused when he received some Arabic verses composed by Mírzá Muḥammad-'Alí,† (a son of Bahá'u'lláh and in his teens), which he claimed were the verses of God, and like those of his Father, sent down by divine Revelation. In these writings he refers to himself as the revealer of the word of God, he who has ushered in the most great revelation, and through whose words all creation had come into being!

Mírzá Muḥammad-'Alí had sent his writings from Adrianople secretly to Qazvín. Three believers in particular had become influenced by his claims and were his principal supporters. They were Mírzá 'Abdu'lláh, Ḥájí Ḥasan and his brother Áqá 'Alí.‡ As a result, a great controversy erupted in Qazvín. The few supporters of Mírzá Muḥammad-'Alí, who regarded their youthful contender as having a station co-equal with his Father, clashed with other believers in Qazvín. There were heated arguments in the community and Shaykh Káẓim-i-Samandar emphatically declared that the writings of Mírzá Muḥammad-'Alí consisted of a string of Arabic sentences and had no relationship to the Words of God. It was mainly because of this controversy that Khalíl sent a letter to Bahá'u'lláh begging Him to clarify His own station and the station of His sons. This was possibly around the time that Bahá'u'lláh moved into the house of Riḍá Big, because He alludes to Khalíl's questions in the *Lawḥ-i-Rúḥ*.§

Bahá'u'lláh severely rebuked Mírzá Muḥammad-'Alí for his preposterous claims and chastised him with His own hand. He revealed a Tablet[23] in answer to Khalíl, declared His own station and explained the position of His sons. The uncertainties

* Literally 'Friend', a designation by which Abraham is known in Islám.

† He later became the arch-enemy of 'Abdu'l-Bahá and the arch-breaker of the Covenant of Bahá'u'lláh.

‡ Bahá'u'lláh especially sent for these two brothers to come from Persia. They attained His presence and recognized their own folly and misjudgement.

§ See p. 181.

agitating the mind of Khalíl were resolved. He became a steadfast believer and the recipient of other Tablets.*

Bahá'u'lláh states that as long as His sons believed in Him, observed the commandments of God, did not deviate from the Faith and did not create divisions in the Cause, they might be regarded as the leaves and branches of His Tree and the members of His Holy Family. Through them the mercy of God would be revealed, and His light diffused. Muḥammad-'Alí did not live up to these standards. Apart from his absurd claim, he inflicted other injuries upon the Cause of God during Bahá'u'lláh's lifetime, and after His ascension he broke His Covenant and rebelled against 'Abdu'l-Bahá.†

In the *Tablet of Khalíl*, Bahá'u'lláh alludes to 'Abdu'l-Bahá in terms which immensely distinguish Him from others. He refers to Him as the One among His sons 'from Whose tongue God will cause the signs of His power to stream forth' and as the One Whom 'God hath specially chosen for His Cause'.[24] And yet during Bahá'u'lláh's lifetime, 'Abdu'l-Bahá was so reluctant to write ‡ anything that at one stage the believers complained. In reply He told them that when the shrill voice of the Pen of the Most High could be heard on every side, it was not appropriate for others to write.

In a Tablet[25] addressed to the Ismu'lláh, Siyyid Mihdíy-i-Dahají, Bahá'u'lláh rebukes some of the believers for having foolishly designated His son as a partner with Him in Divine Revelation. Referring to Muḥammad-'Alí by name, Bahá'u'lláh in this Tablet states that 'He, verily, is but one of My servants . . . Should he for a moment pass out from under the shadow of the Cause, he surely shall be brought to naught'.[26]

In unequivocal language Bahá'u'lláh affirms that the Mani-

* Some excerpts from his Tablets are translated and included in *Gleanings from the Writings of Bahá'u'lláh*, sections XXXIII, XXXVIII, LXXVII, CXXVII.

† For more details of the life and rebellion of Muḥammad-'Alí see *God Passes By* and *The Revelation of Bahá'u'lláh*, vol. I.

‡ From time to time Bahá'u'lláh instructed 'Abdu'l-Bahá to write on certain subjects.

festation of God is exalted above all humanity and cannot join partners with anyone. He asserts in His Writings that God bestows infallibility upon His Manifestations. He refers to this as the Most Great Infallibility which is the prerogative only of the Prophet and no one else. This should not be confused with conferred infallibility which Bahá'u'lláh bestowed upon 'Abdu'l-Bahá.

Lawḥ-i-Siráj

Another person who wrote to Bahá'u'lláh and posed certain questions concerning the position of Mírzá Yaḥyá was Mullá 'Alí-Muḥammad-i-Siráj, a native of Iṣfahán. He had become a Bábí in the early days of the Faith and attained the presence of the Báb in that city. It was his sister Fáṭimih* whom the Báb, after much insistence by Manúchihr Khán, the Governor of Iṣfahán, took as His second wife. Mullá 'Alí-Muḥammad-i-Siráj became a follower of Mírzá Yaḥyá, and although Bahá'u'lláh in this Tablet explained all that was necessary concerning the Cause of God, he remained defiant, and together with his brother, Mullá Rajab-'Alíy-i-Qahír, continued to support the evil activities of Mírzá Yaḥyá.

The Tablet revealed for Siráj is very lengthy,† and like many other Tablets in this period refutes the misrepresentations of Mírzá Yaḥyá and those of his supporters. Bahá'u'lláh declares in moving and tender language that His motive for revealing this Tablet has been to teach the Faith of God, so that perchance a few souls may recognize Him and arise for the triumph of His Cause. He states that there can be no greater injustice in the world than that the Blessed Beauty should need to adduce proofs to establish the truth of His own Mission, in spite of the fact that He is as manifest as the sun, and the outpourings of His

* See vol. I, p. 249.

† Small portions of this Tablet are translated into English by Shoghi Effendi and included in *Gleanings from the Writings of Bahá'u'lláh*, sections L and XCVII.

Revelation have encompassed the world. He affirms that the Cause of God is exalted above proofs and may never be judged by any standard except its own. Yet He has consented, for the sake of the guidance of a few souls, to demonstrate the verities enshrined in His Faith.

The basic question posed by Siráj concerned the exalted titles and position which the Báb had conferred upon Mírzá Yaḥyá. He wanted to know how such a person could be denounced by Bahá'u'lláh as the embodiment of Satan and the focal point of negation.

Bahá'u'lláh's elucidations are both profound and simple, and are mainly based on the Writings of the Báb. To describe them in the absence of a translation is not an easy task. Furthermore, in order to understand them, one would need to become familiar with Islamic and Bábí terminology. However, Bahá'u'lláh's basic explanation is that as long as man remains under the shadow of the Cause of God, his virtues and qualities are praiseworthy, but when he withholds himself from this bounty and opposes the Faith, his virtues turn into vices and his light into darkness.

In many Tablets Bahá'u'lláh dwells on this theme. For instance, in His Tablet to Shaykh Salmán* which was revealed in Adrianople, He states that a believer who is truly faithful to the Cause of God manifests divine virtues. Because of his devotion to God, the Sun of Truth sheds its radiance upon his soul and consequently these virtues come to light. As long as he remains in this state, his praiseworthy attributes, which originate from God, are evident and undeniable.

Should the same individual at a later time repudiate the Cause of God, all his virtues will return to their origin and his achievements become void. Shorn of divine qualities, he may no longer be regarded as the same person. Bahá'u'lláh states that even the clothes he wears, though physically the same as before, are different in reality. For, as long as a person is a true believer, though he may wear the coarsest of cotton, in the sight

* See chapter 13.

of God his clothes are as lustrous as the silk of paradise, while after his denial they are fit only to burn in hell-fire.* To illustrate this point Bahá'u'lláh cites the example of a candle. As long as the candle is lighted, it sheds its radiance around. But if the wind blows it out, the light will be extinguished.

There are many people who have rendered notable services to the Faith and their names are recorded in its annals, yet when the winds of tests blew they were unable to subdue their self and ego. These individuals not only lost their faith, but also their goodness and virtues. They fell from the heights of glory into the abyss of degradation and ignominy.

Jamál-i-Burújirdí, to whom reference has been made previously,† is a telling example. During the ministry of Bahá'u'lláh, he was one of the leading teachers of His Cause. Wherever he went the believers flocked around him in order to partake of his knowledge.

Although Jamál was a deceitful man who lusted for leadership and longed for glory, the great majority of the believers did not realize this. They considered him a man of God and treated him with great respect.

In Islamic communities, men of learning were revered by the people. Bahá'u'lláh has also exhorted His followers to honour the truly learned in the Faith, those whose knowledge and learning have not become the cause of pride and self-glorification. A person who is truly learned in the Faith is one who reaches such heights of detachment that he sincerely regards his learning as utter nothingness compared with the truths of the Cause of God. He becomes the embodiment of humility and self-effacement. The best example is Mírzá Abu'l-Faḍl, to whom a brief reference was made previously.‡ Before embracing the Faith, Mírzá Abu'l-Faḍl often asserted his own knowledge

* Bahá'u'lláh teaches that heaven and hell are not places but conditions. Nearness to God is a state of being in heaven, while remoteness from Him is hell-fire.

† See pp. 118–19.

‡ See p. 45.

and accomplishments. After his recognition of the Faith, however, he became so humble that in all his Bahá'í career he never sought to elevate himself above anybody and he never used the word 'I' to point out, or even allude to, his own achievements. His greatness is not merely in that he did not use the word 'I', but in his genuine belief that he did not have the merit to use the word 'I'.

No doubt it is concerning such men that Bahá'u'lláh reveals in the *Kitáb-i-Aqdas*:

> Happy are ye, O ye the learned ones in Bahá. By the Lord! Ye are the billows of the Most Mighty Ocean, the stars of the firmament of Glory, the standards of triumph waving betwixt earth and heaven. Ye are the manifestations of steadfastness amidst men and the daysprings of Divine Utterance to all that dwell on earth. Well is it with him that turneth unto you and woe betide the froward.[27]

In the earlier days of the Faith, those individuals like Jamál, who considered themselves superior to others in knowledge and exalted in station, and who pretended to be the most distinguished, always proved to be the source of strife and contention. Bahá'u'lláh has seized power and authority from such men and has dismissed as unauthoritative interpretations the assertions of all individuals even though they may be regarded as the most learned in the Faith. He has instead ordained that all matters be referred to the elected institutions of the Faith whose supreme body—the Universal House of Justice—is under His own guidance.

Jamál-i-Burújirdí was for almost forty years one of the foremost teachers of the Faith. During this period he managed to hide his true colours from the eyes of the faithful. But, as we have stated, there were some with insight who found him to be a master of hypocrisy and deceit. One such person was Ustád Muḥammad 'Alíy-i-Salmání* who met Jamál in Adrianople when the latter had gone to attain the presence of Bahá'u'lláh. In his memoirs Salmání recounts the following story:

* See pp. 155–61 for an account of his life.

One day I brought water into the outer apartment of the house of Bahá'u'lláh where I learnt that Áqá Jamál-i-Burújirdí had arrived. I went into the reception room and found him seated in a corner, clad in an 'abá [cloak] and wearing a large turban.* He held his hands in such a way that if anyone was so inclined he could kiss them! † He had not yet attained the presence of Bahá'u'lláh. That creature was a peculiar looking priest.

I used to consider myself to be a schemer and a man of cunning. So I walked in, uttered a casual greeting of 'Alláh'-u-'Abhá,' and without paying any attention to him sat at the other end of the room. Then I lay down on the floor and after some time arose and sat down again. I did all this to hurt his vanity for he was a pompous man who was seated in the reception room of the Blessed Beauty with an air of superiority and a greatly inflated ego. After having treated him disrespectfully in this manner, I looked at him for a while and then said 'How are you?' He merely shook his head at me. I then left him there and went about my own duties until the afternoon when they brought the news that he was summoned to the presence of Bahá'u'lláh. I went in and called him to follow me. I took him to the inner apartments of the house; we went up the stairs into Bahá'u'lláh's room. The Purest Branch ‡ was standing in the presence of the Blessed Beauty.

I stood at the entrance to the room. Jamál went in pretending to be trembling all over and then fell on the ground; this was a mere act. The Blessed Beauty was seated; the Purest Branch went forward to help Jamál to his feet. But Bahá'u'lláh stopped him, saying 'Leave him alone, he will get up himself.'

* Muslim priests wore turbans; the greater the turban, the more important the priest. Jamál during his Bahá'í career did not discard his turban and priestly attire.

† Muslims showed great respect towards the priests who used to display their hands for the public to kiss. Bahá'u'lláh has forbidden the kissing of hands.

‡ Mírzá Mihdí, the youngest brother of 'Abdu'l-Bahá who later died in 'Akká. His death is regarded by Bahá'u'lláh as His own sacrifice. We shall refer later to this illustrious son in the next volume.

After a while he arose; he sat at first and then stood up. Bahá'u'lláh afterwards dismissed him from his presence and did not say anything. Jamál . . . stayed for a few days, then Bahá'u'lláh sent him back to Persia. This man was corrupt from the beginning, his aim was nothing but leadership . . . [28]

It was this insatiable passion for leadership that destroyed Jamál in the end. For the Faith of Bahá'u'lláh does not allow such unwholesome elements to remain within its fold. It intrinsically repels vain and egotistical people. It is like an ocean: when the tide comes in it throws on the shore dead bodies and cleanses itself from their pollution. In the early years of the ministry of 'Abdu'l-Bahá, before the rebellion of Mírzá Muḥammad-'Alí became public, Jamál created a disturbing situation in the community in Ṭihrán by seeking leadership there. Although he had allied himself with Mírzá Muḥammad-'Alí, nevertheless for some time he appeared as one who was loyal to 'Abdu'l-Bahá. During this period he confused the minds of many people and openly contended with the Hands of the Cause of God* in his struggle to gain a position for himself in the Faith. When Mírzá Muḥammad-'Alí's rebellion came into the open, Jamál became one of his lieutenants. He was cast out of the Faith by the power of the Covenant. 'Abdu'l-Bahá has said that Jamál was a poison to the community and his expulsion from the Faith cleansed it from his pollution. The fall of Jamál was as dramatic as his rise. When he rebelled against 'Abdu'l-Bahá, the appointed Centre of the Cause of Bahá'u'lláh, he became spiritually dead and soon perished. His latter days were spent in remorse and destitution. The crowds who once gathered around with enthusiasm to hear his words were disbanded, for the spirit of faith had departed from his soul. Even one of his sons, Mírzá Luṭfu'lláh, who remained steadfast in the Covenant, dissociated himself from him. Mírzá Luṭfu'lláh, who later took the family name of Mawhibat, was an artist of out-

* The functions of the Hands of the Cause, as defined in the Will and Testament of 'Abdu'l-Bahá, are mainly the protection and propagation of the Faith. Those now living were appointed by the Guardian, Shoghi Effendi.

standing talent. He rendered a unique service to the Cause by illuminating a great many Tablets which are preserved in the archives of the Faith. These beautiful illuminations stand as a testimony to his artistic genius as well as to his devotion to the Cause of God.

In His *Lawḥ-i-Siráj*, Bahá'u'lláh states that the followers of Mírzá Yaḥyá in Adrianople had been asserting that just as gold cannot be transmuted into baser metal, so a soul who attains an exalted station (i.e. Mírzá Yaḥyá) can never lose it. In answer to this Bahá'u'lláh has revealed these words:

> Consider the doubts which they who have joined partners with God have instilled into the hearts of the people of this land. 'Is it ever possible,' they ask, 'for copper to be transmuted into gold?' Say, Yes, by my Lord, it is possible. Its secret, however, lieth hidden in Our Knowledge. We will reveal it unto whom We will. Whoso doubteth Our power, let him ask the Lord his God, that He may disclose unto him the secret, and assure him of its truth. That copper can be turned into gold is in itself sufficient proof that gold can, in like manner, be transmuted into copper, if they be of them that can apprehend this truth. Every mineral can be made to acquire the density, form, and substance of each and every other mineral. The knowledge thereof is with Us in the Hidden Book.[29]

The question of alchemy has occupied the minds of people for centuries. During Bahá'u'lláh's ministry it was a live issue and several believers were involved in it. Bahá'u'lláh urged them not to seek to achieve it at that time. However, He confirmed that transmuting baser metal into gold, the dream of the alchemist, was possible. He promised that it would be realized, and asserted that its realization would constitute one of the signs of the coming of age of humanity. He also prophesied that after its discovery a great calamity would await the world unless mankind came under the shelter of the Cause of God.[30] Present-day physicists, through special nuclear processes, are able to transmute various elements into others.

In the *Lawḥ-i-Siráj* Bahá'u'lláh dwells at length upon the misdeeds of Mírzá Yaḥyá, refers to Himself as Joseph, and describes His own sufferings at the hand of His brother whom He lovingly counsels to repent and return to his God.

Concerning the Revelation of His Word, Bahá'u'lláh informs Siráj that the Word of God has been sent down with an intensity and profusion such as 'secretaries are incapable of transcribing. It has, therefore, remained for the most part untranscribed.'[31] He affirms that although a large part of His Writings were cast into the river in Baghdád by His own instruction,* there yet existed the equivalent of one hundred thousand verses in Adrianople, none of which had so far been transcribed. He states that several people had requested to be allowed to compile those of His Tablets which were available into books for circulation among the believers, but He had not permitted this. Instead, He had assured them that God would raise up exalted men in the future who would gather His Writings together and compile them in the best possible form. He states that Revelation of the Word is the function of the Manifestation of God, while its promulgation rests with man. He gives the example of the *Qur'án*, which was compiled after Muḥammad, as the Gospels after Christ.

Today, the followers of Bahá'u'lláh are witnessing the fulfilment of these words. Several volumes of the Tablets of Bahá'u'lláh have so far been compiled in the original Persian and Arabic languages and a few in other languages. This process is now gathering momentum and as time goes on, more will become available. Apart from this, the Universal House of Justice, the supreme body of the Faith, since the early days of its establishment† has set itself the task of collating the Holy Writings, a task which by virtue of its paramount importance plays a significant role in the unfoldment of the Revelation of Bahá'u'lláh.

* See vol. I, p. 69.

† The Universal House of Justice was first elected by the National Spiritual Assemblies of the world on 21 April 1963, the centenary of the Declaration of Bahá'u'lláh.

12

Tests of Faith

The Falling Stars

In November 1866 when Bahá'u'lláh was residing in the house of Riḍá Big, a spectacular meteoric shower took place. Thousands of shooting-stars lit up the sky as they blazed their way through the atmosphere. This event, which has been called the 'star-fall' of 1866, was watched by millions in the East and West and for many the experience was terrifying.*

According to the Gospels, one of the signs of the coming of Christ in the glory of the Father is the falling of stars.† Bahá'u'lláh, in one of His Tablets cited in the *Epistle to the Son of the Wolf*, refers to this:

> O thou who hast set thy face towards the splendours of My Countenance! Vague fancies have encompassed the dwellers of the earth and debarred them from turning towards the Horizon of Certitude, and its brightness, and its manifestations and its lights. Vain imaginings have withheld them from Him Who is the Self-Subsisting. They speak as prompted by their own caprices, and understand not. Among them are those who have said: . . . 'Have the stars fallen?' Say: 'Yea, when He Who is the Self-Subsisting dwelt in the Land of Mystery (Adrianople). Take heed, ye who are endued with discernment!' All the signs appeared when We drew forth the Hand of Power from the bosom of majesty and might.[1]

Although this fascinating display of falling-stars was a literal fulfilment of the prophecies of old, its real significance is to be

* See Appendix I.

† See *Matthew* 24:29.

found in the Writings of Bahá'u'lláh and 'Abdu'l-Bahá where the words of the Gospels are interpreted. Bahá'u'lláh explains that by the falling of stars is meant the fall of religious leaders who, because they denied the Revelation of Bahá'u'lláh, are losing their influence over mankind. Addressing the Christian ecclesiastics, Bahá'u'lláh in one of His Tablets proclaims:

> O concourse of bishops! Ye are the stars of the heaven of My knowledge. My mercy desireth not that ye should fall upon the earth. My justice, however, declareth: 'This is that which the Son (Jesus) hath decreed.' And whatsoever hath proceeded out of His blameless, His truth-speaking, trustworthy mouth, can never be altered.[2]

And again:

> The stars of the heaven of knowledge have fallen, they that adduce the proofs they possess in order to demonstrate the truth of My Cause, and who make mention of God in My name. When I came unto them, in My majesty, however, they turned aside from Me. They, verily, are of the fallen.[3]

As far as recorded history shows, every religion has had its leaders. In past Dispensations, the clergy played a major part in conducting the affairs of religion. They became the most vital element in the fabric of human society, and exerted a powerful influence in the life of the community. They gained a great deal of authority which never waned until the coming of Bahá'u'lláh, when by one stroke of His exalted Pen, he stripped them of a power they had enjoyed since the beginning of time. He wrote in one of His Tablets:

> From two ranks amongst men power hath been seized: kings and ecclesiastics.[4]

The creative influence of the words of Bahá'u'lláh in this and similar pronouncements has set in motion the process of the disintegration of religious institutions and the progressive downfall of their leaders, who are increasingly becoming aware of their impotence to exercise a meaningful influence upon their communities.*

In this Dispensation Bahá'u'lláh has abolished priesthood. He has entrusted the administration of His Faith to the institutions designated by Him as the 'Houses of Justice.'†

Súriy-i-'Ibád

The *Súriy-i-'Ibád* (Súrih of the Servants) was revealed in Arabic in Adrianople in honour of Siyyid Mihdíy-i-Dahají. Siyyid Mihdí, to whom reference was made in a previous chapter,‡ was entitled by Bahá'u'lláh Ismu'lláhu'l-Mihdí (The Name of God, He Who is Guided). He was one of the famous teachers of the Cause during Bahá'u'lláh's ministry, but like Jamál-i-Burújirdí, who was also entitled 'Ismu'lláh', was a proud and ambitious man who in the end broke the Covenant of Bahá'u'lláh and rebelled against 'Abdu'l-Bahá.

Siyyid Mihdí was a native of Dahaj in the province of Yazd. He attained the presence of Bahá'u'lláh in Baghdád, Adrianople and 'Akká and received His unfailing bounties. Like Jamál, he travelled widely throughout Persia and was much honoured by the believers. Yet people who were endowed with discernment found him to be insincere, egotistical and deeply attached to the things of this world. Notable among those who have written their impressions of him is Ḥájí Mírzá Ḥaydar-'Alí, who also wrote about Jamál-i-Burújirdí. A perusal of his narratives makes it clear that these two men had at least one thing in common, namely an insatiable lust for leadership. Siyyid Mihdí

* For a fuller treatment of this subject see *The Promised Day is Come.*

† Apart from the Universal House of Justice, the supreme body of the Faith, Bahá'u'lláh has ordained the establishment of local Houses of Justice in every town or village. These bodies are functioning today in their embryonic form—the Local Spiritual Assemblies.

‡ See pp. 118–19.

ḤÁJÍ ÍMÁN

A devoted follower of Bahá'u'lláh, who visited Him in Adrianople; he suffered persecution for his faith
A photograph taken in prison

ḤÁJÍ MUḤAMMAD IBRÁHÍM-I-KHALÍL

A notable believer of Qazvín
The recipient of the Lawḥ-i-Khalíl

always entered Bahá'í gatherings with an air of superiority. He loved to see a retinue of the faithful walk behind him, and at nights he was preceded by a number of believers who carried lanterns for him.* This made a spectacular scene in those days; for normally one servant or friend with a lantern accompanied a person at night. But in his case some believers vied with each other to perform this service, and Ḥájí Mírzá Ḥaydar-'Alí recalls an evening when no less than fourteen men, with lanterns in hand, escorted him to a meeting!

Men such as these always fall. The Faith of Bahá'u'lláh does not harbour people who are egotistical and seek to glorify themselves. Its hallmark is servitude, and the standard it demands is purity of motive and sincerity. It is not therefore surprising to find that Siyyid Mihdí and Jamál-i-Burújirdí were toppled to the ground when the winds of tests began to blow. They both broke the Covenant of Bahá'u'lláh, and in the hope of becoming the undisputed leaders of the Faith in Persia, joined hands with Mírzá Muḥammad-'Alí† and rebelled against the appointed Centre of the Cause of God.‡ When this became known in Persia, the believers left them to their own devices, and soon their glory was turned into abasement. At first they made a great deal of clamour and noise within the community. They agitated the minds of many, but the power of the Covenant swept them into the abyss of ignominy and cleansed the Faith from their pollution.

During His ministry, Bahá'u'lláh concealed the faults and wrongdoings of Siyyid Mihdí. In His Tablets He showered His loving-kindness upon him and exhorted him to sincerity, purity and detachment. There is scarcely a Tablet revealed in his honour in which these points are not emphasized. When Bahá'u'lláh left Ba<u>gh</u>dád for Constantinople, He bade

* As there was no public lighting in those days, people carried lanterns at night. Important men had their servants carry a lantern in front of them.

† See vol. I and p. 260 above.

‡ 'Abdu'l-Bahá.

Siyyid Mihdí move into His house* and become its caretaker.

While residing in this house a small incident happened which reveals the weakness of his faith and demonstrates his attachment to material things. Some thieves broke into the house and stole some of his personal belongings. The loss of these few small items caused Siyyid Mihdí so much grief that he complained to Bahá'u'lláh. In reply, a Tablet was revealed in which Bahá'u'lláh counsels him to be detached from the things of this world and reminds him that his grievances are as utter nothingness when compared to the sufferings that Bahá'u'lláh Himself had endured in the path of God.

The *Súriy-i-'Ibád* was revealed by Bahá'u'lláh in the early days of His sojourn in Adrianople while Siyyid Mihdí was still caretaker of the Most Great House in Baghdád. In it He urges him to live a pious life, to cleanse his heart from the defilement of the world, and to become detached from his own self and all created things. Bahá'u'lláh extols His own Essence, and states that for many years He had revealed the Words of God in great profusion while hiding His glory behind many veils of concealment. When the appointed hour had struck, however, He unveiled His exalted station and shed an infinitesimal measure of the light of His countenance upon all created things. As a result of this outpouring, the Concourse on high† and the chosen ones of God were awestruck and dumbfounded.

A considerable part of this Tablet recounts the events of the journey from Baghdád to Adrianople. It also serves as a channel of communication between Bahá'u'lláh and the believers in 'Iráq, for in it He addresses the believers in general and a few in particular. He exhorts them to rectitude of conduct, steadfastness in His love and unity among themselves.

Although Siyyid Mihdí's Bahá'í career ended in shame and he perished spiritually, he had a nephew, Ḥájí Siyyid 'Alí-

* This house in Baghdád is known as the 'Most Great House'. See vol. I, pp. 211–12.

† The gathering of holy souls in the Kingdom of God.

Akbar-i-Dahají, an embodiment of faith and servitude and very much loved by Bahá'u'lláh. Concerning this believer, Ḥájí Muḥammad-Ṭáhir-i-Málmírí writes in his unpublished 'History of the Faith in the Province of Yazd':

> The late Ḥájí Siyyid 'Alí-Akbar-i-Dahají was one of the early believers. Seldom has there been a soul so distinguished and pious as he. He was a nephew of Siyyid Mihdí, the Ismu'lláh . . . Physically he was very handsome and had a sweet melodious voice. One might say that whenever he chanted the Words of God, even the Concourse on high and the Denizens of the Kingdom of Abhá were exhilarated by his voice . . . I have never heard anyone chant so beautifully as he did. He attained the presence of the Blessed Beauty several times and became the recipient of Bahá'u'lláh's infinite favours and bounties. His relationship with Him was truly that of a lover and the Beloved. There are many Tablets revealed in his honour. Notable among them is the Tablet of Iḥtiráq.* . . . Ḥájí Siyyid 'Alí-Akbar passed away in Ṭihrán on his way back from the Holy Land after having attained the presence of Bahá'u'lláh for the last time. After his death, Bahá'u'lláh indicated that He was so attached to Hájí Siyyid 'Alí-Akbar that He wished the name of this believer mentioned in His presence. He thereafter instructed that henceforth his uncle Siyyid Mihdí, the Ismu'lláh, be called Siyyid 'Alí-Akbar.[5]

Another person who may be regarded in the same light as Siyyid Mihdí and Jamál-i-Burújirdí is Muḥammad-Javád-i-Qazvíní; although the third did not have the learning of the first two. Bahá'u'lláh conferred upon him the title Ismu'lláhu'l-Javád (The Name of God, the All-Bountiful). He also became a Covenant-breaker and one who inflicted great sufferings upon the person of 'Abdu'l-Bahá. Javád, as a youth, attained the presence of Bahá'u'lláh in Baghdád. In 1867 he went to

* This Tablet is also known by its opening verse as *Qad-Iḥtaraqa'l-Mukhliṣún*. It has become known among the English-speaking believers as the *Fire Tablet*. We shall refer to it in the next volume.

Adrianople in the company of Nabíl-i-A'ẓam and was among those who were permitted to accompany Bahá'u'lláh to 'Akká.

During the ministry of Bahá'u'lláh, Javád enjoyed nearness to Him and in spite of his many shortcomings, Bahá'u'lláh conferred His favours upon him and concealed his faults. But after the ascension of Bahá'u'lláh, Javád, driven by his ambitions and aspirations, joined hands with Mírzá Muḥammad-'Alí, the arch-breaker of the Covenant of Bahá'u'lláh, caused much anguish and pain to 'Abdu'l-Bahá, and severely attacked Him in his venomous writings which contained many inaccuracies, falsehoods and calumnies. Thus ended in tragedy the career of one whom Bahá'u'lláh had exalted through His loving-kindness. It did not take very long before his plans and aspirations were frustrated and, like Jamál and Siyyid Mihdí, he perished ingloriously.

The Test of Gold

Having referred to the downfall of Javád-i-Qazvíní, it is interesting to recount the story of his eldest brother, Ḥájí Muḥammad-Báqir-i-Qazvíní who had an unusual Bahá'í career; he was one who fell from grace, but was saved towards the end of his life. Ḥájí Muḥammad-Báqir attained the presence of Bahá'u'lláh in Baghdád. While there he requested Bahá'u'lláh to bestow wealth upon him. Bahá'u'lláh acceded to his plea and assured him that God would grant his wish. Soon afterwards he became very rich, but as a result grew heedless of the Cause of God.

In the course of Ḥájí Mírzá Ḥaydar-'Alí's account of what appears to be his first audience with Bahá'u'lláh in Adrianople, we find the following story of Ḥájí Muḥammad-Báqir. Having explained that he cannot express in words the excitement, awe and wonder of what he felt in his heart whenever he attained the presence of Bahá'u'lláh, Ḥájí Mírzá Ḥaydar-'Alí writes:

Because it was the early days of the rise of the Day-Star of the World,* Bahá'u'lláh asked me to give Him an account of the state of the believers in Ṭihrán, Qazvín, Zanján and Tabríz, the towns I had passed through. He enquired of their faith, and their love for the Cause. I did not reply.† After we [Ḥájí Mírzá Ḥaydar-'Alí and his two companions] were dismissed from His presence, we were taken to a place where it was arranged for us to stay. There, Bahá'u'lláh sent someone to whom I could recount the conditions of the believers. I reported all I knew about each person, including the late Ḥájí Muḥammad-Báqir who was at that time a well-known merchant, foremost among the believers in faith, certitude and enthusiasm, and was serving the Cause with devotion and self-sacrifice.

The messenger left and after some minutes returned with an exalted Tablet which had been revealed in honour of the Ḥájí. He stated [on behalf of Bahá'u'lláh]: 'This man attained the presence of Bahá'u'lláh in Baghdád. There He wrote a letter to Him and begged for wealth and prosperity. In answer, this exalted and wonderful Tablet was revealed for him. In it Bahá'u'lláh stated that his request would be granted and that the doors of prosperity and wealth would be opened for him from every direction. He warned him, however, to be on his guard and not to allow riches to become a barrier and make him heedless.

Now you are here to attain the presence of Bahá'u'lláh and in the future you will witness that this man [Ḥájí Muḥammad-Báqir] will be overtaken with fear to such an extent that he will renounce God and His Cause. Not long after, he will make substantial losses, following which he will write a letter to Bahá'u'lláh and repent. God will then turn his losses into profit and he will become again highly successful in his business and will emerge as the foremost merchant in Con-

* Bahá'u'lláh. (A.T.)

† It was not unusual for the believers who were in the presence of Bahá'u'lláh not to reply to His questions. In the first place, they were so carried away that they could not utter a word. Secondly, to speak was regarded by many as being contrary to the spirit of utter self-effacement in His presence.

stantinople and Tabríz. However, this time he will wax prouder than before, more heedless and deprived . . . This time he will lose all his possessions, will be unable to continue trading and will become helpless in arranging his affairs. It is then that he will repent and return, and will be content to live as a poor man. He will spend the days of his life in the service of the Cause of God. His end will be blessed and he will receive great confirmations from God.' He then said to me: 'Remember all these things, for they will come to pass, and you shall witness them.'

We were in Adrianople when news came that Javád, the younger brother of the Ḥájí, had been arrested and cast into prison. Ḥájí Muḥammad-Báqir had paid one thousand túmáns* for the release of his brother and had left Tabríz for Constantinople in great haste. Upon arrival he had gone to visit the late Mus͟híru'd-Dawlih, the Persian Ambassador, and there in his presence had recanted his Faith. Bahá'u'lláh affirmed that this was the beginning of his tests and instructed that believers passing through Constantinople should not associate with him.

Later, I left Adrianople for Constantinople where I stayed for fourteen months. There I heard that the Ḥájí had bought enormous quantities of cotton and because the prices had suddenly fallen drastically, not only had he lost all his possessions, but he was also unable to pay his creditors . . . When this happened he wrote a letter supplicating Bahá'u'lláh and repenting. A holy and blessed Tablet was revealed in his honour. In it Bahá'u'lláh gave him the glad-tidings that he would soon make enormous profits. When I went to Egypt, I heard that the price of cotton had risen considerably and the Ḥájí's wealth as a result increased tenfold.[6]

This time Ḥájí Muḥammad-Báqir became very rich and influential. He emerged foremost among the merchants of Constantinople and acquired great fame. However, his wealth again became a barrier between him and God. Again he forsook the Cause, and completely cut off his relationship with Bahá'u'lláh. After some years Bahá'u'lláh asked Ḥájí Abu'l-Ḥasan-i-

* A very large sum of money in those days. (A.T.)

Amín* to establish contact with him and find out how he was. Ḥájí Amín went to see him in Constantinople. He found him to be utterly heedless and forgetful of Bahá'u'lláh and the Cause. The world and its attractions had so possessed him that at one point in the interview, Ḥájí Muḥammad-Báqir pointed to a coffer in his office and said, 'My god is in this box!'

Ḥájí Amín has stated that when he reported this to Bahá'u'lláh, He became very sad. As He was pacing up and down, He stopped, held out His hand, palm open, and said 'With this hand We conferred upon him riches.' Then with a sudden movement, He withdrew, closed His hand, and said, 'Now with the same hand We take it back from him.'

Soon Ḥájí Muḥammad-Báqir lost all his possessions. He again became repentant and wrote to Bahá'u'lláh. This time a Tablet was revealed for him in which Bahá'u'lláh clearly stated that God took away his wealth so that he might return to Him and become steadfast in His love. He directed Ḥájí Muḥammad-Báqir to leave Constantinople and occupy himself with transcribing the holy Writings.

After this incident, Ḥájí Muḥammad-Báqir lived the remainder of his life in the utmost poverty. He grew strong in his faith and devoted his time to the service of the Cause. Ḥájí Mírzá Ḥaydar-'Alí, who met him after this event, writes:

> . . . I met him [Ḥájí Muḥammad-Báqir] in Tabríz. He said 'After the revelation of the Tablet of Bahá'u'lláh, it was as if the nails in the wall, the curtains in the room, and everything else had ears to hear and were carrying out the command of Bahá'u'lláh. I lost everything that I had earned. The house I live in now is owned by my wife and the clothes I wear are tailored by my children.'[7]

Ḥájí Muḥammad-Báqir was not the only one who had asked Bahá'u'lláh to bestow upon him riches through the power of God. There were others, some of whom became utterly heedless of the Cause after their success in life. It is man's nature to

* The Trustee of Bahá'u'lláh. For further information see vol. III.

become attracted to material things. However, if he allows worldly riches to possess him and rule over his soul, then he will be deprived of the bounties of God, and will perish spiritually. Wealth and attachment to material things are some of the greatest tests for the soul of man. Bahá'u'lláh states in *The Hidden Words*:

> O Son of Being!
> Busy not thyself with this world, for with fire We test the gold, and with gold We test Our servants.[8]

As we have previously stated,* there is nothing in the Writings of Bahá'u'lláh to condemn wealth as long as it does not become a barrier between man and God. On the contrary He glorifies the station of a rich person whose riches have not prevented him from recognizing His Cause and serving Him with devotion. The view that one must be poor in order to become godly and spiritual is not necessarily correct. The criterion for nearness to God is detachment, and although it is more difficult for the rich to attain to this lofty station, a poor person often has to fight many battles within himself before he becomes detached from this world.

'Abdu'l-Bahá in one of His Tablets[9] explains that it is a basic requirement for the order of creation to have both rich and poor in human society.† If all were equal the balance in this world would be upset, and human progress would halt.

Nature also confirms 'Abdu'l-Bahá's explanation and demonstrates the falsity and impracticability of those ideologies which seek to establish equality in human society. That all human beings have equal rights and privileges is one of the basic teachings of Bahá'u'lláh. But it is also made clear that people are not equal in their capacity, intelligence and accomplish-

* See vol. I, pp. 75–7.

† It is important to note that while the Bahá'í teachings maintain that human society should consist of many levels, they advocate the abolition of extreme poverty and wealth.

ments. Therefore society must comprise within itself men of all ranks and position who are related to each other in their various functions.

'Abdu'l-Bahá states, in the fore-mentioned Tablet, that poverty is meritorious in the sight of God if it comes about in His path. He gives the example of those who were persecuted and lost all their possessions because they followed the Cause of God. There are many Tablets in which Bahá'u'lláh and 'Abdu'l-Bahá have exhorted the believers to be patient and content in poverty and generous in prosperity. In *The Hidden Words* Bahá'u'lláh reveals:

> O Son of My Handmaid!
> Be not troubled in poverty nor confident in riches, for poverty is followed by riches, and riches are followed by poverty. Yet to be poor in all save God is a wondrous gift, belittle not the value thereof, for in the end it will make thee rich in God, and thus thou shalt know the meaning of the utterance, 'In truth ye are the poor,' and the holy words, 'God is the all-possessing,' shall even as the true morn break forth gloriously resplendent upon the horizon of the lover's heart, and abide secure on the throne of wealth.[10]

In the course of one of His talks to His companions[11] 'Abdu'l-Bahá states that a poor man who is patient and forbearing is better than a rich man who is thankful. However, a poor man who is thankful is more praiseworthy than the one who is patient, while more meritorious than all is the rich man who expends his wealth for others.

It is clear from the teachings of Bahá'u'lláh that man must earn his living in this life by engaging in some form of work, trade or profession. In *The Hidden Words* Bahá'u'lláh says:

> O My Servants!
> Ye are the trees of My garden; ye must give forth goodly and wondrous fruits, that ye yourselves and others may profit therefrom. Thus it is incumbent on every one to engage in

crafts and professions, for therein lies the secret of wealth, O men of understanding! For results depend upon means, and the grace of God shall be all-sufficient unto you. Trees that yield no fruit have been and will ever be for the fire.

O My Servant!

The best of men are they that earn a livelihood by their calling and spend upon themselves and upon their kindred for the love of God, the Lord of all worlds.[12]

However, one of the most important attributes for one who earns his living is to be content and resigned to whatever God has ordained for him. 'The source of all good,' Bahá'u'lláh states, 'is trust in God, submission unto His command, and contentment in His holy will and pleasure.'[13]

13

Lawḥ-i-Salmán

A Tablet which in its profundity and wealth of knowledge stands out as one of the most significant among Bahá'u'lláh's Writings is the *Lawḥ-i-Salmán* (Tablet of Salmán),* revealed in Adrianople in honour of Shaykh Salmán. We have referred to part of this Tablet previously.† Shaykh Salmán, whose life story is given in the first volume,‡ was a devoted servant of Bahá'u'lláh and dedicated his life to travelling for Him. He carried His Writings to the believers in Persia and brought back their letters and news to Him. He rendered this service with such care that none of Bahá'u'lláh's Tablets ever fell into the hands of the enemy. It is recorded that on one occasion when he realized that he was about to be searched by the authorities in a Persian town, he ate the few Tablets he was carrying in order to protect the Cause and the believers for whom they were intended!

Salmán was pure-hearted and very simple. The believers always enjoyed his company but there were some friends in high positions who were embarrassed and sometimes afraid to meet him because of his simplicity and frankness. Ḥájí Mírzá Ḥaydar-'Alí writes of this in his *Bihjatu'ṣ-Ṣudúr*:

I spent some time in Shíráz where I used to attain the pres-

* In the list 'Bahá'u'lláh's best known Works' prepared by Shoghi Effendi, in volumes of *The Bahá'í World*, this Tablet is described as *Lawḥ-i-Salmán I*. It is mainly in Persian and parts of it are translated by Shoghi Effendi and included in *Gleanings from the Writings of Bahá'u'lláh*, sections XXI, CXLVIII, CLIV.

† See pp. 263–4.

‡ See vol. I, pp. 109–13.

ence of the celebrated Salmán . . . I was filled with infinite joy by associating with him. He was truly a brilliant lamp. Outwardly he was an illiterate person and very simple, but inwardly he was the essence of wisdom and knowledge who could solve difficult problems and explain abstruse questions in simple language. Salmán was the essence of selflessness, he had no ego whatsoever. He was in no way able to flatter people or to deal deceitfully with them. It was for this reason that the pure in heart among the believers were truly devoted to him. But those who were sophisticated and conventional were not keen to associate with him. For they feared that he might ruin their prestige in the gatherings of the friends. It is commonly known and is true, that once the Ancient Beauty told Salmán to show respect towards important people in the meetings, and not to speak unkindly about them. Salmán replied, 'I do not consider anybody great except the Ancient Beauty and the Master. The so-called great are nothing but pompous men.' This remark amused Bahá'u'lláh.[1]

In the *Tablet of Salmán* Bahá'u'lláh bids him to journey throughout the land with feet of steadfastness, wings of detachment and a heart ablaze with the fire of the love of God, so that the forces of evil may be powerless to prevent him from carrying out his mission.

Revealed at the time when Mírzá Yaḥyá had openly arisen against Bahá'u'lláh, this Tablet also contains many passages concerning the unfaithfulness, the treachery, the ungodliness of Mírzá Yaḥyá and his shameful activities including his plans to take the life of Bahá'u'lláh. In moving language, He pours out His heart to Salmán and speaks of the anguish of His own heart, of His pains and sufferings which were inflicted by one whom He had brought up with such loving-kindness, care and consideration. He recalls the times when Mírzá Yaḥyá was in constant attendance by day and night. He would stand humbly in His presence and listen to the Words of God which were revealed with great power and majesty. But as the Cause began to grow, he was enticed by the prospect of his own fame. His whole being was so filled with the love of leadership that he left his Lord and rebelled against Him. Bahá'u'lláh in this Tablet intimates to Shaykh Salmán that He is so encompassed by grief and sorrow that His Pen is prevented from bestowing the knowledge of God upon people and revealing some of the mysteries of His Cause.

A great part of the *Tablet of Salmán* is in answer to a question concerning the meaning of a line from a poem by Mawlaví.* In order to appreciate Bahá'u'lláh's profound explanations, one must be well versed in Islamic philosophy and the meaning of mystical terms. Otherwise it is not an easy task to understand this part of the Tablet. Furthermore, Bahá'u'lláh states that He is reluctant to expound the works of the mystics and sages of the past. For, He proclaims, the Sun of Truth has risen and oceans of knowledge have surged forth through His Revelation. Therefore there is no need to dwell on the words and teachings of old. Gnostics and men of learning must needs turn to Him as the Source of knowledge and receive enlightenment from Him.

Bahá'u'lláh calls on Salmán to meet the servants of God and counsel them on His behalf. They should cleanse their hearts so that they may be enabled to recognize the Beauty of His countenance, walk in His ways, meditate upon His Words, and know that if the worlds of God were limited to this one, the Báb would never have allowed Himself to fall into the hands of His enemy, nor would He have sacrificed His life in the path of God. In another Tablet [2] Bahá'u'lláh states that if there were any merit in this mortal world, He Himself would have occupied its highest thrones and owned all its treasures. The fact that the Creator of this world has not set His own affection upon it is a proof that there are spiritual worlds far more glorious than this one. It is to these worlds that the soul of the believer repairs after its separation from the body.†

Bahá'u'lláh in the *Tablet of Salmán* promises that through the

* Jaláli'd-Dín-i-Rúmí, the author of the *Mathnaví*.

† There are many Tablets concerning life after death. Some of these will feature in the next volumes.

influence of His Revelation, some souls will arise who, renouncing the world, will turn fully to Him with the utmost devotion, and regard the sacrifice of life in His path as the easiest of all things. He affirms that God has chosen these souls for His own Self, and that the dwellers of the realms on high long to attain their presence.

The history of the Cause records with pride many episodes in the lives of such believers, who have shed a great lustre upon the Faith of Bahá'u'lláh. The tree of the Cause of God in this day has grown and flourished mainly as a result of two factors: one, the outpouring of the Revelation of Bahá'u'lláh which, like the rays of the sun, has imparted to it a measure of its vivifying energies; the other, the blood of the martyrs who willingly gave their lives in order to nourish and water it.

Bahá'u'lláh in this Tablet confers an exalted station upon the soul of the believer. He states that if the glory of such a station be revealed in this world, even to the extent of a needle's eye, every soul will expire through ecstasy. Because of this, the station of the true believer is kept hidden in this life. In another Tablet revealed in 'Akká Bahá'u'lláh makes a similar statement:

> Blessed is the soul which, at the hour of its separation from the body, is sanctified from the vain imaginings of the peoples of the world. Such a soul liveth and moveth in accordance with the Will of its Creator . . . If any man be told that which hath been ordained for such a soul in the worlds of God, the Lord of the throne on high and of earth below, his whole being will instantly blaze out in his great longing to attain that most exalted, that sanctified and resplendent station . . .[3]

In the *Tablet of Salmán* Bahá'u'lláh explains one of the most interesting mysteries in the *Qur'án*, a mystery which had hitherto remained unnoticed. He refers to the well-known phrase, 'There is no God but Him'. This is the cardinal statement of faith which every Muslim must make, and which is the basis of the Islamic religion.

As we have previously written,* the Word of God has many significances which are beyond the ken of men. There are inner meanings enshrined in the Word of God which only His Manifestation and those whom He guides understand. Bahá'u'lláh explains that in this phrase 'There is no God but Him', the letter of negation precedes that of affirmation. Therefore as a result of the creative influence of this phrase, ever since it was revealed, the violators of the Cause of God, representing the letter of negation, dominated over the faithful in the past. All the sufferings which the hands of the breakers of the Covenant of God inflicted upon the steadfast Muslims and their apparent superiority, were the fulfilment of the Words uttered by Muḥammad. God had, through His wisdom, so destined that those who were impure and rebellious should dominate those who were true and sincere.

It is a Bahá'í belief that those who usurped the right of Imám 'Alí, the lawful successor of Muḥammad and the interpreter of His Word, were acting against the expressed wishes of their Prophet. They disregarded the injunctions of Muḥammad concerning His successor, became the primary cause of division within the Faith of Islám, brought about the death of the holy Imáms and persecuted their followers. They were the letters of negation and till the end of the Dispensation of Muḥammad, dominated His faithful followers.†

History demonstrates that great differences arose among the followers of each religion soon after the death of its Founder. These differences led to schisms and divisions which have increased with the passage of time. This process, however, must not be so misunderstood as to lead us to believe that the Founders of the world's great religions in the past were incapable of establishing ways and means of uniting their followers, or of staying the hands of the unfaithful from corrupting the religion of God.

That religions have divided into sects is not due to the teach-

* See vol. I, chapter 3.

† For a more detailed account of these events, see vol. I, pp. 126–8.

ings of their Founders, but rather to the immaturity of their followers. Just as children are too young to be held responsible for keeping their clothes clean as they play outside, so humanity in past dispensations had not acquired sufficient maturity to protect the religion of God from disunity and discord.

Even in Islám, the most recent of the older religions, men were not sufficiently mature to receive from Muḥammad a firm Covenant, similar to that established by Bahá'u'lláh, a Covenant which would require His followers strictly to follow His Faith without creating division within it. On the contrary, as we have already observed from the fore-mentioned phrase in the *Qur'án*, Muḥammad knew that His followers would not be capable of maintaining their unity after Him. He knew that if He were to establish an irrevocable covenant in writing, the people of Islám would not have had the maturity and capacity at that time to observe its provisions strictly. But this is not to be regarded as a failure on the part of Islám, or of older religions which became similarly divided. It was only natural for humanity, which had not come of age, to neglect its duty and conduct itself irresponsibly. However, through God's forbearance and justice, the followers of past religions received their spiritual sustenance regardless of the sects they created.

For example, the primacy of Peter is acknowledged in the Gospels. However, differences arose and the followers of Christ became divided. Nevertheless each sect received a measure of the bounties of Christ. The tree of Christianity blossomed even after acquiring several branches, and each one remained verdant and flourishing until the advent of Islám when the Dispensation of Christ was closed. Similarly, the two major branches of Islám remained part of that religion. Even those who violated the wishes of the Prophet were not cut off from the Tree of Islám; all received their sustenance from it until the advent of the Báb when the Dispensation of Islám came to an end.

However, the Dispensation of Bahá'u'lláh has ushered in a new day. Through the potency of His Revelation mankind is destined to come of age and Bahá'u'lláh has given it responsibility. He established an irrefutable Covenant with His followers, appointed its Centre, 'Abdu'l-Bahá, exhorted the believers to follow Him and made it clear that in this Dispensation there would be no room for disunity and division. The Cause of God is one and indivisible, and man, having left behind the stages of childhood and adolescence, must now play a responsible part in maintaining its unity, in consolidating its world-wide structure and in protecting its nascent institutions from the unfaithful.

Referring to the fore-mentioned phrase 'There is no God but Him', Bahá'u'lláh, in the *Tablet of Salmán*, proclaims in majestic and powerful language that He has removed the letter of negation which had been placed before that of affirmation. This phrase, which the Prophet of Islám, through His all-encompassing wisdom, regarded to be the cornerstone of His Faith, is now, in the Dispensation of Bahá'u'lláh, symbolically replaced by the affirmative phrase 'He is God', signifying that the Revealer of the Cause of God holds within His hands the reins of authority, and, unlike the Dispensations of the past, no one has the power to wrest it from Him. The violators and the breakers of Bahá'u'lláh's Covenant, as history has shown, have been utterly impotent to introduce divisions within His Faith, to arrest its onward march or influence its glorious destiny.

How striking are the evidences of the creative power of the words of Bahá'u'lláh, that through but a movement of His Pen He reversed a process which had persisted for centuries, which had created schisms within religions and placed the true exponents of the Faith of God under the domination of the unfaithful. After the ascension of Bahá'u'lláh, 'Abdu'l-Bahá was opposed by no less a person than His brother Mírzá Muḥammad-'Alí. This son of Bahá'u'lláh tried, against the provisions of the Will and Testament of His Father and in company with a number of outstanding teachers of the Faith, to undermine the exalted position which Bahá'u'lláh had conferred upon 'Abdu'l-Bahá. In the end, the power of the Covenant of Bahá'u'lláh swept

Mírzá Muḥammad-'Alí into the abyss of ignominy and he perished ingloriously. Through the same power, the breakers of the Covenant during the ministry of Shoghi Effendi were also struck down.

It is important to note that those who rebelled against 'Abdu'l-Bahá and broke the Covenant were not of a foolish and senseless type. On the contrary, most of them were intelligent and capable men; some were highly knowledgeable teachers and immensely respected by the community. Jamál-i-Burújirdí was a distinguished *mujtahid* with a keen mind, Siyyid Mihdíy-i-Dahají was an erudite person and a powerful speaker. There were several others like them who were once outstanding followers of Bahá'u'lláh, who served the Faith with distinction but whose ego destroyed them in the end. Covenant-breaking is a deadly spiritual disease. It existed in the Dispensations of the past, but as already explained, it resulted in schisms and divisions. This disease is contagious and, if not checked, can destroy the very foundations of religion. It is for this reason that Bahá'u'lláh and 'Abdu'l-Bahá have warned the believers not to associate with those who break the Covenant. Through this vital commandment, which is entirely new in the history of religion, the Cause of God, which since its inception has been betrayed many times by proud and vainglorious men, and whose appointed Centres were ruthlessly opposed by bands of egotistical followers, has emerged triumphant from these most severe crises, its unity unimpaired and its solidarity further enhanced.

Bearing in mind the turmoil of the age in which we live and the spirit of rebellion which agitates human society today, we realize that the Cause of Bahá'u'lláh would have been divided by now into hundreds of sects had it not been for the power of the Covenant of Bahá'u'lláh and the creative influence of His Words in which we find the assurance that this is 'the Day which shall not be followed by night'.* [4]

* For a further discussion of this subject, see vol. I, pp. 129–37, and pp. 240–42.

14

Confrontation with Mírzá Yaḥyá

Foremost among the 'letters of negation' referred to by Bahá'u'lláh in the *Tablet of Salmán* was Mírzá Yaḥyá, who was swiftly struck down by the hand of power and might.

During the one-year period that Bahá'u'lláh stayed in the house of Riḍá Big and His subsequent return to the house of Amru'lláh, He never met Mírzá Yaḥyá or Siyyid Muḥammad whom He had expelled from His presence. Mírzá Yaḥyá with his family now lived in a separate house, and Siyyid Muḥammad was living among the Muslims in the city. After a stay of about three months in the house of Amru'lláh, Bahá'u'lláh moved His residence to the house of 'Izzat Áqá which was situated in the same quarter of the city. He remained there till the end of His stay in Adrianople.

Soon after transferring His residence to this house, an event of the utmost significance occurred which toppled Mírzá Yaḥyá to his doom and degraded him in the eyes of his supporters as well as the authorities in Adrianople. This was in the month of Jamádíyu'l-Avval, 1284 A.H. (September 1867). Having for years observed the exemplary patience with which Bahá'u'lláh had endured all the calumnies and falsehoods which Mírzá Yaḥyá had heaped upon Him while counting on His forbearance, knowing that He did not generally seek to appear in public and assuming that He would never consider meeting His unfaithful brother face to face, Siyyid Muḥammad-i-Iṣfahání, in order to strengthen his own position, expressed to a few Persians of Muslim faith in Adrianople that, whereas he and Mírzá Yaḥyá were ready to confront Bahá'u'lláh in public he was sure that Bahá'u'lláh would not respond to the challenge.

This form of confrontation, known as *mubáhilih*, had taken place in Islám. For instance, when a deputation of the Christians of Najrán in Medina were talking of offering a challenge to the Prophet Muḥammad, it was to be a confrontation in the form of *mubáhilih*. This is a challenge between truth and falsehood; the two parties come together, each one invoking God to annihilate the other, and calling on His wrath to strike down the faithless. It is expected in these circumstances that the power of Truth will destroy the forces of falsehood.

The person who became instrumental in bringing this matter to its conclusion was Mír Muḥammad-i-Mukárí from Shíráz, a caravan-driver who had accompanied the Báb on His pilgrimage to Mecca, and later Bahá'u'lláh from Baghdád to Constantinople.* Although he was uneducated, Mír Muḥammad was a man of great discernment, wisdom and courage. He was a Bábí and, being confused with the differences which had arisen in the Faith, he travelled especially to Adrianople in order to investigate the truth for himself. While in that city, he moved freely among the companions of Bahá'u'lláh and the supporters of Mírzá Yaḥyá alike.

Soon after his arrival he heard Siyyid Muḥammad's propaganda about a confrontation with Bahá'u'lláh. This created great interest in Mír Muḥammad who urged Siyyid Muḥammad to induce Mírzá Yaḥyá to meet Bahá'u'lláh in a public place for a *mubáhilih*. He in turn promised personally to invite Bahá'u'lláh to accept the challenge. This is how Shoghi Effendi describes this important event:

> A certain Mír Muḥammad, a Bábí of Shíráz, greatly resenting alike the claims and the cowardly seclusion of Mírzá Yaḥyá, succeeded in forcing Siyyid Muḥammad to induce him to meet Bahá'u'lláh face to face, so that a discrimination might be publicly effected between the true and the false. Foolishly assuming that his illustrious Brother would never countenance such a proposition, Mírzá Yaḥyá appointed the mosque

* See p. 409.

of Sulṭán Salím as the place for their encounter. No sooner had Bahá'u'lláh been informed of this arrangement than He set forth, on foot, in the heat of midday, and accompanied by this same Mír Muḥammad, for the afore-mentioned mosque, which was situated in a distant part of the city, reciting, as He walked, through the streets and markets, verses, in a voice and in a manner that greatly astonished those who saw and heard Him.

'O Muḥammad!', are some of the words He uttered on that memorable occasion, as testified by Himself in a Tablet, 'He Who is the Spirit hath, verily, issued from His habitation, and with Him have come forth the souls of God's chosen ones and the realities of His Messengers. Behold, then, the dwellers of the realms on high above Mine head, and all the testimonies of the Prophets in My grasp. Say: Were all the divines, all the wise men, all the kings and rulers on earth to gather together, I, in very truth, would confront them, and would proclaim the verses of God, the Sovereign, the Almighty, the All-Wise. I am He Who feareth no one, though all who are in heaven and all who are on earth rise up against me . . . This is Mine hand which God hath turned white for all the worlds to behold. This is My staff; were We to cast it down, it would, of a truth, swallow up all created things.'* Mír Muḥammad, who had been sent ahead to announce Bahá'u'lláh's arrival, soon returned, and informed Him that he who had challenged His authority wished, owing to unforeseen circumstances, to postpone for a day or two the interview. Upon His return to His house Bahá'u'lláh revealed a Tablet, wherein He recounted what had happened, fixed the time for the postponed interview, sealed the Tablet with His seal, entrusted it to Nabíl, and instructed him to deliver it to one of the new believers, Mullá Muḥammad-i-Tabrízí, for the information of Siyyid Muḥammad, who was in the habit of frequenting that believer's shop. It was arranged to demand from Siyyid Muḥammad, ere the delivery of that Tablet, a sealed note pledging Mírzá Yaḥyá, in the event of failing to appear at the trysting-place, to affirm in writing that

* Part of the *Tablet of Mubáhilih*, addressed to Mullá Ṣádiq-i-Khurásání. See vol. I and *Memorials of the Faithful*. (A.T.)

his claims were false. Siyyid Muḥammad promised that he would produce the next day the document required, and though Nabíl, for three successive days, waited in that shop for the reply, neither did the Siyyid appear, nor was such a note sent by him. That undelivered Tablet, Nabíl, recording twenty-three years later this historic episode in his chronicle, affirms was still in his possession, 'as fresh as the day on Which the Most Great Branch had penned it, and the seal of the Ancient Beauty had sealed and adorned it,' a tangible and irrefutable testimony to Bahá'u'lláh's ascendancy over a routed opponent.[1]

Mírzá Áqá Ján mentions[2] that when Bahá'u'lláh left for the mosque with Mír Muḥammad, he himself was not in the house, as he had gone to attend to some business in town. He heard the news and hastened back. On his way he saw a large crowd on both sides of the street and they told him that Bahá'u'lláh had just gone to the mosque of Sulṭán Salím. Mírzá Áqá Ján immediately went to the mosque, where he found Bahá'u'lláh uttering the verses of God in majestic tone and in great profusion. None of the companions of Bahá'u'lláh was permitted by Him to accompany Him except Mír Muḥammad and Mírzá Áqá Ján who followed. Those members of the public who were in the mosque were amazed by what they saw. So powerful were the words of Bahá'u'lláh that a Persian man who heard them was awestruck; he was trembling all over and tears flowed from his eyes. Bahá'u'lláh at one point ordered Mír Muḥammad to go and call Mírzá Yaḥyá to come with all his sins and transgressions and face his Lord.[3] Bahá'u'lláh remained in the mosque till near sunset, while Mírzá Yaḥyá and Siyyid Muḥammad stayed at home and gave some excuses to Mír Muḥammad for not attending.

Ḥájí Mírzá Ḥaydar-'Alí, who was in Adrianople at the time, has written the account of that day. This is a translation of some of his reminiscences:

> The meeting was to be on Friday at the mosque of Sulṭán Salím at the time of the congregational prayer when the

Muslims gather inside in great numbers . . . Mír Muḥammad-i-Mukárí from Shíráz who was a Bábí . . . could not imagine that Azal had broken the Covenant. So he begged the Blessed Beauty to enlighten him. Bahá'u'lláh said to him that if ever Azal came face to face with Him at a meeting place, then he could consider Azal's claims to be true. Mír Muḥammad accepted this statement as a criterion for distinguishing between truth and falsehood, and he endeavoured to bring this meeting about.

The news and date of the confrontation became known among the peoples of Muslim, Christian and Jewish religions in the city. All of them had heard of the miracles of Moses and the story of His confrontation with Pharaoh. And now they were expecting the meeting face to face in the mosque between His Holiness the Shaykh Effendi (a designation by which the people called Bahá'u'lláh to express their reverence for Him) and Mírzá 'Alí who had denied Him. (For fear of being recognized, Azal had called himself by this name.) Therefore, from the morning of Friday until before noon, a large multitude drawn from the followers of these three religions had thronged the area between the house of Amru'lláh . . . and the entrance to the mosque. The crowd was so large that it was difficult to move about.* Bahá'u'lláh, the Day-Star of Glory, emerged from His home . . . and as He passed through the crowd, people showed such reverence as is difficult to describe. They greeted Him with salutations, bowed and opened the way for Him to pass. Many of them

* The statement by Ḥájí Mírzá Ḥaydar-'Alí that the public had gathered in the streets to watch Bahá'u'lláh going to the mosque need not be viewed as contrary to Shoghi Effendi's statement that Bahá'u'lláh set off for the mosque as soon as he was informed of the arrangement. We must bear in mind that for some time Siyyid Muḥammad had been telling some of the Muslims about Mírzá Yaḥyá's readiness for a *mubáhilih*. Bahá'u'lláh obviously knew about this propaganda. When Mírzá Yaḥyá appointed the mosque of Sulṭán Salím, the sensational news spread very rapidly among the people. It appears that Mír Muḥammad, who had acted all along as a focal point for this confrontation, went to the house of Bahá'u'lláh on Friday and informed Him of the arrangements; Bahá'u'lláh then readily set off for the mosque with him. (A.T.)

prostrated themselves at His feet and kissed them. Bahá'u'lláh, the Countenance of majesty and omnipotence, in acknowledgement greeted the crowd by raising His hands (as was customary among the Ottomans), and expressed His good wishes. This continued all the way to the mosque. As soon as He entered the mosque, the preacher, who was delivering his discourse, became speechless or perhaps he forgot his words. Bahá'u'lláh went forward, seated Himself and then gave permission to the preacher to continue. Eventually the preaching and prayers came to an end. But Azal did not turn up. We heard that he had feigned illness and asked to be excused.

In every city in the Ottoman Empire, there are Mawlavís, who are dervishes and followers of Mawlaví,* the author of *Mat͟hnaví*. Every Friday they hold their services in their *takyihs* (centres of congregation) when they whirl around their master and chant certain words in unison. Inside its chambers some play music and sing delightful melodies. When Bahá'u'lláh was about to leave the mosque He said: 'We owe a visit to the Mawlavís. We had better go to their *takyih*.' As He rose to go, the Governor of Adrianople and other dignitaries, together with the divines, availed themselves of the opportunity to be in His presence and so they accompanied Him. As a token of their humility and courtesy, the Governor, the S͟hayk͟hu'l-Islám,† the 'Ulamá ‡ and other dignitaries walked four or five steps behind Bahá'u'lláh while the stream of His utterance was flowing.§ Sometimes, through His grace and loving-kindness, Bahá'u'lláh would stop and beckon the Governor and the others to walk in front. But they would refuse to do so. In this way, with

* Jaláli'd-Dín-i-Rúmí.

† The head of the Muslim ecclesiastical institution in the city.

‡ Divines and men of learning.

§ When an important person walked it was considered discourteous if his subordinates walked in front of, or abreast of him except at night when someone carried a lantern before him. In order to show their humility they always walked a few steps behind. This is how, for example, the oriental believers conducted themselves when they were walking with Bahá'u'lláh, 'Abdu'l-Bahá or Shoghi Effendi.

majesty and glory born of God, Bahá'u'lláh arrived in the *takyih*. At that time the <u>Sh</u>ay<u>kh</u> of the Mawlavís was standing in the centre and the dervishes were circling around and chanting. As soon as their eyes beheld Him, they all stopped their service without any reason. They bowed and showed their respect for Him and became absolutely silent. Bahá'u'lláh then seated Himself, permitted others who were with Him to be seated, and then He gave permission to the <u>Sh</u>ay<u>kh</u> to resume his service again.

The news was widely circulated in Adrianople that when <u>Sh</u>ay<u>kh</u> Effendi* had entered the mosque the preacher was unable to deliver his sermon and when he went to the *taykih*, the dervishes and their leader forgot their words and stopped their service. The following evening some believers attained His presence and I was among them . . . Bahá'u'lláh made these remarks: 'When We entered the crowded mosque, the preacher forgot the words of his sermon, and when We arrived inside the *takyih*, the dervishes were suddenly filled with such awe and wonder that they became speechless and silent. However, since people are brought up in vain imaginings, they foolishly consider such events as supernatural acts and regard them as miracles!' †[4]

Ḥájí Mírzá Ḥaydar-'Alí then describes how much he was touched by these words of Bahá'u'lláh. Through these words he clearly saw the difference between the ways of God and those of man. He recalls his meetings with men of eminence, leaders of religion and outstanding personalities who, without exception, were eager to publicize their slightest achievements and to exploit every opportunity through which they could enhance their fame and consolidate their positions. But this is not so with the Manifestations of God. Bahá'u'lláh, in this instance, by refuting the claims of the people who attributed miracles to Him, demonstrated that His glory does not depend upon the

* Bahá'u'lláh.

† These are not the exact words of Bahá'u'lláh, but convey their import. (A.T.)

praise of men and their actions. He stands far above the human world and is its Ruler.

The detailed news of the *mubáhilih* and Mírzá Yaḥyá's failure to appear before Bahá'u'lláh was communicated to the believers in Persia by a certain Áqá Mírzá Hádíy-i-Shírází. He wrote a full account of this event and quoted those Tablets which Bahá'u'lláh had revealed for this particular occasion. His account was widely circulated among the believers. This event, which established Bahá'u'lláh's ascendancy in the eyes of the public over one who is stigmatized by Him as the 'source of perversion', removed the veil from the eyes of many among the followers of the Báb and enabled them to embrace the Cause of Bahá'u'lláh.

It may interest the student of the Bible to note that, according to Shoghi Effendi, the Guardian of the Bahá'í Faith, the rise and fall of Mírzá Yaḥyá was clearly foretold by St. Paul in the following passages:

> Let no man deceive you by any means; for that day shall not come, except there come a falling away first, and that man of sin be revealed, the son of perdition; who opposeth and exalteth himself above all that is called God, or that is worshipped; so that he as God sitteth in the temple of God, showing himself that he is God . . .
> And then shall that Wicked be revealed, whom the Lord shall consume with the spirit of His mouth, and shall destroy with the brightness of His coming . . .[5]

Mírzá Yaḥyá's dramatic fall was accompanied by an unprecedented outpouring of revelation by Bahá'u'lláh which soon afterwards resulted in the proclamation of His Message to the kings and rulers of the world.

Shoghi Effendi, in his masterly writings, has described the momentous upsurge of Bahá'u'lláh's Revelation in these words:

The 'Most Great Idol,'* had at the bidding and through the

* Mírzá Yaḥyá. (A.T.)

power of Him Who is the Fountain-head of the Most Great Justice been cast out of the community of the Most Great Name, confounded, abhorred and broken. Cleansed from this pollution, delivered from this horrible possession, God's infant Faith could now forge ahead, and, despite the turmoil that had convulsed it, demonstrate its capacity to fight further battles, capture loftier heights, and win mightier victories.

A temporary breach had admittedly been made in the ranks of its supporters. Its glory had been eclipsed, and its annals stained forever. Its name, however, could not be obliterated, its spirit was far from broken, nor could this so-called schism tear its fabric asunder. The Covenant of the Báb, to which reference has already been made, with its immutable truths, incontrovertible prophecies, and repeated warnings, stood guard over that Faith, insuring its integrity, demonstrating its incorruptibility, and perpetuating its influence.

Though He Himself was bent with sorrow, and still suffered from the effects of the attempt on His life, and though He was well aware a further banishment was probably impending, yet, undaunted by the blow which His Cause had sustained, and the perils with which it was encompassed, Bahá'u'lláh arose with matchless power, even before the ordeal was overpast, to proclaim the Mission with which He had been entrusted to those who, in East and West, had the reins of supreme temporal authority in their grasp. The day-star of His Revelation was, through this very Proclamation, destined to shine in its meridian glory, and His Faith manifest the plenitude of its divine power.

A period of prodigious activity ensued which, in its repercussions, outshone the vernal years of Bahá'u'lláh's ministry. 'Day and night,' an eye-witness has written, 'the Divine verses were raining down in such number that it was impossible to record them. Mírzá Áqá Ján wrote them as they were dictated, while the Most Great Branch was continually occupied in transcribing them. There was not a moment to spare.' 'A number of secretaries,' Nabíl has testified, 'were busy day and night and yet they were unable to cope with the task. Among them was Mírzá Báqir-i-Shírází . . . He alone transcribed no less than two thousand verses every day. He laboured during six or seven months. Every month the equivalent of several volumes would be transcribed by him and sent to Persia. About twenty volumes, in his fine penmanship, he left behind as a remembrance for Mírzá Áqá Ján.' Bahá'u'lláh, Himself, referring to the verses revealed by Him, has written: 'Such are the out-pourings . . . from the clouds of Divine Bounty that within the space of an hour the equivalent of a thousand verses hath been revealed.' 'So great is the grace vouchsafed in this day that in a single day and night, were an amanuensis capable of accomplishing it to be found, the equivalent of the Persian Bayán would be sent down from the heaven of Divine holiness.' 'I swear by God!' He, in another connection has affirmed, 'In those days the equivalent of all that hath been sent down aforetime unto the Prophets hath been revealed.' 'That which hath already been revealed in this land (Adrianople),' He, furthermore, referring to the copiousness of His writings, has declared, 'secretaries are incapable of transcribing. It has, therefore, remained for the most part untranscribed.'[6]

15

Súriy-i-Mulúk

The unprecedented outpouring of the Revelation of Bahá'u'lláh which took place immediately after the downfall of Mírzá Yaḥyá reached its climax with the revelation of the *Súriy-i-Mulúk* (Súrih of Kings). This most momentous of the Tablets of Bahá'u'lláh is chiefly addressed to the kings of the world collectively. Revealed in Arabic, it proclaims in unequivocal terms the claims of its Author and His station in language of might and power.* To a sincere and unbiased observer, the opening paragraph alone portrays the authority and majesty of the One who announces Himself as the Vicegerent of God on earth and summons the kings and rulers of the world to renounce their possessions and embrace His Cause:

> O Kings of the earth! Give ear unto the Voice of God, calling from this sublime, this fruit-laden Tree, that hath sprung out of the Crimson Hill, upon the holy Plain, intoning the words: 'There is none other God but He, the Mighty, the All-Powerful, the All-Wise.' . . . Fear God, O concourse of kings, and suffer not yourselves to be deprived of this most sublime grace. Fling away, then, the things ye possess, and take fast hold on the Handle of God, the Exalted, the Great. Set your hearts towards the Face of God, and abandon that which your desires have bidden you to follow, and be not of those who perish.[1]

Bahá'u'lláh unveiled His station gradually and in stages. His

* Shoghi Effendi, the Guardian of the Faith, has translated parts of this Tablet into English. They are found mainly in *Gleanings from the Writings of Bahá'u'lláh*, sections LXV, LXVI, CXIII, CXIV, CXVI, CXVIII and *The Promised Day is Come*, pp. 20–21.

Declaration took place in the Garden of Riḍván in 1863.* On that historic occasion, which may be regarded as the initial stage of His announcement of the advent of the Day of God, He revealed the transcendent glory of His station to only a few of His Companions. Many of the Bábís who were assembled in that Garden to pay their last homage to Him on the day of His departure for Constantinople, had no knowledge of this declaration; they learnt of it months later. Mírzá Asadu'lláh-i-Ká<u>sh</u>ání in his spoken chronicle mentions this fact. He was a self-appointed guard of Bahá'u'lláh in Ba<u>gh</u>dád, a devoted servant who against Bahá'u'lláh's advice and in spite of his very short stature, carried a dagger under his clothes and walked behind Him in public. This is how he describes Bahá'u'lláh's departure from the Garden of Riḍván and the state of the believers left behind in Ba<u>gh</u>dád:

> Although Bahá'u'lláh had commanded the friends not to follow them, I was so loath to let Him go out of my sight, that I ran after them for three hours.
>
> He saw me, and getting down from His horse, waited for me, telling me with His beautiful voice, full of love and kindness, to go back to Ba<u>gh</u>dád, and, with the friends, to set about our work, not slothfully, but with energy:
>
> 'Be not overcome with sorrow—I am leaving friends I love in Ba<u>gh</u>dád. I will surely send to them tidings of our welfare. Be steadfast in your service to God, who doeth whatsoever He willeth. Live in such peace as will be permitted to you.' †
>
> We watched them disappear into the darkness with sinking hearts, for their enemies were powerful and cruel! And we knew not where they were being taken.
>
> An unknown destination!
>
> Weeping bitterly, we turned our faces towards Ba<u>gh</u>dád, determining to live according to His command.
>
> We had not been, at that time, informed of the great event

* See vol. I, chapter 16.

† These are not the exact words of Bahá'u'lláh, but convey the sense of what He said. (A.T.)

of the 'Declaration', that our revered and beloved Bahá'u'lláh was He Who should come—'He Whom God shall make Manifest'—but we again felt that unspeakable joy, which surged within us, overcoming our bitter sorrow with a great and mysterious radiancy.[2]

Mírzá Asadu'lláh then describes how after some time, one of the believers brought a Tablet from Adrianople and through it the friends in 'Iráq learnt of Bahá'u'lláh's well-being, His Declaration in the Garden of Riḍván and His public proclamation in Adrianople.

The second stage in the revealing of the station of Bahá'u'lláh was its announcement mainly to the members of the Bábí community, through the revelation of innumerable Tablets from Adrianople as well as the teaching exploits of some of His outstanding disciples.

And now, the final stage was this majestic proclamation to the world at large through the kings and leaders who at that time wielded great power and, together with the ecclesiastical authorities, dominated the minds of their subjects.

Centuries before, Muḥammad had sent emissaries to rulers of some neighbouring lands announcing His mission and inviting them to embrace His Faith. Those whom Muslim historians have recorded as being addressed by Muḥammad were the Sháh of Persia, the Negus of Ethiopia, the Emperor of Byzantium, the ruler of Egypt, the Governor of Damascus, and the Imám of Yamámah.*

The Báb, who had addressed the 'concourse of kings and sons of kings' in His *Qayyúmu'l-Asmá'*, and summoned them to deliver His Message to the peoples of the world, sent Tablets to only two monarchs of His day—Muḥammad Sháh of Persia and Sulṭán 'Abdu'l-Majíd of Turkey.

Bahá'u'lláh, the Supreme Manifestation of God whose

* The names of these rulers are respectively as follows: Khusraw Parvíz (Chosroes II), Aḍjamih Abjur, Heraclius, Maqawqis, al-Ḥárith Ibn Abí-Shimr, and Hawdhah Ibn 'Alí.

mission was to unite the human race under one universal Faith, issued His clarion call to the kings of the world collectively, proclaimed His Message, summoned them to embrace His Cause, urged them to carry out His counsels and warned them of the dire consequences of disobeying His exhortations.

The study of the *Súriy-i-Mulúk* and of His subsequent Tablets to individual crowned heads of the world, brings to light remarkable features of Bahá'u'lláh's indomitable spirit, His courage and His uncompromising attitude in revealing the Truth enshrined within His Revelation. Any man who, over a century ago, addressed the potentates and monarchs of the world, especially such despots as Náṣirid'-Dín Shláh of Persia and Sulṭán 'Abdu'l-'Azíz of Turkey, needed to be a master in the art of diplomacy and to couch his words in such terms as to represent himself as a humble servant at their threshold. The pomp and majesty of the kings were so awesome that in most cases a stout-hearted man would feel inhibited to approach them or express his opinions, especially if they were not in conformity with those of the kings. No man of sound mind would have attempted, a hundred years ago, to address the kings in a language ringing with authority and command, especially if he were a prisoner captive in the hands of a despotic ruler.

Who else but the Vicegerent of God on earth could have had such power and authority as to address the kings in the manner that Bahá'u'lláh would address them from 'Akká in the *Kitáb-i-Aqdas*:

> O kings of the earth! He Who is the sovereign Lord of all is come. The Kingdom is God's, the omnipotent Protector, the Self-Subsisting. Worship none but God, and, with radiant hearts, lift up your faces unto your Lord, the Lord of all names. This is a Revelation to which whatever ye possess can never be compared, could ye but know it . . .
>
> Ye are but vassals, O kings of the earth! He Who is the King of Kings hath appeared, arrayed in His most wondrous glory, and is summoning you unto Himself, the Help in

MOSQUE OF SULṬÁN SALÍM

This famous mosque in Adrianople was visited occasionally by Bahá'u'lláh

ḤUSAYN-I-ÁSHCHÍ

The cook in the household of Bahá'u'lláh
and one of his sincere followers

Peril, the Self-Subsisting. Take heed lest pride deter you from recognizing the Source of Revelation, lest the things of this world shut you out as by a veil from Him Who is the Creator of heaven. Arise, and serve Him Who is the Desire of all nations, Who hath created you through a word from Him, and ordained you to be, for all time, the emblems of His sovereignty.[3]

Some Important Themes of the *Súriy-i-Mulúk*

The responsibility of the kings

In the *Súriy-i-Mulúk*, Bahá'u'lláh admonishes the kings for their failure to heed the Message of the Báb. He addresses them in these words:

> Relate unto them, O Servant,* the story of 'Alí (the Báb), when He came unto them with truth, bearing His glorious and weighty Book, and holding in His hands a testimony and proof from God, and holy and blessed tokens from Him. Ye, however, O kings, have failed to heed the Remembrance of God in His days and to be guided by the lights which arose and shone forth above the horizon of a resplendent Heaven. Ye examined not His Cause when so to do would have been better for you than all that the sun shineth upon, could ye but perceive it. Ye remained careless until the divines of Persia—those cruel ones—pronounced judgement against Him, and unjustly slew Him. His spirit ascended unto God, and the eyes of the inmates of Paradise and the angels that are nigh unto Him wept sore by reason of this cruelty. Beware that ye be not careless henceforth as ye have been careless aforetime. Return, then, unto God, your Maker, and be not of the heedless . . .[4]

These words give us new insight into the fact that Bahá'u'lláh expected the kings, many of whom were uninformed of the Message of the Báb, to have investigated His claims and embraced His Cause. He does not entertain the thought that

* Bahá'u'lláh. (A.T.)

most of them might have been unaware of His coming or unfamiliar with His claims. On the contrary, He rebukes them for their ignorance and reveals for them the verses of God regardless of the fact that most of them were unfamiliar with His terminology. In summoning them to His Cause, He did not alter His usual style and mode of expression to suit the understanding of His readers. Thus He wrote: 'Relate unto them, O Servant, the story of 'Alí when He came unto them with truth . . .' The kings ought to have known who 'Alí was. It is the duty of man to follow the Word of God, to understand it, and to educate himself through it. Since the disciples of Bahá'u'lláh achieved this, it is expected that all men, regardless of their background and knowledge—and this includes the kings—are capable of grasping the utterances of Bahá'u'lláh which constitute the Word of God for this age.

Bahá'u'lláh further rebukes the kings for not having recognized His own Revelation. He admonishes them to turn to Him in these words:

> My face hath come forth from the veils, and shed its radiance upon all that is in heaven and on earth; and yet, ye turned not towards Him, notwithstanding that ye were created for Him, O concourse of kings! Follow, therefore, that which I speak unto you, and hearken unto it with your hearts, and be not of such as have turned aside.[5]

In another passage, Bahá'u'lláh reminds the kings of their failure to prevent the enemy from persecuting Him and His followers. He thus rebukes them:

> Twenty years have passed, O kings, during which We have, each day, tasted the agony of a fresh tribulation. No one of them that were before Us hath endured the things We have endured. Would that ye could perceive it! They that rose up against Us have put us to death, have shed our blood, have plundered our property, and violated our honour. Though aware of most of our afflictions, ye, nevertheless,

have failed to stay the hand of the aggressor. For is it not your clear duty to restrain the tyranny of the oppressor, and to deal equitably with your subjects, that your high sense of justice may be fully demonstrated to all mankind?

God hath committed into your hands the reins of the government of the people, that ye may rule with justice over them, safeguard the rights of the down-trodden, and punish the wrong-doers. If ye neglect the duty prescribed unto you by God in His Book, your names shall be numbered with those of the unjust in His sight. Grievous, indeed, will be your error. Cleave ye to that which your imaginations have devised, and cast behind your backs the commandments of God, the Most Exalted, the Inaccessible, the All-Compelling, the Almighty? Cast away the things ye possess, and cling to that which God hath bidden you observe. Seek ye His grace, for he that seeketh it treadeth His straight Path.[6]

And again:

If ye stay not the hand of the oppressor, if ye fail to safeguard the rights of the downtrodden, what right have ye then to vaunt yourselves among men? What is it of which ye can rightly boast? Is it on your food and your drink that ye pride yourselves, on the riches ye lay up in your treasuries, on the diversity and the cost of the ornaments with which ye deck yourselves? If true glory were to consist in the possession of such perishable things, then the earth on which ye walk must needs vaunt itself over you, because it supplieth you, and bestoweth upon you, these very things, by the decree of the Almighty. In its bowels are contained, according to what God hath ordained, all that ye possess. From it, as a sign of His mercy, ye derive your riches. Behold then your state, the thing in which ye glory! Would that ye could perceive it!

Nay! By Him Who holdeth in His grasp the kingdom of the entire creation! Nowhere doth your true and abiding glory reside except in your firm adherence unto the precepts of God, your whole-hearted observance of His laws, your resolution to see that they do not remain unenforced, and to pursue steadfastly the right course.[7]

General counsels to the kings

Some outstanding features of the *Súriy-i-Mulúk* are Bahá'u'lláh's counsels to the kings. He outlines for them those qualities which must adorn every crowned head. These are some of His exhortations:

> Lay not aside the fear of God, O kings of the earth, and beware that ye transgress not the bounds which the Almighty hath fixed. Observe the injunctions laid upon you in His Book, and take good heed not to overstep their limits. Be vigilant, that ye may not do injustice to anyone, be it to the extent of a grain of mustard seed. Tread ye the path of justice, for this, verily, is the straight path.
>
> Compose your differences, and reduce your armaments, that the burden of your expenditures may be lightened, and that your minds and hearts may be tranquillized. Heal the dissensions that divide you, and ye will no longer be in need of any armaments except what the protection of your cities and territories demandeth. Fear ye God, and take heed not to outstrip the bounds of moderation, and be numbered among the extravagant.
>
> We have learned that you are increasing your outlay every year, and are laying the burden thereof on your subjects. This, verily, is more than they can bear, and is a grievous injustice. Decide justly between men, and be ye the emblems of justice amongst them. This, if ye judge fairly, is the thing that behoveth you, and beseemeth your station.
>
> Beware not to deal unjustly with any one that appealeth to you, and entereth beneath your shadow. Walk ye in the fear of God, and be ye of them that lead a godly life. Rest not on your power, your armies and your treasures. Put your whole trust and confidence in God, Who hath created you, and seek ye His help in all your affairs. Succour cometh from Him alone. He succoureth whom He willeth with the hosts of the heavens and of the earth.
>
> Know ye that the poor are the trust of God in your midst. Watch that ye betray not His trust, that ye deal not unjustly with them and that ye walk not in the ways of the treacherous.

> Ye will most certainly be called upon to answer for His trust on the day when the Balance of Justice shall be set, the day when unto every one shall be rendered his due, when the doings of all men, be they rich or poor, shall be weighed.[8]

The consequences of rejection

Having counselled the rulers of the world, Bahá'u'lláh then issued an ominous warning:

> If ye pay no heed unto the counsels which, in peerless and unequivocal language, We have revealed in this Tablet, Divine chastisement shall assail you from every direction, and the sentence of His justice shall be pronounced against you. On that day ye shall have no power to resist Him, and shall recognize your own impotence. Have mercy on yourselves and on those beneath you.[9]

The call of Bahá'u'lláh and his summons to the kings fell on deaf ears. Consequently, mankind has increasingly experienced harrowing afflictions of war and the breakdown of order everywhere. The world has been plunged into such chaos and conflict that none may be found among its leaders, whether political or religious, who have the ability to rescue it from its doom and downfall. The sufferings and tribulations which have descended upon man, as foreshadowed by Bahá'u'lláh, are increasing day by day, and the process of the collapse of the old order is accelerating with the passage of time.

Grievous as is the plight of humanity, more grievous still is the fact that the generality of mankind, its leaders and its wise men, have not been able to discover the cause of their sufferings and the reason for such conflict and disorder in the world. Only those who have recognized the station of Bahá'u'lláh and embraced His Faith know that these calamities are the direct consequence of the rejection of the call of Bahá'u'lláh by mankind in general and by the kings and leaders of the world in particular. They firmly believe that there is no refuge for man today unless and until he comes under the shadow of the Cause of God.

Not only in the *Súriy-i-Mulúk* has Bahá'u'lláh warned mankind of the consequences of rejecting His call, but also in numerous Tablets revealed later He has clearly foreshadowed the torment and trials which would afflict an unbelieving humanity which turned away from its God and rejected His supreme Manifestation. These passages gleaned from the Writings of Bahá'u'lláh portray the spectacle awaiting a world steeped in perversity and heedlessness:

> 'The time for the destruction of the world and its people hath arrived.' 'The hour is approaching when the most great convulsion will have appeared.' 'The promised day is come, the day when tormenting trials will have surged above your heads, and beneath your feet, saying: "Taste ye what your hands have wrought!"' 'Soon shall the blasts of His chastisement beat upon you, and the dust of hell enshroud you.' 'And when the appointed hour is come, there shall suddenly appear that which shall cause the limbs of mankind to quake.' 'The day is approaching when its [civilization's] flame will devour the cities, when the Tongue of Grandeur will proclaim: "The Kingdom is God's, the Almighty, the All-Praised!"'[10]

Although the present day and the immediate future, as foretold by Bahá'u'lláh, are calamitous and very dark, we are reassured by His promise that the distant future is so glorious that no man can as yet visualize it. He states:

> After a time, all the governments on earth will change. Oppression will envelop the world. And following a universal convulsion, the sun of justice will rise from the horizon of the unseen realm.[11]

And again:

> The whole earth is now in a state of pregnancy. The day is approaching when it will have yielded its noblest fruits,

when from it will have sprung forth the loftiest trees, the most enchanting blossoms, the most heavenly blessings.[12]

Having familiarized the kings with His Message in the *Súriy-i-Mulúk* and having warned them of the terrible consequences which would follow if they paid no heed to it, the Tongue of Grandeur* addresses Bahá'u'lláh in these words:

> Warn and acquaint the people, O Servant, with the things We have sent down unto Thee, and let the fear of no one dismay Thee, and be Thou not of them that waver. The day is approaching when God will have exalted His Cause and magnified His testimony in the eyes of all who are in the heavens and all who are on the earth. Place, in all circumstances, Thy whole trust in Thy Lord, and fix Thy gaze upon Him, and turn away from all them that repudiate His truth. Let God, Thy Lord, be Thy sufficing succourer and helper. We have pledged Ourselves to secure Thy triumph upon earth and to exalt Our Cause above all men, though no king be found who would turn his face towards Thee.[13]

To the Christians

A challenging call awaits the 'kings of Christendom' in the *Súriy-i-Mulúk*:

> O kings of Christendom! Heard ye not the saying of Jesus, the Spirit of God, 'I go away, and come again unto you'? Wherefore, then, did ye fail, when He did come again unto you in the clouds of heaven, to draw nigh unto Him, that ye might behold His face, and be of them that attained His Presence? In another passage He saith: 'When He, the Spirit of Truth, is come, He will guide you into all truth.' And yet, behold how, when He did bring the truth, ye refused to turn your faces towards Him, and persisted in disporting yourselves with your pastimes and fancies. Ye welcomed Him not, neither did ye seek His Presence, that ye might hear

* The voice of God speaking to Bahá'u'lláh.

the verses of God from His own mouth, and partake of the manifold wisdom of the Almighty, the All-Glorious, the All-Wise. Ye have, by reason of your failure, hindered the breath of God from being wafted over you, and have withheld from your souls the sweetness of its fragrance. Ye continue roving with delight in the valley of your corrupt desires. Ye, and all ye possess, shall pass away. Ye shall, most certainly, return to God, and shall be called to account for your doings in the presence of Him Who shall gather together the entire creation . . .[14]

To the Sulṭán of Turkey

The only monarch addressed individually in the *Súriy-i-Mulúk* is Sulṭán 'Abdu'l-'Azíz of Turkey, whose royal edicts had caused Bahá'u'lláh to be confined in the city of Adrianople, designated by Him as the 'remote prison', and later in the city of 'Akká, the 'Most Great Prison'. A great part of His address is translated into English.* The opening passage alone demonstrates the majesty of Bahá'u'lláh. His words, uttered with divine authority, portray the King as a mere vassal:

> Hearken, O King (Sulṭán 'Abdu'l-'Azíz), to the speech of Him that speaketh the truth, Him that doth not ask thee to recompense Him with the things God hath chosen to bestow upon thee, Him Who unerringly treadeth the straight Path. He it is Who summoneth thee unto God, thy Lord, Who showeth thee the right course, the way that leadeth to true felicity, that haply thou mayest be of them with whom it shall be well.[15]

Bahá'u'lláh reproves the King for having entrusted his affairs to ministers who are not trustworthy and God-fearing. The corruption which existed in the court of the Sulṭán, coupled with an oppressive regime, had caused unbearable sufferings for Bahá'u'lláh and His companions. 'Álí Pá<u>sh</u>á, the Grand Vizir, and Fu'ád Pá<u>sh</u>á, the Foreign Minister, in com-

* *Gleanings*, section CXIV.

pany with other men, had been the source of oppression and tyranny in that land. No wonder that Bahá'u'lláh, the Judge and the Counsellor for mankind, should have devoted a considerable part of His address to the Sulṭán admonishing him in these words:

> Beware, O King, that thou gather not around thee such ministers as follow the desires of a corrupt inclination, as have cast behind their backs that which hath been committed into their hands and manifestly betrayed their trust. Be bounteous to others as God hath been bounteous to thee, and abandon not the interests of thy people to the mercy of such ministers as these. Lay not aside the fear of God, and be thou of them that act uprightly. Gather around thee those ministers from whom thou canst perceive the fragrance of faith and of justice, and take thou counsel with them, and choose whatever is best in thy sight, and be of them that act generously . . .
>
> Take heed that thou resign not the reins of the affairs of thy state into the hands of others, and repose not thy confidence in ministers unworthy of thy trust, and be not of them that live in heedlessness. Shun them whose hearts are turned away from thee, and place not thy confidence in them, and entrust them not with thine affairs and the affairs of such as profess thy faith. Beware that thou allow not the wolf to become the shepherd of God's flock, and surrender not the fate of His loved ones to the mercy of the malicious. Expect not that they who violate the ordinances of God will be trustworthy or sincere in the faith they profess. Avoid them, and preserve strict guard over thyself, lest their devices and mischief hurt thee. Turn away from them, and fix thy gaze upon God, thy Lord, the All-Glorious, the Most Bountiful.[16]

In addressing the Sulṭán, Bahá'u'lláh makes one of the most thought-provoking statements in this Tablet. He affirms:

> Know thou for a certainty that whoso disbelieveth in God is neither trustworthy nor truthful. This, indeed, is the truth, the undoubted truth. He that acteth treacherously towards

God will, also, act treacherously towards his king. Nothing whatever can deter such a man from evil, nothing can hinder him from betraying his neighbour, nothing can induce him to walk uprightly.[17]

In order to appreciate this statement let us remember that many people who disbelieve in God may be truthful and honest in a normal situation. But the real criterion of a man's truthfulness and honesty is his attitude at the time of temptation. When severe tests and trials descend upon man, the only thing which keeps him truthful is his faith in God. If he does not believe in God, there is no motivation within him to resist temptation.

Bahá'u'lláh continues to offer His counsels to the Sulṭán with great mercy and compassion. These few passages gleaned from His exhortations amply demonstrate Bahá'u'lláh's loving-kindness, as well as His authority.

Wert thou to incline thine ear unto My speech and observe My counsel, God would exalt thee to so eminent a position that the designs of no man on the whole earth can ever touch or hurt thee. Observe, O King, with thine inmost heart and with thy whole being, the precepts of God, and walk not in the paths of the oppressor . . .

Place not thy reliance on thy treasures. Put thy whole confidence in the grace of God, thy Lord. Let Him be thy trust in whatever thou doest, and be of them that have submitted themselves to His Will. Let Him be thy helper and enrich thyself with His treasures, for with Him are the treasuries of the heavens and of the earth . . .

Overstep not the bounds of moderation, and deal justly with them that serve thee. Bestow upon them according to their needs, and not to the extent that will enable them to lay up riches for themselves, to deck their persons, to embellish their homes, to acquire the things that are of no benefit unto them, and to be numbered with the extravagant. Deal with them with undeviating justice, so that none among them may either suffer want, or be pampered with luxuries. This is but manifest justice.

Allow not the abject to rule over and dominate them who are noble and worthy of honour, and suffer not the high-minded to be at the mercy of the contemptible and worthless, for this is what We observed upon Our arrival in the City (Constantinople), and to it We bear witness. We found among its inhabitants some who were possessed of an affluent fortune and lived in the midst of excessive riches, whilst others were in dire want and abject poverty. This ill beseemeth thy sovereignty, and is unworthy of thy rank . . .

Set before thine eyes God's unerring Balance and, as one standing in His Presence, weigh in that Balance thine actions every day, every moment of thy life. Bring thyself to account ere thou art summoned to a reckoning, on the Day when no man shall have strength to stand for fear of God, the Day when the hearts of the heedless ones shall be made to tremble.

It behoveth every king to be as bountiful as the sun, which fostereth the growth of all beings, and giveth to each its due, whose benefits are not inherent in itself, but are ordained by Him Who is the Most Powerful, the Almighty. The King should be as generous, as liberal in his mercy as the clouds, the outpourings of whose bounty are showered upon every land, by the behest of Him Who is the Supreme Ordainer, the All-Knowing . . .

Thou art God's shadow on earth. Strive, therefore, to act in such a manner as befitteth so eminent, so august a station. If thou dost depart from following the things We have caused to descend upon thee and taught thee, thou wilt, assuredly, be derogating from that great and priceless honour. Return, then, and cleave wholly unto God, and cleanse thine heart from the world and all its vanities, and suffer not the love of any stranger to enter and dwell therein . . .

Let thine ear be attentive, O King, to the words We have addressed to thee. Let the oppressor desist from his tyranny, and cut off the perpetrators of injustice from among them that profess thy faith.[18]

To the ministers of the Sulṭán

In the *Súriy-i-Mulúk* Bahá'u'lláh addresses the ministers of the Sulṭán, and reproaches them for their actions. These are a few passages:

> Say: It behoveth you, O Ministers of State, to keep the precepts of God, and to forsake your own laws and regulations, and to be of them who are guided aright. Better is this for you than all ye possess, did ye but know it. If ye transgress the commandment of God, not one jot or tittle of all your works shall be acceptable in His sight. Ye shall, erelong, discover the consequences of that which ye shall have done in this vain life, and shall be repaid for them. This verily, is the truth, the undoubted truth . . .
>
> Say: What! Cleave ye to your own devices, and cast behind your backs the precepts of God? Ye, indeed, have wronged your own selves and others. Would that ye could perceive it! Say: If your rules and principles be founded on justice, why is it, then, that ye follow those which accord with your corrupt inclinations and reject such as conflict with your desires? By what right claim ye, then, to judge fairly between men? Are your rules and principles such as to justify your persecution of Him Who, at your bidding, hath presented Himself before you, your rejection of Him, and your infliction on Him every day of grievous injury? Hath He ever, though it be for one short moment, disobeyed you? All the inhabitants of 'Iráq, and beyond them every discerning observer, will bear witness to the truth of My words.[19]

Bahá'u'lláh assures the ministers that His Mission is not to lay His hands on their treasures and earthly goods. He affirms His detachment from all else save God and states that all the treasures of the world appear as a handful of dust in His estimation and in the estimation of His loved ones. For everything shall perish except the splendours of the Cause of God. He warns the ministers of their fate:

> Know ye that the world and its vanities and its embellish-

ments shall pass away. Nothing will endure except God's Kingdom which pertaineth to none but Him, the Sovereign Lord of all, the Help in Peril, the All-Glorious, the Almighty. The days of your life shall roll away, and all the things with which ye are occupied and of which ye boast yourselves shall perish, and ye shall, most certainly, be summoned by a company of His angels to appear at the spot where the limbs of the entire creation shall be made to tremble, and the flesh of every oppressor to creep. Ye shall be asked of the things your hands have wrought in this, your vain life, and shall be repaid for your doings. This is the day that shall inevitably come upon you, the hour that none can put back. To this the Tongue of Him that speaketh the truth and is the Knower of all things hath testified.[20]

To the citizens of Constantinople

To the inhabitants of Constantinople Bahá'u'lláh also directs His admonitions and counsels. He exorts them to fear God, to incline their ears to His call, to rid themselves of pride, and to detach themselves from this world. These are some of His exhortations:

Fear God, ye inhabitants of the City (Constantinople), and sow not the seeds of dissension amongst men. Walk not in the paths of the Evil One. Walk ye, during the few remaining days of your life, in the ways of the one true God. Your days shall pass away as have the days of them who were before you. To dust shall ye return, even as your fathers of old did return . . .

Incline your ears to the counsels which this Servant giveth you for the sake of God. He, verily, asketh no recompense from you and is resigned to what God hath ordained for Him, and is entirely submissive to God's Will.

The days of your life are far spent, O people, and your end is fast approaching. Put away, therefore, the things ye have devised and to which ye cleave, and take firm hold on the precepts of God, that haply ye may attain that which He hath purposed for you, and be of them that pursue a right course . . .

Beware that ye swell not with pride before God, and disdainfully reject His loved ones. Defer ye humbly to the faithful, they that have believed in God and in His signs, whose hearts witness to His unity, whose tongues proclaim His oneness, and who speak not except by His leave. Thus do We exhort you with justice, and warn you with truth, lest perchance ye may be awakened.

Lay not on any soul a load which ye would not wish to be laid upon you, and desire not for any one the things ye would not desire for yourselves. This is My best counsel unto you, did ye but observe it.[21]

In addressing the people of Constantinople Bahá'u'lláh makes His own position clear to them:

Know ye that I am afraid of none except God. In none but Him have I placed My trust; to none will I cleave but Him, and wish for naught except the thing He hath wished for Me. This, indeed, is My heart's desire, did ye but know it. I have offered up My soul and My body as a sacrifice for God, the Lord of all worlds. Whoso hath known God shall know none but Him, and he that feareth God shall be afraid of no one except Him, though the powers of the whole earth rise up and be arrayed against him. I speak naught except at His bidding, and follow not, through the power of God and His might, except His truth. He, verily, shall recompense the truthful . . .

The day is approaching when God will have raised up a people who will call to remembrance Our days, who will tell the tale of Our trials, who will demand the restitution of Our rights from them that, without a tittle of evidence, have treated Us with manifest injustice.[22]

It is interesting to note that in His exhortations to the inhabitants of Constantinople, most of whom were Sunnís, Bahá'u'lláh extols in glowing terms the virtues and exalted station of

Imám Ḥusayn, describes his sacrifice, and prays that He Himself may similarly lay down His life in the path of God.

To the divines and philosophers

The ecclesiastical leaders of Constantinople are denounced in the *Súriy-i-Mulúk* for their waywardness and negligence in that they did not seek to attain His presence and did not investigate His Cause. Bahá'u'lláh rebukes them for being worshippers of 'names', and lovers of leadership. He grieves that they failed to recognize Him as their Lord and reckons them as being spiritually dead.

Bahá'u'lláh addresses the 'wise men' of Constantinople and the philosophers of the world. He warns them not to become proud of their learning, for the essence of wisdom and knowledge is the fear of God and the recognition of His Manifestation. He rebukes them for their failure to seek enlightenment from Him, and counsels them not to violate the laws of God, nor to pay attention to the ways of men and their habits.

To the French Ambassador

Bahá'u'lláh reproaches the French Ambassador in Constantinople for having combined with the Persian Ambassador in acting against Him without enquiring into His case. He tells the French Ambassador that he has neglected the exhortations of Jesus Christ as recorded in the Gospels, otherwise he would not have united himself with the Persian Ambassador. He warns him that soon his glory will pass away and he will have to answer for his doings in the presence of his Lord. He counsels him, and those like him, to tread the path of justice and not to follow the promptings of the evil within their own selves.

To the Persian Ambassador

A considerable portion of the *Súriy-i-Mulúk* is addressed to Ḥájí Mírzá Ḥusayn Khán, the Mushíru'd-Dawlih, the Persian Ambassador in Constantinople.* We have already referred to his activities against Bahá'u'lláh.† He was a native of Qazvín, one of the ablest statesmen of Persia, who remained in his post as Persian Ambassador in Constantinople for about fifteen years from 1270–85 A.H. (1853–68). In 1288 A.H. (1871) he was promoted to the post of Foreign Minister. Later he was dismissed. Having incurred the Sháh's displeasure he was installed as the custodian of the Shrine of Imám Riḍá in Mashhad‡ and there he died suddenly in 1298 A.H. (1881) at the age of fifty-seven. It is commonly believed that he was offered a cup of poisoned coffee by the order of the Sháh.

In the *Súriy-i-Mulúk*, Bahá'u'lláh addresses him in these challenging words:

> Dost thou imagine, O Minister of the Sháh in the City (Constantinople), that I hold within My grasp the ultimate destiny of the Cause of God? Thinkest thou that My imprisonment, or the shame I have been made to suffer, or even My death and utter annihilation, can deflect its course? Wretched is what thou hast imagined in thine heart! Thou art indeed of them that walk after the vain imaginings which their hearts devise. No God is there but Him. Powerful is He to manifest His Cause, and to exalt His testimony, and to establish whatsoever is His Will, and to elevate it to so eminent a position that neither thine own hands, nor the hands of them that have turned away from Him, can ever touch or harm it.
>
> Dost thou believe thou hast the power to frustrate His

* The full text of this particular part of the *Súriy-i-Mulúk* is translated into English and included in *Gleanings from the Writings of Bahá'u'lláh*, section CXIII.

† See chapter 3.

‡ Meshed.

Will, to hinder Him from executing His judgment, or to deter Him from exercising His sovereignty? Pretendest thou that aught in the heavens or in the earth can resist His Faith? No, by Him Who is the Eternal Truth! Nothing whatsoever in the whole of creation can thwart His Purpose. Cast away, therefore, the mere conceit thou dost follow, for mere conceit can never take the place of truth. Be thou of them that have truly repented and returned to God, the God Who hath created thee, Who hath nourished thee, and made thee a minister among them that profess thy faith . . .

If this Cause be of God, no man can prevail against it; and if it be not of God, the divines amongst you, and they that follow their corrupt desires and such as have rebelled against Him will surely suffice to overpower it.[23]

Bahá'u'lláh sternly rebukes the Ambassador, as a representative of his country, for the persecutions and sufferings which had been heaped upon the believers in Persia and especially for the supreme crime of the execution of the Báb. These are a few passages:

. . . How many those who every year, and every month, have because of you been put to death! How manifold the injustices ye have perpetrated—injustices the like of which the eye of creation hath not seen, which no chronicler hath ever recorded! How numerous the babes and sucklings who were made orphans, and the fathers who lost their sons, because of your cruelty, O ye unjust doers! How oft hath a sister pined away and mourned over her brother, and how oft hath a wife lamented after her husband and sole sustainer!

Your iniquity waxed greater and greater until ye slew Him* Who had never taken His eyes away from the face of God, the Most Exalted, the Most Great. Would that ye had put Him to death after the manner men are wont to put one another to death! Ye slew Him, however, in such circumstances as no man hath ever witnessed. The heavens wept sore over Him, and the souls of them who are nigh unto God cried out for

* The Báb. (A.T.)

His affliction. Was He not a Scion of your Prophet's ancient House? Had not His fame as a direct descendant of the Apostle been spread abroad amongst you? Why, then, did ye inflict upon Him what no man, however far ye may look back, hath inflicted upon another? By God! The eye of creation hath never beheld your like. Ye slay Him Who is a Scion of your Prophet's House, and rejoice and make merry while seated on your seats of honour! . . .[24]

Bahá'u'lláh continues in this vein and states:

Ye have persisted in your waywardness until ye rose up against Us, though We had committed nothing to justify your enmity. Fear ye not God who hath created you, and fashioned you, and caused you to attain your strength, and joined you with them that have resigned themselves to Him (Muslims)? How long will ye persist in your waywardness? How long will ye refuse to reflect? How long ere ye shake off your slumber and are roused from your heedlessness? How long will ye remain unaware of the truth? . . .

Ye perpetrate every day a fresh injustice, and treat Me as ye treated Me in times past, though I never attempted to meddle with your affairs. At no time have I opposed you, neither have I rebelled against your laws. Behold how ye have, at the last, made Me a prisoner in this far-off land! Know for a certainty, however, that whatever your hands or the hands of the infidels have wrought will never, as they never did of old, change the Cause of God or alter His ways.

Give heed to My warning, ye people of Persia! If I be slain at your hands, God will assuredly raise up one who will fill the seat made vacant through My death, for such is God's method carried into effect of old, and no change can ye find in God's method of dealing. Seek ye to put out God's light that shineth upon His earth? Averse is God from what ye desire. He shall perfect His light, albeit ye abhor it in the secret of your hearts.[25]

Having rebuked the Ambassador for the injustices inflicted on the Cause of God, Bahá'u'lláh addressed him in these words:

Despite what thou hast done I entertain—and to this God is My witness—no ill-will against thee, nor against any one, though from thee and others We receive such hurt as no believer in the unity of God can sustain. My cause is in the hand of none except God, and My trust is in no one else but Him. Erelong shall your days pass away, as shall pass away the days of those who now, with flagrant pride, vaunt themselves over their neighbour. Soon shall ye be gathered together in the presence of God, and shall be asked of your doings, and shall be repaid for what your hands have wrought, and wretched is the abode of the wicked doers!

By God! Wert thou to realize what thou hast done, thou wouldst surely weep sore over thyself, and wouldst flee for refuge to God, and wouldst pine away and mourn all the days of thy life, till God will have forgiven thee, for He, verily, is the Most Generous, the All-Bountiful . . .

I know not the path ye have chosen and which ye tread, O congregation of My ill-wishers! We summon you to God, We remind you of His Day, We announce unto you tidings of your reunion with Him, We draw you nigh unto His court, and send down upon you tokens of His wondrous wisdom, and yet lo, behold how ye reject Us, how ye condemn Us, through the things which your lying mouths have uttered, as an infidel, how ye devise your devices against Us! . . .[26]

In this part of the *Súriy-i-Mulúk* Bahá'u'lláh alludes to Mírzá Buzurg Khán,* the Persian Consul-General in Baghdád who was His implacable enemy and who had played a major part in His exile to Constantinople. He refers to him as the Minister whose name His pen was loth to mention. He denounces this haughty and arrogant man in the following passage:

For eleven years We dwelt in that land,† until the Minister representing thy government arrived, whose name Our pen is loth to mention, who was given to wine, who followed his

* For more details see vol. I, pp. 143–7, passim.

† 'Iráq. (A.T.)

lusts, and committed wickedness, and was corrupt and corrupted 'Iráq. To this will bear witness most of the inhabitants of Baghdád, wert thou to inquire of them, and be of such as seek the truth. He it was who wrongfully seized the substance of his fellow-men, who forsook all the commandments of God, and perpetrated whatever God had forbidden. Eventually, he, following his desires, rose up against Us, and walked in the ways of the unjust. He accused Us, in his letter to thee, and thou didst believe him and followed in his way, without seeking any proof or trustworthy evidence from him. Thou didst ask for no explanation, nor didst thou attempt either to investigate or ascertain the matter, that the truth might be distinguished from falsehood in thy sight, and that thou mightest be clear in thy discernment. Find out for thyself the sort of man he was by asking those Ministers who were, at that time, in 'Iráq, as well as the Governor of the City (Baghdád) and its high Counsellor, that the truth may be revealed to thee, and that thou mayest be of the well-informed.[27]

And finally, the closing passages of His address to the Ambassador reveal Bahá'u'lláh's loving-kindness as He exhorts him to piety, justice, and humility before God and His loved ones:

It is not Our purpose in addressing thee these words to lighten the burden of Our woe, or to induce thee to intercede for Us with any one. No, by Him Who is the Lord of all worlds! We have set forth the whole matter before thee, if perchance thou might realize what thou hast done, might desist from inflicting on others the hurt thou hast inflicted on Us, and might be of them that have truly repented to God, Who created thee and created all things, and might act with discernment in the future. Better is this for thee than all thou dost possess, than thy ministry whose days are numbered.

Beware lest thou be led to connive at injustice. Set thy heart firmly upon justice, and alter not the Cause of God, and be of them whose eyes are directed towards the things that have been revealed in His Book. Follow not, under any condition, the promptings of thy evil desires. Keep thou the law of God, thy Lord, the Beneficent, the Ancient of Days. Thou shalt most certainly return to dust, and shalt perish like all the things in which thou takest delight. This is what the Tongue of truth and glory hath spoken.

Rememberest thou not God's warning uttered in times past, that thou mayest be of them that heed His warning? He said, and He, verily, speaketh the truth: 'From it (earth) have We created you, and unto it will We return you, and out of it will We bring you forth a second time.' This is what God ordained unto all them that dwell on earth, be they high or low. It behoveth not, therefore, him who was created from dust, who will return unto it, and will again be brought forth out of it, to swell with pride before God, and before His loved ones, to proudly scorn them, and be filled with disdainful arrogance. Nay, rather it behoveth thee and those like thee to submit yourselves to them Who are the Manifestations of the unity of God, and to defer humbly to the faithful, who have forsaken their all for the sake of God, and have detached themselves from the things which engross men's attention, and lead them astray from the path of God, the All-Glorious, the All-Praised. Thus do We send down upon you that which shall profit you and profit them that have placed their whole trust and confidence in their Lord.[28]

Moves Towards a Further Banishment

This Persian Ambassador, the Mus͟híru'd-Dawlih, who had already succeeded in his efforts to induce the Turkish Government to banish Bahá'u'lláh twice, played an important part also in bringing about His exile to 'Akká.

Soon after the 'Most Great Separation' had begun, when the followers of Bahá'u'lláh dissociated themselves from Mírzá Yaḥyá and his supporters, Siyyid Muḥammad-i-Iṣfahání began to intensify his campaign of misrepresentations against Bahá'u'lláh. He went to Constantinople and met several times with the Persian Ambassador. In the course of these interviews he complained about Bahá'u'lláh and poisoned the mind of the Ambassador with so much falsehood and calumny that some of the authorities, who had previously been impressed by Bahá'u'lláh's uprightness and dignity, became disillusioned. And at last he succeeded, through misrepresentations and exaggerated statements, in arousing the fears and suspicion of the Ambassador. Siyyid Muḥammad also contacted high officials in the Sublime Porte and spoke to them about Mírzá Yaḥyá in highly complimentary terms, while referring to Bahá'u'lláh's activities as subversive and aimed at overthrowing the Ottoman Government.

In these shameful representations, Siyyid Muḥammad was ably aided by his accomplice, a certain Áqá Ján* known as Kaj Kuláh (Skew-cap), a retired artillery officer in the Turkish army. This man, who created many troubles for Bahá'u'lláh and His companions both in Adrianople and 'Akká, was a native of Salmás in Á<u>dh</u>irbáyján. He was originally an officer in the Persian army, then defected to the Ottomans, was installed in the Turkish army, promoted to the rank of Colonel and after some years retired in 1283 A.H. (1866). He came in contact with Siyyid Muḥammad in Constantinople and became influenced by his satanic spirit. So potent was this influence that Áqá Ján became a faithful ally and followed in the footsteps of his master till the end. When interrogated by the authorities on 1 April 1868, in Constantinople, after his arrest in that city, he testified that he had never met Mírzá Yaḥyá, but had been in communication with him through Siyyid Muḥammad. He admitted that he did not understand the writings of Mírzá Yaḥyá, nor had he seen any miracles from him. His motive for following him had been to serve the Ottoman Government. To prove this, Áqá Ján made an utterly fantastic statement. He claimed that the great majority of the people of Persia, including the wives of Náṣiri'd-Dín <u>Sh</u>áh, were the followers of Mírzá Yaḥyá! He expressed his belief that if the Ottoman Government were to support the cause of Mírzá Yaḥyá, the Persian people would relinquish their Government and come under the rule of the Ottomans. Áqá Ján pleaded that he had prepared a written

* Not to be confused with Mírzá Áqá Ján, Bahá'u'lláh's amanuensis.

statement on this subject to convince the authorities, but had not yet been able to release it.

In the course of this interrogation, Áqá Ján explained his relationship with Siyyid Muḥammad. He gave testimony that he had accompanied Siyyid Muḥammad in 1867 to the Foreign Office where they had had an interview with a certain high-ranking official. The purpose of this visit, according to him, had been to convince the Government that Mírzá Yaḥyá ought to be the recipient of the monthly allowance* and not Bahá'u'lláh. Áqá Ján affirmed that he had twice visited the Sublime Porte and delivered a petition by Mírzá Yaḥyá to the Prime Minister concerning this allowance.

It is important to note at this juncture that when the news of Mírzá Yaḥyá's misrepresentation concerning the monthly allowance reached Bahá'u'lláh, He declined to draw this allowance any more. According to the testimony of Muḥammad-Báqir-i-Qahvih-chí, who was arrested in Constantinople and interrogated on 7 April 1868, Bahá'u'lláh's refusal to receive the allowance dated from about August 1867. From that time onwards, Bahá'u'lláh had to sell some of His belongings in order to provide the barest necessities for Himself and those who were dependent on Him.

As to Siyyid Muḥammad and Áqá Ján, those two men of evil exerted every effort for a long time to discredit Bahá'u'lláh in the eyes of the authorities, while representing Mírzá Yaḥyá as a man of God endowed with great qualities. A few Turkish government officials were misled by their propaganda. Among them were a certain 'Iṣmat Effendi and Ḥájí Muḥammad Núrí. Siyyid Muḥammad, master of deception and hypocrisy, had managed to win them over by promising great favours when Mírzá Yaḥyá had established his ascendancy. One of the tricks was that he and Mírzá Yaḥyá inscribed a few words within a circle, added their numerical values and claimed that the result indicated that the conquest of Constantinople would take place in the year 1286 A.H. (1869). This circle is referred to by

* See p. 57.

Bahá'u'lláh, in one of His letters to the Governor of Adrianople, as a circle which was designed to stir up sedition. It was circulated among certain people and a copy of it reached the authorities in Adrianople and Constantinople. Mírzá Yaḥyá promised his Turkish supporters in government circles that he would emerge victorious in the struggle and would richly reward them for their help. He conferred upon Áqá Ján the title of Sayfu'l-Ḥaq (The Sword of Truth) and promised him that he would achieve the conquest of 'Iráq, while to the amusement of many, the evil-minded Siyyid Muḥammad was designated as Quddús (Holy), an appellation which was widely used in official circles.

At the same time that this propaganda was going on, Siyyid Muḥammad succeeded in creating fear in the minds of the authorities by stating that Bahá'u'lláh, with the help of His followers—many of whom were visiting Adrianople—and assisted by the Bulgarian leaders, was preparing to launch an attack on Constantinople! These false reports alarmed the Prime Minister and the Foreign Minister and resulted in the formulation of new policies which eventually led to Bahá'u'lláh's imprisonment in the fortress of 'Akká.

Interrogations in Constantinople

In order to allay the fears and clear the misgivings which Siyyid Muḥammad had instilled in the mind of the Persian Ambassador, Bahá'u'lláh sent to Constantinople from Adrianople two of His faithful disciples, Mis͟hkín-Qalam* and 'Alíy-i-Sayyáḥ.† A third believer, Jamshíd-i-Gurjí, was sent with them, mainly to help and serve them while in that city. Mis͟hkín-Qalam and Sayyáḥ had some interviews with the Ambassador, but the calumnies and misrepresentations of Siyyid Muḥammad and Áqá Ján had already made an abiding impression upon his mind. Soon their machinations resulted in the arrest and

* See vol. I, pp. 26–8.

† See above pp. 209–13.

imprisonment of Bahá'u'lláh's emissaries. Mishkín-Qalam, Sayyáḥ and Jamshíd-i-Gurjí were taken into custody in Constantinople.

Some months before this, a devoted believer from Baghdád, Ḥájí Mírzá Músáy-i-Javáhirí,* entitled Ḥarf-i-Baqá, had sent three exquisite Arab horses as a gift to Bahá'u'lláh. And now in this period, when He and His companions were living in great austerity, there was no alternative but to sell these horses. Bahá'u'lláh therefore instructed three of His servants, Ustád Muḥammad-'Alíy-i-Salmání, Darvísh Ṣidq-'Alí, and Muḥammad-Báqir-i-Qahvih-chí, to take the horses to Constantinople and sell them there with the help of 'Abdu'l-Ghaffár.† Not knowing that Mishkín-Qalam and Sayyáḥ had been taken to prison, these men went straight to a certain inn known as Kahrabárjí Khán where the former three had stayed. Upon their arrival, however, they were arrested by the soldiers who were posted in the Khán, and conducted to prison. 'Abdu'l-Ghaffár was also taken into custody. Apart from these seven Bahá'ís, the Government also arrested Áqá Ján and they were all interrogated by a commission which later submitted its findings to the Sublime Porte.

In these interrogations, which began in April 1868 and lasted several weeks, Áqá Ján tried very hard to disentangle himself from Mírzá Yaḥyá. He claimed that his own activities were aimed at gaining great political power for the Ottoman Government. But the prosecutors clearly were not impressed by his devious claims, for he was later condemned to life imprisonment in 'Akká. Each of the seven Bahá'í prisoners was interrogated according to the same general pattern. The questions they were asked were similar in every case. One of the main questions concerned the claims of Bahá'u'lláh. The Bahá'í prisoners were very discreet in their statements, for they did not wish to say anything which might play into the hands of Bahá'u'lláh's enemies. When one reads the account of the

* See vol. I, p. 211.
† See p. 411.

interrogations,[29] one marvels at their wisdom. Although some of them were uneducated, their recognition of the Faith and their understanding of the need for its protection were very profound.

One of these men was Muḥammad-Báqir-i-Qahvih-chí. He had been occupied day and night with domestic work in the household of Bahá'u'lláh. His main task was making tea for the visitors and pilgrims. Yet he spoke with truth and wisdom. When asked about the claims of Bahá'u'lláh and whether he had heard Him claim to be the Mihdí (The Promised One of Islám), Muḥammad-Báqir stated that he had never heard Him say that. The prosecutor, however, was anxious to find out who had claimed to be the Mihdí. Muḥammad-Báqir told him that it was the Báb and then spoke about His Revelation and martyrdom.

At this juncture it is important to remember that Bahá'u'lláh had advised His followers not to teach the Faith among the Ottomans. Among the many wise considerations in this injunction was the protection of the Faith. This counsel was uppermost in the minds of these prisoners when being interrogated.

Darvísh Ṣidq-'Alí was another servant of Bahá'u'lláh whose heart overflowed with His love. He spoke about the Báb and His Revelation, and when asked whether Bahá'u'lláh had claimed to be the Mihdí, he replied that he never heard Him make such a claim. Further to this question, the prosecutor wanted to know if Bahá'u'lláh had made any other claim. The Darvísh replied that Bahá'u'lláh counselled His followers to pray and fast, to observe the commandments of God and to be loving towards each other. When questioned about his own beliefs, he affirmed that he was only a servant of Bahá'u'lláh and believed in the words of His Master. He was asked what would be his attitude if Bahá'u'lláh claimed to be a Prophet of God. The Darvísh stated that he would believe in Him.

Ustád Muḥammad 'Alíy-i-Salmání was asked similar questions about Bahá'u'lláh's claims and he also responded in the same way. When Ustád Muḥammad-'Alí denied that Bahá'u'lláh had claimed to be the Mihdí, he was pressed to say what his reaction would be if Bahá'u'lláh did make such a claim? He responded by saying that obviously he would have to make his decision if and when this happened.

One of the important questions which the authorities were anxious to investigate was the nature of Bahá'u'lláh's activities in Adrianople. There were many wild rumours circulating at the time, all originating from Mírzá Yaḥyá and Siyyid Muḥammad. As we have already stated, Bahá'u'lláh did not associate with the people of Adrianople in general, nor did He involve any of them in the Faith. Yet many dignitaries of the city, including its former governors and especially Khurshíd Páshá, the Governor at the time, were attracted to Him and were among His admirers. On several occasions, Khurshíd Páshá called on Bahá'u'lláh and humbly sat at His feet. One of the most cherished yearnings of his heart was fulfilled when Bahá'u'lláh, after much pleading and insistence by the Governor, accepted his invitation and was entertained by him one evening during the month of fasting.

In the course of these interrogations the followers of Bahá'u'lláh stated that Bahá'u'lláh did not associate with people of the city, and that He met only with His own companions who would gather in His presence. When asked, one of the Bahá'í prisoners described the nature of such gatherings, and said that they met together, recited the words of God, and listened to Bahá'u'lláh's exhortations—which were to follow the teachings of God and to live in unity and peace with their fellow men.

Another important question was the relationship between Bahá'u'lláh and Mírzá Yaḥyá. They wanted to know who Mírzá Yaḥyá was, and what was the extent of his knowledge and his following. Every one of the Bahá'í prisoners testified that he did not associate with him and was not therefore in a position to know much about him. Most of them, however, said that Mírzá Yaḥyá was as a drop compared with the ocean of Bahá'u'lláh's knowledge. Here we can see again their wisdom in dealing with this controversial subject. They did not speak of Mírzá Yaḥyá's activities. They only made it clear that Bahá'u'lláh was as the light and that light and darkness cannot come together. When Darvísh Ṣidq-'Alí was asked 'How many of Bahá'u'lláh's brothers were in Adrianople?', he replied that there were only two, Mírzá Músá and Mírzá Muḥammad-Qulí! When asked who then Mírzá Yaḥyá was, he replied that he was no longer a brother of Bahá'u'lláh and was cut off from Him.*

Persecution in Egypt and 'Iráq

At the same time that the Turkish authorities had begun to put pressure upon the followers of Bahá'u'lláh and persecute them, Ḥájí Mírzá Ḥusayn Khán, the Persian Ambassador, informed Mírzá Ḥasan Khán-i-Khú'í and Mírzá Buzurg Khán, the Persian Consuls in Egypt and 'Iráq respectively, that the Ottomans had withdrawn their protection from the Bábís. Emboldened by this news, these two men embarked upon a campaign of persecution against the believers in these countries. Through the instigations of Mírzá Ḥasan Khán the authorities in Cairo arrested Ḥájí Mírzá Ḥaydar-'Alí and six other believers,† and sent them as prisoners to the Sudan, where they endured almost unbearable hardships for many years.

In 'Iráq the fore-mentioned Mírzá Buzurg Khán, assisted by Shaykh 'Abdu'l-Ḥusayn-i-'Iráqí,‡ a diabolical Muslim divine and an inveterate enemy of Bahá'u'lláh since His days in Baghdád, stirred up mischief and brought about a wave of persecutions against the defenceless community of Bahá'u'lláh's followers in that land.

At the instigation of these two men, who incited the people to rise up against the followers of Bahá'u'lláh, Áqá 'Abdu'r-

* See p. 408 for the fate of these seven prisoners.

† See Appendix III.

‡ Identical with Shaykh 'Abdu'l-Ḥusayn-i-Ṭihrání. See vol. I, pp. 142–7 passim. It is interesting to note that a grandson of the Shaykh embraced the Faith of Bahá'u'lláh and became one of its active teachers.

Rasúl-i-Qumí was stabbed to death in Ba<u>gh</u>dád. He was a devoted believer on whom Bahá'u'lláh conferred the honour of being the Saqqá* (water supplier) of His Most Great House in that city. For five years he served in this capacity with exemplary faithfulness and dedication. Before him, it was Mírzá Áqá Ján, Bahá'u'lláh's amanuensis, who carried out this function. Áqá 'Abdu'r-Rasúl and his brother Áqá Ḥusayn had embraced the Cause of the Báb in the early days of the Faith in their native city of Qum. Upon becoming Bábís they were taken to Ṭihrán and imprisoned there. The hardships in the dungeon were so severe that after two years Áqá Ḥusayn passed away. But Áqá 'Abdu'r-Rasúl endured his great sufferings for seven years of imprisonment. When he was released he went to Ba<u>gh</u>dád where he attained the presence of Bahá'u'lláh and became filled with the spirit of faith.

One day, towards the end of Bahá'u'lláh's stay in Adrianople, as Áqá 'Abdu'r-Rasúl was carrying the skin of water to the House of Bahá'u'lláh, two men approached and stabbed him fatally. He managed to drag himself to that House where he expired. Later a crowd of people gathered at the Muslim graveyard to prevent his burial there. Eventually the authorities intervened and he was buried by their order. Bahá'u'lláh, in some of His Tablets, has mentioned 'Abdu'r-Rasúl, recounted his sufferings and remembered him with much tenderness and affection. After his martyrdom He revealed a Tablet of Visitation for him and showered His bounties upon his soul.

The martyrdom of 'Abdu'r-Rasúl was only a signal for other atrocities which were committed against the members of the community in 'Iráq. Mírzá Buzurg <u>Kh</u>án, following the advice of <u>Sh</u>ay<u>kh</u> 'Abdu'l-Ḥusayn, decided to exile all the believers from Ba<u>gh</u>dád and neighbouring cities. His initial move was to arrest three believers in Karbilá and escort them to Ba<u>gh</u>dád in chains. They were the fore-mentioned <u>Sh</u>ay<u>kh</u> Ḥasan-i-Zunúzí,

* Since there was no running water in the houses, there were men whose occupation it was to carry skins full of water for household use and sometimes gardening.

Mullá Muḥammad-Ḥasan-i-Qazvíní and 'Askar-i-Ṣáḥib. These three were to be sent to Persia and handed over to the authorities in Kirmánsháh. The hardships of the journey, and the weight of chains and fetters, brought about the death of Mullá Muḥammad-Ḥasan in Baghdád, while Shaykh Ḥasan passed away in Kirmánsháh. But 'Askar-i-Ṣáḥib, who was a survivor of this torturous journey, was taken to the dungeon in Ṭihrán. However, the sufferings and privations which were inflicted upon him were so severe that after one week his soul also took its flight to the abode of the Beloved and joined its two illustrious companions in the realms of the spirit.

After these tragic events, the Consul-General continued to plot against the community in Baghdád. He tried very hard until the Governor of Baghdád agreed to banish them to Mosul. Consequently about seventy men, women and children were exiled from Baghdád amidst scenes of public derision. The Governor did everything in his power to protect the company of exiles from the onslaught of the enemy. He provided a military escort to protect them on the way to Mosul.

These refugees were subjected to severe hardships in Mosul. When they arrived, some of the inhabitants crowded on to the rooftops and threw stones at them. The shopkeepers refused to sell them food and no one would give them shelter. It took a long time for them to settle in Mosul. After much privation and difficulties most of them managed to engage in some work, sharing their modest income with each other. They remained in Mosul for about twenty years. During this period Bahá'í pilgrims going to 'Akká and returning to Persia often travelled *via* Mosul, bringing much joy and spiritual upliftment to the refugees. They also delivered gifts such as clothing and other goods from Bahá'u'lláh who wished to alleviate some of the hardship of their lives.

Notable among those who sent generous contributions were the two illustrious disciples of Bahá'u'lláh, designated by Him the 'King of the Martyrs' and the 'Beloved of the Martyrs'.*

* A more detailed story of their lives will appear in a future volume.

Their financial aid played an important part in bringing relief to the community. The pilgrims became carriers of divine love and bounty from Bahá'u'lláh. Through receiving many Tablets which He revealed for them, and through the visits of the pilgrims, the believers in Mosul remained faithful to Bahá'u'lláh and steadfast in His Cause.

One who rendered unique and valued services to the community was Mullá Zaynu'l-'Ábidín, surnamed by Bahá'u'lláh Zaynu'l-Muqarrabín* (The Ornament of Those Who are Nigh). He was one of the exiles to Mosul. For about eighteen years he acted as a shepherd to the community. Under his supervision a 'charity fund' was established—the first fund of that kind in any Bahá'í community. His knowledge and learning, his understanding of the Faith, his intelligent and well-balanced personality, together with a delightful sense of humour, endeared him to the believers and made him the focal point of the community. Bahá'u'lláh had also instructed him in His Tablets to gather the friends together, exhort them to unity and love, encourage them to deepen in the Faith, and help them to attain heavenly qualities. He spent most of his time transcribing the Writings of Bahá'u'lláh and making them available to the friends. In particular he had to make several copies of those Tablets which were addressed to some or all of the believers in Mosul, and give each one a copy.

In the course of one of his journeys, Ḥájí Mírzá Ḥaydar-'Alí visited Mosul. These few lines extracted and translated from his narrative describe the state of the community there.

> ... I attained the presence of Zaynu'l-Muqarrabín and other loved ones of God in Mosul including Áqá Mírzá Muḥammad-i-Vakíl.† The latter, owing to destitution, had to work as a cobbler in spite of old age ... The friends in Mosul, together with the person of Zaynu'l-Muqarrabín, made one remember the days spent in Bahá'u'lláh's holy presence in the

* For a brief account of his life, see vol. I, pp. 25–6.

† See *Memorials of the Faithful* for a brief account of his life. (A.T.)

holy city of 'Akká. These believers were living in the utmost unity and harmony. They vied with each other in their efforts and their services. They had no desire except first, to gain the good pleasure of the Blessed Beauty, and secondly, to attain His presence.[30]

Zaynu'l-Muqarrabín carried the weight of the community on his shoulders with great zeal and devotion until in 1885 Bahá'u'lláh advised him in a Tablet to proceed to 'Akká provided such a move did not jeopardize the state of the community. Responding to this call, he left Mosul in 1303 A.H. (1886), and with great joy entered the presence of his Beloved. He spent the rest of his life in that holy spot.

About the same time that Zaynu'l-Muqarrabín left, Bahá'u'lláh advised the friends in Mosul to proceed towards Persia or other parts of 'Iráq; He particularly stipulated that they should not go to the Holy Land. They were to be cautious and leave gradually and in small numbers. So the believers left Mosul and it ceased to be a Bahá'í centre.

16

Two Kings are Summoned

The *Súriy-i-Mulúk* was not the only Tablet addressed to the kings. Bahá'u'lláh also revealed a number of Tablets to certain kings, rulers and religious leaders individually. Two of them were revealed in Adrianople: the *Lawḥ-i-Sulṭán* (Tablet to Náṣiri'd-Dín Sháh) and the first tablet to Napoleon III.

Themes of the *Lawḥ-i-Sulṭán*

Náṣiri'd-Dín Sháh was the only monarch to have been closely involved with the Faith of the Báb from the first. He had been informed of its birth soon after the disciples of the Báb began to spread His Faith and he had witnessed its meteoric rise. His was the privilege as Crown Prince of meeting its Author face to face and hearing Him declare in ringing tones to an assembled gathering of the divines and dignitaries of Ádhirbáyján, these majestic words: 'I am, I am, I am the Promised One! I am the One Whose name you have for a thousand years invoked, at Whose mention you have risen, Whose advent you have longed to witness, and the hour of Whose Revelation you have prayed God to hasten. Verily, I say, it is incumbent upon the peoples of both the East and the West to obey My word, and to pledge allegiance to My person.'[1]

Having observed the overpowering zeal and enthusiasm of the Bábís, and having watched with fear and dismay the humiliating defeats they had inflicted on his army,* he arose

* In the days of the Báb, the believers defended themselves against their enemies. This resulted in many bloody struggles in which the Bábís

with the aid of his ministers and at the instigation of the clergy to wipe out the newly-born community from the land of Persia. The execution of the Báb, the martyrdom of thousands of His followers, the imprisonment of Bahá'u'lláh and His exile to 'Iráq, together with many atrocities which were committed against an oppressed community, all took place during his reign.

It is for this reason that Bahá'u'lláh in one of His Tablets denounces Náṣiri'd-Dín Sháh in these words:

> Among them (kings of the earth) is the King of Persia, who suspended Him Who is the Temple of the Cause (the Báb) in the air, and put Him to death with such cruelty that all created things, and the inmates of Paradise, and the Concourse on high wept for Him. He slew, moreover, some of Our kindred, and plundered Our property, and made Our family captives in the hands of the oppressors. Once and again he imprisoned Me. By God, the True One! None can reckon the things which befell Me in prison, save God, the Reckoner, the Omniscient, the Almighty. Subsequently he banished Me and My family from My country, whereupon We arrived in 'Iráq in evident sorrow. We tarried there until the time when the King of Rúm (Sulṭán of Turkey) arose against Us, and summoned Us unto the seat of his sovereignty. When We reached it there flowed over Us that whereat the King of Persia rejoiced. Later We entered this Prison, wherein the hands of Our loved ones were torn from the hem of Our robe. In such a manner hath he dealt with Us![2]

In the light of these statements, the Tablet of Bahá'u'lláh addressed to Náṣiri'd-Dín Sháh assumes a special significance. Not only was he familiar with Bahá'u'lláh Himself, whose followers he was persecuting, but because of his religious background he could follow Bahá'u'lláh's reasoning and

---

triumphed over their adversaries. Bahá'u'lláh has enjoined on His followers not to resort to force when attacked in the path of God. For a more detailed discussion of this subject, see vol. I, pp. 278–9, and above, p. 258.

terminology. However, it appears that in revealing this Tablet Bahá'u'lláh chose, in certain parts, to use unusually difficult Arabic words and phrases, so that the monarch might be forced to seek the help of the divines in reading it. And this is exactly what the King did. He passed it on to the divines and requested them to write an answer to it—a task which they did not fulfil.

The *Lawḥ-i-Sulṭán* is the lengthiest Tablet revealed to any monarch. It is partly in Arabic and partly in Persian and is composed with beauty and eloquence. A small portion of it is translated into English by Shoghi Effendi.* Although revealed in Adrianople, this Tablet was sent from 'Akká. A youth of seventeen, Badí', accepting martyrdom, took it to Ṭihrán and personally handed it to the Sháh. We shall record the life and sacrifice of this youth, 'The Pride of the Martyrs', in the next volume.

In this Tablet Bahá'u'lláh invites the monarch to look upon his people with the eyes of loving-kindness and to rule them with justice. He states that both the pomp and grandeur of this world and its abasement shall pass away. He demonstrates its transitory nature by remarking that should one open the grave of a king and that of a pauper, it would be impossible to distinguish the remains of one from the other. In that state there is no difference between rich and poor, between ruler and subject. He teaches that distinction for man lies in his deeds of righteousness and piety.

In several passages Bahá'u'lláh exhorts the King not to fix his attention on this mortal life, reminds him that there were many eminent rulers before him who have departed from this world and that no one remembers them today: their palaces lie in ruins, their treasures are dissipated, and their glory has vanished. Men of learning, scholars, and noblemen, have come in countless numbers and have gone, leaving no trace behind. Their power and influence have been obliterated and their names forgotten.

* Cited in *The Promised Day Is Come*, pp. 40–43, 46 and 75.

More than once Bahá'u'lláh urges the King to be just, and invites him to judge between Him and His enemies. These are His own words:

> Look upon this Youth, O King, with the eyes of justice; judge thou, then, with truth concerning what hath befallen Him. Of a verity, God hath made thee His shadow amongst men, and the sign of His power unto all that dwell on earth. Judge thou between Us and them that have wronged Us without proof and without an enlightening Book. They that surround thee love thee for their own sakes, whereas this Youth loveth thee for thine own sake, and hath had no desire except to draw thee nigh unto the seat of grace, and to turn thee toward the right-hand of justice. Thy Lord beareth witness unto that which I declare.[3]

Persecution of the Bábís

There is another passage in the Tablet concerning those officials who serve the King 'for their own sakes'. Bahá'u'lláh condemns the activities of these men and states that instead of working for the prosperity of the nation, their service to the King consists mainly in denouncing a few souls as Bábís, and then engaging in killing them and plundering their properties.

The history of the Faith clearly demonstrates this fact. In Persia for many decades, the authorities acquired fame and popularity among the people by persecuting the followers of the Báb and Bahá'u'lláh. The best way to destroy one's enemy was to accuse him of becoming a Bábí. The onslaught against such a man would be almost instantaneous and often fatal. Before the victim could prove his innocence, he would be faced with the most serious persecution, including death.

Ḥájí Mírzá Ḥaydar-'Alí has written the comical story of a Siyyid in Iṣfahán which illustrates this point. He says that in the early days of the Faith in Iṣfahán, he came in contact with a Siyyid who was a theological student. They became friends and Ḥájí spoke to him about the Bábí Faith. Soon he accepted the

Faith and was introduced to a few of the friends and was given some of the Writings of the Báb to read. Later, Ḥájí heard from an authoritative source that the Siyyid was not a sincere person, but that he was an informer and his real purpose was to find out the identity of the believers so as to pass this information to the enemies. Ḥájí knew that danger was looming ahead and that the believers would become a target for persecution and martyrdom. He hit on an idea which demonstrates his vigilance as well as his resourcefulness. He decided that the best way to get rid of the Siyyid was to denounce him as a Bábí. Such an accusation was sufficient to drive him out of the city. Concerning this he writes:

> I knew that the Siyyid was lodging in the school of Bídábád . . . I went to the school and informed its head . . . that the Siyyid was a Bábí and that he had in his possession some of the Bábí writings. At the same time, at my instigation, some one frightened the Siyyid and advised him to be on the alert. The Siyyid was so scared that he left all his books and belongings behind, fled the city and did not return![4]

Another story which demonstrates the dangers of being labelled as a Bábí is that of Mullá Muḥammad-i-Qá'iní, surnamed Nabíl-i-Akbar.* It is extracted from his spoken chronicle as recorded by his illustrious nephew Shaykh Muḥammad-'Alíy-i-Qá'iní. The story took place when Bahá'u'lláh was imprisoned in the Síyáh-Chál of Ṭihrán and a great campaign to exterminate the Bábís had been mounted by the Government. Nabíl-i-Akbar, a very learned and erudite divine, was not a Bábí at that time. He had arrived in Ṭihrán at the height of persecutions against the Bábís and was on his way to the cities of Karbilá and Najaf in 'Iráq. While in Ṭihrán he took up residence in a theological school headed by a certain Shaykh 'Abdu'l-Ḥusayn. This is how he describes his days in Ṭihrán:

* For more information about Nabíl-i-Akbar, see vol. I, pp. 91–5.

Shaykh 'Abdu'l-Ḥusayn [the head of the school] was not informed of divine philosophy and metaphysics.* But being interested in these subjects he used to invite me to dinner in the evenings in order to find out my views and those of other learned philosophers.

It was during this period that one of the Bábís made an attempt on the life of the Sháh.† Consequently the fire of the King's anger spread and the order to exterminate the Bábís was issued by him. In Ṭihrán two officers were made responsible for carrying out this order. They were 'Azíz Khán-i-Sardár and Maḥmúd Khán-i-Kalántar. Each day a number of people were captured and executed. The situation was so serious that any person who was falsely accused of being a Bábí would suffer the same fate and had no way of escape.

It happened that some of the students who were against my involvement in philosophy and disliked philosophers altogether . . . had gone to Maḥmúd Khán to vilify me and had accused me of being a Bábí. I was spending the night in the district of Sangilaj in the home of a physician who was a friend and well-wisher. While I was there some soldiers arrived in the early morning and took me to the home of Maḥmúd Khán-i-Kalántar. However, I managed to write a few lines to Shaykh 'Abdu'l-Ḥusayn and apprise him of my situation.

In the house of the Kalántar, I was taken to the upstairs quarters where I met an old man . . . who was arrested for the same reason. He became very sad when he saw me, expressed sympathy for me and with tears in his eyes begged God for my deliverance.

Then a strange commotion started elsewhere in the house. We heard the cries and groaning of people and realized that some others who had been arrested were being tortured and beaten by the Kalántar. Afterwards, the Kalántar came upstairs to a room opposite ours. A few minutes later, without seeking his permission I walked up to him, and

* Nabíl-i-Akbar, in his earlier days, had mastered the subjects of divine philosophy and metaphysics. It was later in his life that he went to 'Iráq, became a renowned *mujtahid* and acquired great fame.

† See *God Passes By*.

uttered words of salutation. He did not reciprocate my greetings; instead he became angry and ignored me. I asked, 'What is the reason for summoning me here?' He said, 'To carry out the orders of the Sháh.' 'What am I guilty of?' I enquired. 'Is there a greater crime', he replied, 'than being a Bábí, an enemy of religion and government?' 'This is a false accusation against me', I pleaded, 'whoever has reported me as a Bábí is my enemy and had no intention other than harming me.' I saw that my words did not make any impression upon him. Therefore I did not pursue the matter any further and submitted myself to my fate.

In the midst of all this, the secretary of Shaykh 'Abdu'l-Ḥusayn arrived and handed him a letter. After reading it, he became relaxed and happy, and began to apologize. He said 'The Shaykh wants to see you. You had better go at once.' As I rose to go, he also arose and accompanied me to the door and several times expressed his apologies.

I went to the school. The Shaykh and others were waiting for me. He was delighted to see me arrive. Curious about my arrest, he wanted to know what had caused the incident. I said, 'Ask this question from your arrogant students who wrongfully made false accusations and, without any justification, vilified me.' On hearing this, Shaykh 'Abdu'l-Ḥusayn became very angry. Addressing his pupils sternly, he rebuked them and promised severe punishment and expulsion for the culprit.

However, this incident, though without foundation, resulted in my becoming known as a Bábí among the divines and the theological students. In the end they came to the conclusion that I was a Bábí and had been arrested, but had been released as a result of intervention by Shaykh 'Abdu'l-Ḥusayn. I became so well known as a Bábí that the people in the streets and bazaars were pointing at me. Some of the theological students shunned me in the streets and kept their distance so that their cloaks would not touch mine.*

One evening, after I had become known as a Bábí, a certain Siyyid Ya'qúb, a native of Qá'in, who was living in

* The clergy had introduced this practice. They taught that if a Muslim touched a Bábí, he would be defiled.

the same school, came to visit me. Later it became apparent that he was a Bábí who had been hiding his faith. Jokingly, he said to me, 'Do you realize that you have become known in this city as a Bábí? The divines and the students call you by the name Bábí, and consider you a member of that community.' I replied, 'But these rumours are without foundation. I know nothing about this community except a mere name, have not read even one line of their writings, and have not met with any of them.' He said, 'In any case you have now become known as a Bábí. People's opinion about you is not going to change whether you read the Writings of the Báb or not. I have come across some of these Writings, but I don't understand them. Since I have found you to be without prejudice and a trustworthy person, endowed with discernment and good taste, I have brought them here with me so that you may read them. I would be grateful if you would tell me your findings and conclusions.' He then took some papers from his pocket, handed them to me and left.

I glanced through the papers carelessly and only for amusement. Because my mind was full of the words of philosophers and accustomed to their terminology, these Writings did not impress me in the least. I found them weak and devoid of any truth or wisdom. Therefore I hid them underneath my books.

Siyyid Ya'qúb came the following evening to enquire about my findings. I said, 'I had a cursory glance at the Writings, but did not find any subject worthy of attention. These poor people [i.e. the Bábís] place themselves in perilous situations in vain, and sacrifice their lives in the path of error. The common people may be excused, for they are unable to distinguish between right and wrong. But why should some men of learning tread this path and become the cause of misleading the common people? It is clear and evident that the claims of the Báb are false, and there is no need to prove that the Bábís have erred.'

Siyyid Ya'qúb became disturbed by hearing these words. For some time he remained silent and did not look at me . . . then as he arose to go he recited this poem:

How often knowledge and intelligence
Turn into a monstrous thief and rob the wayfarer.

He then addressed me in these words:

'. . . Turn thy gaze upon the inner significances and truth of these Writings so that you may see what no eye has seen, and hear what no ear has heard and feel what no heart has felt.' Then looking disappointed, Siyyid Ya'qúb left the room. For a while I meditated upon the state of the Siyyid and his thoughts. I became perturbed by his disappointment. I suspected that he was a Bábí and was aiming to mislead me . . .

In order to demonstrate to the Siyyid the falsity of the claims of the Báb and to save him from following the path of error, I took out the Writings of the Báb and began to read them carefully in order to prove the invalidity of His claims from His Own Writings. Although this was my reason for reading these Writings, nevertheless my inner being was overtaken with fear and trembling and I was disturbed. I found myself to be placed on the Ṣiráṭ * at the crossroads between death and deliverance. However, this time as I read them, to my amazement I found that each line opened a new door of knowledge before my face and a new world appeared in front of my eyes. I could not sleep that night. My astonishment increased every moment as I read and re-read these Writings. I immersed myself in that billowing sea, and like a diver acquired gems of great value. It came to pass that the truth of the Cause of the Primal Point † became as clear to me as the sun in its midmost point in the sky. I found myself possessed of a new heart, a new eye, a new soul and a new strength. All the knowledge and philosophy that I had previously learned and which were a source of pride to me, appeared as utter nothingness . . .

The following evening Siyyid Ya'qúb arrived. He became so filled with ecstasy and rapture when he heard my story that he prostrated himself on the ground. He was captivated and stunned by the news. Tears flowed down his cheeks

* See p. 74, f.n. (A.T.)
† The Báb.

and his laughter resounded through the room. After that he kept bringing more Writings to me . . .[5]

The Station of Bahá'u'lláh

Returning to the *Lawḥ-i-Sulṭán*, there is a celebrated passage in which Bahá'u'lláh describes His own Revelation in language of beauty and power:

> O king! I was but a man like others, asleep upon My couch, when lo, the breezes of the All-Glorious were wafted over Me, and taught Me the knowledge of all that hath been. This thing is not from Me, but from One Who is Almighty and All-Knowing. And He bade Me lift up My voice between earth and heaven, and for this there befell Me what hath caused the tears of every man of understanding to flow. The learning current amongst men I studied not; their schools I entered not. Ask of the city wherein I dwelt, that thou mayest be well assured that I am not of them who speak falsely. This is but a leaf which the winds of the will of thy Lord, the Almighty, the All-Praised, have stirred. Can it be still when the tempestuous winds are blowing? Nay, by Him Who is the Lord of all Names and attributes! They move it as they list. The evanescent is as nothing before Him Who is the Ever-Abiding. His all-compelling summons hath reached Me, and caused Me to speak His praise amidst all people. I was indeed as one dead when His behest was uttered. The hand of the will of thy Lord, the Compassionate, the Merciful, transformed Me. Can any one speak forth of his own accord that for which all men, both high and low, will protest against him? Nay, by Him Who taught the Pen the eternal mysteries, save him whom the grace of the Almighty, the All-Powerful, hath strengthened . . .[6]

These words attest the sublimity of the station of Bahá'u'lláh. For He attributes His Revelation to God alone, proclaims His knowledge to be innate and not acquired, describes His own utter submissiveness to the command of the Almighty and indicates that every act of His is that of God. Any unbiased observer who has spiritual insight may readily discover, from the above quoted passages, the truth of the Cause of Bahá'u'lláh. For no human being of sound mind and self-motivated, can make such a staggering claim, announce it to the kings, be persecuted as a result and stand by it till the end. Only a Manifestation of God can speak as Bahá'u'lláh did.

There is an interesting comment made by 'Abdu'l-Bahá in connection with the fore-mentioned passage: 'I was but a man like others, asleep upon My couch, when lo, the breezes of the All-Glorious were wafted over Me, and taught Me the knowledge of all that hath been.' He explains:

> This is the state of manifestation . . . it is an intellectual reality, exempt and freed from time, from past, present, and future; it is an explanation, a simile, a metaphor, and is not to be accepted literally; it is not a state that can be comprehended by man. Sleeping and waking is passing from one state to another. Sleeping is the condition of repose, and wakefulness is the condition of movement; sleeping is the state of silence, wakefulness is the state of speech; sleeping is the state of mystery, wakefulness is the state of manifestation.
>
> For example, it is a Persian and Arabic expression to say that the earth was asleep, and the spring came and it awoke; or the earth was dead, and the spring came and it revived. These expressions are metaphors, allegories, mystic explanations in the world of signification.
>
> Briefly, the Holy Manifestations have ever been, and ever will be, Luminous Realities; no change or variation takes place in Their essence. Before declaring Their manifestation, They are silent and quiet like a sleeper, and after Their manifestation, They speak and are illuminated, like one who is awake.[7]

We have previously referred to 'Abdu'l-Bahá's explanation* that a Manifestation of God is always a Manifestation and that

* See vol. I, p. 208.

He has within Him all the divine attributes long before He receives the call of Prophethood. In one of His Tablets Bahá'u'lláh gives us a glimpse of the stirrings of God's Revelation within Him in His early life. Although we shall never be able to understand fully the reality and all the implications of what took place, nevertheless the story is awe-inspiring. Bahá'u'lláh states[8] that once during His childhood, He read* the story of the bloodshed which resulted from the massacre of the tribe of Qurayẓah,† as narrated by Mullá Muḥammad Báqir-i-Majlisí.‡ He relates how He was overtaken by feelings of intense sadness and grief as a result of reading this episode. At that time He beheld the limitless ocean of God's forgiveness and mercy surging before Him. Then he beseeched God to vouchsafe unto all the peoples of the world that which would establish unity and love among them. He then describes how suddenly on a certain day before dawn, He was overcome by a condition which completely affected His manners, His thoughts and His words. It was a transfiguration which gave Him the tidings of ascendancy and exaltation, and which continued for twelve days. After this He testifies that the ocean of His utterance began to surge,§ and the Sun of Assurance shone forth and He continued in this state until He manifested Himself to man. He further testifies in the same Tablet that in this Dispensation, He has, on the one hand, removed from religion anything which could become the cause of suffering and disunity and, on the other, ordained

* In the days of Bahá'u'lláh, one of the first books children learnt to read was the *Qur'án*, followed by other books on the Islamic religion and poetry.

† The details are well known in the history of Islám.

‡ A famous divine, the author of a series of books known as *Biḥaru'l-Anvár* containing traditions of Islám and other accounts. The S͟hí'ah cherish this series as an encyclopedia of S͟hí'ah religious knowledge.

§ God bestows upon His Manifestation the power of His Words. Those who have attained the presence of Bahá'u'lláh have testified that when He spoke it was as if an ocean had gushed forth. His words were at once tender and powerful.

those teachings which would bring about the unity of the human race.

In the *Lawḥ-i-Sulṭán* Bahá'u'lláh informs the King of the exalted station which awaits him should he recognize the Source of Divine Revelation in this day. He addresses him in these words:

> O King! Wert thou to incline thine ear unto the shrill of the Pen of Glory and the cooing of the Dove of Eternity which, on the branches of the Lote-Tree beyond which there is no passing, uttereth praises to God, the Maker of all names and Creator of earth and heaven, thou wouldst attain unto a station from which thou wouldst behold in the world of being naught save the effulgence of the Adored One, and wouldst regard thy sovereignty as the most contemptible of thy possessions, abandoning it to whosoever might desire it, and setting thy face toward the Horizon aglow with the light of His countenance. Neither wouldst thou ever be willing to bear the burden of dominion save for the purpose of helping thy Lord, the Exalted, the Most High. Then would the Concourse on high bless thee. O how excellent is this most sublime station, couldst thou ascend thereunto through the power of a sovereignty recognized as derived from the Name of God! . . .[9]

The Challenge to the Divines

In this Tablet to the Sháh, Bahá'u'lláh has made a proposition of the utmost significance, a proposition which no Manifestation of God in earliest days had ever produced. He states:

> Would that the world-adorning wish of His Majesty might decree that this Servant be brought face to face with the divines of the age, and produce proofs and testimonies in the presence of His Majesty the Sháh! This Servant is ready, and taketh hope in God, that such a gathering may be

convened in order that the truth of the matter may be made clear and manifest before His Majesty the Sháh. It is then for thee to command, and I stand ready before the throne of thy sovereignty. Decide, then, for Me or against Me.[10]

With this challenging statement Bahá'u'lláh has not fallen short of His duty to establish the truth of His Cause among the peoples of the world.

In this Tablet He speaks of the divines, points out their insincerity and lack of understanding, quotes certain traditions of Islám which foreshadow the wickedness of the divines in the latter days, and states that the following passages revealed by Him in *The Hidden Words* are addressed to such people who are outwardly noted for their learning and piety, but who are inwardly subservient to their passions and lust:

'O ye that are foolish, yet have a name to be wise! Wherefore do ye wear the guise of the shepherd, when inwardly ye have become wolves, intent upon My flock? Ye are even as the star, which riseth ere the dawn, and which, though it seem radiant and luminous, leadeth the wayfarers of My city astray into the paths of perdition.'

And likewise He saith: 'O ye seeming fair yet inwardly foul! Ye are like clear but bitter water, which to outward seeming is crystal pure but of which, when tested by the Divine Assayer, not a drop is accepted. Yea, the sunbeam falls alike upon the dust and the mirror, yet differ they in reflection even as doth the star from the earth: nay, immeasurable is the difference!'

And also He saith: 'O essence of desire! At many a dawn have I turned from the realms of the Placeless unto thine abode, and found thee on the bed of ease busied with others than Myself. Thereupon, even as the flash of the spirit, I returned to the realms of celestial glory, and breathed it not in My retreats above unto the hosts of holiness.'

And again He saith: 'O bond slave of the world! Many a dawn hath the breeze of My loving-kindness wafted over thee and found thee upon the bed of heedlessness fast asleep. Bewailing then thy plight it returned whence it came.'[11]

The 'Sword of Wisdom and Utterance'

In the *Lawḥ-i-Sulṭán* Bahá'u'lláh tries to dispel some of the doubts and misgivings in the mind of the Sháh concerning the activities of the believers. We must recall that since the birth of the Bábí Faith, the authorities in Persia had been fearful of the influence of the Bábí community. The manner in which the followers of the Báb defended themselves against the onslaught of their adversaries had earned them the reputation of being men of fierce courage and immense self-sacrifice. At the same time the majority of the people were apprehensive of their intentions in furthering the interests of their Faith. The Government had accused the believers of being men of violence ever since a few irresponsible Bábís had made an attempt on the life of the Sháh in 1852. Bahá'u'lláh assures the King in convincing terms that since His arrival in 'Iráq, He has exhorted the members of the community to abandon fighting and strife, to lay down the sword, and to conquer the cities of the hearts of men with the sword of wisdom and of utterance. Bahá'u'lláh quotes passages from one of His Tablets in which He counsels the friends that it is better for them to be slain in the path of God than to slay. He states that people have misunderstood the meaning of the word 'victory' which appears in heavenly Books. Victory is not won by fighting; it is achieved by good deeds and a stainless life.

In this connection it is important to note that the followers of the Báb who defended themselves against the onslaught of the enemy, did so because of the special circumstances under which the Faith of the Báb was born and His Message propagated. To appreciate this, we must become familiar with the conditions prevailing at that time in Persia within the Shí'ah community, and the nature of the Revelation of the Báb.

Let us recall that all the Manifestations of God prior to the Revelation of the Báb appeared within the cycle of prophecy which began with Adam,* as the first Manifestation of God of that cycle, and culminated with the Dispensation of Muḥammad who was the Seal of the Prophets. They, one and all, prophesied the advent of the Day of God and recounted their visions of the 'Glory of God' manifesting Himself to mankind.

The main objects of the Báb in revealing Himself were to herald the Revelation of Bahá'u'lláh and prepare the people for His coming, to close the cycle of prophecy and to open the cycle of fulfilment when the 'Glory of God' would be manifested as foretold in the heavenly Books.† Islám, the last Dispensation in the chain of the Prophetic Cycle, was therefore more closely involved with the Revelation of the Báb than any other religion.

The Báb appeared among the people of Islám. His Message was eagerly anticipated by them, as both Shí'ah and Sunní expected the appearance of the Qá'im or Mihdí respectively. This expectation was based on the prophecies of Muḥammad and the Imáms, especially the latter who had left thousands of traditions concerning the appearance of the Qá'im.‡ To the Islamic community, the coming of the Promised One was real and had been explicitly foretold. The Shí'ah among whom the Báb appeared lauded the glory of the Qá'im in their meetings, fervently prayed for His advent and rose to their feet at the mention of His name. That the Báb had a special link with Islám is not due merely to the fact that He was born a Muslim and was Himself a Siyyid, a descendant of the Prophet Muḥammad, but lies in His special Mission to terminate the Dispensation of Muḥammad and abrogate its laws. So tremendous was this function that its mere contemplation cast terror into the hearts and souls of men in Persia. Even some of the followers of the Báb, those who had not fully appreciated the significance

* According to Bahá'í belief the Biblical story of Adam is allegorical and He was the first Manifestation of God in recorded history (see *Some Answered Questions* by 'Abdu'l-Bahá).

† See pp. 16–18.

‡ See vol. I, pp. 193–4.

and potency of His Revelation, lost their faith when they heard the annulment of Qur'ánic Law being proclaimed at the conference of Badasht* by a distinguished band of His disciples a little more than four years after the Declaration of the Báb. To abrogate the twelve-hundred-year-old law of Islám was not a light matter. People had cherished it for centuries and had shaped their lives and conduct in accord with its provisions. To annul these by a stroke of the Pen needed not only divine power, but also divine wisdom and mercy.

The Manifestations of God do not change the laws of old suddenly or prematurely, nor do they reveal new laws until their followers are ready and able to carry them out. Bahá'u'lláh explains:

> Know of a certainty that in every Dispensation the light of Divine Revelation has been vouchsafed to men in direct proportion to their spiritual capacity. Consider the sun. How feeble its rays the moment it appeareth above the horizon. How gradually its warmth and potency increase as it approacheth its zenith, enabling meanwhile all created things to adapt themselves to the growing intensity of its light. How steadily it declines until it reacheth its setting point. Were it all of a sudden to manifest the energies latent within it, it would no doubt cause injury to all created things . . . In like manner, if the Sun of Truth were suddenly to reveal, at the earliest stages of its manifestation, the full measure of the potencies which the providence of the Almighty hath bestowed upon it, the earth of human understanding would waste away and be consumed; for men's hearts would neither sustain the intensity of its revelation, nor be able to mirror forth the radiance of its light. Dismayed and overpowered, they would cease to exist.[12]

Through His mercy, the Manifestation of God introduces new laws and ordinances gradually, and leads His followers from one world into another, stage by stage, knowing too

* For more information see *The Dawn-Breakers*.

well that they are attached to their age-long traditions and habits. For instance, when Muḥammad appeared, the Arabs consumed intoxicating drinks to excess. But the Prophet did not forbid drinking at once. At first, He merely remarked that it had advantages and disadvantages but stated that the harm such drinks inflicted on them was far greater than the good. Later in His ministry He forbade those who were drunk to take part in congregational prayer and, later still, when His followers had acquired maturity, He denounced drinking categorically and enjoined on them to abstain.*

The Báb and Bahá'u'lláh have likewise revealed the laws of religion at those times in Their ministries when Their followers were ready to receive them. The Báb did not reveal the bulk of His laws until half-way through His ministry. Bahá'u'lláh also revealed the *Kitáb-i-Aqdas*, the Book of His Laws, when His ministry had run half its course, and even then, it was some years before He released a copy of this Book to His followers.

Another feature of the Revelation of the Báb, relating to this subject, is the fact that His Dispensation was destined to be very short in duration and was to be superseded by the Revelation of Bahá'u'lláh. This meant that the Báb formulated only those laws and teachings which were vital to the progress of His Cause during a short space of time. Knowing that His Revelation was only a stepping-stone to a universal Revelation, He deliberately refrained from touching upon those teachings which were premature and which were ordained later by Bahá'u'lláh as His followers acquired capacity for them.

One such teaching practised in Islám and which the Báb did not alter because of the conditions prevailing at the time, was that of taking up arms and defending oneself for the sake of one's religion. That is why the Bábís took part in many battles which were defensive in nature. They were seldom involved in an offensive whether individually or collectively. The struggles of Mázindarán, Zanján and Nayríz are clear examples.†

* See *Qur'án* ii. 219, iv. 43 and v. 93–4.

† See *The Dawn-Breakers*.

From the early days of His ministry, Bahá'u'lláh on numerous occasions counselled the Bábís to abandon this age-old practice of fighting for one's religion. But it was some years before the believers realized that a new day had dawned and that they were to sheathe their swords for good. Eventually Bahá'u'lláh, in the *Kitáb-i-Aqdas*, prohibited the carrying of arms by individuals unless it was essential.

The Sufferings of Bahá'u'lláh

In the following passages in the *Lawḥ-i-Sulṭán* Bahá'u'lláh dwells on the sufferings which He had endured in the path of God:

> I have seen, O Sháh, in the path of God what eye hath not seen nor ear heard . . . How numerous the tribulations which have rained, and will soon rain, upon Me! I advance with My face set towards Him Who is the Almighty, the All-Bounteous, whilst behind Me glideth the serpent. Mine eyes have rained down tears until My bed is drenched. I sorrow not for Myself, however. By God! Mine head yearneth for the spear out of love for its Lord. I never passed a tree, but Mine heart addressed it saying: 'O would that thou wert cut down in My name, and My body crucified upon thee, in the path of My Lord!' . . . By God! Though weariness lay Me low, and hunger consume Me, and the bare rock be My bed, and My fellows the beasts of the field, I will not complain, but will endure patiently as those endued with constancy and firmness have endured patiently, through the power of God, the Eternal King and Creator of the nations, and will render thanks unto God under all conditions. We pray that, out of His bounty—exalted be He—He may release, through this imprisonment, the necks of men from chains and fetters, and cause them to turn, with sincere faces, towards His Face, Who is the Mighty, the Bounteous. Ready is He to answer whosoever calleth upon Him, and nigh is He unto such as commune with Him.[13]

Bahá'u'lláh also reminds the King that all the Prophets and

Messengers of God have suffered at the hands of their own people, and yet no one reflects on the cause of such behaviour. He speaks of Muḥammad and names some of His enemies who strenuously opposed and denounced Him. He also tells the story of Jesus and the cruel judgement passed on Him by religious leaders.

In the *Lawḥ-i-Sulṭán*, Bahá'u'lláh dwells on the trials and persecutions which He Himself has endured in the path of God. He speaks about His imprisonment in the Síyáh-Chál, recounts the sufferings which were inflicted upon Him in that dark and pestilential subterranean dungeon, recalls His deliverance from that prison through the power of God, and His exile to 'Iráq by the order of the King, after His innocence had been established. He further acquaints the Sháh with conditions in 'Iráq: the opposition of the Shí'ah clergy, their plotting and vicious attacks which resulted in His advising some of His companions to seek the protection of the Governor of 'Iráq.* He describes His arrival in Constantinople, and foretells His future exile to and imprisonment in 'Akká, a city described by Him in these words:

> According to what they say, it is the most desolate of the cities of the world, the most unsightly of them in appearance, the most detestable in climate, and the foulest in water. It is as though it were the metropolis of the owl.[14]

In a passage in the *Lawḥ-i-Sulṭán* written with great eloquence and power, Bahá'u'lláh prophesies in unequivocal language the triumph of His Cause when people will enter it in troops.

He declares that in past Dispensations, God established the ascendancy of His Cause through afflictions and sufferings. He prays that in this day these calamities may also act as a buckler to protect His Faith, and makes the following statement concerning trials and tribulations suffered in the path of God:

* This is a reference to those companions whom Bahá'u'lláh advised to enrol themselves as subjects of the Ottoman Government.

By Him Who is the Truth! I fear no tribulation in His path, nor any affliction in My love for Him. Verily God hath made adversity as a morning dew upon His green pasture, and a wick for His lamp which lighteth earth and heaven.[15]

The Story of a Martyr

Concerning the believers in this Dispensation, Bahá'u'lláh states that they regard their religion to be the true Faith of God and therefore have renounced their lives in His path and for His sake. He affirms that this act alone is evidence of the truth of their Cause. For no person will normally renounce his life unless he is insane. Bahá'u'lláh, however, dismisses the charge of insanity on the grounds that it cannot be brought against countless men of distinguished conduct and virtuous character who have sacrified their lives in the path of God. He describes some of the persecutions which were, for twenty years, inflicted upon the community by order of the King. So fierce had been the onslaught that there was no land which had not been dyed with their blood! How many children had been made fatherless, how many fathers had lost their children, and how many mothers had not dared, through fear and dread, to mourn over their slaughtered children! Yet, He testifies, the fire of divine love which burned within the hearts of these people was so bright that even if they were to be hewn in pieces, they would not forswear the love of their Lord.

The history of the Faith depicts the lives and martyrdom of thousands of believers throughout Persia, and amply testifies to their faith and detachment, their heroism and self-sacrifice. It also vividly portrays the harrowing circumstances in which the families of martyrs suffered, and recounts the excruciating afflictions which assailed them from every direction. The stories of the martyrs in various parts of Persia have been written in detail and some have been published. A great wave of sadness descends upon the heart when one reads them. For instance, the accounts of the suffering and persecution heaped upon the martyrs and their families, as portrayed in the *History of the Martyrs of Yazd*, are so heart-rending that seldom can one read even a few pages without being overcome with deep sorrow and agonizing grief.

The martyrdom of Ḥájí Mírzáy-i-Ḥalabí-Sáz (tinsmith), one of the most devoted followers of Bahá'u'lláh in Yazd, is an episode from that history. It happened during one of the most grievous upheavals in Yazd in the summer of 1903 when a great number of Bahá'ís were savagely martyred within a few days:

> On the anniversary of the birth of the Prophet Muḥammad [17 Rabí'u'l-Avval], a religious festival, a group of men gathered outside the house of Ḥájí Mírzá. For a considerable time they viciously pelted the door of the house with stones and broke all the windows. They behaved with such vulgarity that eventually Ḥájí Mírzá appeared on the roof of the house* above the porch and demanded an explanation. Some of the men felt embarrassed as soon as they saw Ḥájí Mírzá; they bowed their heads in shame and left. Some of the younger ones continued their acts of violence but were eventually calmed by Ḥájí Mírzá's words and left also . . . However they returned again after sunset and continued throwing stones into the courtyard for about three hours.
>
> Following his usual practice, Ḥájí Mírzá left in the early hours of the morning for the home of Ḥájí Mírzá Maḥmúd-i-Afnán † where the friends gathered to pray at the Mashriqu'l-Adhkár.‡ He stayed there until the prayers ended just

* Houses in Yazd have flat roofs easily accessible by a staircase from inside. (A.T.)

† Son of the illustrious Ḥájí Muḥammad-Taqí, the Vakílu'd-Dawlih, a cousin of the Báb. (A.T.)

‡ Literally, 'The Dawning-Place of the mention of God', a Bahá'í House of Worship. Although there were not 'Houses of Worship' in Yazd, the believers gathered at someone's home and referred to it as the Mashriqu'l-Adhkár. Bahá'u'lláh has particularly indicated the merits of attending the service before dawn; prayers said at that time have a special potency. (A.T.)

before sunrise. As everybody was about to go, Ḥájí Mírzá expressed a desire to bid farewell to them all, as he thought that he might never see them again.* He embraced everyone and said farewell to them. Ḥájí Mírzá Maḥmúd advised Ḥájí Mírzá not to go home for a while but to wait and see what would transpire during the day. But he went home saying 'Whatever is God's will, will happen.'

Ḥájí Mírzá was busy working at home during the morning when a number of men appeared outside his door, headed by a certain Ḥasan-i-Mihrízí, an unusually strong and well-built person. He kicked the door open and the crowd poured in. Ḥájí Mírzá was cutting a piece of glass at the time, while his wife and three young children sat beside him. Ḥasan-i-Mihrízí, who was at the front of the crowd and carried a heavy chain,† took Ḥájí Mírzá by the hand, violently dragged him out of the house and beat him savagely with the chain. The crowd surged forward and everybody began beating the victim. They attacked him fiercely, some with sticks or stones, others with chains, yet others with bare hands. They beat him so much that he fell on the ground dazed and bleeding all over.

The wife of Ḥájí Mírzá, in desperation, pushed her way through the crowd and threw herself on the wounded body of her husband.‡ But the crowd beat her with sticks and chains, and wounded her badly. They tried hard to push her away from the body of her beloved, but she clung on top of him for some time. The children, near the crowd, were

* The upheaval in Yazd, although it lasted only a few days, witnessed the martyrdom of many people. Every Bahá'í family was engulfed in its fury and no one felt safe. (A.T.)

† Violent men in those days carried a large steel chain as a weapon. A few lashings of the chain often caused serious injuries. (A.T.)

‡ Women in those days did not usually become involved in public affairs. They led a sheltered life and in public wore a *c͟hádur* (a large piece of cloth which covers the head and all other clothing and reaches almost to the ground). It was against the laws of religion for a man who was not married to a woman, or not a close relative, to see her face, how much more shocking to touch her body. The fact that Ḥájí Mírzá's wife, wearing her *c͟hádur*, pushed her away through a crowd of men, is indicative of her utter desperation and distress. (A.T.)

screaming and frightened to death. God knows what the children went through. The eldest son, 'Ináyatu'lláh, was eleven, the eldest daughter, Riḍván, was nine and the youngest, Ṭúbá, was six years old. After a while, the attackers succeeded in separating husband and wife. Although his body was battered and covered with blood from head to toe, Ḥájí Mírzá was dragged towards the home of the Imám-Jum'ih,* accompanied by a crowd which by now numbered about two hundred. No sooner did they drag him a few steps then his wife managed to throw herself on his body again, but the crowd removed her. Nevertheless she managed to cling to him yet again. This time they beat her harder than before until she fell unconscious in the street. Then they took Ḥájí Mírzá away. In the meantime a number of people had entered the house and were busy plundering everything they could find . . .

As to the children of that glorious martyr, they were wailing and weeping beside their beloved mother who had fallen on the ground unconscious . . . Then a few women arrived and took away a scarf which had covered her head.† Her body had been so badly beaten by chains and sticks, and kicked by so many, that her thin dress was torn and she lay almost naked on the ground. At last a certain woman by the name of Rubábih, who was known to be a prostitute, showed a truly magnanimous spirit. She went to her home, which was close to the house of Ḥájí Mírzá, brought an old *chádur*, spread it over the injured woman and tried in vain to revive her. In the meantime the children were sobbing unceasingly; their grief knew no bounds. Rubábih did all

* The religious dignitary of the city who leads men in prayer in the mosque. It was the practice to bring any one accused of being a Bahá'í to the presence of a *mujtahid*, where he would be required to recant his faith if he wished to be set free. The *mujtahids* would pass the death sentence on those who refused to recant. But quite often in that upheaval in Yazd, the attackers killed their victims before going through this procedure. (A.T.)

† This act was designed to further humiliate the wife of Ḥájí Mírzá, as it was considered grossly unchaste if a woman displayed her hair in public. (A.T.)

she could to comfort them, and carried their mother on her back to her home.* There she prepared a herbal infusion, gave some to the children and administered some to their mother, who regained consciousness after about two hours. But the children had cried so much that they were exhausted.

As soon as she was able, Ḥájí Mírzá's wife . . . asked for news of her husband and was told that he was taken to the Castle [Government headquarters] and that the Prince † was treating him with the utmost kindness . . . On hearing this she broke down in tears. Rubábih consoled her, saying, 'Thanks to God, Ḥájí is safe, you should try not to weep in front of the children as they have suffered greatly' . . . She helped Ḥájí Mírzá's wife . . . to her feet and carried her home with the children. The house was thoroughly plundered. The furniture, carpets, clothes, even doors of the rooms were taken away. Nothing of any value was left. They could not close the door of the house as it had been broken and thrown on the ground.

The mother, covered all over with wounds, and the grief-stricken children, took refuge in the house and were sobbing most bitterly until about midday, when a woman ‡ brought tidings from Ḥájí Mírzá Maḥmúd-i-Afnán that Ḥájí Mírzá had walked unaided to the Castle and was well. She conveyed further words of comfort from Afnán, as-

* In this incident Rubábih showed great courage in going to help the victim. Normally in such circumstances, no one dared to extend assistance to a Bahá'í, for he himself would then be accused of being one. In this case, it appears that Rubábih, herself an outcast because she was a prostitute, did not fear retaliation from the public. (A.T.)

† Prince Maḥmúd Mírzá, the Jalálu'd-Dawlih, a son of Prince Mas'úd Mírzá, the Ẓillu's-Sulṭán. He tried to stop the massacre of Bahá'ís but failed. For three days he lost effective control and during this time many lost their lives. Some years later he was in London at the time when 'Abdu'l-Bahá visited that city. He went especially to attain the presence of 'Abdu'l-Bahá, threw himself at His feet and asked for forgiveness. (A.T.)

‡ In the massacre of 1903 in Yazd, it was mainly Bahá'í women who acted as news carriers and messengers. It was not easy for the public to detect their identity, because they wore veils. (A.T.)

suring her that Ḥájí Mírzá was now in a safe place and would return home in the evening. This news brought some relief. Rubábih although fearful that she might be attacked, managed to bring some food for the children and their mother. In the meantime, since the house had no door, women and children* came in frequently to see if there was anything left to take away.

The mother and her children had taken refuge in the corner of a room waiting for darkness and Ḥájí Mírzá's arrival . . . with the help of Rubábih they cooked a simple broth to be served to Ḥájí Mírzá when he should return. But he did not come.

As to Ḥájí Mírzá, the crowd were taking him to the home of the Imám-Jum'ih. When they reached the entrance of Muṣallá,† however, a certain man by the name of Ḥasan the son of Rasúl-i-Mu'ayyidí stepped forward and called on Ḥájí Mírzá to utter imprecations against the Bahá'í Faith. Ḥájí Mírzá only gazed at him and did not respond. Ḥasan repeated his demand. Ḥájí said 'You are neither a judge of religious law nor of common law. It is none of your business. When they take me to the proper authority I shall answer questions.' On hearing this, Ḥasan went to the nearby butcher's shop, took a cleaver, and with a powerful stroke slashed Ḥájí Mírzá's skull open. With another stroke he hacked off his arm . . .

In the meantime two or three government officials arrived at the scene and took the injured man to the Government house at the Castle. Ḥájí Mírzá possessed such spiritual strength that in spite of his severe injuries he managed to walk to the Castle. Only upon arrival inside the corridor did he fall to the ground, but regained consciousness a few minutes later . . . The crowd went as far as the Castle and then dispersed . . . Ḥájí Mírzá took out his American watch which was adorned with the picture of the Master on the

* It was against the principle of chastity if men went into someone's house without giving ample warning to allow the women to retire to the inner apartments, or to wear their veils. But women could walk in freely. (A.T.)

† A mosque in Yazd. (A.T.)

back and gave it to a certain Áqá Mullá Muḥammad-'Alí* to deliver it to his wife and children . . . In the meantime the executioner had tied his own apron on Ḥájí's head, but blood was pouring out and he was becoming weaker . . . until he expired. Thus he attained to the exalted station of martyrdom. The executioner unwound the apron from Ḥájí Mírzá's head and placed it on his face . . .

After dark the Governor . . . sent for Ḥájí Mírzá Maḥmúd-i-Afnán and asked him to send someone to remove the body about two hours after sunset and bury it. Accordingly . . . the custodian of the Buq'atu'l-Khaḍrá † called at the Castle. He carried the body of Ḥájí Mírzá on his back to the Buq'atu'l-Khaḍrá and buried it there. Ḥájí Mírzá was thirty-eight years old when martyred.

The family of Ḥájí Mírzá remained unaware of his martyrdom that night. They stayed awake till morning, anxious and expectant of his safe arrival home. The children were tense and continually asked about their father. The mother did her best to assure them that he would come soon. But time passed, and when it was four hours after sunset the night curfew guards went on duty around the city. Thus any hope of Ḥájí Mírzá's arrival faded. The children could not sleep. The mother, in pain from her many wounds and injuries, was highly distressed and could not sleep either. She waited till the dawn and when her husband did not return, she went, in spite of her condition, to the home of Ḥájí Mírzá Maḥmúd-i-Afnán to enquire about him. As soon as his eyes fell on her, Ḥájí Mírzá Maḥmúd could not contain his grief and began to weep. This was how Ḥájí Mírzá's wife learned of the martyrdom of her husband. God alone knows the state of her mind at that time and the agony that

* He was one of the believers who were taken into custody by order of the Imám-Jum'ih. These men were there when Ḥájí Mírzá arrived and watched him die. (A.T.)

† The Afnán family in Yazd built a private cemetery not far from the Castle. This was later offered for use as a Bahá'í burial ground. Bahá'u'lláh designated it the Buq'atu'l-Khaḍrá (The Verdant Spot). Several of the Afnáns, Bahá'í martyrs, and eminent Bahá'ís are buried there. The cemetery is no longer in use. (A.T.)

she went through! She wept ceaselessly, and returned home broken and shattered. The children, on the other hand, were waiting for their mother to bring their father back. But when they saw her alone and in such a state of anguish, they realized what had happened. Their heart-rending cries and wails of lamentation could be heard in all directions. We can feel the agony of their hearts when we reflect on their condition. The house was completely empty, the father had been killed, the mother wounded and the people had arisen against them.

Two days later, a woman maliciously spread rumours that Ḥájí Mírzá's wife had been putting poison in public cisterns* in the town. This gross accusation was an excuse for some . . . women to make an attempt on her life. As she was sitting with her children in a corner of the house lamenting her bereavement and praying to God, suddenly a group of women, sixty or seventy strong, entered the house, pushed her down on the ground and began to beat her with the intention of taking her life. The children were thrown about by that cruel and bloodthirsty mob, which created a great commotion in the house. However, the Kad-Khudá † and his men were speedily informed. They rushed to the spot, forced their way through the crowd and found that Ḥájí Mírzá's wife had been unconscious on the ground for about half an hour and the attackers were still beating her . . . These savage women were convinced that she was dead when the Kad-Khudá and his men drove them out.

Ḥájí Mírzá's wife lay on the ground, her clothes torn, her body naked and her flesh covered in blood and dust. Pieces of her torn clothing could be seen scattered around her. The Kad-Khudá, overcome by feelings of shame, was embarrassed to look at her exposed body and therefore left. The children who had been brutally handled for a long time, found themselves standing around the battered body of their

* Public cisterns with cooling towers built in each district of the city used to supply drinking water to the public. People filled jugs of water at the cistern and took them home. (A.T.)

† The chief officer of a district.

mother. There was no one to look after them except an old grandmother who was herself an invalid.

But God demonstrated His might and power that day. His mercy and compassion descended upon the children. After an hour, the lifeless body of their mother began to move. Soon she regained consciousness. Rubábih brought some clothes and put them on her.

On hearing that Ḥájí Mírzá's wife was alive, the group of women were determined to go back and put an end to her life. But in spite of the fact that she was unable to move, the Kad-Khudá managed to carry her out of the house. She was taken to the Government house in the Castle . . . Shaykh Muḥammad-Ja'far-i-Sabzivárí, who was a *mujtahid*, undertook to protect her . . . He sent for a certain woman, Bíbí Bagum . . . and asked her to keep the unfortunate woman in her home and to look after her until the situation improved.

For twenty days, Ḥájí Mírzá's wife was kept in the home of Bíbí Bagum. During this period the innocent young children, wronged and oppressed, their parents taken from them, stayed in the ruins of their plundered home with an old sick grandmother. They merely existed, in a state of perpetual fear and expectation,—they feared for their lives, thinking they would be killed too, while their hearts were in a state of expectation of their mother's return. The children suffered so much that after twenty days their bodies looked like mere skeletons, and their faces had the colour of a corpse. Many people who passed by threw stones into the house, reviled them and used foul language.* Each time they heard the shouts of cursing and execration, the children thought the people were coming to kill them and would be frightened to death. They would run towards the frail body of their grandmother and throw themselves on her bosom. The agony of bereavement so tortured the eldest son,

* In many cities, especially in Yazd, the enemies of the Faith often gathered outside the houses of the believers where they shouted curses and execrated the names of the Founders of the Faith. These fanatical and savage outbursts throughout the years, and especially during the massacre of 1903, cast terror into the hearts of the inhabitants of these houses. (A.T.)

'Ináyatu'lláh, that he became seriously ill and lay in the corner of a room. The other children suffered so much that they came very close to death. They often asked their grandmother 'What have we done that people kill us?' No pen can bear to write the agony which the children went through . . .

Eventually, after twenty days, when the situation had become somewhat more peaceful, the mother came back with much fear and trepidation.[16]

Ḥájí Muḥammad-Ṭáhir-i-Málmírí, the author of the *History of the Martyrs of Yazd*, concludes the account of Ḥájí Mírzá's martyrdom with the following words of his widow. She recounted to him the agony of her heart when she returned home and found her children almost lifeless.

'God is my witness, when I arrived home, I saw three children whom I could not recognize as my own. I wanted to know where my children were; my mother said to me: "These are your children!" When I was assured that they were indeed my children, I was plunged into such a state of agony and distress that all my sufferings of the past paled into insignificance.' She said to me, 'Even now as I recount the story after all these years, my whole body is seized with fear and trembling.'[17]

The same author, in his unpublished 'History of the Faith in the Province of Yazd', has written the following account giving us another glimpse of the sufferings inflicted upon the children of Ḥájí Mírzá while their mother was kept in custody:

Zaynal-i-'Arab was a neighbour of Ḥájí Mírzá. The roof of his house was joined to that of Ḥájí Mírzá's house. One evening during the upheaval of Yazd, Zaynal was told by some violent men in Mír-Chaqmáq* that, since he was a neighbour of Ḥájí Mírzá's, they suspected him of being a

* An important square in Yazd with a famous mosque and minaret. In those days it was a centre of religious festivities.

Bahá'í. The fact however was that Zaynal, far from being a Bahá'í, was a vile man and foremost among the trouble-makers of Yazd. When such an accusation was levelled against him, he became so angry that he decided to go and kill the wife of Ḥájí Mírzá and her three children. He went home immediately, took up his revolver, tied a cartridge belt around his waist and went up the stairs onto the roof* of his own house. From there he crossed to the roof of Ḥájí Mírzá's house and began to shout abuse and utter curses. He loaded the gun and announced in a loud voice in vulgar terms his intention of going down the steps to kill the ... children of Ḥájí Mírzá. At that time the children were sitting in a corner around their old grandmother. The ugly figure of Zaynal, shouting abuse and standing on the roof with a revolver in his hand, frightened the innocent children terribly. They cried, screamed and begged.

While Zaynal was on his way down the steps to the court-yard of the house, another neighbour, Áqá Ḥusayn, a son of Áqá Riḍá, who had heard the commotion, appeared on the roof just in time to avert a tragedy. He ran towards Zaynal and tried to stop him. He asked 'Why do you want to kill these children?' 'This evening,' Zaynal replied, 'a number of people in Mír-Chaqmáq accused me of being a Bahá'í, because I am a neighbour of Ḥájí Mírzá's. I am therefore determined to wipe out this family. No one can stop me from carrying out my intention.'

Áqá Ḥusayn counselled Zaynal to calm down and began to explain that the children were innocent. He said 'Their father, who was a Bahá'í, has been put to death, and no one knows the fate of their mother. These children have been orphaned; their father was assaulted in front of their eyes and later died, their mother was beaten so much that it is not yet known whether she is dead or alive. The children now live in a ruined house; they don't get enough food. Look at their pitiful condition. They are reduced to mere skeletons. How can your conscience allow you to carry out your design? The Prophet of Islám exhorted His followers to honour their neighbours even if they were infidels. You

* See p. 358, f.n.

are a follower of the Prophet, how can you do such a thing to these innocent children?'

These words of Áqá Ḥusayn, however, had no effect on Zaynal. Eventually Áqá Ḥusayn urged him to postpone the intended murder, to go to his house instead for a smoke, have a cup of tea and relax for a while . . . And at last Áqá Ḥuṣayn managed to take Zaynal to his home. Through loving-kindness and much exhortation he succeeded in changing Zaynal's mind.

As to the children, God alone knows the measure of their anguish and fear that night! . . . One of them said to me: 'We sat all night in the dark and were literally trembling with fear. Our eyes were fixed in the direction of the stairs expecting Zaynal to come down at any time. The slightest noise would scare us to death for we thought that he was coming downstairs. We shall never forget the horrors and the dread of that night.'[18]

Bahá'u'lláh's First Tablet to Napoleon III

This Tablet was revealed by Bahá'u'lláh in Adrianople and forwarded to the Emperor through one of his ministers. Shoghi Effendi writes concerning it:

> In His first Tablet Bahá'u'lláh, wishing to test the sincerity of the Emperor's motives, and deliberately assuming a meek and unprovocative tone, had, after expatiating on the sufferings He had endured, addressed him the following words: 'Two statements graciously uttered by the king of the age have reached the ears of these wronged ones. These pronouncements are, in truth, the king of all pronouncements, the like of which have never been heard from any sovereign. The first was the answer given the Russian Government when it inquired why the war (Crimean) was waged against it. Thou didst reply: "The cry of the oppressed who, without guilt or blame, were drowned in the Black Sea wakened me at dawn. Wherefore, I took up arms against thee." These oppressed ones, however, have suffered a greater wrong, and are in greater distress. Whereas

the trials inflicted upon those people lasted but one day, the troubles borne by these servants have continued for twenty and five years, every moment of which has held for us a grievous affliction. The other weighty statement, which was indeed a wondrous statement manifested to the world, was this: "Ours is the responsibility to avenge the oppressed and succour the helpless." The fame of the Emperor's justice and fairness hath brought hope to a great many souls. It beseemeth the king of the age to inquire into the condition of such as have been wronged, and it behooveth him to extend his care to the weak. Verily, there hath not been, nor is there now, on earth any one as oppressed as we are, or as helpless as these wanderers.'[19]

In another passage Shoghi Effendi writes:

Bahá'u'lláh's previous Message, forwarded through one of the French ministers to the Emperor, had been accorded a welcome the nature of which can be conjectured from the words recorded in the 'Epistle to the Son of the Wolf': 'To this (first Tablet), however, he did not reply. After Our arrival in the Most Great Prison there reached Us a letter from his minister, the first part of which was in Persian, and the latter in his own handwriting. In it he was cordial, and wrote the following: "I have, as requested by you, delivered your letter, and until now have received no answer. We have, however, issued the necessary recommendations to our Minister in Constantinople and our consuls in those regions. If there be anything you wish done, inform us, and we will carry it out." From his words it became apparent that he understood the purpose of this Servant to have been a request for material assistance.'[20]

It is reported that upon reading it the Emperor flung down the Tablet of Bahá'u'lláh and stated 'If this man is God, I am two Gods!'

Soon after His arrival in 'Akká, Bahá'u'lláh despatched a most challenging Tablet to Napoleon. We shall write about this Tablet in the next volume.

17

The *Kitáb-i-Badí'*

The *Kitáb-i-Badí'* is Bahá'u'lláh's apologia written in defence of His Faith and to demonstrate the validity and the truth of His Own Mission. It is mainly in Persian, but also contains many passages in Arabic. This book may be regarded in the same light as the *Kitáb-i-Íqán*, in which Bahá'u'lláh establishes the authenticity and truth of the Message of the Báb. A contrasting feature of these two books is that, whereas the *Kitáb-i-Íqán* was addressed to the Báb's illustrious uncle* who as a result of reading it became illumined by the light of faith and acknowledged the truth of the Cause of God, the *Kitáb-i-Badí'* was addressed to the notorious Mírzá Mihdíy-i-Gílání, a so-called Bábí and a man of perfidy and hypocrisy. It was revealed in response to several venomous comments which he had made in a letter to one of the companions of Bahá'u'lláh. In the early days of the Faith, Mírzá Mihdí had entered the fold of the Bábí community in Ṭihrán and was a close friend of Áqá Muḥammad-'Alíy-i-Tambákú-Furúsh. Mírzá Mihdí, however, was known among the Bábís as a man who lived an impious life and whose deeds were contrary to the teachings of God.

When Ḥájí Mírzá Ḥaydar-'Alí was preparing to go to Adrianople, Mírzá Mihdí decided to accompany him. They were both in Ṭihrán at the time. The former at first agreed, but then refused to travel with him when he observed Mírzá Mihdí's reprehensible conduct and attitude. They parted company and Mírzá Mihdí went on his own to Constantinople, but not to Adrianople. Ḥájí Mírzá Ḥusayn Khán, the Persian

* See vol. I, chapter 10.

Ambassador in Constantinople, was impressed by Mírzá Mihdí and appointed him as the judge of the Persian Shí'ah community in the capital. It was at this juncture in his life that he came in contact with Siyyid Muḥammad-i-Iṣfahání who had gone to Constantinople to stir up trouble for Bahá'u'lláh and His companions.

As a result of this association a new chapter opened in the life of Mírzá Mihdí. As a corrupt and arrogant mischief-maker himself, he discovered in Siyyid Muḥammad an affinity and likeness which soon resulted in his becoming an ardent follower and a willing tool. Under the guidance of his new-found teacher, he learned new lessons in intrigue, became acquainted with those misrepresentations and lies which characterized the activities of Siyyid Muḥammad, and arose in enmity and opposition to Bahá'u'lláh.

At the instigation of Siyyid Muḥammad, Mírzá Mihdí wrote a letter to his old friend Áqá Muḥammad-'Alíy-i-Tambákú-Furúsh who was one of Bahá'u'lláh's companions in Adrianople. This venomous letter, loaded with calumnies against Bahá'u'lláh, was obviously written with the help of Siyyid Muḥammad, and probably composed by him. Most of its arguments were aimed at proving the falseness of the claims of Bahá'u'lláh to be 'He Whom God shall make manifest', the One promised by the Báb. Not only were his objections utterly false themselves, but some of them were couched in discourteous language and were disrespectful to Bahá'u'lláh.

Áqá Muḥammad-'Alí, to whom this letter was addressed, was a devoted companion of Bahá'u'lláh. We have already stated* that he had accompanied Bahá'u'lláh from Baghdád to Constantinople and Adrianople, and he was also among those who later journeyed with Him to 'Akká. He was a man who enjoyed a good life in spite of the hardships and privations suffered during these banishments. Of him 'Abdu'l-Bahá writes:

* See vol. I, p. 287.

> . . . he had little to live on, but was happy and content. A man of excellent disposition, he was congenial to believers and others alike . . . In Adrianople as well, his days passed happily, under the protection of Bahá'u'lláh. He would carry on some business which, however trifling, would bring in surprisingly abundant returns . . .
>
> He spent his days in utter bliss. Here,* too, he carried on a small business, which occupied him from morning till noon. In the afternoons he would take his samovar, wrap it in a dark-coloured pouch made from a saddle-bag, and go off somewhere to a garden or meadow, or out in a field, and have his tea. Sometimes he would be found at the farm of Mazra'ih, or again in the Riḍván Garden; or, at the Mansion, he would have the honour of attending upon Bahá'u'lláh.
>
> Muḥammad-'Alí would carefully consider every blessing that came his way. 'How delicious my tea is today,' he would comment. 'What perfume, what colour! How lovely this meadow is, and the flowers so bright!' He used to say that everything, even air and water, had its own special fragrance. For him the days passed in indescribable delight. Even kings were not so happy as this old man, the people said. 'He is completely free of the world,' they would declare. 'He lives in joy.' It also happened that his food was of the very best, and that his home was situated in the very best part of 'Akká. Gracious God! Here he was, a prisoner, and yet experiencing comfort, peace and joy.[1]

Áqá Muḥammad-'Alí had a great sense of humour and was a delightful companion to Bahá'u'lláh. Once in 'Akká Bahá'u'lláh attended a memorial meeting for one of the believers who had died. Áqá Muḥammad-'Alí was present. He noticed how the bounties of Bahá'u'lláh and His loving-kindness were being showered upon the soul of the deceased. Longing for the same treatment, he is reported to have said to Him, 'I shall be honoured if you would presume that I am dead also, and give me the privilege of inviting you to attend a memorial meeting

* 'Akká. (A.T.)

for me!' Thereupon he gave a lavish feast in which he entertained Bahá'u'lláh and the believers in 'Akká.

As soon as he read Mírzá Mihdí's distasteful letter, Áqá Muḥammad-'Alí took it to Bahá'u'lláh. The *Kitáb-i-Badí'* was written to refute the accusations of Mírzá Mihdí. Bahá'u'lláh revealed this book on three successive days. Each day He dictated for about two hours and Áqá Muḥammad-'Alí took the words down. We have stated previously* that while some of Bahá'u'lláh's Writings appear to have been composed by his amanuensis Mírzá Áqá Ján, yet every word was dictated by Bahá'u'lláh Himself. The *Kitáb-i-Badí'* is a similar case. Although it is written in the words of Áqá Muḥammad-'Alí, in fact it is revealed by Bahá'u'lláh from beginning to end.

This book, almost twice the size of the *Kitáb-i-Íqán* and written in defence of the Faith of Bahá'u'lláh, occupies a significant position among His Writings. It gives the reader remarkable insight into the prophecies of the Báb concerning 'Him Whom God shall make manifest', and clearly demonstrates that the advent of the Revelation of Bahá'u'lláh was the ultimate aim of the Báb and the fulfilment of all that He had cherished in His heart. The book exerted a great influence upon the members of the Bábí community, especially those who were confused and vacillating. It resolved many of their doubts and perplexities and enabled them to recognize the exalted station of Bahá'u'lláh as 'He Whom God shall make manifest'. For those who are well versed in the Writings of the Báb, this book may be regarded as a key to many of the mysteries which are to be found in the Revelations of the Báb and Bahá'u'lláh. It is one of the most challenging works of Bahá'u'lláh, written with forcefulness and clarity. It also gives an account of some of Bahá'u'lláh's teachings as well as some aspects of the history of His Cause. One of its outstanding features is the way in which Bahá'u'lláh refutes the objections and accusations of Mírzá Mihdí with such convincing proofs

* See vol. I, pp. 40–42.

that the reader becomes utterly overwhelmed by the irrefutable power of His reasoning.

There is no doubt that the *Kitáb-i-Badí'* shattered the idle fancies of the breakers of the Covenant of the Báb who had sought assiduously to undermine the Faith of Bahá'u'lláh through the dissemination of misleading and untrue reports. The arguments put forward by Mírzá Mihdí were feeble and misguided. They contained many false statements, misrepresentations and lies which originated from Siyyid Muḥammad.

The manner in which the *Kitáb-i-Badí'* is revealed is such that Bahá'u'lláh quotes a few lines from the letter of Mírzá Mihdí and then reveals pages in reply. He continues in this way until all points and accusations embodied in the letter are fully answered. A remarkable feature of these answers is the compelling vigour of Bahá'u'lláh's pronouncements. So powerful are His words that Mírzá Mihdí seems like a puny bird held in the claws of a mighty falcon and reduced to utter nothingness. The force of Bahá'u'lláh's arguments, the clarity of His explanations, the profundity of His utterances, are matched only by His all-encompassing knowledge of the Writings of the Báb which He quotes profusely in support of His theme. And this in spite of the fact that, as He Himself attests,* He had not read everything from the Writings of the Báb, including the *Bayán*! This is an evidence of His divine knowledge.

In the *Kitáb-i-Badí'*, Bahá'u'lláh at times uses very strong language in condemning the actions of Mírzá Mihdí and his master, Siyyid Muḥammad. Mírzá Mihdí is denounced as the 'wicked one', 'the evil plotter', 'the impious', 'the impudent', 'the outcast', 'the faithless soul', 'the froward', 'he who contends with God', 'one from whose pen had flowed what caused the Báb to lament in the Kingdom and with Him the souls of all the chosen ones of God'. Repeatedly, Bahá'u'lláh calls on him to withhold his pen and warns him that God, through His wrath, will soon strike him down. Indeed, it was not long before Mírzá Mihdí died. Bahá'u'lláh refers to this in the

* See *Epistle to the Son of the Wolf*, pp. 165, 167.

*Lawḥ-i-Fu'ád** where He describes the tormenting agony of his soul when the wrathful vengeance of God descended upon him. There are also many passages in the *Kitáb-i-Badí'* in which Siyyid Muḥammad is stigmatized in such terms as the 'one who joined partners with God', 'the prime mover of mischief', 'the embodiment of wickedness and impiety', and 'one accursed of God'. That Bahá'u'lláh addressed these men in such strong language is indicative of His supreme authority as the Judge and Ruler of mankind. Let us ponder upon the power of the Manifestation of God. He, and He alone, can reveal all the attributes of God to man, and one of God's attributes is His wrath. It is through the operation of this attribute that God casts out those who rise up to oppose Him.

From the study of the Writings of Bahá'u'lláh it becomes clear that God's mercy and forgiveness overshadow the whole of creation. Through these attributes God has vouchsafed His protection to humanity. If it were not for His mercy and grace, no man could survive the operation of His justice. The loving and forgiving God overlooks the sins and shortcomings of man, immerses him in the ocean of His mercy and, without his deserving, bestows upon him everlasting life. But when a person breaks His Covenant and consciously rebels against the One who manifests Him, then His wrath is invoked and the soul of that individual becomes deprived of the bounties of God. Siyyid Muḥammad and Mírzá Mihdí were of this category, and Bahá'u'lláh, in denouncing them, is doing no more than revealing the true condition of their souls. An important point to bear in mind, however, is that no man has the vision or the authority to condemn another soul. It is solely the function of the Manifestation of God and those upon whom He confers infallibility and authority.

* This Tablet was revealed in 1869 in 'Akká.

Condemnation of the Covenant-breakers

The *Kitáb-i-Badí'* is also replete with passages in condemnation of the centre of rebellion, Mírzá Yaḥyá. Bahá'u'lláh refutes his claims to be the appointed successor of the Báb and quotes numerous passages from the Writings of the Báb in support of His arguments. He makes it very clear that the only thing which the Báb promised to His followers was the advent of the Revelation of 'Him Whom God shall make manifest'. Since Mírzá Yaḥyá was one of the 'Mirrors' of the Bábí Dispensation*—and he used to employ this title to impress the followers of the Báb—Bahá'u'lláh clarifies the position of the 'Mirrors'. He quotes many statements of the Báb that the 'Mirrors' had no light of their own, that their radiance depended upon their turning to the source of light, 'Him Whom God shall make manifest'. The Báb reveals:

> He †—glorified be His mention—resembleth the sun. Were unnumbered mirrors to be placed before it, each would, according to its capacity, reflect the splendour of that sun, and were none to be placed before it, it would still continue to rise and set, and the mirrors alone would be veiled from its light. I, verily, have not fallen short of My duty to admonish that people, and to devise means whereby they may turn towards God, their Lord, and believe in God, their Creator. If, on the day of His Revelation, all that are on earth bear Him allegiance, Mine inmost being will rejoice, inasmuch as all will have attained the summit of their existence, and will have been brought face to face with their Beloved, and will have recognized, to the fullest extent attainable in the world of being, the splendour of Him Who is the Desire of their hearts. If not, My soul will indeed be saddened. I truly have nurtured all things for this purpose. How, then, can anyone be veiled from Him? For this have I called upon God, and will continue to call upon Him. He, verily, is nigh, ready to answer.[2]

* The Báb had bestowed the title 'Mirror' upon several of His followers.

† He Whom God shall make manifest. (A.T.)

Even in one of His Own Writings, the Báb, addressing Ḥájí Siyyid Javád-i-Karbilá'í, complains that the Mirrors have not detached themselves from the things of this world and have turned to Him with sullied hearts. These are His words:

> I complain unto thee, O Mirror of My generosity,* against all the other Mirrors. All look upon Me through their own colours.[3]

And again:

> O Sun-like Mirrors! Look ye upon the Sun of Truth. Ye, verily, depend upon it, were ye to perceive it. Ye are all as fishes, moving in the waters of the sea, veiling yourselves therefrom, and yet asking what it is on which ye depend.[4]

In the *Kitáb-i-Badí'* Bahá'u'lláh stigmatizes Mírzá Yaḥyá as the idol of the Bábí community, states that all his accomplishments were in the field of deceit and lies, discloses the extent of his shallowness and ignorance, declares that his words contained the essence of falsehood, any truth found in them having been borrowed from Bahá'u'lláh, refers to the fact that with the help of Siyyid Muḥammad he had disseminated some of Bahá'u'lláh's Writings among the believers in his own name, explains that He did not expel Mírzá Yaḥyá from His presence until he publicly rose up against the Cause of God, denounces him for his malicious and slanderous letters, and portrays, in a number of lengthy passages and in moving and dramatic language, the lamentations of a pen held between the fingers of Mírzá Yaḥyá pleading to its God for deliverance from such a vile and perfidious master!

Writings of the Báb concerning 'Him Whom God shall make manifest'

A considerable part of the *Kitáb-i-Badí'* relates to the circumstances of the rebellion of Mírzá Yaḥyá and Siyyid Muḥam-

* Ḥájí Siyyid Javád-i-Karbilá'í. (A.T.)

mad. But the major part of the book is devoted to the exalted theme of 'Him Whom God shall make manifest', Bahá'u'lláh, the Promised One of the *Bayán*. Bahá'u'lláh quotes numerous passages from the Writings of the Báb in which He extols the station, the glory, the transcendental majesty and the authority of 'Him Whom God shall make manifest'. It suffices to quote only a few passages from the Writings of the Báb all of which Bahá'u'lláh quotes in the *Kitáb-i-Badí'*. It should be noted that the Báb's Writings are replete with similar statements about Bahá'u'lláh:

> I have written down in My mention of Him* these gem-like words: 'No allusion of Mine can allude unto Him, neither anything mentioned in the Bayán.' . . . Exalted and glorified is He above the power of any one to reveal Him except Himself, or the description of any of His creatures. I Myself am but the first servant to believe in Him and in His signs, and to partake of the sweet savours of His words from the first-fruits of the Paradise of His knowledge. Yea, by His glory! He is the Truth. There is none other God but Him. All have arisen at His bidding.[5]

The study of the *Kitáb-i-Badí'* makes it clear that the purpose of the Báb in revealing Himself was none other than to prepare His followers for the coming of Bahá'u'lláh. There are many passages in the Writings of the Báb in which He makes a firm covenant with His followers concerning 'Him Whom God shall make manifest'. In one of these He states:

> Glorified art Thou, O My God! Bear Thou witness that, through this Book, I have covenanted with all created things concerning the Mission of Him Whom Thou shalt make manifest, ere the covenant concerning Mine own Mission had been established. Sufficient witness art Thou and they that have believed in Thy signs. Thou, verily, sufficest Me. In Thee have I placed My trust, and Thou, verily, taketh count of all things.[6]

* Him Whom God shall make manifest. (A.T.)

There are also many quotations concerning the *Bayán*, the Mother Book of the Bábí Dispensation, and its relationship to 'Him Whom God shall make manifest'. The Báb states:

The whole of the Bayán is only a leaf amongst the leaves of His Paradise.[7]

And again:

The Bayán is, from beginning to end, the repository of all His* attributes, and the treasury of both His fire and His light.[8]

The Báb warned His followers not to allow anything in this world, including the *Bayán*, to become a barrier between them and Bahá'u'lláh. He states:

Suffer not the Bayán and all that hath been revealed therein to withhold you from that Essence of Being and Lord of the visible and invisible.[9]

In another passage He affirms:

Suffer not yourselves to be shut out as by a veil from God after He hath revealed Himself. For all that hath been exalted in the Bayán is but as a ring upon My hand, and I Myself am, verily, but a ring upon the hand of Him Whom God shall make manifest—glorified be His mention! He turneth it as He pleaseth, for whatsoever He pleaseth, and through whatsoever He pleaseth. He, verily, is the Help in Peril, the Most High.[10]

The Báb declares that one line from the Writings of Bahá'u'lláh is more meritorious in the sight of God than all that has been revealed by the Manifestations of the past. In another instance the Báb reveals:

* Bahá'u'lláh. (A.T.)

> Better is it for thee to recite but one of the verses of Him Whom God shall make manifest than to set down the whole of the Bayán, for on that Day that one verse can save thee, whereas the entire Bayán cannot save thee.[11]

He testifies to the exalted station of Bahá'u'lláh by the pronouncement that He, Bahá'u'lláh, can bestow the station of prophethood upon whomsoever He wishes. These are the words of the Báb:

> Were He to make of every one on earth a Prophet, all would, in very truth, be accounted as Prophets in the sight of God . . . In the day of the revelation of Him Whom God shall make manifest all that dwell on earth will be equal in His estimation. Whomsoever He ordaineth as a Prophet, he, verily, hath been a Prophet from the beginning that hath no beginning, and will thus remain until the end that hath no end, inasmuch as this is an act of God. And whosoever is made a Viceregent by Him, shall be a Viceregent in all the worlds, for this is an act of God. For the will of God can in no wise be revealed except through His will, nor His wish be manifested save through His wish. He, verily, is the All-Conquering, the All-Powerful, the All-Highest.[12]

The Báb states that no one can recognize 'Him Whom God shall make manifest' except by His own standard. He affirms:

> Look not upon Him with any eye except His own. For whosoever looketh upon Him with His eye, will recognize Him; otherwise he will be veiled from Him. Shouldst thou seek God and His Presence, seek thou Him and gaze upon Him.[13]

In one of His Writings, the Báb declares that at the time of the coming of 'Him Whom God shall make manifest', all those who dwell in the Sinai of God's Revelation will be found awe-struck at His glory. He urges the learned among His followers to withhold their pens from writing epistles and books when 'Him Whom God shall make manifest' has revealed Himself. He further urges His followers to recognize and acknowledge Bahá'u'lláh with no hesitation or delay and warns them:

> Recognize Him by His verses. The greater your neglect in seeking to know Him, the more grievously will ye be veiled in fire.[14]

These, and many more tributes which the Báb paid to Bahá'u'lláh, are recorded in the *Kitáb-i-Badí'*. We have already quoted some of these passages in the former volume and devoted an entire chapter to this subject.*

In the *Kitáb-i-Badí'*, Bahá'u'lláh demonstrates the validity of His Cause, glorifies His own Revelation, proclaims His mission and re-affirms the statement He had made in the Garden of Riḍván—that no other Manifestation of God would appear before a thousand years had passed.† He describes the outpouring of the verses of God from His Pen and invites Mírzá Mihdí to attain His presence so that he may witness the rapidity with which the Words of God are revealed in this day. He also recounts many outstanding events which took place during His sojourn in Baghdád and Adrianople, describes the devotion and self-sacrifice of some of His followers, dwells on the sufferings which were inflicted on Him by the hand of Mírzá Yaḥyá and which culminated in the 'Most Great Separation', and enumerates some of the grievous transgressions committed by him, such as his orders to kill some of the outstanding Bábís, and his most flagrant crime, the repugnant violation of the honour of the Báb.‡

* See vol. I, chapter 18: 'Him Whom God shall make manifest'.
† See vol. I, pp. 279–80.
‡ See vol. I, p. 249.

Khadíjih-Bagum

In the *Kitáb-i-Badí'* Bahá'u'lláh extols the virtues and exalted station of Fáṭimih-Bagum, the mother of the Báb,* and His wife Khadíjih-Bagum, designates them both as the Khayru'n Nisá' (The Most Virtuous among Women) and enjoins on His loved ones to venerate and honour them.

Khadíjih-Bagum was of noble lineage. She was a paternal cousin of the mother of the Báb. Her marriage with the Báb took place almost two years before His declaration. Through the purity of her heart, Khadíjih-Bagum recognized the station of her beloved Husband and acknowledged the truth of His Cause in the early days of His ministry. She was an eye-witness to that transforming power which emanated from the person of the Báb, a power which revolutionized the lives and conduct of His early disciples and the heroes of the Bábí Faith. Concerning Khadíjih-Bagum, Nabíl-i-A'ẓam writes in his narrative:

> The wife of the Báb, unlike His mother, perceived at the earliest dawn of His Revelation the glory and uniqueness of His Mission, and felt from the very beginning the intensity of its force. No one except Ṭáhirih, among the women of her generation, surpassed her in the spontaneous character of her devotion nor excelled the fervour of her faith. To her the Báb confided the secret of His future sufferings, and unfolded to her eyes the significance of the events that were to transpire in His Day. He bade her not to divulge this secret to His mother and counselled her to be patient and resigned to the will of God. He entrusted her with a special prayer, revealed and written by Himself, the reading of which, He assured her, would remove her difficulties and lighten the burden of her woes. 'In the hour of your perplexity,' He directed her, 'recite this prayer ere you go to sleep. I Myself will appear to you and will banish your anxiety.' Faithful to His advice, every time she turned to Him in prayer, the

* For a brief outline of her distinguished career, see vol. I, pp. 154–5.

light of His unfailing guidance illumined her path and resolved her problems.[15]

Khadíjih-Bagum recognized the station of Bahá'u'lláh from the early days in Baghdád and remained one of His most devoted followers.

In his narratives, the late Ḥájí Mírzá Ḥabíbu'lláh-i-Afnán* writes the following account concerning the wife of the Báb.

> ... The Blessed Beauty after His arrival in Baghdád sent many Tablets, with His own signature, 152,† (which signifies Bahá) to various parts of Persia. These were taken to their intended destinations by some trustworthy individuals. Among these was a Tablet revealed in honour of the Exalted Leaf,‡ the wife of the Báb. At that time no one among the family of the Afnán§ had embraced the Faith, and therefore the wife of the Báb had no close friend in whom she could confide. For this reason, she entered into conversation about the Faith with the father of the writer, Jináb-i-Afnán, Áqá Mírzá Áqá,¶ who was her nephew (her sister's son), and was then thirteen years of age.
> ... Because of the purity of her heart, Áqá Mírzá Áqá was deeply attracted to the Cause of God, recognized its truth

* A devoted follower of Bahá'u'lláh who for some time was custodian of the House of the Báb in Shíráz.

† The numerical values of the letters B, H, A, which constitute the word Bahá, are 2, 5 and 1 respectively. Some Tablets of Bahá'u'lláh are signed in this way by Him.

‡ In some of His Tablets Bahá'u'lláh has addressed Khadíjih-Bagum as the Exalted Leaf.

§ Descendants of the maternal uncles of the Báb and those of the two brothers and the sister of the wife of the Báb are known as the Afnán (The Twigs).

¶ Áqá Mírzá Áqá was one of the outstanding members of the Afnán family. He was instrumental in encouraging Ḥájí Siyyid Muḥammad, the uncle of the Báb, to proceed to Baghdád and attain the presence of Bahá'u'lláh. He rendered distinguished services to the Faith. Bahá'u'lláh has granted him and his descendants the custodianship of the House of the Báb in Shíráz. We shall refer to him again in future volumes. (A.T.)

and was filled with such enthusiasm that he was unable to withhold himself from teaching it, and proceeded to do so with courage and steadfastness. First he succeeded in teaching his own father . . . and then his own mother, the sister of the Báb's wife.[16]

When Bahá'u'lláh summoned Munírih Khánum* to 'Akká He instructed Shaykh Salmán to accompany her. The party started from Iṣfahán for Búshihr via Shíráz. Arrangements were made for her to stay a short while in Shíráz in the home of Ḥájí Mírzá Siyyid Muḥammad, the uncle of the Báb. She arrived in the month of Dhi'l-Q'adih 1288 A.H. (January–February 1872) and had the privilege of meeting the wife of the Báb several times. The following is taken from Munírih Khánum's memoirs concerning one of her interviews with Khadíjih-Bagum:

> . . . I asked the wife of the Báb to recount for me some reminiscences of her association with the Báb, of attaining His presence and of her marriage with Him. She said, 'I do not remember every detail but will tell you what I can remember . . .
>
> 'We were three sisters.† One night I dreamt that Fáṭimih [the daughter of the Prophet Muḥammad, the holiest woman in Islám] came to our house as a suitor to propose‡ marriage. With great joy and ecstasy my sisters and I went to her. She then came forward to me and kissed my forehead. I understood in the dream that she had chosen me. When I woke up in the morning I felt very happy and joyous, but I felt too shy to share my dream with anybody. In the afternoon of the same day, the mother of the Báb came to our house. My

* Munírih Khánum became the wife of 'Abdu'l-Bahá. See pp. 205–9.

† One of the three sisters was a half-sister who married Ḥájí Mírzá Siyyid 'Alí, the uncle of the Báb who was martyred in Ṭihrán. (A.T.)

‡ In those days it was the custom for mothers, sisters or close female relatives of a man who wished to get married to propose to the parents of a girl. Once the agreement was reached, the girl would be informed and later married. (A.T.)

sister and I went to her. Exactly as I had dreamt, she came forward, kissed my forehead and embraced me. She then left. My eldest sister said to me, 'The mother of the Báb came to propose and has asked for your hand in marriage [with her son].' I replied, 'This is a great felicity for me.' I recounted my dream and expressed the happiness of my heart because of its implications.

'After a few days . . . they sent some gifts as a token of engagement,* and the Báb went to Búshihr on business in company with His uncle. Although the mother of the Báb and I were cousins, yet, because of my dream every time I met her, I showed great courtesy and respect towards her. I cannot recall the duration of the Báb's journey.

'When He was in Búshihr, I dreamt one night that I was sitting in the presence of the Báb. It appeared as though it was the evening of our wedding. The Báb was dressed in a green cloak around the borders of which were inscribed the verses of the Qur'án . . . and light was emanating from Him. Seeing Him in this way, I was filled with such joy and gladness that I woke up. After this dream I was assured in my heart that the Báb was a distinguished personage. I cherished a love for Him in my heart, but did not disclose my feelings to anybody. Eventually He returned from Búshihr and His uncle arranged the wedding.

'After the wedding, I entertained no thought of earthly things in my mind. My heart was entirely attracted to the person of the Báb. From His words and conduct, His magnanimity and solemnity, it became clear to me that He was a distinguished person. But the thought never occurred to me that He could be the Qá'im, the Promised One. Most of the time He was engaged in praying and reading verses . . . As was customary among merchants, He would ask in the evenings for His business papers and account books. But I noticed that they were not business papers. Sometimes I used to ask Him what the papers were. He once said 'It is

* Engagement was a family affair. It was improper for a man engaged to a woman to associate with her until married. In any case it was not permitted even to see the face of his fiancée until after marriage. Of course a couple who were close relatives would have seen each other before. (A.T.)

the Book of the accounts of all the peoples of the world.' Should any visitor suddenly arrive, He would spread a handkerchief over the papers. All close relatives such as His uncles and aunts were fully conscious of His exalted personality. They revered Him and showed the utmost respect towards Him, until the fateful night of the 5th of Jamádíyu'l-Avval 1260 A.H. (22 May 1844) arrived. It was the night that Jináb-i-Bábu'l-Báb, Mullá Ḥusayn-i-Bushrú'í* attained the presence of the Báb and acknowledged the truth of His Cause. That was indeed a memorable evening. The Báb intimated that we were having a guest who was dear to Him. He was as if on fire and in the utmost excitement. I was very eager to hear His blessed words, but He bade me go to bed. Although I was lying awake the whole night, I remained in bed as I did not wish to disobey Him. I could hear His voice until morning as He conversed with Jináb-i-Bábu'l-Báb. He was reading the verses of God and adducing proofs. Later I observed that every day a strange guest would arrive and the Báb would engage in similar talks.

'If I attempt to describe the sufferings and persecutions of those days, I will not be able to endure talking about them, neither will you have the fortitude to listen to them . . .

'One night, I woke up about midnight to find that the . . . Chief Constable 'Abdu'l-Ḥamíd had entered the house from the roof with his men and, without giving any reasons, took the Báb with him.† I never attained His presence again . . .'[17]

Munírih Khánum describes in her memoirs how eager the wife of the Báb was for her to prolong the visit, but Shaykh Salmán had instructions from Bahá'u'lláh to proceed to 'Akká in company with the caravan which was taking the Muslim pilgrims to Mecca and time was running out.

After we bade farewell to her, the wife of the Báb said, 'Please supplicate the Blessed Perfection to grant two wishes of mine. One, that one of the exalted Leaves of the blessed

* The first believer of the Bábí Dispensation. (A.T.)

† For more information, see *The Dawn-Breakers*. (A.T.)

Family* may be permitted to join in wedlock with a member of the family of the Báb, so that the two holy trees may be outwardly knit together. The other, to grant me permission to attain His presence.' I conveyed this message when I attained the presence of Bahá'u'lláh; He readily assented to both her requests.[18]

The person whom the wife of the Báb had in mind for this marriage was Ḥájí Siyyid 'Alíy-i-Afnán, a son of her brother, the 'Great Afnán', Ḥájí Mírzá Siyyid Ḥasan. Bahá'u'lláh granted the wish of the wife of the Báb, and Ḥájí Siyyid 'Alí was joined in wedlock with Furúghíyyih Khánum, a daughter of Bahá'u'lláh.†

As to the second wish, however, circumstances prevented the wife of the Báb from attaining the presence of Bahá'u'lláh.‡ This was a grievous blow to her and she could not be consoled. It is reported that she wept so much that her health was seriously impaired. Grief-stricken, she passed away a few months afterwards, on the evening of the 29th day of Dhi'l-Qa'dih 1299 A.H (11 November 1882). Strangely on the same evening her maid (Fiḍḍih) who had served her since the days of the Báb also passed away.

The news of the passing of the wife of the Báb brought sadness to Bahá'u'lláh. He revealed a special Tablet of Visitation for her and later He composed a verse to be inscribed on her tombstone. During her lifetime too, Bahá'u'lláh had revealed many Tablets in her honour.

* Female member of Bahá'u'lláh's family; here a daughter of Bahá'u'lláh was intended. (A.T.)

† They both became Covenant-breakers during the ministry of 'Abdu'l-Bahá. But the wishes of the wife of the Báb were fulfilled in the marriage of Mírzá Hádíy-i-Afnán with Ḍíyá'íyyih Khánum, a daughter of 'Abdu'l-Bahá. They were the parents of Shoghi Effendi.

‡ Knowing that he had no chance of securing this marriage on his own, and knowing also how eager the wife of the Báb was to attain the presence of Bahá'u'lláh, Ḥájí Siyyid 'Alí promised that he would accompany her to 'Akká if she arranged this marriage for him. But he did not fulfil his promise.

18

Súriy-i-Ghuṣn

An important Tablet revealed in Adrianople is the *Súriy-i-Ghuṣn* (Súrih of the Branch). It is in Arabic and addressed to Mírzá 'Alí-Riḍáy-i-Mustawfí, a native of Khurásán. This believer was a titled person—the Mustasháru'd-Dawlih. He had a prominent position in government circles in the district of Khurásán and was a man of great influence there. His teacher was no less a person than Mullá Ḥusayn* who taught him the Faith in Mashhad.

Mírzá 'Alí-Riḍá became a dedicated believer who in spite of his rank and position never hesitated to assist the friends whenever they faced difficulties; he always helped the poor and downtrodden among them. He was the one mainly responsible for providing the horses and finance for Mullá Ḥusayn and his companions when they were leaving Mashhad for Mázindarán on a mission of great importance.† With the help of Mullá Ṣádiq-i-Khurásání, the renowned teacher of the Faith, he succeeded in converting his younger brother Mírzá Muḥammad-Riḍá, the Mu'taminu's-Salṭanih, who became a devoted believer. When Mírzá 'Alí-Riḍá retired, it was this same brother who succeeded him in office. It is interesting to note that in a Tablet, Bahá'u'lláh comments on a photograph of Mu'taminu's-Salṭanih, saying that it bears a striking resemblance to Himself.

The main theme of the *Súriy-i-Ghuṣn* is the unveiling of the station of 'Abdu'l-Bahá. In it 'Abdu'l-Bahá is referred to as 'the Trust of God', 'this sacred and glorious Being', 'this Branch of

* The first of the Báb's disciples.

† See *The Dawn-Breakers*.

Holiness', 'the Limb of the Law of God', 'this sublime, this blessed, this mighty, this exalted Handiwork', 'the most great Favour', 'the most perfect bounty'.[1] Bahá'u'lláh also makes this significant statement about 'Abdu'l-Bahá:

> Well is it with him that hath sought His ['Abdu'l-Bahá's] shelter and abideth beneath His shadow . . . They who deprive themselves of the shadow of the Branch, are lost in the wilderness of error, . . . and are of those who will assuredly perish.*[2]

These lofty attributes revealing the station of the Master heralded His appointment, later in 'Akká, as the Centre of Bahá'u'lláh's Covenant and the Interpreter of His words—an appointment announced in the *Kitáb-i-Aqdas* and the *Kitáb-i-'Ahdí* (The Book of My Covenant). The praise and glorification of 'Abdu'l-Bahá did not surprise any of Bahá'u'lláh's followers. Even Bahá'u'lláh's enemies confessed the exalted character and greatness of 'Abdu'l-Bahá. For instance, Mírzá Aḥmad-i-Kirmání, an inveterate enemy of the Cause stigmatized by Bahá'u'lláh as a 'foreboder of evil', and to whose reprehensible deeds He has alluded in the *Kitáb-i-Aqdas*, once announced from the pulpit that if there was one proof by which Bahá'u'lláh could substantiate His claims, it would be that He had reared a son such as 'Abbás Effendi.†

From His childhood, 'Abdu'l-Bahá displayed outstanding qualities of faith and virtue. He did not attend any school except for a short period in Ṭihrán. As a child of nine, He not only recognized the station of His Father,‡ but manifested such understanding and knowledge that He excelled the learned and erudite. In Baghdád, while He was in His early teens, 'Abdu'l-Bahá attended a gathering of those divines who were friendly.

* Part of this Tablet is translated into English and cited in *The World Order of Bahá'u'lláh*, p. 135. See also *The Revelation of Bahá'u'lláh*, vol. I, p. 135.

† 'Abdu'l-Bahá.

‡ See p. 14.

They always enjoyed 'Abdu'l-Bahá's company and listened when he spoke. In the course of discussion someone mentioned that in one of his writings Ḥájí Mírzá Karím Khán* had used a certain Persian word as Arabic. All the divines agreed that he had made a mistake. However, 'Abdu'l-Bahá stated that although Ḥájí Mírzá Karím Khán was an enemy of the Faith of the Báb, He had to say that in this particular instance he had not erred. The word in question, although used in the Persian language, was originally an Arabic word. The divines still maintained their view, until 'Abdu'l-Bahá asked them to look up the word in the dictionary. To their amazement they discovered that it was indeed Arabic.

It was in Baghdád that 'Alí Shawkat Páshá, one of the dignitaries of 'Iráq, requested Bahá'u'lláh to elucidate for him the inner significances of a certain tradition of Islám which brings to light the relationship between God and man and reveals the purpose of creation. The voice of God proclaims in this tradition: 'I was a hidden treasure, I loved to be known therefore I created beings to know [Me].'

Bahá'u'lláh instructed 'Abdu'l-Bahá, who was then in his adolescence, to write a commentary on this tradition. 'Abdu'l-Bahá wrote a most profound and lengthy commentary which astounded the Páshá and opened before his eyes the vistas of knowledge and understanding. He thereupon became an ardent admirer of the Master. Not only was 'Alí Shawkat Páshá deeply impressed by 'Abdu'l-Bahá's elucidations, but generally, every person who read this illuminating commentary was deeply moved and became aware of His extraordinary knowledge and wisdom. Once the renowned Ḥájí Siyyid Javád-i-Karbilá'í, to whom we have referred previously, said in reply to a person who demanded proofs of the authenticity of the Mission of Bahá'u'lláh, that one unmistakable token of the truth of His Cause was that His son 'Abdu'l-Bahá, during His adolescence, had written such a superb treatise shedding so much light on this subject.

* See vol. I, Appendix IV.

Among many people of note who became particularly attracted to 'Abdu'l-Bahá and recognized His greatness was Khurshíd Páshá, the Governor of Adrianople. Shoghi Effendi writes:

> It was His ['Abdu'l-Bahá's] discussions and discourses with the learned doctors with whom He came in contact in Baghdád that first aroused that general admiration for Him and for His knowledge which was steadily to increase as the circle of His acquaintances was widened, at a later date, first in Adrianople and then in 'Akká. It was to Him that the highly accomplished Khurshíd Páshá, the governor of Adrianople, had been moved to pay a public and glowing tribute when, in the presence of a number of distinguished divines of that city, his youthful Guest had, briefly and amazingly, resolved the intricacies of a problem that had baffled the minds of the assembled company—an achievement that affected so deeply the Páshá that from that time onwards he could hardly reconcile himself to that Youth's absence from such gatherings.[3]

'Abdu'l-Bahá shouldered many responsibilities from childhood. He was ten years of age when His Father withdrew to the mountains of Sulaymáníyyih. During the years of Bahá'u'lláh's absence, He took upon Himself, at this tender age, and while disconsolate in His separation from His Father, the burden of managing the affairs of the family. Later He intimated to Nabíl that He felt that He had grown old while still in His childhood. He endured His share of the sufferings and privations which were heaped upon His Father during forty years of His ministry, and beyond that during His own ministry.

One aspect of the life of 'Abdu'l-Bahá becomes clear from the statements He made about His own health. For instance, once in Paris in 1913 when He became ill, He spoke to His companions about this. He testified that His life was sustained not through physical laws, but through the decree of Providence. He stated that there was a wisdom in His becoming ill in Paris. Had it not been for this illness He would not have stayed more than one month. Yet He remained there for well-nigh four months. When we survey His work in Paris we realize that one important aspect of it was that during His stay several prominent statesmen and influential personalities from the East attained His presence, felt the radiance of His spirit and were humbled by the power of His words and the charm of His character. Among them was the haughty Prince Masú'd Mírzá, the Ẓillu's-Sulṭán, the eldest son of Náṣiri'd-Dín Sháh, once the Governor of Iṣfahán during whose rule the two illustrious brothers, the 'King of the Martyrs' and the 'Beloved of the Martyrs', were put to death.

Speaking about His illness, 'Abdu'l-Bahá told His companions in Paris that His life was not governed by the laws of nature. This illness was not due to physical causes, but to the will of God. He recounted the story of His illness at the age of seven, when He was afflicted with consumption and His case was thought hopeless. But the hand of God was behind this illness. Its wisdom became clear later. For had He been healthy, He would have been sent to live in the ancestral home of Bahá'u'lláh in Mázindarán, whereas because of His illness He had to remain in Ṭihrán up to the time of Bahá'u'llah's imprisonment, witness the birth of His Revelation, and then proceed to Baghdád in His company. Then suddenly and against the verdict of the doctors who had pronounced Him incurable, He recovered perfect health.

The relationship between Bahá'u'lláh and 'Abdu'l-Bahá is one of the most fascinating features of their lives. 'Abdu'l-Bahá had so fully recognized the station of His Father, that throughout His life He showed the utmost humility and reverence to Him. He never allowed the family relationship of father and son to interfere. No one else in this Dispensation has had the capacity and vision to recognize the true station of His Lord as 'Abdu'l-Bahá did, and it is for this reason that He was able to manifest the most profound measure of self-effacement towards Bahá'u'lláh and consider Himself as utter nothingness in relation to Him.

To cite one example: when 'Abdu'l-Bahá went to attain the presence of His Father in the Mansion of Bahjí outside 'Akká, He often rode a donkey. But as soon as He could see the Mansion from a distance, He would dismount as a sign of humility. He was a true servant of Bahá'u'lláh and a servant does not ride into the presence of his Lord. Not only did 'Abdu'l-Bahá show humility towards Bahá'u'lláh, but by example He taught the companions of Bahá'u'lláh and His disciples lessons in self-effacement and servitude at the threshold of His Father. When pilgrims arrived, it was 'Abdu'l-Bahá who prepared them in every way for that glorious moment when they were to enter the presence of their Lord. He even arranged their attire and helped them to become selfless when in His presence.

Bahá'u'lláh, on the other hand, always showered His special love and affection upon 'Abdu'l-Bahá. He extolled and glorified the person of 'Abdu'l-Bahá, and conferred upon Him exalted titles. Bahá'u'lláh's adoration for 'Abdu'l-Bahá knew no bounds. For example, when 'Abdu'l-Bahá was to visit the Mansion of Bahjí, Bahá'u'lláh evinced great joy and yearning to meet His beloved Son. He would often send His other sons and male members of the family some distance from the Mansion to await the coming of the Master, to act as a welcoming party and to escort Him to the Mansion; while sometimes Bahá'u'lláh Himself would stand on the balcony to see Him arrive, and as 'Abdu'l-Bahá walked, He often pointed to His majesty and praised the beauty of His countenance and the strength of His character. But alas, at times this great adoration for the Master had to be suppressed by Bahá'u'lláh, so that 'Abdu'l-Bahá's brothers and other members of the family who did not have spiritual qualities would not become upset through jealousy.

'Abdu'l-Bahá's life was distinguished by His virtues and perfections. There is no need to dwell on this aspect which is universally acknowledged. Many writers, both oriental and occidental, have extolled in glowing terms the nobility of His character and testified to His divine qualities. The Revelation of

Bahá'u'lláh, of which He was the recipient, had so filled His soul that He became its perfect mirror reflecting the light of His Father's Faith upon the whole of mankind and manifesting to their eyes the resplendent characteristics of a perfect Bahá'í.

It is one of the unique bounties of God that in this age Bahá'u'lláh vouchsafed to humanity not only His Revelation, but a priceless gift in the person of 'Abdu'l-Bahá who occupies a unique position in His Dispensation. Though not invested with the rank of the Manifestation of God, the authority which Bahá'u'lláh has conferred on Him is such that His words have the same validity as those of Bahá'u'lláh and the Báb.

Soon after the ascension of Bahá'u'lláh there were differences among the believers concerning the station of 'Abdu'l-Bahá. Some regarded Him as having the same identity as Bahá'u'lláh —a belief which runs counter to the basic verities enshrined within the Faith. In several Tablets 'Abdu'l-Bahá clarified His own position. He explained that although He was the Centre of the Covenant of Bahá'u'lláh and the Interpreter of His words, He was nevertheless a lowly servant at the threshold of Bahá'u'lláh. In one of His Tablets 'Abdu'l-Bahá writes:

> This is my firm, my unshakable conviction, the essence of my unconcealed and explicit belief—a conviction and belief which the denizens of the Abhá Kingdom fully share: The Blessed Beauty is the Sun of Truth, and His light the light of truth. The Báb is likewise the Sun of Truth, and His light the light of truth . . . My station is the station of servitude—a servitude which is complete, pure and real, firmly established, enduring, obvious, explicitly revealed and subject to no interpretation whatever . . . I am the Interpreter of the Word of God; such is my interpretation.[4]

At one time Ḥájí Mírzá Ḥaydar-'Alí, to whom we have referred previously, wrote a letter to 'Abdu'l-Bahá and asked Him to explain the significance of Bahá'u'lláh's utterances in the *Súriy-i-Ghuṣn* and other Tablets including certain verses in the *Mathnaví* concerning the exalted station of the Branch. In reply, 'Abdu'l-Bahá wrote a Tablet in which He announced most eloquently His station of servitude and besought the Almighty to immerse Him in the ocean of servitude. He then made the following statement:

I am according to the explicit texts of the Kitáb-i-Aqdas and the Kitáb-i-'Ahd the manifest Interpreter of the Word of God . . . Whoso deviates from my interpretation is a victim of his own fancy . . . I affirm that the true meaning, the real significance, the innermost secret of these verses,* of these very words, is my own servitude to the sacred Threshold of the Abhá Beauty, my complete self-effacement, my utter nothingness before Him. This is my resplendent crown, my most precious adorning. On this I pride myself in the kingdom of earth and heaven. Therein I glory among the company of the well-favoured! [5]

Concerning the station of the Master, Shoghi Effendi writes:

. . . Though moving in a sphere of His own and holding a rank radically different from that of the Author and the Forerunner of the Bahá'í Revelation, He, by virtue of the station ordained for Him through the Covenant of Bahá'u'lláh, forms together with them what may be termed the Three Central Figures of a Faith that stands unapproached in the world's spiritual history. He towers, in conjunction with them, above the destinies of this infant Faith of God from a level to which no individual or body ministering to its needs after Him, and for no less a period than a full thousand years, can ever hope to rise. [6]

He is, and should for all time be regarded, first and foremost, as the Centre and Pivot of Bahá'u'lláh's peerless and all-enfolding Covenant, His most exalted handiwork, the stainless Mirror of His light, the perfect Exemplar of His teachings, the unerring Interpreter of His Word, the embodiment of every Bahá'í ideal, the incarnation of every Bahá'í

* Verses of the *Súriy-i-Ghuṣn* and the *Mathnaví* which glorify the station of 'Abdu'l-Bahá. (A.T.)

virtue, the Most Mighty Branch sprung from the Ancient Root, the Limb of the Law of God, the Being 'round Whom all names revolve', the Mainspring of the Oneness of Humanity, the Ensign of the Most Great Peacc, the Moon of the Central Orb of this most holy Dispensation—styles and titles that are implicit and find their truest, their highest and fairest expression in the magic name 'Abdu'l-Bahá. He is, above and beyond these appellations, the 'Mystery of God'—an expression by which Bahá'u'lláh Himself has chosen to designate Him, and which, while it does not by any means justify us to assign to him the station of Prophethood, indicates how in the person of 'Abdu'l-Bahá the incompatible characteristics of a human nature and superhuman knowledge and perfection have been blended and are completely harmonized.[7]

19

Bahá'u'lláh's Departure from Adrianople

The activities of Bahá'u'lláh's enemies, who intended to impose upon Him the strictest of confinements, gathered momentum in the early part of the year 1868. The most glorious, yet the most turbulent period in Bahá'u'lláh's ministry—a period of almost five years—was drawing to a close. It had been a time notable for its dynamism, its tests and trials, its challenging events, its unfaithful who turned to evil and its heroes who stood steadfast against the unfaithful; and above all it had seen the mighty Revelation of God poured out and His Message proclaimed to the rulers of the world collectively.

The Tablets revealed by Bahá'u'lláh in this period are so vast in number that their mere volume is bound to astonish the unbiased observer. If we were to write in detail even about the best-known Tablets revealed in Adrianople, this book would assume such impossible proportions as to necessitate several volumes. All we can do in the circumstances is to list a few of the more well-known Tablets: *Súriy-i-Bayán*, *Munájátháy-i-Ṣiyám* (prayers for fasting), *Lawḥ-i-Tuqá*, *Lawḥ-i-Riḍván*, *Lawḥ-i-Nuqṭih*, *Súriy-i-Hijr*, *Súriy-i-Qalam*, *Súriy-i-Qamíṣ*, *Súriy-i-Aḥzán*, *Riḍvánu'l-Iqrár*.

The revelation of so many important Tablets, and the proclamation of Bahá'u'lláh's Message to the kings and rulers of the world, had endowed the Faith with such ascendancy that by the summer of 1868 the authorities in Constantinople had become apprehensive of its rising prestige and power. The exaggerated reports and calumnies of Siyyid Muḥammad and his accomplice Áqá Ján together with further representations by the Mushíru'd-Dawlih, the Persian Ambassador, to the Sublime Porte, induced the Ottoman Government to remove the Author of such a dynamic Faith from the mainland and sentence Him to solitary confinement in a far-off prison.

The authorities in Constantinople were alarmed by the news that several outstanding personalities, including Khurshíd Páshá, the Governor of Adrianople, were among the fervent admirers of Bahá'u'lláh, were frequenting His house and showing Him veneration worthy of a king. They knew that the consuls of foreign governments had also been attracted to Him and often spoke about His greatness. The movement of many pilgrims in and out of Adrianople further aggravated the situation. Fu'ád Páshá, the Turkish Foreign Minister, passed through Adrianople, made a tour of inspection and submitted exaggerated reports about the status and activities of the community. Furthermore, a few among the authorities had come across some of Bahá'u'lláh's Writings and become aware of His stupendous claims. All these were important factors in deciding the fate of Bahá'u'lláh and His companions.

Those mainly responsible for Bahá'u'lláh's final banishment were the Prime Minister, 'Álí Páshá, the Foreign Minister, Fu'ád Páshá and the Persian Ambassador, Ḥájí Mírzá Ḥusayn Khán (the Mushíru'd-Dawlih). These three worked together closely until they succeeded in their efforts to banish Bahá'u'lláh to 'Akká and to impose on Him life imprisonment within the walls of that prison city. Bahá'u'lláh prophesied that 'Álí Páshá and Fu'ád Páshá would be struck down by the hand of God as a punishment for their action; we shall refer to their fate in the next volume.

As to the Mushíru'd-Dawlih, Bahá'u'lláh had at one time sent him a strong message through Ḥájí Mírzá Ḥasan-i-Ṣafá,* saying that if the Ambassador's aim in opposing Him was to destroy His person, there was nothing to stop him from carrying out his intentions against a Prisoner in the land. However, if he was

* See p. 55.

trying to exterminate the Cause of God, then he should know that no power on earth could quench this Fire which God had kindled on the earth. Its flame would soon encompass the whole world.

However, the Mushíru'd-Dawlih did everything in his power to enforce Bahá'u'lláh's imprisonment in 'Akká. The following is a translation of a letter he wrote to his Government a little over a year after Bahá'u'lláh's arrival in 'Akká.

> I have issued telegraphic and written instructions, forbidding that He (Bahá'u'lláh) associate with any one except His wives and children, or leave under any circumstances, the house wherein He is imprisoned. 'Abbás-Qulí Khán, the Consul-General in Damascus . . . I have, three days ago, sent back, instructing him to proceed direct to 'Akká . . . confer with its governor regarding all necessary measures for the strict maintenance of their imprisonment . . . and appoint, before his return to Damascus, a representative on the spot to insure that the orders issued by the Sublime Porte will, in no wise, be disobeyed. I have, likewise, instructed him that once every three months he should proceed from Damascus to 'Akká, and personally watch over them, and submit his report to the Legation.[1]

As the years went by, however, the Mushíru'd-Dawlih began to realize that the accusations made against Bahá'u'lláh by His enemies were unfounded. He saw in Him divine attributes and was impressed by His integrity and loftiness of purpose. After leaving his post in Constantinople, he spoke highly in Government circles in Persia of Bahá'u'lláh's uprightness and dignity. In Ṭihrán he is reported to have said that the only person outside Persia who had brought honour to the nation was Bahá'u'lláh, and later he assured Náṣirid-Dín Sháh that the followers of Bahá'u'lláh were not, as alleged, working against the interests of the country.

In the *Epistle to the Son of the Wolf* Bahá'u'lláh has commended him in these words:

His Excellency, the late Mírzá Ḥusayn Khán, Mushíru'd-Dawlih—may God forgive him—hath known this Wronged One, and he, no doubt, must have given to the Authorities a circumstantial account of the arrival of this Wronged One at the Sublime Porte, and of the things which He said and did . . . That which was done by his late Excellency—may God exalt his station—was not actuated by his friendship towards this Wronged One, but rather was prompted by his own sagacious judgment, and by his desire to accomplish the service he secretly contemplated rendering his Government. I testify that he was so faithful in his service to his Government that dishonesty played no part, and was held in contempt, in the domain of his activities. It was he who was responsible for the arrival of these wronged ones in the Most Great Prison ('Akká). As he was faithful, however, in the discharge of his duty, he deserveth Our commendation . . .[2]

Shaykh Káẓim-i-Samandar, to whom we have referred previously, has recorded the following account in his narratives:

Once Shaykh Salmán was arrested and imprisoned in Aleppo by the Persian Consul because he was carrying a number of letters and some goods from the believers to Bahá'u'lláh. Ḥájí Mírzá Ḥusayn Khán-i-Qazvíní was the Ambassador in those days. He happened to be passing through Aleppo at that time and therefore he carefully read all the letters, which numbered about three hundred. He noticed that none of them contained any political or worldly subjects. They were all supplications and questions on spiritual matters. He therefore ordered that all the letters and goods be returned to their owner. He then called Shaykh Salmán to his office and asked him to convey his greetings to Bahá'u'lláh. When this servant, the writer, was in the presence of the Blessed Beauty in the year 1291 A.H. (1874–5), He asked me once about the attitude and behaviour of Ḥájí Mírzá Ḥusayn Khán who was then the most outstanding personality in Persia. In the course of His talks Bahá'u'lláh stated that Ḥájí Mírzá Ḥusayn Khán was more prudent than the rest of the authorities in Persia, and had eventually mended his attitude towards Him.[3]

ÁQÁ RIḌÁY-I-QANNÁḌ OF SHÍRÁZ

A loyal companion of Bahá'u'lláh throughout His exile from Baghdád to 'Akká

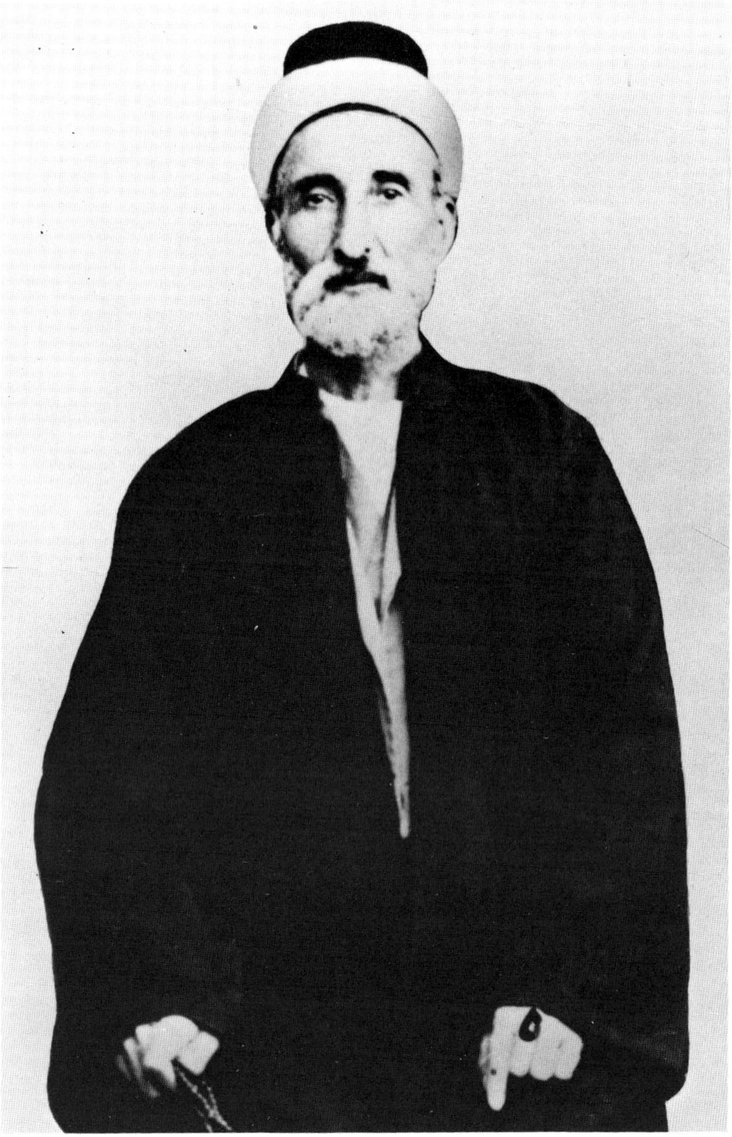

MÍRZÁ MAḤMUD-I-KÁSHÁNÍ

A selfless and trusted companion of Bahá'u'lláh throughout His exile from Baghdád to 'Akká

Speaking about Ḥájí Mírzá Ḥusayn Khán, Bahá'u'lláh in one of His Tablets has said that since he had changed his attitude and because he was related to a believer, God might through His bounty, forgive his misdeeds. The believer to whom the Mushíru'd-Dawlih was related was Mírzá Muḥammad-'Alíy-i-Kad-Khudá, a native of Qazvín. He was a devoted follower of Bahá'u'lláh described by Shaykh Káẓim-i-Samandar as 'a man adorned with spiritual qualities and human virtues, knowledgeable and sincere in faith, one who manifested these qualities to the full in his associations with people and in business circles'.[4]

The statement that God may forgive a soul because of kinship to a believer is explicit in the Writings of Bahá'u'lláh. In one of His Tablets[5] He states that one of the special bounties of God in this Dispensation is that in the next world His forgiveness and mercy will surround the souls of those who although bearing no allegiance to His Cause, are related to a believer, provided they have done no disservice to the Faith of Bahá'u'lláh, nor caused any harm to His loved ones during their lives.

This bounty is especially true of parents who do not embrace the Faith. In a Tablet[6] Bahá'u'lláh states that in this Revelation God has vouchsafed a special bounty to those believers whose parents are untouched by the light of the Faith. He affirms that in the next life God will illumine the souls of the parents through His favours and mercy. In one of His Tablets[7] 'Abdu'l-Bahá writes that the believers should earnestly pray for the souls of their departed non-Bahá'í parents. They should tearfully supplicate God for His forgiveness and carry out acts of beneficence on their behalf so that God may, through His grace, enable their souls to progress in His spiritual worlds.

While the authorities in Constantinople were actively engaged in their campaign of opposition to Bahá'u'lláh, Khurshíd Páshá, the Governor of Adrianople, did everything in his power to change their course of action but failed in his efforts. At last 'Álí Páshá, the Prime Minister, succeeded in securing from Sulṭán 'Abdu'l-'Azíz an imperial edict dated 5th Rabí'u'l-

Ákhir 1285 A.H. (26 July 1868) ordering Bahá'u'lláh's exile to the Fortress of 'Akká and His life imprisonment within the walls of that prison-city. In the same edict five others, mentioned by name, were to be exiled with Him. They were: the two faithful brothers of Bahá'u'lláh, Áqáy-i-Kalím and Mírzá Muḥammad-Qulí, His faithful servant Darvísh Ṣidq-'Alí, the Antichrist of the Bahá'í Revelation Siyyid Muḥammad-i-Iṣfahání, and his accomplice Áqá Ján Big. Mírzá Yaḥyá was condemned to life imprisonment in Famagusta along with four of Bahá'u'lláh's followers: Mírzá Ḥusayn entitled Mishkín Qalam, 'Alíy-i-Sayyáḥ, Muḥammad-Báqir-i-Qahvih-chí and 'Abdu'l-Ghaffár.

Strict orders were issued in the edict to the authorities in 'Akká directing them to accommodate the prisoners inside a house in the Fortress, to guard it most effectively and to ensure that the exiles did not associate with anyone.

When Khurshíd Páshá was informed of the edict and learnt of Bahá'u'lláh's immediate banishment he knew that he could not bring himself to notify Bahá'u'lláh of the contents of the Sulṭán's order. He was so embarrassed that he absented himself from his office and left the task to the registrar.

Mírzá Áqá Ján, Bahá'u'lláh's amanuensis, has described[8] the events leading to Bahá'u'lláh's departure from Adrianople. He states that one evening late at night Bahá'u'lláh instructed Jamál-i-Burújirdí and two believers from Persia who had come for the purpose of attaining His presence, to leave the city immediately and return to Persia. No one understood the wisdom of this action at the time, but it became evident on the following morning, when some Government officials called to ask Jamál's whereabouts, and were told that he had left the city a few hours earlier. (At this juncture it is appropriate to mention that before going to Adrianople Jamál-i-Burújirdí had rendered an important service to the Faith in Persia. He and Mullá 'Alí-Akbar-i-Shahmírzádí, known as Ḥájí Ákhúnd,* whom Bahá'u'lláh later appointed a Hand of the Cause of God,

* A brief account of his life will appear in a future volume.

had been instructed by Him in 1284 A.H. (1867–8) to transfer the remains of the Báb which were concealed within the Shrine of Imám-Zádih Ma'ṣúm to another place of safety. The details of this and subsequent transfers until the remains were laid to rest for ever in the bosom of God's holy mountain, Mount Carmel, constitute one of the most interesting episodes in the annals of the Faith.)*

Mírzá Áqá Ján states that the day after Jamál left Adrianople, the members of the community were rounded up early in the morning, and brought to Government headquarters. They were kept in custody while soldiers surrounded the house of Bahá'u'lláh and posted sentinels at its gates. An officer representing the Sublime Porte called and informed 'Abdu'l-Bahá that Bahá'u'lláh and His family were to proceed to Gallipoli.† According to Mírzá Áqá Ján's testimony, the officers had indicated that only those twelve companions who had accompanied Bahá'u'lláh to Adrianople were to travel with Him to Gallipoli. But the rest of the believers were extremely agitated by this proposition. They all wanted to accompany their Lord. Several of them who owned trading establishments in the city gave up their businesses, sold up what they could at very low prices and left many of their goods behind.

Áqá Riḍáy-i-Shírází,‡ known as Áqá Riḍáy-i-Qannád (candy maker), one of the companions of Bahá'u'lláh, who had come with him from Baghdád, has written about the reaction of the people of Adrianople to these developments:

> A great tumult seized the people. All were perplexed and full of regret . . . Some expressed their sympathy, others consoled us, and wept over us . . . Most of our possessions were auctioned at half their value.' [9]

* Shoghi Effendi has written a brief account of it in *God Passes By*, pp. 273–6.

† It appears that not until the exiles arrived at Gallipoli were they informed of their ultimate destination as set out in the Royal edict.

‡ See vol. I, pp. 288–9, and *Memorials of the Faithful*.

Another believer, Ḥusayn-i-Áshchí,* who served Bahá'u'lláh as a cook for many years, has left the following account † concerning the events leading to Bahá'u'lláh's departure for Gallipoli:

> Orders were issued from Constantinople for Bahá'u'lláh's exile to Syria. Since Khurshíd Páshá failed in his efforts to alter the course of events he felt ashamed to attain the presence of Bahá'u'lláh and therefore he announced his departure for another city. He left Adrianople leaving the affairs of the Government in the hands of an officer. However, he did not travel to another city; he merely retired to a summer residence on the outskirts of Adrianople. One afternoon after working in the kitchen I went to the bazaar. I visited Áqá Riḍáy-i-Shírází and Mírzá Maḥmúd-i-Káshání ‡ at their shop. I had been there only a few minutes when two soldiers called and summoned the two of them to the Government headquarters. I attempted to leave the shop but the soldiers caught me and took me with them. I noticed that all the friends who had shops in the bazaar had been taken to the headquarters. We were all counted,§ then each one's particulars were recorded. When they realized that I was a cook in Bahá'u'lláh's household, a soldier was called in and instructed to escort me to the house of Bahá'u'lláh . . .
>
> When we came near the house, I noticed that a number of soldiers were on duty and sentinels had been placed outside the gate. I was frightened by what I saw. I was stopped as I attempted to enter the house, even though the soldier who had escorted me had explained the circumstances. I was told that only the officer in charge could issue permission for entry, and he was in the outer apartment conversing with 'Abdu'l-Bahá . . . Eventually I was allowed in and was ushered straight into the presence of Bahá'u'lláh. He

* See pp. 169–70.

† This account is edited by the present writer.

‡ See vol. I, pp. 288–9.

§ Several times before this the members of the community had been taken to Government headquarters and counted.

enquired about the situation in town, but I was so frightened* that I could hardly speak. My mouth dried up with fear. I came out of the room and asked for water to drink. Then I felt better and went again to attain the presence of Bahá'u'lláh. He looked at me, smiled, and jokingly said, 'Was the Káshí frightened?' †

I told him the whole story. He then sent me to the house of Áqáy-i-Kalím with a message to come at once . . . I accompanied Áqáy-i-Kalím to the gate of Bahá'u'lláh's house. I was allowed in, but the soldiers stopped Áqáy-i-Kalím who sent a message to Bahá'u'lláh saying that since he was free to move in the city, was there anything he could do to help? When I conveyed this to Him, He said, 'Tell Áqáy-i-Kalím to come in. We seek help from no one, our affairs are not in the hands of anyone, they are in the hands of God.' ‡ I went to 'Abdu'l-Bahá and told Him this, and He asked the officer to let Áqáy-i-Kalím in and he did. It was this officer who had conveyed to 'Abdu'l-Bahá the news that the Governor, Khurshíd Páshá, was not available and that he was deputized to notify Him of the orders from Constantinople requiring Bahá'u'lláh's departure to Syria within two days . . .

Bahá'u'lláh, however, told the authorities that two days were not adequate time to prepare for the journey. He informed them that His household steward owed money to some suppliers in the bazaar. He required the authorities to free his men who were imprisoned in Constantinople and to allow them to sell the three horses§ so that every creditor in the bazaar might be paid. Then it would become possible to leave . . . Each day officers would arrive in the outer apartment and meet 'Abdu'l-Bahá. The soldiers had surrounded

* We should note that Ḥusayn-i-Áshchí at that time was a youth who for some years had enjoyed a sheltered life in Bahá'u'lláh's household protected from persecution.

† A native of Káshán is referred to as Káshí or Káshání. Persians often make fun of the Káshís alleging them to be faint-hearted and timid. This of course is purely fictitious.

‡ These are not the exact words of Báhá'u'lláh, but they convey the import of what He said.

§ See pp. 329.

the house and were on duty day and night. This situation lasted for eight days . . .

Several consuls of foreign powers arrived to attain the presence of Bahá'u'lláh and the soldiers did not prevent them from entering. They one and all showed genuine respect and humility towards Bahá'u'lláh and offered Him the protection of their respective governments. But Bahá'u'lláh clearly stated that He would not seek help from any government. His sole refuge was God . . . The consuls came several times, and no matter how much they persisted, Bahá'u'lláh rejected their offers and reaffirmed that He put His trust in God and turned to Him at all times . . .

On one occasion Bahá'u'lláh counselled some of the friends who had recently arrived to stay away and not to become part of the community of exiles. He spoke to them words of consolation, and told them that His destination was unknown . . . Among those whom Bahá'u'lláh counselled to stay away were two brothers, Ḥájí Ja'far-i-Tabrízí and Karbilá'í Taqí . . . who had come to Adrianople to attain the presence of Bahá'u'lláh. They were men of courage, tall in stature, enthusiastic and full of excitement. After hearing Bahá'u'lláh's advice that they should not think of accompanying Him, Ḥájí Ja'far privately decided that he preferred to die than to live away from His Lord. He took a razor with him to the outer apartment of the house which was crowded with military officers and government officials, put his head out of a window which opened onto the street, and cut his own throat.* Standing nearby in the room was Áqá Muḥammad-'Alíy-i-Tambákú-Furúsh who heard a terrifying shout coming from Ḥájí Ja'far. He pulled him into the room and found his throat cut. Immediately they called 'Abdu'l-Bahá. Everyone was appalled at the sight. At that moment I arrived in the outer apartment to count the number of people so that I could bring supper for everybody. The Greatest Holy Leaf was in the kitchen waiting for me to tell her the number. But when I saw Ḥájí Ja'far in that state staggering

* We have briefly referred to this incident in vol. I, pp. 97–8. It should be noted that the surgeon who attended to him later found that the carotid artery had not been cut.

all over the place with blood pouring out I was riveted to the scene before me, dazed and in a state of shock. The soldiers were telling Ḥájí Ja'far that a surgeon would be coming to attend to his wounds, but although he could not speak, he made it clear to them by sign language that even if the surgeon was able to stitch his wounds he would cut his throat again . . .

As I did not return to the kitchen the Greatest Holy Leaf sent the widow of Mírzá Muṣṭafá* to come and fetch me at once. But when she saw Ḥájí Ja'far in that frightful state she fainted and fell unconscious on the ground. Then from the kitchen they sent another person—a Christian maid—to come and see what was the cause of delay. She also fainted and dropped beside the widow of Mírzá Muṣṭafá!

In the meantime 'Abdu'l-Bahá sent me into the inner apartments of the house to bring some of His own clothes so that He could change Ḥájí Ja'far's clothes. On my way I found the two women fallen unconscious at the gate; I sprinkled water on their faces and massaged them until they regained consciousness. The three of us entered the kitchen together. When the holy family saw us in such a state, frightened and trembling, they wanted to know what had happened, especially when I asked for the Master's clothes. I said the Master had perspired a lot in the crowd and wished to change! But the Greatest Holy Leaf did not believe me. She said, 'Tell me the truth, what is the matter? Why are you all so frightened?' I still tried to hide the news from her, but she lovingly urged me to tell the truth pointing out that my hiding it would cause distress to everybody in the household. So I told the story . . . and suggested that the news be kept from Bahá'u'lláh until after He had had supper. The Greatest Holy Leaf dismissed my idea as a feeble one and admonished me saying that this was not the first time that such a thing had happened; already thousands of lovers had shed their blood in the path of the Blessed Beauty . . .

As to Ḥájí Ja'far, 'Abdu'l-Bahá urged him to co-operate with the surgeon when he came and promised him that he would be allowed to join Bahá'u'lláh. They placed some

* He had been martyred in Persia, see pp. 60–61.

cotton over his wound until a competent surgeon by the name of Muḥammad arrived. But Ḥájí Ja'far was unwilling for his throat to be stitched up. He kept on saying 'Away from my Beloved this life is useless to me . . .' Eventually the Ancient Beauty came to his bedside . . . and with His hands touched Ḥájí Ja'far's head and face, and assured him that He would summon him to His new place of exile as soon as his wounds were healed. He urged him to remain in Adrianople until he was completely recovered.* When Bahá'u'lláh returned to His room the surgeon started to stitch the wound, but the thread kept breaking. He had to repeat the operation several times. During this ordeal Ḥájí Ja'far remained motionless. He endured the pain with such strength that he did not even screw up his face once!

As to Bahá'u'lláh's departure for Gallipoli, the authorities responded favourably to His demand concerning the release of the prisoners in Constantinople . . . and forwarded a sum of money towards the value of the horses. Then preparations began for the journey and the standard of bereavement was hoisted in the city. The souls of many people burnt in the fire of separation from their Beloved and their hearts cried out in their remoteness from Him . . . All the furniture was auctioned at a very low price. It took eight days before everything was ready. Then they brought about fifty carriages for all of us. Many people, Muslims, Christians and Jews crowded around the carriages, sobbing and grief-stricken . . . The scenes of lamentation were more heart-rending than those of a few years before at the time of Bahá'u'lláh's departure from Baghdád . . . Bahá'u'lláh spoke words of comfort to all and bade them farewell . . . At Gallipoli we housed all our belongings in a caravanserai while we stayed in a house. Bahá'u'lláh, the holy family and the females among the party stayed upstairs and the rest of us downstairs.'[10]

Among those who arrived in Gallipoli from the prison in Constantinople were Mishkín-Qalam, 'Alíy-i-Sayyáḥ, 'Abdu'l-Ghaffár and Muḥammad-Báqir-i-Qahvih-chí, all of whom were

* Ḥájí Ja'far and his brother were able to proceed to 'Akká soon after Bahá'u'lláh's departure to that city. See *Memorials of the Faithful*.

condemned to accompany Mírzá Yaḥyá to Cyprus, while Darvís̲h̲ Ṣidq-'Alí, whose name was recorded in the Royal edict, was to accompany Bahá'u'lláh to 'Akká. The other two prisoners, Ustád Muḥammad-'Alíy-i-Salmání and Jams̲h̲íd-i-Gurjí, were deported to the borders of Persia. It appears that these two were released from prison partly through the prompt intervention of Mír Muḥammad-i-Mukárí,* who, on learning that these two had not been freed, went to the Sublime Porte and vehemently demanded their immediate release.

Salmání and Jams̲h̲íd-i-Gurjí were taken as prisoners to one of the border towns and handed over to the Kurdish authorities for transfer to Persia. The Kurds, finding the prisoners to be men of integrity, and innocent of any crime, set them free, and the two of them managed to find their way to the Prison of 'Akká where they were reunited with their Lord.

Shoghi Effendi has briefly described Bahá'u'lláh's departure from Adrianople:

> On the twenty-second of the month of Rabí'u't̲h̲-T̲h̲ání 1285 A.H. (12 August 1868) Bahá'u'lláh and His family, escorted by a Turkish captain, Ḥasan Effendi by name, and other soldiers appointed by the local government, set out on their four-day journey to Gallipoli, riding in carriages and stopping on their way at Uzún-Kúprú and Kás̲h̲ánih, at which latter place the Súriy-i-Ra'ís was revealed. 'The inhabitants of the quarter in which Bahá'u'lláh had been living, and the neighbours who had gathered to bid Him farewell, came one after the other,' writes an eye-witness, 'with the utmost sadness and regret to kiss His hands and the hem of His robe, expressing meanwhile their sorrow at His departure. That day, too, was a strange day. Methinks the city, its walls and its gates bemoaned their imminent separation from Him.' 'On that day,' writes another eye-witness, 'there was a wonderful concourse of Muslims and Christians at the door of our Master's house. The hour of departure was a memorable one. Most of those present were weeping and wailing,

* See chapter 14.

especially the Christians.' '*Say*,' Bahá'u'lláh Himself declares in the Súriy-i-Ra'ís, '*this Youth hath departed out of this country and deposited beneath every tree and every stone a trust, which God will erelong bring forth through the power of truth.*'

Several of the companions who had been brought from Constantinople were awaiting them in Gallipoli. On his arrival Bahá'u'lláh made the following pronouncement to Ḥasan Effendi, who, his duty discharged, was taking his leave: '*Tell the king that this territory will pass out of his hands, and his affairs will be thrown into confusion.*' 'To this,' Áqá Riḍá, the recorder of that scene has written, 'Bahá'u'lláh furthermore added: "Not I speak these words, but God speaketh them." In those moments He was uttering verses which we, who were downstairs, could overhear. They were spoken with such vehemence and power that, methinks, the foundations of the house itself trembled.'

Even in Gallipoli, where three nights were spent, no one knew what Bahá'u'lláh's destination would be. Some believed that He and His brothers would be banished to one place, and the remainder dispersed, and sent into exile. Others thought that His companions would be sent back to Persia, while still others expected their immediate extermination. The Government's original order was to banish Bahá'u'lláh, Áqáy-i-Kalím and Mírzá Muḥammad-Qulí, with a servant to 'Akká, while the rest were to proceed to Constantinople. This order, which provoked scenes of indescribable distress, was, however, at the insistence of Bahá'u'lláh, and by the instrumentality of 'Umar Effendi, a major appointed to accompany the exiles, revoked. It was eventually decided that all the exiles, numbering about seventy, should be banished to 'Akká. Instructions were, moreover, issued that a certain number of the adherents of Mírzá Yaḥyá, among whom were Siyyid Muḥammad and Áqá Ján, should accompany these exiles, whilst four of the companions of Bahá'u'lláh were ordered to depart with the Azalís for Cyprus.

So grievous were the dangers and trials confronting Bahá'u'lláh at the hour of His departure from Gallipoli that He warned His companions that '*this journey will be unlike any of the previous journeys*', and that whoever did not feel himself '*man enough to face the future*' had best '*depart to whatever place he pleaseth, and be preserved from tests, for hereafter he will find himself unable to leave*'—a warning which His companions unanimously chose to disregard.

On the morning of the 2nd of Jamádíyu'l-Avval 1285 A.H. (21 August 1868) they all embarked in an Austrian-Lloyd steamer for Alexandria, touching at Madellí, and stopping for two days at Smyrna, where Jináb-i-Munír, surnamed Ismu'lláhu'l-Muníb, became gravely ill, and had, to his great distress, to be left behind in a hospital where he soon after died. In Alexandria* they transhipped into a steamer of the same company, bound for Haifa, where, after brief stops at Port Said and Jaffa, they landed, setting out, a few hours later, in a sailing vessel, for 'Akká, where they disembarked, in the course of the afternoon of the 12th of Jamádíyu'l-Avval 1285 A.H. (31 August 1868). It was at the moment when Bahá'u'lláh had stepped into the boat which was to carry Him to the landing-stage in Haifa that 'Abdu'l-Ghaffár, one of the four companions condemned to share the exile of Mírzá Yaḥyá, and whose '*detachment, love and trust in God*' Bahá'u'lláh had greatly praised, cast himself, in his despair, into the sea, shouting 'Yá Bahá'u'l-Abhá', and was subsequently rescued and resuscitated with the greatest difficulty, only to be forced by adamant officials to continue his voyage, with Mírzá Yaḥyá's party, to the destination originally appointed for him.†[11]

Súriy-i-Ra'ís

The *Súriy-i-Ra'ís* was revealed in honour of Ḥájí Muḥammad Ismá'íl-i-Káshání, entitled Dhabíḥ (Sacrifice) and Anís (Companion) by Bahá'u'lláh. It is in Arabic‡ and is addressed to 'Álí Páshá, the Grand Vizir of Turkey. Dhabíḥ, unlike his half-

* See vol. I, p. 204. (A.T.)
† See vol. I, pp. 287–8. (A.T.)
‡ Not to be confused with *Lawḥ-i-Ra'ís* in Persian, revealed in 'Akká and also addressed to 'Álí Páshá.

brother Ḥájí Mírzá Aḥmad,* was a faithful believer and a man of piety. He arrived in Adrianople during the time that the House of Bahá'u'lláh was surrounded by soldiers. He therefore could not attain the presence of Bahá'u'lláh and was advised by Him to proceed to Gallipoli. Dhabíḥ wrote a letter to Bahá'u'lláh and this Tablet was revealed in his honour. It was after the revelation of the *Súriy-i-Ra'ís* and with Bahá'u'lláh's permission that he attained His presence in the public bath in Gallipoli.

The following is a brief account of the life and activities of Dhabíḥ as outlined by Shaykh Káẓim-i-Samandar in his memoirs:

> . . . Ḥájí Muḥammad Ismá'íl-i-Dhabíḥ of Káshán was a brother of the late Ḥájí Mírzá Jání. When the Báb was on His way to Ṭihrán, . . . He honoured these brothers by staying in their home † . . . In the early days of the Faith these two brothers worked together in the promotion of the Cause of God, until Ḥájí Mírzá Jání was martyred.‡ After the declaration of Bahá'u'lláh and as a result of much investigation and endeavour on his part, Dhabíḥ became an ardent follower of Bahá'u'lláh. Since that time he engaged in teaching the Faith and transcribing the Writings. He travelled to Adrianople, but his journey coincided with the time of troubles and persecution in that land, a time when the house of Bahá'u'lláh and those of the believers were guarded by troops and no one was admitted. Dhabíḥ and those who were with him proceeded to Gallipoli. The *Súriy-i-Ra'ís* was revealed in those days . . .
>
> After returning from this journey he devoted his time to teaching the Cause and diffusing the fragrances of God with the utmost vigour and steadfastness. He exerted such an influence in Ṭihrán that the Náyibu's-Salṭanih § arrested and imprisoned him. During the interrogations which ensued, Dhabíḥ openly taught the Faith. The authorities took a

* See p. 137.

† See p. 110.

‡ See *The Dawn-Breakers*.

§ Prince Kámrán Mírzá, a son of Náṣiri'd-Dín Sháh. He was Governor of Ṭihrán for some years.

photograph of him for presentation to the Sháh and copies of it are available from some of the friends. Lately he went *via* Qazvín to Tabríz where he passed away* to the realms of eternity . . .[12]

In one of His Tablets[13] addressed to Dhabíḥ, Bahá'u'lláh urges him to arise and teach His Cause, as God has created him for this purpose. In another Tablet addressed to Dhabíḥ's son Ghulám-'Alí, Bahá'u'lláh states that Dhabíḥ wished to lay down his life in the path of God and affirms that he had the station of a martyr in the sight of God and was honoured with the appellation Dhabíḥ (Sacrifice) by the Pen of the Most High.

The revelation of the *Súriy-i-Ra'ís* began soon after Bahá'u'lláh left Adrianople in the village of Káshánih and was completed at Gyáwur-Kyuy on His way to Gallipoli.

The first part of this Súrih is addressed to 'Álí Páshá, whom Bahá'u'lláh calls Ra'ís (Chief). This is one of the most challenging Tablets of Bahá'u'lláh, in which the Prime Minister is reprimanded by the Tongue of power and might. In its opening passage Bahá'u'lláh bids 'Álí Páshá hearken to the voice of God, calling throughout earth and heaven and summoning mankind to Himself. He states that no power on earth can frustrate Him from proclaiming His Message, and in strong language He unequivocally declares that neither 'Álí Páshá's opposition nor that of his associates can hinder Him from carrying out His purpose. He rebukes 'Álí Páshá for having united with the Persian ambassador in committing that which had caused Muḥammad, the Prophet of God, to lament in the most exalted paradise. He proclaims the greatness of His Revelation and the exalted station of its Author, affirms that should He unveil His glory which is kept hidden because of the weakness of man, the whole of creation would sacrifice itself in His path.

In this Tablet Bahá'u'lláh identifies 'Álí Páshá with those who denied the Manifestations of past Dispensations and rose up against them. He recalls the arrogance of the Persian Emperor

* This was around 1297–8 A.H. (1880–81).

in the days of Muḥammad, the transgressions of Pharaoh against Moses and the wicked acts perpetrated by Nimrod against Abraham. Addressing 'Álí Pá<u>sh</u>á directly, Bahá'u'lláh asserts that his efforts to extinguish the fire of the Cause which the hands of God have ignited will be of no consequence; on the contrary they will help to fan it into flame. He prophesies that ere long it will encompass the whole world and that His Revelation will quicken the souls of all mankind.

The *Súriy-i-Ra'ís* was revealed at a time when Bahá'u'lláh and His companions were outwardly afflicted with tribulations and indignities on the eve of their banishment to 'Akká, yet from the Pen of the Most High these ominous warnings were issued to one who was the head of the Turkish Government at the time and the main perpetrator of the cruel injustices against Bahá'u'lláh.

> The day is approaching when the Land of Mystery (Adrianople), and what is beside it shall be changed, and shall pass out of the hands of the king, and commotions shall appear, and the voice of lamentation shall be raised, and the evidences of mischief shall be revealed on all sides, and confusion shall spread by reason of that which hath befallen these captives at the hands of the hosts of oppression. The course of things shall be altered, and conditions shall wax so grievous, that the very sands on the desolate hills will moan, and the trees on the mountain will weep, and blood will flow out of all things. Then wilt thou behold the people in sore distress.*[14]

At one point in the *Súriy-i-Ra'ís*, Bahá'u'lláh turns His attention away from 'Álí Pá<u>sh</u>á and addresses <u>Dh</u>abíḥ in words of

* These prophecies, and others which were uttered by Bahá'u'lláh in 'Akká, foreshadowing the downfall of Sulṭán 'Abdu'l-'Azíz, 'Álí Pá<u>sh</u>á and Fu'ád Pá<u>sh</u>á were remarkably fulfilled. The Russian troops occupied Adrianople, Serbia, Montenegro and Rumania and announced their independence; Cyprus and Egypt were occupied; Eastern Rumelia was ceded to Bulgaria which became a self-governing state. In brief the Ottoman Empire was dismembered. We shall refer to these events in more detail in a future volume.

loving-kindness and appreciation. He states that as the soldiers were keeping guard, He found Himself in a state of immense joy and gladness, for nothing would be more meritorious in His sight than martyrdom in the path of God. He recounts the tragic actions of the Government authorities when they sent troops to surround His residence and those of His loved ones, and states that the believers and His family were left without food on the first night of the siege, and in the following words, depicts the scenes of lamentation by the inhabitants of Adrianople on the day of His departure from the city:

> The people surrounded the house, and Muslims and Christians wept over Us . . . We perceived that the weeping of the people of the Son (Christians) exceeded the weeping of others—a sign for such as ponder.[15]

He describes the attempt by Ḥájí Ja'far-i-Tabrízí to take his own life because of the love he cherished for his Lord, testifies that such an act was 'unheard of in bygone centuries'; it was an act that 'God hath set apart for this Revelation, as an evidence of the power of His might'.[16] He recalls a similar incident in Baghdád when Siyyid Ismá'íl of Zavárih had been so carried away by the ocean of love which surged within his heart as to take his own life by cutting his throat.* Bahá'u'lláh declares that these souls were so magnetized by His love that they were driven by an uncontrollable urge to sacrifice their lives, and affirms that in spite of the fact that in so doing, they acted against His commandments, they are immersed in the ocean of His forgiveness and have attained an exalted station in the realms of God.

In the *Súriy-i-Ra'ís* Bahá'u'lláh affirms that tribulations and sufferings inflicted upon the believers will act as oil for the lamp of the Cause of God and add to its radiance and glory. He states that the Cause is immeasurably great, that nothing can undermine its rise and establishment even though all the forces of

* See vol. I, pp. 101–3.

earth and heaven league against it and the kings and rulers rise up to oppose it. He further prophesies:

> Ere long will God raise up from among the kings one who will aid His loved ones. He, verily, encompasseth all things. He will instill in the hearts the love of His loved ones. This, indeed, is irrevocably decreed by One Who is the Almighty, the Beneficent.[17]

So great is this Revelation that Bahá'u'lláh proclaims in the *Súriy-i-Ra'ís*:

> Had Muḥammad, the Apostle of God, attained this Day, He would have exclaimed: 'I have truly recognized Thee, O Thou the Desire of the Divine Messengers!' Had Abraham attained it, He too, falling prostrate upon the ground, and in the utmost lowliness before the Lord thy God, would have cried: 'Mine heart is filled with peace, O Thou Lord of all that is in heaven and on earth! I testify that Thou hast unveiled before mine eyes all the glory of Thy power and the full majesty of Thy law!' . . . Had Moses Himself attained it, He, likewise, would have raised His voice saying: 'All praise be to Thee for having lifted upon me the light of Thy countenance and enrolled me among them that have been privileged to behold Thy face!'[18]

One of the unique features of the Manifestation of God is that, unlike the human being, His thoughts and actions are not necessarily directed to the immediate issue of the time no matter how vital and pressing the situation may be. He can never be absorbed in one particular problem to the exclusion of others.* For He does not abide in the world of limitations. Although He dwells on earth, He is animated by the Spirit of God and, as stated in Islám, 'Nothing whatsoever keepeth Him from being occupied with any other thing.'[19]

This characteristic of the Manifestation of God is clearly

* For a further discussion see vol. I, pp. 262–3.

demonstrated in the person of Bahá'u'lláh as He revealed the *Súriy-i-Ra'ís* in the midst of calamities and afflictions which even threatened His life and that of His family and companions. For in response to a question by Dhabíḥ, He describes the nature of the rational soul, and elucidates the conditions under which it can acquire different qualities. He explains that the soul may progress in two different directions. If it moves towards God it will acquire spiritual qualities, and after its separation from the body it will abide in the realms of God adorned with divine attributes. If it turns away from Him, however, it will become satanic and devoid of spiritual characteristics. Bahá'u'lláh dwells on this subject at great length; a detailed study of His explanations is beyond the scope of this volume.*

Concerning the significance of the *Súriy-i-Ra'ís*, Bahá'u'lláh in one of His Tablets revealed in 'Akká states:

> So blind hath become the human heart that neither the disruption of the city, nor the reduction of the mountain in dust, nor even the cleaving of the earth, can shake off its torpor. The allusions made in the Scriptures have been unfolded, and the signs recorded therein have been revealed, and the prophetic cry is continually being raised. And yet all, except such as God was pleased to guide, are bewildered in the drunkenness of their heedlessness!
>
> Witness how the world is being afflicted with a fresh calamity every day. Its tribulation is continually deepening. From the moment the *Súriy-i-Ra'ís* (Tablet to Ra'ís) was revealed until the present day, neither hath the world been tranquillized, nor have the hearts of its peoples been at rest. At one time it hath been agitated by contentions and disputes, at another it hath been convulsed by wars, and fallen a victim to inveterate diseases. Its sickness is approaching the stage of utter hopelessness, inasmuch as the true Physician is debarred from administering the remedy, whilst unskilled practitioners

* The subject of the soul and its immortality are explained by Bahá'u'lláh and 'Abdu'l-Bahá in many Tablets. They will be discussed in the next volume.

are regarded with favour, and are accorded full freedom to act . . . The dust of sedition hath clouded the hearts of men, and blinded their eyes. Erelong, they will perceive the consequences of what their hands have wrought in the Day of God. Thus warneth you He Who is the All-Informed, as bidden by One Who is the Most Powerful, the Almighty.[20]

These warnings uttered by Bahá'u'lláh over a century ago and soon after His clarion call to the kings and rulers of the world in the *Súriy-i-Mulúk*, in which similar warnings were issued, have set in motion an immense cataclysmic process, breaking up the old order and destroying the foundations of human society everywhere on the planet. Helpless and agonized, mankind is held in the clutches of its devastating fury not knowing where to turn and how to stem the tide of its catastrophic course. And yet we live at a time when man's knowledge and material achievements, compared with the past, are phenomenal.

To the followers of Bahá'u'lláh the cause of these calamitous trends is clear and simple. The plight of man today is similar to that of a gardener who toils and labours in vain because he has planted his seeds in fertile soil but in a dark pit far away from the rays of the sun. Man has turned his back on the Sun of Truth. Not until he recognizes Him and turns to Him will he find peace on this earth and tranquillity in his heart.

Almost four decades ago, in the midst of the Second World War, Shoghi Effendi wrote a most illuminating analysis * of the world-engulfing calamities afflicting the human race, delineated their origin, and depicted their outcome. In this masterly work he describes on the one hand the inevitability of the breaking up of the old order and the suffering that it entails, and on the other the glorious vistas of the distant future when the Golden Age of the Faith of Bahá'u'lláh will usher in an era of unsurpassed blissfulness and unity for the whole human race.

Enumerating the manifold persecutions and sufferings which

* *The Promised Day is Come.*

the human race, for almost eight decades, inflicted upon Bahá'u'lláh, the Báb and 'Abdu'l-Bahá, Shoghi Effendi writes:[21]

> ... Alas, a thousand times alas, that a Revelation so incomparably great, so infinitely precious, so mightily potent, so manifestly innocent, should have received, at the hands of a generation so blind and so perverse, so infamous a treatment! 'O My servants!' Bahá'u'lláh Himself testifies, 'The one true God is My witness! This most great, this fathomless and surging ocean is near, astonishingly near, unto you. Behold it is closer to you than your life-vein! Swift as the twinkling of an eye ye can, if ye but wish it, reach and partake of this imperishable favour, this God-given grace, this incorruptible gift, this most potent and unspeakably glorious bounty.'

After a revolution of well nigh one hundred years what is it that the eye encounters as one surveys the international scene and looks back upon the early beginnings of Bahá'í history? A world convulsed by the agonies of contending systems, races and nations, entangled in the mesh of its accumulated falsities, receding farther and farther from Him Who is the sole Author of its destinies, and sinking deeper and deeper into a suicidal carnage which its neglect and persecution of Him Who is its Redeemer have precipitated. A Faith, still proscribed, yet bursting through its chrysalis, emerging from the obscurity of a century-old repression, face to face with the awful evidences of God's wrathful anger, and destined to arise above the ruins of a smitten civilization. A world spiritually destitute, morally bankrupt, politically disrupted, socially convulsed, economically paralyzed, writhing, bleeding and breaking up beneath the avenging rod of God. A Faith Whose call remained unanswered, Whose claims were rejected, Whose warnings were brushed aside, Whose followers were mowed down, Whose aims and purposes were maligned, Whose summons to the rulers of the earth were ignored, Whose Herald drained the cup of martyrdom, over the head of Whose Author swept a sea of unheard-of tribulations, and Whose Exemplar sank beneath the weight of life-long sorrows and dire misfortunes. A world that has lost its bearings, in which the bright flame of religion is fast dying out, in which the forces of a blatant nationalism and racialism have usurped the rights and prerogatives of God Himself, in which a flagrant secularism—the direct offspring of irreligion—has raised its triumphant head and is protruding its ugly features, . . . and in which the virus of prejudice and corruption is eating into the vitals of an already gravely disordered society . . .

We are indeed living in an age which, if we would correctly appraise it, should be regarded as one which is witnessing a dual phenomenon. The first signalizes the death-pangs of an order, effete and godless, that has stubbornly refused, despite the signs and portents of a century-old Revelation, to attune its processes to the precepts and ideals which that Heaven-sent Faith proffered it. The second proclaims the birth-pangs of an Order, divine and redemptive, that will inevitably supplant the former, and within whose administrative structure an embryonic civilization, incomparable and world-embracing, is imperceptibly maturing. The one is being rolled up, and is crashing in oppression, bloodshed, and ruin. The other opens up vistas of a justice, a unity, a peace, a culture, such as no age has ever seen. The former has spent its force, demonstrated its falsity and barrenness, lost irretrievably its opportunity, and is hurrying to its doom. The latter, virile and unconquerable, is plucking asunder its chains, and is vindicating its title to be the one refuge within which a sore-tried humanity, purged from its dross, can attain its destiny.

'Soon,' Bahá'u'lláh Himself has prophesied, 'will the present day order be rolled up, and a new one spread out in its stead.' And again 'By Myself! The day is approaching when We will have rolled up the world and all that is therein, and spread out a new Order in its stead.' . . .

'The whole earth,' He, moreover, has stated, 'is now in a state of pregnancy. The day is approaching when it will have yielded its noblest fruits, when from it will have sprung forth the loftiest trees, the most enchanting blossoms, the most heavenly blessings.' 'All nations and kindreds,' 'Abdu'l-Bahá likewise has written, '. . . will become a single nation.

Religious and sectarian antagonism, the hostility of races and peoples, and differences among nations, will be eliminated. All men will adhere to one religion, will have one common faith, will be blended into one race, and become a single people. All will dwell in one common fatherland, which is the planet itself.'

APPENDIX I

The Star-fall of 1866 *

The spectacular shower of meteors in the early hours of the morning of 14 November 1866 was observed all over Europe. It was an extraordinary event exciting comment from professional astronomers and laymen alike. The following accounts have been chosen from the many reports and letters in contemporary newspapers.

The Times
Saturday, 17 November 1866.

> The Rev. Robert Main, the Radcliffe Observer at Oxford, gives the following account of the meteorological phenomenon of Tuesday night last:—
> '. . . This great display began about 13h. (or 1 o'clock in the morning), and reached its maximum at about 13h.24m., after which time it gradually began to slacken. The watch, however, was kept up till 18h., though after 15h., there were not many meteors seen. In all there were observed not fewer than 3,000 during the night, of which about 2,000 fell between 13h. and 14h., or between 1 a.m. and 2 a.m. As to the general appearance of the meteors, it was noticed that the majority of them were of a whitish or yellowish colour. Some, however, were reddish or orange-coloured, and one meteor was noticed to be bluish. The brightest left generally a train behind them, which was to be seen for a few seconds after the meteor disappeared.'

* For its significance see p. 270

poznač si...

IV The worship ... Writings 35, 36, 65, 66, 68, 69.

III 30, 31, 32, 33 – 51, 54, 79, 80, 82, 83, 84, 93, 94, 126, 128, 141.

247

The Times
Thursday, 15 November 1866.

Sir:—
The predicted display of shooting stars was observed here on a magnificent scale during the early hours of this morning, and, as the sky may have possibly been in few places so clear as here, the notes I made may perhaps be interesting to some of your numerous readers.

During the half-hour preceding midnight about 66 were observed.
From midnight to 12.30 about 200 were observed.
From 12.30 to 12.50 about 201 were observed.
From 12.50 to 12.58 about 190 were observed.
From 12.58 to 1.2 about 201 were observed in 4 minutes.
From 1.2 to 1.5 about 206 were observed in 3 minutes.
From 1.5 to 1.10 about 214 were observed in 5 minutes.
From 1.10 to 1.11 about 100 were observed in 1 minute.
From 1.11 to 1.13 about 206 were observed in 2 minutes.

The falls now became so incessant that it was impossible to count numbers fast enough . . .

I am, Sir, your obedient Servant
M.

Cowes, Isle of Wight, Nov. 14.

The Times
Thursday, 15 November 1866.

Sir:—
The following observations of last night's phenomena were made near Corley, the highest point of Warwickshire, by myself and a friend . . . The meteors took a direction from E. to W., with but very few exceptions. They may be divided into three classes. The most numerous were the ordinary shooting stars interspersed with some very large ones, which left a long blue (and sometimes green) streak of light varying in width. At the moment of extinction there was nothing extraordinary but the intense brilliancy of the head. Another class occurred at intervals of a few minutes,

and seemed to be balls of copper-coloured fire, which left no path, nor varied in brightness before vanishing. The most remarkable series were also infrequent. The path they took was an irregular curve, short, but well defined, and which remained in view two or three minutes.

Some of the largest meteors appeared to burst, and then reappear, leaving two nodes of light connected by a luminous line.

It would be impossible to exaggerate the grandeur of the heavens between 1 and 3 o'clock . . .

I am, Sir, yours &c.,
W. W. TYLER

Coventry, Nov. 14.

The Times
Thursday, 15 November 1866.

Sir:—

The predicted shower of meteors has been witnessed here during the past night under very favourable atmospheric circumstances . . . From midnight to 1 o'clock a.m., Greenwich time, one thousand one hundred and twenty meteors were noted, the number gradually increasing. From 1 a.m. to 1h.7m.5s. no less than five hundred and fourteen were counted, and we were conscious of having missed very many, owing to the rapidity of their succession. At the latter moment there was a rather sudden increase to an extent which rendered it impossible to count the number, but after a hundred and twenty a decline became perceptible. The maximum was judged to have taken place about 1.10, and at this time the appearance of the whole heavens was very beautiful, not to say magnificent . . . while the meteors in the opposite corners of the sky traversed arks of many degrees, in the vicinity of the diverging point they shone out for a few seconds without appreciable motion, and might have been momentarily mistaken for stars by anyone to whom the configuration of the heavens in that direction was not familiar . . .

I am, Sir, your obedient servant,
J. R. HIND.

Mr. Bishop's Observatory, Twickenham, Nov. 14.

The Times
Saturday, 17 November 1866.

Sir:—

Last night, the 14th of November, I witnessed a very extraordinary display of 'falling stars', and as I think I have understood that this particular night of the year is remarkable for the appearance of these meteors, a short account of their occurrence on the occasion may not be without interest to some of your readers. For several weeks past the sky in this part of Spain has been without a cloud, and consequently the display of last night was seen under circumstances which could only very rarely occur in England. My attention was first directed to the falling stars at about 12 o'clock at night, by observing groups of people in the narrow streets of Saragossa conversing together with a certain degree of excitement. 'Mira Usted es como si fue en el tiempo del sito' ('Look, it is just as if it were in the time of the siege') was the reply to my question as to what was the matter, and on looking up the appearance certainly was as if the city was being shelled. Showers of meteors seemed to be pouring into the place, a score or more at a time, exploding with a brilliant flame at different points, and leaving long luminous trains behind them, some of which lasted as streaks in the sky several instants after the explosion of the meteor. I hastened to an open space, and I much regret that the sight I witnessed did not fall to the lot of a scientific observer. The meteors seemed to be more abundant towards the north and north-west, and I noticed a particular stream of them not far from the constellation of the Great Bear. The direction of their flight was mostly from right to left downwards at various angles of inclination; but on arriving at my own room afterwards I observed from the window, which commanded a somewhat different view, a succession of meteors, which seemed to fall nearly in a vertical direction from about the same point in the sky. I may notice that the luminous tracks at this point were occasionally seen crossing at acute angles those which were projected from right to left, but I did not observe a single instance of the tracks crossing in other directions, or, in other words, of meteors projected from the opposite side. It was evident to me that the stars were being projected in one or more fixed lines of flight. Those which fell in a nearly vertical direction appeared to be much more brilliant than the others; they all left a well defined trail or track of sparks of a pale bluish colour, and they finally exploded with a brilliant white or yellow flame; in some instances the flame appeared tinged on the edges with a vivid emerald green colour, and others exhibited tints of pink or crimson and blue. Some idea may be formed of their number and brilliancy from the fact that when I went to bed, though the field of sky visible through my window as I lay was very small, it was being continually crossed by the meteors, and a looking-glass which hung on the wall was every moment brilliantly lit up with the reflection of the explosions which occurred. During the short time I observed them many hundreds of meteors fell, and, as there was no perceptible diminution in their number, I have no doubt during the night the number must have been tens of thousands.

I am, Sir, your obedient servant.

J. C. ROBINSON.

Saragossa, Nov. 15.

APPENDIX II

A Visit to Adrianople from an article by Martha L. Root[1]

. . . We know He [Bahá'u'lláh] arrived with His family and friends on Saturday, 12 December 1863, and remained until Wednesday, 12 August 1868; He was forty-six years old when He came and His son, 'Abbás Effendi known as 'Abdu'l-Bahá, was a youth of nineteen years while His daughter, Bahíyyih Khánum, was a girl seventeen years old. How different was their journey from Constantinople to the present luxurious Oriental Express trip when the train speeds swiftly over the distance in exactly six hours' time! Their journey to Adrianople, evidently hurried and enforced, for they were not prepared and were only thinly clad, took twelve days and was full of hardships as the weather was bitterly cold. Bahíyyih Khánum said long years after that she was a strong, well girl before those terrible exile journeys.

Their first lodging in Adrianople was in the Khán-i-'Arab Caravanserai where they stayed three nights. All one knew about it was that it was near the house of 'Izzat Áqá. Then they lived for one week in a house in the Murádíyyih quarter near the Takyiy-i-Mawlaví and then changed to a winter house close by. Twice Bahá'u'lláh lived in the house of Amru'lláh Big, which has been spoken of by Áqá Riḍá in his early account as a three-storey house to the North of Sulṭán Salím Mosque. Another house in which He lived was the home of Riḍá Big. Then He returned to the residence of Amru'lláh Big, but the last eleven months of His stay were spent in the home of 'Izzat Áqá. We know, too, that He was sometimes in the

Murádíyyih Mosque and very often in the Sulṭán Salím Mosque where He met and spoke with thinkers . . .

Miss Marion E. Jack, a Bahá'í who is a painter from Canada and the writer, a Bahá'í who is a journalist and magazine writer from the United States, came to Adrianople, on 17 October 1933, to look for 'traces of the Traceless Friend'. Their quest was 'to seek, to find and not to fail' to portray Adrianople to the Bahá'í world . . . Miss Jack through her brush and the writer through her pen . . .

The beautiful road lighted by the moon was lined on each side with great poplar, plane and willow trees mystic with shadows, and as we came over the fine Maritza bridge the lights of the city gleamed a welcome in this 'Land of Mystery' . . .

This Adrianople, which the Turks call Edirne, was a city of two hundred thousand inhabitants before the Balkan wars and the world war. Now it numbers only forty thousand. It is on the direct Oriental Express route from Constantinople to Paris, and is also on the main motoring way from Central Asia to Western Europe. One remembers, too, that in 1360 Adrianople was made the capital of the great Turkish Empire and became the centre from which radiated the light of Islám to a Western world. Its mosque architecture is extraordinarily beautiful. Adrianople is interesting, too, because it is so typically Turkish, much more so than is Constantinople, which is now considerably westernized . . .

The first morning it rained. Down through the stone-cobbled streets the water poured in little torrents. Standing at our window, we saw the people of Adrianople trying to cross these fiercely flowing rivulets but none could do it without immersing their feet far down in the pools. However, after mid-day dinner the skies suddenly cleared, the streams disappeared leaving the cobble stones clean and white. The sun came out in glory, shedding its warmth generously, and we took a horse and carriage driven by a kind Turk whose name was Muṣṭafá.

We rode through Government Street, the principal thoroughfare, picturesque with its vistas of bazaars and its brightly coloured rugs hanging outside the shops, but most interesting of all we passed some of the most beautiful mosques to be found anywhere in the world. We drove over the cobbled stones of some extremely narrow streets till we came into a more open road which led to the Murádíyyih district. Leaving Muṣṭafá and the carriage at the foot of the hill, we walked up the steep, needle-eye road lined on each side with little shops and a mill where a horse goes round and round turning wheels to grind the olive into oil. The Murádíyyih Mosque crowns the slope and, just as we were coming, the muezzin came out on a parapet of the slender, graceful minaret and using his hand as funnel loud-speaker chanted the call to prayer.

When we reached the historic mosque we did not go in at once because a Ḥájí and some others were engrossed in their daily devotions. We walked about looking at this noble mass of splendid architecture, but most of all scanning the horizon to see where Bahá'u'lláh might have lived. Murádíyyih section in Bahá'u'lláh's day was one of the most fashionable residential summer districts of Adrianople, even the Sulṭán had a summer palace in that quarter. The air is most pure and fresh on this mountain slope and the grapes there were world renowned. The route to Bulgaria and on to Central and Western Europe and the road to Constantinople wind like broad white ribbons through the plains below stretching on and on until out of sight.

We found the Takyiy-i-Mawlaví, a building for dervishes in the last century, it is just in front of the mosque—and we knew that Bahá'u'lláh's houses, one at least, was very near to that. Miss Jack took her pencil and sketch book to draw this Takyiy-i-Mawlaví and the fountain in front of it where women were carrying away heavy pails of water hung on poles balanced over their shoulders. What Water of Life the women of Bahá'u'lláh's time could have carried away when He was at that well!

I went into the mosque, for now it was quite empty except for the kindly old caretaker whose eyes were filled with peace. It is a beautiful interior, high and lofty and the blue faience, of various hues from the delicate Chinese green-blue of the East to the deep rich Sèvres' blue of the West, is marvellously colourful although now it is more than five hundred years old. No wonder a man from Poland famous in tile designing has just come to make a study of these tiles and that many come from the United States just to see this faience work. It was made by a Persian whom the Turks invited to come and decorate this mosque.

Quotations from the holy Qur'án illumined the walls. All colours were soft and harmonious, such rich old tones are seldom seen in our modern churches; but the outer things were almost as if I did not see them, so absorbed was I in the consciousness that this was a place where He had prayed and where God had spoken to Him as of old He had spoken to Moses in the Burning Bush! I was impressed how in all His exiles, Bahá'u'lláh seemed always to live close to the mosques—the symbols of the divine in the earth-plane. In His hours of prayer in these terrestrial edifices God certainly revealed to Him how the dead world was to be revivified. What wonderful Works were written by Bahá'u'lláh in Adrianople! There were fourteen that we know of, and among these were the Tablets to the Kings, the Prayers on Fasting, the first Tablet to Napoleon III, and the great Tablet to the Sháh of Persia which have been translated into our Western languages.

Kneeling with forehead to the rugs in this memorable mosque, the writer felt with a throb of wonder how far Bahá'u'lláh had come to meet our Western world! Adrianople was His closest approach—in the outer plane—to our Occident: but all these thoughts dropped into subconsciousness as one bowed in silent love in His Living presence. He was there in that mosque! And the one listening heard anew that His Teachings, the Logos, carry in Themselves the Power that will make of this world of earth a high paradise. The moments there were sublime, not to be described but experienced!

Later when the writer lifted her eyes from devotion, she glanced once more about the mosque before arising from her knees. As she saw the Verses from the Qur'án upon the walls, she thought of 'Abdu'l-Bahá's Words when He was asked what we in the United States and Canada should do with the Tablets He revealed to the United States and Canada and sent to us in 1919. He replied to put them into the Mashriqu'l-Adhkár in Chicago, not into the vaults but upon the walls. Our new Bahá'í temple in the West and probably other Mashriqu'l-Adhkárs in various parts of the globe will become renowned later as the great new architecture and the new ideal of spiritual edifices conceived in the twentieth century. The Bahá'í architecture will reflect the essential traits of our Bahá'í believers—universality, spiritual solidarity, spiritual refinement, beauty, joyousness, sincerity and light. More than any other edifice in the world, the new Mashriqu'l-Adhkár in Chicago presents in concrete, in bronze, in quartz a gleaming reflection of all these inner qualities. How little we realize that we, too, are building for the centuries ahead in our new architecture, and that the name of our Louis Bourgeois, who designed this first Mashriqu'l-Adhkár in the Americas, will be much more known and praised five hundred years from now even than it is today in the West. Sometimes it is good to see the famous mosques of Sinán and other Muḥammadan architects who lived in the epoch of a former World Teacher; it quickens in us a realization of the stupendous spiritual age in which we ourselves are living.

As the days went by we kept coming back to this Murádíyyih section so often, that Muṣṭafá, our driver, said to the neighbours gathered about us to see the sketches, that we seemed to love Murádíyyih the best of all the places in Adrianople. Then after nearly two weeks' time we found the sites of the two houses where Bahá'u'lláh had lived; how we found all the sites is as interesting as a novel, but space does not permit its telling.

An old man, Muḥammad Ḥilmí Big, a fine type of Turk, told us that he had been a neighbour, that his boyhood home had been just across the roadway from Bahá'u'lláh's house and he showed us the old structure of his place. He explained that there had been two 'Bahá'í Bigs'*—one great Persian, who lived in the mansion just adjoining the entrance gate to the Murádíyyih Mosque, seldom went out, but the other one, 'Abbás Big, used to go everywhere and used to treat the boys with much friendliness; but the great Bahá'í Big, too, was good to the boys. He had pilau given to them. This man told us too, and showed us what an immense house had been the mansion of Bahá'u'lláh; it had eighteen rooms and a Turkish bath—one can see from the site that it had been a very great mansion. The house was demolished in the Russian war fifty years ago; a cheap house had been built twenty-five years ago on the part of the lot nearest to the entrance gate, but most of that, too, had been razed in the last Balkan war. Muḥammad Ḥilmí Big showed us that just beyond the wall of Bahá'u'lláh's house was a stretch of land through which runs a brook, and the Bahá'ís also had that entire place which extended down to the river in that time. There were several different buildings including stables and a large, long garden. He told us that these Persians had beautiful Arabian horses and two donkeys. There had been a house rather larger than the others in this garden enclosure, situated at the lower bend of the grounds and several people told us that Bahá'u'lláh had also lived there for a short time. That house overlooked the summer palace of the Sulṭán which stood lower on an opposite slope still in the Murádíyyih section. Now there is only the site of Bahá'u'lláh's house, all his houses were demolished in the wars. We think that Bahá'u'lláh might have lived in this lower house the first week as it was close to the Takyiy-i-Mawlaví, just as an early historian relates. It could be reached from Takyiy-i-Mawlaví and Murádíyyih Mosque by going down a steep, narrow pathway part of which is stone steps, or one could have approached it through the garden.

Muḥammad Ḥilmí Big told us there were more than fifty Persians living in these places and that very many visitors came; they, too, were entertained there. This genial man explained

* 'Big' is a Turkish title meaning a person of high rank, a Lord. (A.T.)

Sulṭán Salím Mosque; one could walk to it easily from either location. Muṣṭafá Big said to us: 'Oh, how many grapes did we receive from the hand of Bahá'í Big! He gave us so many grapes always!' I heard that the grapes of Adrianople were very celebrated then; later in the wars the grapevines were all destroyed. I was very impressed how in every place Bahá'u'lláh lived in His exiles, He had a garden.

One day when Miss Jack and I went again to the vacant lot where the house of Amru'lláh Big had stood, Muṣṭafá Big came over to us, cane in hand, with the firm eager tread of one who knows and wishes us to know all the history of the place. He showed how one part was the quarter for the women, another the suites for the men and he pointed to the great fireplace in the rear where the cooking was done. However, he pointed to a two-storey house with the middle portion three storeys just across the street but a little further down, and he said that some of Bahá'u'lláh's followers lived in that house, that most of the cooking was done over there. He said that generally the food was prepared and brought to Bahá'u'lláh at the Amru'lláh mansion—though I did understand him to say sometimes the cooking would all be done in the Amru'lláh 'kitchen' fireplace and carried over to the green house where most of the Persian friends ate their meals. He told us that this old house, which was green in colour in Bahá'u'lláh's time, has now been remodelled and is painted pink. He made it very clear that Bahá'u'lláh Himself never lived there. (A pretty Turkish girl came out from the pink house when we took a photograph and a sketch; she asked about the great Man whose friends had eaten in her home!)

This much at least we learned, that Bahá'u'lláh lived for a long time in the home of Amru'lláh Big; the old man told us He lived in Adrianople nearly five years. We know that when the Prince of Peace lived and walked in Adrianople He was an honoured member in three of the great Turkish families, He lived in some splendid mansions of that great former metropolis, and He was loved and reverenced by those who knew Him. Is it not significant that the one man in Adrianople who said: 'I saw Bahá'u'lláh!' tells us that he received pilau and grapes and that Bahá'u'lláh loved the poor and had a kitchen for them!

It seems to me that it must have been in this house of Amru'lláh Big or in the house adjacent that Ṣubḥ-i-Azal poisoned the food of Bahá'u'lláh, for he was living there in the latter time of His stay, and then left this house and went to live in the home of 'Izzat Áqá for the last eleven months of His sojourn in Adrianople . . .

There is not very much to be said about the ruins of the houses of Riḍá Big and 'Izzat Áqá except that one can see from the old stone walls and baths and fireplaces what extraordinarily large mansions they were. Certainly from them one would have a glorious view of the Sulṭán Salím Mosque. We were told that the house of 'Izzat Áqá had a very large library 'where the Bahá'ís studied'—perhaps they meant where Bahá'u'lláh wrote or received the thinkers and seekers. It was the room where the three fireplaces are, . . . The fact that Bahá'u'lláh was living in the homes of these three great citizens of Adrianople proves in itself that He was loved and honoured in their midst. We hope that others coming after us will find out more about these two houses.

Concerning the Khán-i-'Arab Caravanserai, we searched for that for nearly three weeks; in going to the old caravanserais we saw what luxurious hostelries they must have been in that epoch, but we were told later that the Khán-i-'Arab Caravanserai was not one of the great fashionable ones but was for the Arab middle and poorer classes. Probably Bahá'u'lláh and His followers were taken there by the Turkish officials from Constantinople who brought them to Roumelia. There were said to be two Khán-i-'Arab caravanserais—or some persons said that one was called 'Arab-i-Khán, or simply Arab Caravanserai—there were great differences of opinion but both sites are now used for large schools. We took a photograph of the one they said was Khán-i-'Arab Caravanserai near to the house of 'Izzat

'ABDU'L-GHAFFÁR
One of Bahá'u'lláh's most devoted servants
He threw himself into the sea when he was prevented from accompanying Bahá'u'lláh

ḤÁJÍ MUḤAMMAD ISMÁ'ÍL-I-KÁSHÁNÍ

Entitled Dhabíḥ
An outstanding teacher of the Faith of Bahá'u'lláh and one of His most devoted followers. He was the recipient of the Súriy-i-Ra'ís

that one of the members of Bahá'u'lláh's family gave Persian lessons to the head of the Mevlevi Cherleri dervishes.*

Our kind Adrianople friend, Muḥammad Ḥilmí Bey, at the end of our visit said very softly that perhaps we knew they were exiles because they changed religion, but he added most sincerely and with love straight from the heart: 'They were very, very kind, they didn't harm anybody and they did good to everybody!'

Then he said good-bye to us and with a questioning smile—before he started cane in hand to stride slowly down the hill to his house—this brave, true man who has seen three Balkan wars and the world war despoil Adrianople said to us: 'How have you liked us Turks? Do you find Turkish folks don't eat people from other countries!' Beloved Turkish brother whose boyhood home was close beside the house of Bahá'u'lláh, if only we could express to you how lovely we found you and how kind we found the citizens of Adrianople! And to learn from you and others that your citizens here were good to Bahá'u'lláh endears us forever to your historic city!

The home of Amru'lláh Big was the third residence where Bahá'u'lláh lived in Adrianople; this site was the easiest to find and was verified by the greatest number of citizens. This great house stood just near the main entrance to the magnificent Sulṭán Salím Mosque, . . . Also, a man in public life showed us this place—and walked with us on through two or three other streets and pointed out the sites of the houses of Riḍá Big and 'Izzat Áqá and the Khán-i-'Arab Caravanserai site very near the grounds of 'Izzat Áqá. We could see from the ruins that the

* Dervishes no longer hold their services in these buildings at Takyiy-i-Mawlaví, but one man there who used to be dervish told us that Bahá'u'lláh had lived in this lower house and then later in the one up by the entrance gate. He said that Bahá'ís had used the kitchen, the dining-room and the bathroom of the Takyiy-i-Mawlaví and showed us these rooms—and probably they did in those first few days until they could get established. The dervishes then were a large and flourishing group, they had four buildings right beside the mosque. Some of the photographs of earlier meetings show that they all wore the high táj headdress.

three residences were all remarkably large mansions and we heard that all three hosts were distinguished men of Adrianople at that time.

Now this Amru'lláh Big lot, which is like one whole block—and the house covered all of it—is only a place of ruins; the ground is covered with crumbled stones, flowering thistles and weeds. Part of the old wall still stands and a large portion of an enormous old fireplace which the Turks call the 'kitchen'.

We heard of an old man, Muṣṭafá Big, eighty-five years old, who had seen Bahá'u'lláh. When we met him he told us that he had been a neighbour living near the house of Amru'lláh Big and that he had carried yogurt to 'Bahá'í Big' (Bahá'u'lláh), and the latter always had pilau given to him to carry home. His eyes shone as he spoke of Bahá'u'lláh, and he tried to show us how noble He was; this kindly, sincere old man, a Turk, stood up and tried to make us understand how Bahá'í Big walked with such a dignity and power, and how He bowed to people who saluted Him—he told us that all people saluted Bahá'u'lláh, that every one loved and revered Him.

We were informed that Bahá'u'lláh had a kitchen for the poor.

This man told us, too, that Bahá'u'lláh had a great vineyard—from his description we think it was like a garden with an arbour in the centre. He said that Bahá'u'lláh went there often, sometimes alone to spend the day, sometimes He went there with His friends and they walked up and down. When He would return at night with his cortége, this man told us, that Bahá'u'lláh's twenty servants (followers) would all stand together outside the house to salute Him and He always returned their greeting so lovingly.

We took this good friend with us and went out to the vineyard site. He measured off the distances and showed us where the entrance gate had been. The grounds would cover in area about three city blocks; the land is on an elevation and the place is only about seven minutes' walk from Sulṭán Salím Mosque. This vineyard was between the Murádíyyih Mosque slope and

Áqá, and a sketch of the other one which is not far from the Sulṭán Salím Mosque.

Sulṭán Salím Mosque, where Bahá'u'lláh often went, is considered to be the most beautiful mosque in Turkey and was designed by Sinán, the great Turkish architect. Certainly its wide cloisters would be ideal as a place to sit and speak of matters divine, and its interior is full of beauty. Miss Jack and I were each asked to write our impressions of this mosque to be used in a Turkish book and we did so.

. . . I feel happy that we could meet the man who had seen 'Abbás Big and knew the Murádíyyih house well, and that we had explained to us the Amru'lláh Big house and the Vineyard by a man who was a neighbour and who saw Bahá'u'lláh.

[Note: the Persian names in this article have been transliterated in accordance with the system used in this book.]

APPENDIX III

Ḥájí Mírzá Ḥaydar-'Alí of Iṣfahán

Ḥájí Mírzá Ḥaydar-'Alí was one of the outstanding disciples of Bahá'u'lláh and foremost among His trusted teachers who travelled extensively throughout Persia. He is to be forever regarded as one of the most able defenders of the Covenant of Bahá'u'lláh, one who championed the Cause of God during the Ministry of 'Abdu'l-Bahá, helped to protect it from the onslaught of the Covenant-breakers and rallied the believers around the Centre of the Covenant.

Ḥájí Mírzá Ḥaydar-'Alí was born into a Shaykhí family in Iṣfahán. He spent his youth in Kirmán in the service of Ḥájí Mírzá Karím Khán,* the arch-enemy of the Faith of the Báb. But soon he discovered that the man he was serving was devoid of spiritual qualities. Disillusioned, he returned to his native town of Iṣfahán. In that city, a few years after the martyrdom of the Báb, he came across one of the Báb's followers who familiarized him with the Faith. Through study of the Writings and especially through the steadfastness of the believers in the face of persecution and martyrdom, he recognized the truth of the new-born Faith of God.

Soon after his recognition of the Faith, Ḥájí Mírzá Ḥaydar-'Alí was introduced to other believers including Zaynu'l-Muqarrabín.† But meeting the friends demanded the utmost caution, otherwise their lives would be endangered. Ḥájí Mírzá Ḥaydar-'Alí himself recounts the story of how he used to go at the dead of night to the house of one of the Bábí friends. To ensure that no one would see him leave his house, he had to

* See vol. I, Appendix IV.

† See vol. I, pp. 25–6.

climb out through a window and return the same way. At the home of his friend, they used to hide their lamp in a hole inside a room, then hold the Writings of the Báb beside the hole, read the verses of God and receive spiritual sustenance through them.

Soon Ḥájí Mírzá Ḥaydar-'Alí became confirmed in his faith and conversant with the Writings of the Báb. One thing which above all captured his imagination and overwhelmed his mind was the glad-tidings of the coming of 'Him Whom God shall make manifest'. To recognize Him when He revealed Himself, and to attain His presence, was Ḥájí Mírzá Ḥaydar-'Alí's ardent desire and the sole object of his life. Through the purity of his heart he also realized that Mírzá Yaḥyá, although the nominee of the Báb, had none of the requisite spiritual qualities.

Ḥájí Mírzá Ḥaydar-'Alí travelled around Persia, visited the believers and spoke to them about the advent of 'Him Whom God shall make manifest'. In the course of these visits he suffered persecution from the enemies and sometimes opposition from those friends who had set their affections upon Mírzá Yaḥyá.

From the early days, Ḥájí Mírzá Ḥaydar-'Alí became attracted to Bahá'u'lláh, especially when he read the *Kitáb-i-Íqán*. Then he acquired new vision and was further confirmed in his faith. He regarded Bahá'u'lláh as the source of Divine Revelation and championed His cause after His declaration. He travelled to Adrianople, attained His presence and as a result became a new creation and a spiritual giant of this age. We have already referred to some of his experiences in Adrianople and Constantinople.

After spending about fourteen months in the capital of the Ottoman Empire, where he served the Faith acting as a channel of communication between Bahá'u'lláh and the friends, he was directed by Bahá'u'lláh to proceed to Egypt to teach His cause. He was particularly advised to be very discreet and cautious in his teaching work and not to arouse the antagonism of fanatics. In a Tablet to him Bahá'u'lláh had prophesied that he would be afflicted by ordeals and persecutions, had counselled him to be thankful and joyous when sufferings were inflicted upon him in the path of God, had exhorted him to remain steadfast and immovable as a mountain in His Cause and had assured him of ultimate deliverance and protection. Bahá'u'lláh had also promised Ḥájí Mírzá Ḥaydar-'Alí, both in person and in writing, that his eyes would once again behold the beauty of His Lord and that he would attain His presence. These prophetic words were fulfilled. Ḥájí Mírzá Ḥaydar-'Alí went through the most harrowing afflictions during his life in Egypt and the Sudan, afflictions that lasted almost ten years.

He succeeded in teaching the Faith to a number of Persians resident in Egypt, but soon news of his activities spread among that community. Mírzá Ḥasan Kh́án-i-Kh́ú'í, the Consul General and a vicious enemy of the Cause, disguised himself as a seeker of truth and invited Ḥájí Mírzá Ḥaydar-'Alí to his home. After several meetings at which Ḥájí spoke openly about the Faith, the Consul arrested him along with two other friends and imprisoned them in the Consulate. Their feet were placed in stocks and chains put on their necks. Later the number of prisoners was increased to seven Persians who were charged with being followers of the new Faith and one Egyptian who had befriended Ḥájí Mírzá Ḥaydar-'Alí, but was not a believer.

In the meantime the Consul succeeded in arousing the anxiety of the Egyptian authorities by introducing the prisoners as subversive elements teaching a new religion and working against the security of the state. He managed to secure an order condemning them to an indefinite period of imprisonment in the Sudan. The story of the ordeal of this journey to the Sudan and their imprisonment there is recorded in detail by Ḥájí Mírzá Ḥaydar-'Alí and is one of the most heart-rending episodes in the history of the Faith.

The prisoners, chained and fettered, endured many hardships in the Consulate. Their daily food consisted of a slice of bread each and a small cup of water. The Consul did everything possible to humiliate them in the eyes of the public. Ḥájí Mírzá Ḥaydar-'Alí writes:

> During the forty-five days we spent in the home of the Consul we suffered as in hell because of his staff and servants, but the soul was in the utmost joy beyond description.[1]

Eventually they were handed over to the Egyptian authorities and placed in a government jail. Later they were transferred to another jail, and were tied together with a chain and placed inside a dark cell. Into this locked cell no light could enter, nor was there a lamp. The end of the chain was brought out through a hole in the door and was held by a guard.

Ḥájí Mírzá Ḥaydar-'Alí decided that this was an occasion for rejoicing. He taught his companions to chant the *Lawḥ-i-Náqús*. The voice of the prisoners chanting this aloud and in unison echoed through the building. The guards who heard those soul-stirring verses were attracted by them and soon they realized that the prisoners were men of God and not criminals. They opened the cell, took the chains away, gave them a light and would only lock the door when an officer was coming. The prisoners stayed in this prison for about fifty days during which time their bodies recovered from the effects of malnutrition and their souls were in the utmost joy. Ḥájí writes:

> We were very happy because we were freed from this world and willing to lay down our lives in His path.[2]

However, they were then transferred to yet another jail where they faced the hardest ordeal of their life. One day, the authorities called blacksmiths and carpenters to the jail to chain the prisoners permanently for their journey to the Sudan. Four of the prisoners each had their right foot inserted in a huge iron collar and the other four their left foot. Each collar had a large iron loop attached to it. Then they were tied in pairs by joining the two loops with a heavy chain of about two yards long. Ḥájí Mírzá Ḥaydar-'Alí writes:

> The fastening of the iron collars and their connecting chains was such a painful operation that we could not control ourselves. We yelled, screamed and also laughed. The guards, officers, blacksmiths, carpenters, and all the others who were present wept over us and condemned their own jobs and professions for forcing them to torment the servants of God.[3]

Then came the turn of the carpenters. They were to make stocks for the prisoners' hands. A heavy piece of timber about one yard in length and very thick was constructed having two grooves in which the right and left hands of the same couple were placed. Then another piece of timber was securely nailed on the top thus closing the grooves. Ḥájí Mírzá Ḥaydar-'Alí writes:

> The stocks caused greater hardship than the chain and the collar upon our feet. For we might have been able to lighten the burden on our feet by lifting the chain with our hands when walking. But the stocks had tied each pair so inflexibly that our movements became extremely restricted and difficult. The placing of chains and stocks took a long time to complete. It started about two hours before noon and ended soon after sunset.[4]

Immediately after this, the prisoners were moved to a ship and were accommodated in an enclosed quarter which served as a store.

The Persian Consul had so wickedly misrepresented the prisoners to the Egyptian authorities that the Government had become alarmed. They had been led to believe that these men were the most vicious criminals, whose aim was to wipe out the religion of Islám, assassinate the king and overthrow the Government. Therefore orders were issued that the prisoners must be kept in chains, and guarded all the time. The journey, which involved travelling by ship and crossing the desert, sometimes on foot and sometimes by camel, lasted about five months.

Until the prisoners arrived in the Khartoum prison where the chains and stocks were removed and replaced with smaller chains, Ḥájí Mírzá Ḥaydar-'Alí and his companions bore the weight of these gruesome tools of torture. They suffered agony and hardship beyond description. Tied in pairs in this appalling fashion, they sat, slept, and were forced to walk for miles together. During this period the rigours of the journey, the agony of being in chains and fetters, the effects of starvation, malnutrition and gross ill-treatment, the pains of associating with the vilest of men, criminals and murderers, and the crushing force of many other unspeakable sufferings which were inflicted upon them, reduced them to such physical frailty that several times they were brought to the verge of death.

But because of the spiritual powers of Ḥájí Mírzá Ḥaydar-'Alí the prisoners were content and happy. It was also through the influence of his radiant personality that the authorities were charmed by his character and recognized his greatness.

It so happened that as the prisoners were travelling to the Sudan, Ja'far Pá<u>sh</u>á, the Governor of the Sudan was on his way to Khartoum. He met Ḥájí Mírzá Ḥaydar-'Alí at Aswan and was so struck by his spirituality and greatness that he ordered the officers to extend more consideration towards the prisoners. Ḥájí Mírzá Ḥaydar-'Alí writes:

> He [Ja'far Pá<u>sh</u>á] assured us that he would see that we were more comfortable, and he instructed the guards to show as much kindness as was in their power. The Pá<u>sh</u>á left us and we stayed in that spot for three days. On the day that we were to resume the journey we were handed to new soldiers who brought camels for us to ride. But as we were tied together, it was difficult to mount . . . They placed both tied feet and hands of each couple on the saddle, one person hanging on one side of the camel, the other on the other side, and tied the hanging bodies to the camel with the help of cotton sheets. Remaining in this position was extremely difficult. One cannot think of a torture more agonizing than this. But the fact is that there was no alternative. This journey took five or

> six hours, during which time they halted five or six times. They untied us, and helped us to dismount to have a rest. The guards expressed their sympathy and apologized, saying that previously they had escorted thieves and murderers to the Sudan similarly chained, but they had to walk. In our case, however, Ja'far Pá<u>sh</u>á had ordered that we ride and they could not think of a better way . . . Although we were in great pain and torture, nevertheless as we watched each other hanging, we used to laugh very heartily, and managed to reach the Nile alive . . .[5]

After these and many more grievous experiences, the prisoners arrived in Berber in the Sudan and were transferred to a prison which was so overcrowded with thieves and murderers that it was difficult to find a place to sit without being attacked by the inmates or stung by the scorpions. For about forty-five days they stayed in that area until they embarked in a sailing ship on the last leg of their journey. This lasted no less than thirty-six days, during which they endured many more afflictions. At last they arrived in Khartoum and were placed in a prison which was more crowded than the one in Berber. Later, by the orders of Ja'far Pá<u>sh</u>á, mentioned above, the prison authorities removed the ghastly chains and stocks and replaced them with a lighter chain. They were also allowed to sleep in a small hut made of reed and timber which was especially erected for them.

For about nine months the prisoners remained in the Khartoum jail, but soon people recognized the heavenly qualities and spiritual gifts of Ḥájí Mírzá Ḥaydar-'Alí. He wrote a letter to tha <u>Sh</u>ay<u>kh</u>u'l-Islám of Khartoum, proclaimed the mission of the Báb and Bahá'u'lláh to him, described their sufferings, expatiated on Bahá'u'lláh's glory and majesty, His loftiness and grandeur, extolled in glowing terms the qualities of 'Abdu'l-Bahá, explained all the circumstances of his own imprisonment and that of his companions and demanded the intervention of the <u>Sh</u>ay<u>kh</u>u'l-Islám in order to secure the release of the prisoners. The <u>Sh</u>ay<u>kh</u>u'l-Islám shared the letter with Ja'far

Pá<u>sh</u>á who was moved by the story. He went to the prison and issued orders to remove the chains from the prisoners, to issue wheat flour to them instead of corn and to supply them with meat and other necessities to which they were not entitled. He permitted them to leave the prison during the day and return at night. He also requested the authorities in Egypt to relax their restrictions and allow the prisoners to live freely in Khartoum. Two of the prisoners engaged in work as engravers, one practised medicine, and Ḥájí Mírzá Ḥaydar-'Alí was asked by the Governor to become a scribe. Soon many of the inhabitants of Khartoum became aware of the wonderful character and qualities of Ḥájí Mírzá Ḥaydar-'Alí. Some even attributed miracles to him. Many officials flocked to see him in the evenings in the prison where he spent all his earnings and entertained them. His prison chamber became the centre of attraction for the learned and wise who sat at his feet and enjoyed his company.

Then Ja'far Pá<u>sh</u>á's term of office came to an end and a new Governor arrived. It was during the latter's reign that the Egyptian authorities agreed to the request by the former Governor to allow the prisoners to leave the jail and live freely in the city. At this time so great was the prestige of Ḥájí Mírzá Ḥaydar-'Alí that the new Governor would turn to him for guidance and enlightenment when in serious difficulties about personal matters affecting his career. Another Governor who admired Ḥájí Mírzá Ḥaydar-'Alí was Ismá'íl Pá<u>sh</u>á. He had known him since his early days of imprisonment, and had a greater appreciation of Ḥájí's wisdom and spiritual gifts than his predecessors had done. He often used to call on Ḥájí for companionship and visit him in his home.

From the early days of his arrival in Khartoum, Ḥájí Mírzá Ḥaydar-'Alí kept on writing to Bahá'u'lláh. For some time, not knowing that Bahá'u'lláh had been exiled to 'Akká about the same time that he was imprisoned in Egypt, Ḥájí continued to send his letters to Adrianople and these never reached Bahá'u'lláh. However, soon after His arrival in the prison of 'Akká,

Bahá'u'lláh established contact with the believers. He sent a special messenger to the Sudan to find Ḥájí Mírzá Ḥaydar-'Alí and the other prisoners and assure them of His bounties and confirmations. The messenger was Ḥájí Jásim-i-Baghdádí who disguised himself as a dervish, travelled on foot to Khartoum and succeeded in contacting Ḥájí during the period that the latter was still a prisoner but free to move about. The arrival of Bahá'u'lláh's special messenger brought indescribable joy and assurance to the prisoners in general and to Ḥájí in particular. For forty days, Ḥájí heard everything about Bahá'u'lláh's whereabouts, His imprisonment and other afflictions from Ḥájí Jásim. Later a Tablet of Bahá'u'lláh reached Ḥájí Mírzá Ḥaydar-'Alí and over this he rejoiced more than over his meeting with Bahá'u'lláh's messenger.

After this initial Tablet about four to five Tablets a year would be revealed for the prisoners and sent to them in the Sudan. It was also arranged that copies of Tablets and various Writings of Bahá'u'lláh would be sent from Alexandria to them, and some years later Bahá'u'lláh sent another messenger to meet the believers in Khartoum.

Concerning his release from the Sudan, Ḥájí Mírzá Ḥaydar-'Alí writes:

> When Bahá'u'lláh sent me away from His presence in the land of mystery [Adrianople], He promised that I should attain His presence again. Similarly, in His holy and blessed Tablets which through His bounty were despatched to Constantinople, Egypt and the Sudan, He clearly gave the joyous tidings of attaining His presence. Therefore, I was assured and confident of my deliverance.[6]

The release of Ḥájí Mírzá Ḥaydar-'Alí from the Sudan was due to the recommendations and influence of General Gordon, known as Gordon Páshá, the British Governor of the Sudan who succeeded Ismá'íl Páshá. When Gordon Páshá arrived, Ḥájí presented him with a beautiful gift which was made under his supervision and with his help. It was a large mirror (about two and a half metres by one and a half) on which a complimentary phrase was inscribed in gold in English. This pleased the General so much that he sent him an order to make a similar one for his sister in England. Ḥájí complied and one day brought the mirror to Gordon Pá<u>sh</u>á. This is how Ḥájí describes the story:

> He [Gordon Pá<u>sh</u>á] thanked me for the article and said 'It is so beautiful that I cannot pay enough for this gift. You yourself fix the price.' I knew this was the opportunity to say something about freedom, so I told him that I did not want anything except to be released and allowed to leave the Sudan. He said 'Write a letter [addressed to the Khedive of Egypt] and plead that you have been imprisoned here without your case being investigated, that you are far from being guilty of the crime they ascribe to you, and that matters relating to one's conscience are not within the jurisdiction of kings. They are concerned with God, the King of Kings. Then beg him to set you free so that you may return to your home and be thankful.[7]

Six of Ḥájí's companions, including the Egyptian, decided to remain in the Sudan. Only Ḥájí Mírzá Ḥaydar-'Alí and Mírzá Ḥusayn-i-<u>Sh</u>írází,* made this application. The text of the letter was cabled to the Khedive. Gordon Pá<u>sh</u>á described this imprisonment and exile as unlawful and recommended the release of the prisoners. Soon orders arrived for their freedom, but they were not allowed to enter Egypt.

Ḥájí Mírzá Ḥaydar-'Alí, accompanied by Mírzá Ḥusayn, set off on the journey to 'Akká *via* Mecca and Beirut. This was in the year 1877. Concerning their departure from Khartoum Ḥájí writes:

> On the day of our departure from Khartoum, the dignitaries

* Known as <u>Kh</u>arṭúmí, he was also promised by Bahá'u'lláh that he would attain His presence. It should be noted that Mírzá Ḥusayn's deeds in Khartoum and later in India were unworthy of a true Bahá'í. After the passing of Bahá'u'lláh, he became a Covenant-breaker.

and authorities of the city, along with great multitudes, came to the ship to bid us farewell. The signs of affection and faithfulness were manifest in the faces of all. A few Muslims and Christians escorted us all the way to Berber. Thus the meekness and abasement of our entry into that city were turned into glory and honour . . . whereas Mírzá Ḥasan Khán, the cruel Consul, was swiftly punished by God. We had not yet arrived in the Sudan when the Persians resident in Egypt complained to the Sháh about his acts of cruelty and injustice . . . Strangely, orders were given to investigate the allegations. The result was that his wickedness and evil character were exposed. He was forced to pay everything he had acquired through extortion . . . and co-incidentally he was taken to Ṭihrán in chains and fetters where he tasted the fruits of his actions.[8]

After all these sufferings the most rewarding moment was when Ḥájí Mírzá Ḥaydar-'Alí was ushered into the presence of His Lord in 'Akká. The ecstasy and contentment that he evinced on those memorable occasions when he sat in the presence of Bahá'u'lláh are indescribable. We hope to share some of his reminiscences in future volumes. After a stay of about three months in 'Akká, he left at the behest of Bahá'u'lláh for Persia *via* 'Iráq. As a result of his attaining the presence of Bahá'u'lláh, he had become like a flame burning with His love, which he radiated to friend and foe alike. For several years he journeyed throughout the length and breadth of Persia strengthening the believers in their faith and imparting to them a measure of the glory of the Cause and the majesty of its Author. Then he returned to 'Akká once again and basked in the sunshine of Bahá'u'lláh's presence. On his second pilgrimage to 'Akká, as on earlier ones, Ḥájí was so enamoured of the glory of Bahá'u'lláh that he was utterly unaware of his own self and it seemed as though he lived in the realms of the spirit, oblivious to the world and all who dwelt in it. However, this pilgrimage was short-lived and lasted only about two months. Bahá'u'lláh sent him again to Persia, where he continued with unflinching loyalty and zeal to invigorate the faith of the believers and teach the Cause to those who were ready to embrace it.

An outstanding feature of the life of Ḥájí Mírzá Ḥaydar-'Alí was his awareness of the station of 'Abdu'l-Bahá. From the first time that he came in contact with Him in Adrianople, he realized that 'Abdu'l-Bahá was endowed by Bahá'u'lláh with supernatural powers and divine attributes far beyond the ken of men. After the passing of Bahá'u'lláh, and in accordance with the provisions of His Will, Ḥájí, like the great majority of the believers, followed 'Abdu'l-Bahá. He turned towards 'Abdu'l-Bahá with the same dedication and self-effacement that he had shown towards Bahá'u'lláh. His passionate love for and devotion to the Centre of the Covenant may be regarded as the distinguishing features of his life after the ascension of Bahá'u'lláh, qualities through which he shed great lustre on one of the most turbulent periods in the Heroic Age of the Faith. His long record of service to the Covenant of Bahá'u'lláh, spanning almost the full period of the Ministry of 'Abdu'l-Bahá, may be regarded as the fruit and glory of a life wholly dedicated to the Cause of God. To recount the stories of his many activities in this period is beyond the scope of this book. Suffice it to say that he defended the Covenant with such faith and vigour that in his confrontations with the Covenant-breakers and especially their leaders such as Jamál-i-Burújirdí and Siyyid Mihdíy-i-Dahají who arose to divide the Faith, he demonstrated, with characteristic resourcefulness, the ascendancy of the Cause of God, and the invincibility of the Covenant. He exposed the evil designs of the Covenant-breakers, pointed to their folly, warned them of the consequences of their actions and urged them to save their souls from ultimate extinction by turning to the Centre of the Covenant. He also helped and inspired thousands of believers throughout Persia and the neighbouring countries to remain steadfast in the Covenant when the Faith of Bahá'u'lláh was plunged into a severe crisis reminiscent of the rebellion of Mírzá Yaḥyá.

Next to attaining the presence of Bahá'u'lláh, the crowning

glory of his life was the inestimable privilege of spending his latter years in the Holy Land under the loving care of the Master whom he served with the utmost devotion and love. For many years he was a trusted companion to 'Abdu'l-Bahá and a true counsellor to the pilgrims and resident believers. He passed away in Haifa at a great age in December 1920, and is buried on Mount Carmel.

BIBLIOGRAPHY

'Abdu'l-Bahá. *Memorials of the Faithful.* Translated from the original Persian text and annotated by Marzieh Gail. Wilmette, Illinois: Bahá'í Publishing Trust, 1971.

——*Some Answered Questions.* Collected and Translated from the Persian of 'Abdu'l-Bahá by Laura Clifford Barney. London: Kegan Paul, Trench, Trubner & Co. Ltd., 1908. Chicago: Bahá'í Publishing Society, 1918. London: Bahá'í Publishing Trust, 1961. Wilmette, Illinois: Bahá'í Publishing Trust, rev. edn. 1964.

Abu'l-Faḍl, Mírzá. *Kitábu'l-Fará'id.* An apologia. Cairo, undated. Written in 1315 A.H. (A.D. 1899).

Báb, The. *Natíjatu'l-Bayán.* (The Fruit of the Bayán). A compilation of the Writings of the Báb. Ṭihrán, Bahá'í Publishing Trust, 105 B.E. (A.D. 1948).

Bahá'í Revelation, The. A Selection from the Bahá'í Holy Writings. London: Bahá'í Publishing Trust, 1955.

Bahá'í World, The. An International Record. Vol. V, 1932–4. New York: Bahá'í Publishing Committee, 1936. Vol. VIII, 1938–40. Wilmette, Illinois: Bahá'í Publishing Committee, 1942. Vol. XV, 1968–73. Haifa, Israel: The Universal House of Justice, 1976.

Bahá'u'lláh. *Á<u>th</u>ár-i-Qalam-i-A'lá.* (The Traces of the Supreme Pen). A compilation of the Writings of Bahá'u'lláh. Ṭihrán: Bahá'í Publishing Trust. Vol. I, 120 B.E. (A.D. 1963); Vol. IV, 125 B.E. (A.D. 1968).

——*Epistle to the Son of the Wolf.* Trans. by Shoghi Effendi. Wilmette, Illinois: Bahá'í Publishing Trust, rev. edn. 1953.

——*Gleanings from the Writings of Bahá'u'lláh.* Trans. by Shoghi Effendi. Wilmette, Illinois: Bahá'í Publishing Trust, 1935; rev. edn. 1952. London: Bahá'í Publishing Trust, 1949.

——*The Hidden Words.* Trans. by Shoghi Effendi with the assistance of some English friends. First published in England 1932. London: Bahá'í Publishing Trust, 1949. Wilmette, Illinois: Bahá'í Publishing Trust, rev. edn. 1954.

——*Iqtidárát.* A compilation of the Tablets of Bahá'u'lláh. 1310 A.H. (A.D. 1892–3).

——*The Kitáb-i-Íqán. The Book of Certitude.* Trans. by Shoghi Effendi. Wilmette, Illinois: Bahá'í Publishing Trust, 1931; 2nd edn. 1950. London: Bahá'í Publishing Trust, 2nd edn. 1961.

——*Majmú'iy-i-Alváḥ.* A compilation of the Tablets of Bahá'u'lláh. Cairo, 1920.

——*Prayers and Meditations of Bahá'u'lláh.* Compiled and trans. by Shoghi Effendi. New York: Bahá'í Publishing Committee, 1938. Reprinted Wilmette, Illinois: Bahá'í Publishing Trust. London: Bahá'í Publishing Trust, 1957.

——*The Proclamation of Bahá'u'lláh* to the kings and leaders of the world. Haifa: Bahá'í World Centre, 1967.

BAYḌÁ'Í, NI'MATU'LLÁH. *Tadhkiriy-i-Shu'aráy-i-Qarn-i-Avval-i-Bahá'í.* (Memorials of the Poets of the First Bahá'í Century). 4 Vols. Ṭihrán: Bahá'í Publishing Trust, 123 B.E. (A.D. 1966).

BLOMFIELD, LADY (Sitárih Khánum). *The Chosen Highway.* London: Bahá'í Publishing Trust, 1940. Wilmette, Illinois: Bahá'í Publishing Trust, 1967.

BROWNE, E. G. (ed.). *A Traveller's Narrative* written to illustrate the Episode of the Báb. Vol. II, English Translation and Notes. Cambridge University Press, 1891.

Covenant of Bahá'u'lláh, The. A Compilation of Bahá'í Writings. London: Bahá'í Publishing Trust, 1963 (rev.).

FÁḌIL-i-MÁZINDARÁNÍ, ASADU'LLÁH, MÍRZÁ. *Amr Va Khalq.* (Revelation and Creation). Ṭihrán: Bahá'í Publishing Trust. Vol. III, 128 B.E. (A.D. 1971).

——*Asráru'l-Áthár.* A glossary of Bahá'í terms. Ṭihrán: Bahá'í Publishing Trust. 5 Vols., 124–9 B.E. (A.D. 1967–72).

FAIZI, MUḤAMMAD-'ALÍ. *Ḥaḍrat-i-Bahá'u'lláh.* (His Holiness

Bahá'u'lláh). Ṭihrán, Bahá'í Publishing Trust, 125 B.E. (A.D. 1968).
——*L'álíy-i-Darakhshán*. A commentary on some of the Writings of Bahá'u'lláh. Ṭihrán: Bahá'í Publishing Trust, 123 B.E. (A.D. 1966).
——*Khánidán-i-Afnán*. A biography of some members of the Afnán family. Ṭihrán: Bahá'í Publishing Trust, 127 B.E. (A.D. 1970).
ḤAYDAR-'ALÍ, ḤÁJÍ MÍRZÁ. *Bihjatu'ṣ-Ṣudúr*. Reminiscences and autobiography. Bombay: 1913.
ISHRÁQ KHÁVARÍ, 'ABDU'L-ḤAMÍD. *Raḥíq-i-Makhtúm*. A commentary on a letter of Shoghi Effendi. 2 Vols. Ṭihrán, Bahá'í Publishing Trust, 103 B.E. (A.D. 1946).
Má'idiy-i-Ásamání. A compilation of Bahá'í Writings. Compiled by 'Abdu'l-Ḥamíd Ishráq Khávarí. 9 Vols. and one index volume. Ṭihrán: Bahá'í Publishing Trust. 129 B.E. (A.D. 1972).
MIṢBÁḤ, MÍRZÁ 'AZÍZU'LLÁH. 'Bazm-i-Ḥaqáyiq' (The Banquet of Realities). Published in *Díván-i-Miṣbáḥ*. Ṭihrán: Bahá'í Publishing Trust, 122 B.E. (A.D. 1965).
MU'AYYAD, DR. ḤABÍB. *Kháṭirát-i-Ḥabíb*. Memoirs of Ḥabíb. Ṭihrán: 1961.
MUḤAMMAD-ṬÁHIR-i-MÁLMÍRÍ, ḤÁJÍ. *Táríkh-i-Shuhadáy-i-Yazd*. (History of the Martyrs of Yazd). Cairo: 1342 A.H. (A.D. 1926).
NABÍL-i-A'ẒAM. (Muḥammad-i-Zarandí). *The Dawn-Breakers*. Nabíl's Narrative of the Early Days of the Bahá'í Revelation. Wilmette, Illinois: Bahá'í Publishing Trust, 1932. London: Bahá'í Publishing Trust, 1953.
SAMANDAR, SHAYKH KÁẒIM. *Táríkh-i-Samandar*. (The History of Samandar). Ṭihrán: Bahá'í Publishing Trust, 131 B.E. (A.D. 1974).
SHOGHI EFFENDI. *The Advent of Divine Justice*. First published 1939. Wilmette, Illinois: Bahá'í Publishing Trust, rev. edn. 1963.
——*God Passes By*. Wilmette, Illinois: Bahá'í Publishing Trust, 1944.

——*The Promised Day Is Come*. First published 1941. Wilmette, Illinois: Bahá'í Publishing Trust, rev. edn. 1961.

——*The World Order of Bahá'u'lláh*. First published 1938. Wilmette, Illinois: Bahá'í Publishing Trust, rev. edn. 1955.

SULAYMÁNÍ, 'AZÍZ'U'LLÁH. *Maṣábíḥ-i-Hidáyat*. Biography of some of the early Bahá'ís. Ṭihrán: Bahá'í Publishing Trust. Vols. I and II, 121 B.E. (A.D. 1964); Vol. VI, 125 B.E. (A.D. 1968).

Synopsis and Codification of the Laws and Ordinances of the Kitáb-i-Aqdas. Haifa, Israel: The Universal House of Justice, 1973.

YUSUF ALI, ABDULLAH. *The Holy Qur-an*. Text, Translation & Commentary. Lahore, Pakistan: Sh. Muhammad Ashraf, 1938; repr. 1969.

ZARQÁNÍ, MÍRZÁ MAḤMÚD-I-. *Kitáb-i-Badáyi'u'l-Á<u>th</u>ár*. Diary of 'Abdu'l-Bahá's travels in Europe and America, written by His secretary. Bombay: Vol. I, 1914; Vol. II, 1921.

REFERENCES

Full details of authors and titles are given in the bibliography. Page numbers are given for both the American and British editions of the *Kitáb-i-Íqán* and *The Dawn-Breakers*. See Notes and Acknowledgements regarding translations from Persian texts and the numbering of verses in the *Qur'án*.

CHAPTER 1: BAHÁ'U'LLÁH IN CONSTANTINOPLE

1. *Micah*, vii. 12.
2. *Amos*, iv. 13.
3. Bahá'u'lláh, *Má'idiy-i-Ásamání*, vol. VII, p. 192.
4. Bahá'u'lláh, *Epistle to the Son of the Wolf*, pp. 137–8.
5. Browne, (ed.), *A Traveller's Narrative*, p. 92.
6. Bahá'u'lláh, *Má'idiy-i-Ásamání*, vol. IV, p. 369.
7. Bahá'u'lláh, *Gleanings from the Writings of Bahá'u'lláh*, section lxvi.
8. Unpublished.
9. Ḥájí Mírzá Ḥaydar-'Alí, *Bihjatu'ṣ-Ṣudúr*, pp. 70–71.
10. *ibid.*, pp. 69–71.
11. Ḥájí Muḥammad-Ṭáhir-i-Málmírí, unpublished memoirs.
12. Ḥájí Mírzá Ḥaydar-'Alí, *Bihjatu'ṣ-Ṣudúr*, p. 161.
13. *A Traveller's Narrative*, pp. xxxix–xl.
14. Quoted by Bahá'u'lláh in the *Kitáb-i-Badí'*, p. 176.
15. Bahá'u'lláh, *Majmú'iy-i-Alváḥ*, pp. 272–4.
16. *Qu'rán*, xxix. 23; quoted by Bahá'u'lláh in the *Kitáb-i-Íqán*, p. 88 (Brit.), pp. 138–9 (U.S.).
17. *ibid.*, xviii. 111.
18. *ibid.*, ii. 46.
19. *ibid.*, xiii. 2.
20. *Revelation*, xxii. 3 and 4
21. *ibid.*, xxi. 3 and 4.
22. *Isaiah*, xxxv. 2.
23. *ibid.*, xxxv. 4.
24. *ibid.*, xl. 5.

25. *ibid.*, lx. 2.
26. Bahá'u'lláh, *Kitáb-i-Íqán*, p. 63 (Brit.), p. 98 (U.S.).
27. Quoted in *The Bahá'í World*, vol. XIV, p. 632.
28. *Qur'án*, xxviii. 5.
29. *Matthew*, v. 5.
30. *Qur'án*, xi. 27.
31. Ḥájí Muḥammad Ṭáhir-i-Málmírí, unpublished memoirs.
32. Quoted by Fáḍil-i-Mázindarání in *Asráru'l-Áthár*, vol. III, p. 242.
33. Bahá'u'lláh, *Kitáb-i-Íqán*, p. 64 (Brit.), p. 99 (U.S.).
34. Quoted by Fáḍil-i-Mázindarání in *Asráru'l-Áthár*, vol. III, p. 243.
35. From an unpublished Tablet.
36. Bahá'u'lláh, *Má'idiy-i-Ásamání*, vol. IV, pp. 31–2.
37. Mírzá Abu'l-Faḍl, *Kitábu'l-Fará'id*, pp. 220–1.

CHAPTER 2: *Mathnavíy-i-Mubárak*

1. Bahá'u'lláh, *Iqtidárát*, pp. 90–91.
2. Bahá'u'lláh, *The Hidden Words*, no. 11, Arabic.
3. *ibid.*, no. 11, Persian.
4. Bahá'u'lláh, *Má'idiy-i-Ásamání*, vol. VII, p. 200.
5. Bahá'u'lláh, *Iqtidárát*, p. 272.
6. Quoted in *The Proclamation* of *Bahá'u'lláh*, p. 95.
7. Bahá'u'lláh, *Má'idiy-i-Ásamání*, vol. VIII, p. 29.
8. *ibid.*, vol. IV, p. 26.
9. Bahá'u'lláh, *The Hidden Words*, no. 4, Arabic.
10. Bahá'u'lláh, *Prayers and Meditations*, clxxxi.
11. Quoted in *Synopsis and Codification of the Kitáb-i-Aqdas*, p. 12.
12. Mírzá 'Azízu'lláh-i-Miṣbáḥ, *Díván-i-Miṣbáḥ*, p. 337.
13. Bahá'u'lláh, *Gleanings from the Writings of Bahá'u'lláh*, section xcvi.
14. Bahá'u'lláh, *Majmú'iy-i-Alváḥ*, pp. 173–4.
15. Quoted in *The Chosen Highway*, p. 165.
16. Quoted by Shoghi Effendi in *The World Order of Bahá'u'lláh*, p. 139.
17. Ḥájí Mírzá Ḥaydar-'Alí, *Bihjatu'ṣ-Ṣudúr*, pp. 189–90.
18. Bahá'u'lláh, *Epistle to the Son of the Wolf*, p. 74.
19. Mírzá 'Azízu'lláh-i-Miṣbáḥ, *Díván-i-Miṣbáḥ*, p. 365.
20. *ibid.*, p. 343.

21. Quoted by Dr. Ḥabíb Mu'ayyad, *Ḥabíb*, vol. II, p. 310.
22. From the *History of the Martyrs of Yazd*, written by the author's father Ḥájí Muḥammad-Ṭáhir-i-Málmírí; this version is edited and translated by Habib Taherzadeh.
23. Unpublished, not to be confused with the published *History of the Martyrs of Yazd* by the same author.
24. Ḥájí Mírzá Ḥaydar-'Alí, *Bihjatu'ṣ-Ṣudúr*, pp. 168–9.
25. Bahá'u'lláh, *Má'idiy-i-Ásamání*, vol. I, p. 68.
26. Quoted in *The Dawn-Breakers*, p. 96 (Brit.), p. 138 (U.S.).

CHAPTER 3: THE EXILE TO ADRIANOPLE

1. Bahá'u'lláh, *Gleanings from the Writings of Bahá'u'lláh*, section lxv.
2. Shoghi Effendi, *God Passes By*, pp. 159–61.
3. 'Abdu'l-Bahá, *Memorials of the Faithful*, p. 149.
4. Quoted by Muḥammad-'Alíy-i-Faizi, *Ḥaḍrat-i-Bahá'u'lláh*, p. 196.
5. Quoted by Shoghi Effendi, *God Passes By*, p. 161.
6. *ibid.*
7. *ibid.*, pp. 161–2.
8. Quoted by Fáḍil-i-Mázindaráni, *Asráru'l-Á<u>th</u>ár*, vol. I, p. 77.

CHAPTER 4: *Súriy-i-Aṣḥáb*

1. Shoghi Effendi, *God Passes By*, p. 151.
2. Ḥájí Mírzá Ḥaydar-'Alí, *Bihjatu'ṣ-Ṣudúr*, p. 23 ff.
3. *ibid.*
4. *ibid.*, p. 51.
5. <u>Sh</u>ay<u>kh</u> Káẓim-i-Samandar, *Táríkh-i-Samandar*, p. 228.
6. Quoted by Shoghi Effendi, *The World Order of Bahá'u'lláh*, pp. 104, 109.
7. ibid., pp. 112–13.
8. Mírzá 'Azízu'lláh-i-Miṣbáḥ, *Díván-i-Miṣbáḥ*, p. 345.
9. ibid.
10. Quoted by Shoghi Effendi, *The World Order of Bahá'u'lláh*, p. 181.
11. Bahá'u'lláh, *Gleanings from the Writings of Bahá'u'lláh*, section xxix.
12. Bahá'u'lláh, *Má'idiy-i-Ásamání*, vol. IV, p. 155.
13. Bahá'u'lláh, *Iqtidárát*, p. 85.
14. Bahá'u'lláh, *The Hidden Words*, no. 1, Arabic.

15. From the *Súriy-i-Aṣḥáb*, translated by Shoghi Effendi, *The World Order of Bahá'u'lláh*, pp. 108–9.
16. Bahá'u'lláh, *Gleanings from the Writings of Bahá'u'lláh*, section xcviii.
17. Bahá'u'lláh, *Má'idiy-i-Ásamání*, vol. IV, p. 18.
18. Bahá'u'lláh, *Gleanings from the Writings of Bahá'u'lláh*, section xliii.
19. *ibid.*, section v.
20. Shoghi Effendi, *The World Order of Bahá'u'lláh*, pp. 195–9 passim.
21. Bahá'u'lláh, *Má'idiy-i-Ásamání*, vol. IV, p. 47.
22. Bahá'u'lláh, *Gleanings from the Writings of Bahá'u'lláh*, section cxxviii.
23. Bahá'u'lláh, quoted by Shoghi Effendi, *The Advent of Divine Justice*, p. 67.
24. Bahá'u'lláh, *Gleanings from the Writings of Bahá'u'lláh*, section cxxviii.
25. ibid., section clviii.
26. Bahá'u'lláh, *Má'idiy-i-Ásamání*, vol. IV, pp. 123–4.
27. Bahá'u'lláh, *The Hidden Words*, no. 31, Arabic.
28. Bahá'u'lláh, *Epistle to the Son of the Wolf*, p. 27.
29. *ibid.*, p. 136.
30. Bahá'u'lláh, *The Bahá'í Revelation*, p. 138.
31. Bahá'u'lláh, *The Hidden Words*, nos. 46 and 47, Arabic.
32. Bahá'u'lláh, *Má'idiy-i-Ásamání*, vol. I, p. 69.
33. Bahá'u'lláh, *Gleanings from the Writings of Bahá'u'lláh*, section clxiii.
34. Quoted by Fáḍil-i-Mázindarání in *Asráru'l-Áthár*, vol. IV, p. 19.
35. Ḥájí Muḥammad-Ṭáhir-i-Málmírí, unpublished memoirs.
36. *ibid.*
37. *ibid.*
38. *ibid.*

CHAPTER 5: *Tablet of Aḥmad* (ARABIC)

1. Ḥájí Muḥammad-Ṭáhir-i-Málmírí, unpublished 'History of the Faith in the Province of Yazd'.
2. A report by the Bahá'í community of 'Ishqábád, quoted by Ishráq Khávarí in *Muḥáḍirát*, p. 653 ff.
3. *ibid.*
4. Unpublished 'History of the Faith in the Province of Yazd'.
5. Account quoted in *Muḥáḍirát*, p. 653 ff.

6. Unpublished 'History of the Faith in the Province of Yazd'.
7. Ḥájí Mírzá Ḥaydar-'Alí, *Bihjatu's-Ṣudúr*, p. 254.
8. Bahá'u'lláh, *Gleanings from the Writings of Bahá'u'lláh*, section cxlii.
9. Bahá'u'lláh, *Iqtidárát*, pp. 294–5.
10. Bahá'u'lláh, 'Tablet of Aḥmad', included in most Bahá'í prayer books.
11. Bahá'u'lláh, *Gleanings from the Writings of Bahá'u'lláh* section lii.
12. *Qur'án*, ii. 23; quoted in the *Kitáb-i-Íqán*, p. 131 (Brit.), p. 204 (U.S.).
13. Bahá'u'lláh, 'Tablet of Aḥmad', included in most Bahá'í prayer books.
14. *Qur'án*, vii. 34.
15. Bahá'u'lláh, 'Tablet of Aḥmad', included in most Bahá'í prayer books.
16. Bahá'u'lláh, *Má'idiy-i-Ásamání*, vol. IV, p. 365.
17. Bahá'u'lláh, quoted by Fáḍil-i-Mázindarání in *Amr Va Khalq*, vol. III, p. 87.
18. Bahá'u'lláh, *Gleanings from the Writings of Bahá'u'lláh*, section clii.
19. Bahá'u'lláh, 'Tablet of Aḥmad', included in most Bahá'í prayer books.
20. Quoted by Muḥammad-'Alíy-i-Faizi, *L'álíy-i-Darakhshán*, p. 191.

CHAPTER 6: *Lawḥ-i-Aḥmad* (PERSIAN)

1. Bahá'u'lláh, quoted by Fáḍil-i-Mázindarání, *Asráru'l-Áthár*, vol. V, p. 106.
2. Bahá'u'lláh, *Gleanings from the Writings of Bahá'u'lláh*, section cliii.
3. *ibid.*, section clii.
4. Nabíl-i-A'ẓam, 'Panj Kanz', unpublished. It should not be assumed that the utterances of Bahá'u'lláh quoted are His exact words.
5. Bahá'u'lláh, quoted by Shoghi Effendi, *The Advent of Divine Justice*, p. 26.
6. Nabíl-i-A'ẓam, 'Panj Kanz'.
7. Bahá'u'lláh, *Gleanings from the Writings of Bahá'u'lláh*, section cliii.
8. Parts of this Tablet were translated by Shoghi Effendi and

included in *Gleanings from the Writings of Bahá'u'lláh*, sections lxxiii, lxxxiii and cxxiv.

9. Bahá'u'lláh, *Gleanings from the Writings of Bahá'u'lláh*, section lxxxiii.
10. *ibid.*
11. The Báb, quoted by Bahá'u'lláh in *Epistle to the Son of the Wolf*, p. 141.
12. Bahá'u'lláh, *Gleanings from the Writings of Bahá'u'lláh*, section cliii.
13. *ibid.*
14. Bahá'u'lláh, *Má'idiy-i-Ásamání*, vol. IV, p. 370.
15. Shoghi Effendi, *God Passes By*, pp. 407–8.
16. Bahá'u'lláh, *Gleanings from the Writings of Bahá'u'lláh*, section clii.
17. *ibid.*, section cliii.

CHAPTER 7: THE FORCES OF EVIL GATHER MOMENTUM

1. Shoghi Effendi, *God Passes By*, pp. 165–6.
2. Quoted by Bahá'u'lláh in the *Kitáb-i-Íqán*, p. 30 (Brit.), p. 46 (U.S.).
3. Quoted by Ni'matu'lláh-i-Bayḍá'í, *Tadhkiray-i-Shu'aráy-i-Qarn-i-Avval-i-Bahá'í*, vol. II, p. 186.
4. Quoted by Ishráq Khávarí, *Raḥíq-i-Makhtúm*, vol. II, p. 1201 ff.
5. *ibid.*
6. Quoted by Shoghi Effendi, *God Passes By*, p. 167.
7. *ibid.*
8. Ḥájí Mírzá Ḥaydar-'Alí, *Bihjatu'ṣ-Ṣudúr*, p. 76.
9. Shoghi Effendi, *God Passes By*, pp. 167–8.
10. *ibid.*, p. 137.
11. Ḥusayn-i-Áshchí, unpublished memoirs.

CHAPTER 8: THE PROMISED ONE OF THE *Bayán*: SOME TABLETS

1. Nabíl-i-A'ẓam, *The Dawn-Breakers*, p. 201 (Brit.), p. 281 (U.S.).
2. *ibid.*, p. 203 (Brit.), pp. 283–4 (U.S.).
3. *ibid.*, p. 195 (Brit.), pp. 273–5 (U.S.).
4. *ibid.*, pp. 203–4 (Brit.), p. 284 (U.S.).
5. Shaykh Káẓim-i-Samandar, *Táríkh-i-Samandar*, pp. 362–6.
6. Quoted by Shoghi Effendi, *The Advent of Divine Justice*, p. 67.
7. The Báb, quoted by Bahá'u'lláh in *Má'idiy-i-Ásamání*, vol. VII, p. 213.
8. The Báb, *Natíjatu'l-Bayán*, p. 12.

9. *John*, xii. 49.
10. *Matthew*, xvi. 27.
11. Bahá'u'lláh, quoted in *The Proclamation of Bahá'u'lláh*, p. 93.
12. *ibid.*, p. 27.
13. Bahá'u'lláh, *Prayers and Meditations*, clxxxiii.
14. Bahá'u'lláh, *Má'idiy-i-Ásamání*, vol. VII, pp. 142–3.
15. Bahá'u'lláh, quoted in *Synopsis and Codification of the Laws and Ordinances of the Kitáb-i-Aqdas*, p. 11.
16. Bahá'u'lláh, *Gleanings from the Writings of Bahá'u'lláh*, section cxlvii.
17. Bahá'u'lláh, *Má'idiy-i-Ásamání*, vol. IV, p. 352.
18. Mírzá 'Azízu'lláh-i-Miṣbáḥ, *Díván-i-Miṣbáḥ*, p. 366.
19. 'Abdu'l-Bahá, *Má'idiy-i-Ásamání*, vol. IX, p. 128.
20. Bahá'u'lláh, *Gleanings from the Writings of Bahá'u'lláh*, section cxxviii.
21. *ibid.*, section cxxxvi.

CHAPTER 9: SOME EARLY PILGRIMS

1. *Qur'án*, cxii.
2. Ḥájí Mírzá Ḥaydar-'Alí, *Bihjatu'ṣ-Ṣudúr*, p. 72 ff.
3. *ibid.*, p. 80 ff.
4. Nabíl-i-A'ẓam, *The Dawn-Breakers*, pp. 149–50 (Brit.), pp. 208–9 (U.S.).
5. *The Bahá'í World*, vol. VIII, pp. 261–2.
6. *ibid.*
7. Nabíl-i-A'ẓam, *The Dawn-Breakers*, pp. 315–16 (Brit.), pp. 431–3 (U.S.).
8. Bahá'u'lláh, quoted by Shoghi Effendi, *God Passes By*, p. 184.
9. Nabíl-i-A'ẓam, quoted by Shoghi Effendi, *God Passes By*, p. 137.
10. Bahá'u'lláh, *The Hidden Words*, no. 59, Arabic.
11. *ibid.*, no. 27, Persian.
12. *ibid.*, no. 26, Persian.
13. *ibid.*, no. 11, Persian.
14. *ibid.*, no. 42, Arabic.
15. *ibid.*, no. 7, Arabic.

CHAPTER 10: ILLUSTRIOUS MARTYRS

1. 'Abdu'l-Bahá, quoted by Fáḍil-i-Mázindarání in *Asráru'l-Á<u>th</u>ár*, vol. V, p. 219.

2. Bahá'u'lláh, *Epistle to the Son of the Wolf*, p. 73.
3. Shoghi Effendi, *God Passes By*, p. 178.
4. Nabíl-i-A'ẓam, *The Dawn-Breakers*, p. 411 (Brit.), p. 562 (U.S.).
5. *ibid.*
6. Bahá'u'lláh, *Gleanings from the Writings of Bahá'u'lláh*, section lxix.
7. Bahá'u'lláh, *Epistle to the Son of the Wolf*, pp. 73–4.
8. Bahá'u'lláh, *Gleanings from the Writings of Bahá'u'lláh*, section lii.
9. Bahá'u'lláh, *Kitáb-i-Íqán*, p. 124 (Brit.), pp. 194–5 (U.S.).
10. Bahá'u'lláh, *The Hidden Words*, no. 5, Arabic.
11. Bahá'u'lláh, *Gleanings from the Writings of Bahá'u'lláh*, section i.

CHAPTER 11: SOME SIGNIFICANT TABLETS

1. 'Abdu'l-Bahá, *Má'idiy-i-Ásamání*, vol. II, p. 35.
2. Bahá'u'lláh, *The Hidden Words*, no. 57, Persian.
3. 'Abdu'l-Bahá, quoted in *The Covenant of Bahá'u'lláh*, p. 144.
4. Bahá'u'lláh, *Gleanings from the Writings of Bahá'u'lláh*, section xxxix.
5. Bahá'u'lláh, *Á<u>th</u>ár-i-Qalam-i-A'lá*, vol. IV, pp. 368–72.
6. Bahá'u'lláh, *Gleanings from the Writings of Bahá'u'lláh*, section cxxxi.
7. *ibid.*, section xlvi.
8. *ibid.*, section lx.
9. Bahá'u'lláh, *Epistle to the Son of the Wolf*, p. 72.
10. Bahá'u'lláh, *Gleanings from the Writings of Bahá'u'lláh*, section lxxv.
11. *ibid.*, section liii.
12. *Qur'án*, xli. 53.
13. Bahá'u'lláh, *Gleanings from the Writings of Bahá'u'lláh*, section xiv.
14. The Báb, quoted by Shoghi Effendi, *God Passes By*, p. 30.
15. Bahá'u'lláh, *Gleanings from the Writings of Bahá'u'lláh*, section xliii.
16. Bahá'u'lláh, quoted by Shoghi Effendi, *God Passes By*, p. 171.
17. Quoted by Nabíl-i-A'ẓam, *The Dawn-Breakers*, p. 44 (Brit.), p. 65 (U.S.).
18. *ibid.*, pp. 347–8 (Brit.), pp. 471–2 (U.S.).
19. *ibid.*, pp. 348–9 (Brit.), p. 473 (U.S.).
20. Quoted by Muḥammad 'Alíy-i-Faizí, *L'álíy-i-Dara<u>khsh</u>án*, p. 458.
21. *Matthew*, xvii. 20.

22. Bahá'u'lláh, *Má'idiy-i-Ásamání*, vol. IV, pp. 175–6.
23. *ibid.*, vol. I, p. 65.
24. Quoted by Shoghi Effendi, *God Passes By*, p. 242.
25. Bahá'u'lláh, *Má'idiy-i-Ásamání*, vol. VIII, p. 40.
26. Quoted by Shoghi Effendi, *God Passes By*, p. 251.
27. Bahá'u'lláh, quoted in *Synopsis and Codification of Laws and Ordinances of the Kitáb-i-Aqdas*, p. 27.
28. Ustád Muḥammad 'Alíy-i-Salmání, unpublished memoirs, quoted by Ishráq Khávarí, *Raḥíq-i-Makhtúm*, vol. I, pp. 315–16.
29. Bahá'u'lláh, *Gleanings from the Writings of Bahá'u'lláh*, section xcvii.
30. Bahá'u'lláh, *Má'idiy-i-Ásamání*, vol. I, p. 41.
31. Bahá'u'lláh, quoted by Shoghi Effendi, *God Passes By*, p. 171.

CHAPTER 12: TESTS OF FAITH

1. Bahá'u'lláh, *Epistle to the Son of the Wolf*, pp. 131–2.
2. Bahá'u'lláh, quoted by Shoghi Effendi, *The Promised Day is Come*, p. 105.
3. *ibid.*
4. *ibid.*, p. 72.
5. Ḥájí Muḥammad-Ṭáhir-i-Málmírí, unpublished 'History of the Faith in the Province of Yazd'.
6. Ḥájí Mírzá Ḥaydar-'Alí, *Bihjatu'ṣ-Ṣudúr*, p. 74 ff.
7. *ibid.*, pp. 75–6.
8. Bahá'u'lláh, *The Hidden Words*, no. 55, Arabic.
9. 'Abdu'l-Bahá, *Má'idiy-i-Ásamání*, vol. II, p. 86.
10. Bahá'u'lláh, *The Hidden Words*, no. 51, Persian.
11. 'Abdu'l-Bahá, quoted by Mírzá Maḥmúd-i-Zarqání, *Kitáb-i-Badáyi'u'l-Áthár*, vol. I, p. 185.
12. Bahá'u'lláh, *The Hidden Words*, nos. 80 and 82, Persian.
13. Bahá'u'lláh, 'Words of Wisdom', *The Bahá'í Revelation*, p. 138.

CHAPTER 13: *Lawḥ-i-Salmán*

1. Ḥájí Mírzá Ḥaydar-'Alí, *Bihjatu'ṣ-Ṣudúr*, p. 346.
2. Bahá'u'lláh, from a handwritten collection of Tablets.
3. Bahá'u'lláh, *Gleanings from the Writings of Bahá'u'lláh*, section lxxxi.
4. Bahá'u'lláh, quoted by Shoghi Effendi, *God Passes By*, p. 245.

CHAPTER 14: CONFRONTATION WITH MÍRZÁ YAḤYÁ

1. Shoghi Effendi, *God Passes By*, pp. 168–9.
2. *Má'idiy-i-Ásamání*, vol. VII, p. 240.
3. *ibid.*, p. 241.
4. Ḥájí Mírzá Ḥaydar-'Alí, *Bihjatu'ṣ-Ṣudúr*, pp. 77–9.
5. II *Thessalonians*, ii. vv. 3, 4, 8; stated by Shoghi Effendi in a letter to Isfandíyár-i-Majzúb, 17 November 1935.
6. Shoghi Effendi, *God Passes By*, pp. 170–1.

CHAPTER 15: *Súriy-i-Mulúk*

1. Bahá'u'lláh, quoted by Shoghi Effendi, *The Promised Day Is Come*, p. 20.
2. Quoted by Lady Blomfield, *The Chosen Highway*, p. 123.
3. Bahá'u'lláh, *Gleanings from the Writings of Bahá'u'lláh*, section cv.
4. Bahá'u'lláh, quoted by Shoghi Effendi, *The Promised Day Is Come*, pp. 20–21.
5. *ibid.*, p. 21.
6. Bahá'u'lláh, *Gleanings from the Writings of Bahá'u'lláh*, section cxvi.
7. *ibid.*, section cxviii.
8. *ibid.*
9. *ibid.*
10. Bahá'u'lláh, quoted by Shoghi Effendi, *The Promised Day Is Come*, p. 1.
11. *ibid.*, p. 121.
12. *ibid.*
13. Bahá'u'lláh, *Gleanings from the Writings of Bahá'u'lláh*, section cxvi.
14. *ibid.*
15. *ibid.*, section cxiv.
16. *ibid.*
17. *ibid.*
18. *ibid.*
19. *ibid.*, section lxv.
20. *ibid.*
21. *ibid.*, section lxvi.
22. *ibid.*
23. *ibid.*, section cxiii.

24. *ibid.*
25. *ibid.*
26. *ibid.*
27. *ibid.*
28. *ibid.*
29. From an unpublished source.
30. Ḥájí Mírzá Ḥaydar-'Alí, *Bihjatu'ṣ-Ṣudúr*, p. 164.

CHAPTER 16: TWO KINGS ARE SUMMONED

1. The Báb, quoted by Shoghi Effendi, *God Passes By*, p. 21.
2. Bahá'u'lláh, quoted by Shoghi Effendi, *The Promised Day Is Come*, p. 70.
3. *ibid.*, p. 41.
4. Ḥájí Mírzá Ḥaydar-'Alí, *Bihjatu'ṣ-Ṣudúr*, pp. 21–3.
5. Quoted by 'Azízu'lláh Sulaymání, *Maṣábíḥ-i-Hidáyat*, vol. I, pp. 436–43.
6. Bahá'u'lláh, quoted by Shoghi Effendi, *The Promised Day Is Come*, pp. 40–41.
7. 'Abdu'l-Bahá, *Some Answered Questions*, p. 79 (Brit.), pp. 97–8 (U.S.).
8. Bahá'u'lláh, quoted by Fáḍil-i-Mázindarání, *Asráru'l-Áthár*, vol. II, pp. 17–18.
9. Bahá'u'lláh, quoted by Shoghi Effendi, *The Promised Day Is Come*, pp. 41–2.
10. *ibid.*, p. 46.
11. Bahá'u'lláh, *Epistle to the Son of the Wolf*, p. 16.
12. Bahá'u'lláh, quoted by Shoghi Effendi, 'The Dispensation of Bahá'u'lláh', *The World Order of Bahá'u'lláh*, p. 117.
13. Bahá'u'lláh, quoted by Shoghi Effendi, *The Promised Day Is Come*, pp. 42–3.
14. Bahá'u'lláh, quoted by Shoghi Effendi, *God Passes By*, p. 186.
15. Bahá'u'lláh, *Epistle to the Son of the Wolf*, p. 17.
16. Ḥájí Muḥammad-Ṭáhir-i-Málmírí, *History of the Martyrs of Yazd*, p. 95 ff.
17. *ibid.*, p. 110.
18. Ḥájí Muḥammad-Ṭáhir-i-Málmírí, unpublished 'History of the Faith in the Province of Yazd'.
19. Shoghi Effendi, *The Promised Day Is Come*, pp. 51–2.
20. *ibid.*, p. 51.

CHAPTER 17: THE *Kitáb-i-Badí'*

1. 'Abdu'l-Bahá, *Memorials of the Faithful*, pp. 24–5.
2. The Báb, quoted by Bahá'u'lláh, in the *Kitáb-i-Badí'*, and also in English in *Epistle to the Son of the Wolf*, p. 156.
3. *ibid.*, p. 160.
4. *ibid.*
5. *ibid.*, p. 141.
6. *ibid.*, p. 160.
7. The Báb, quoted by Shoghi Effendi, *God Passes By*, p. 30.
8. *ibid.*, p. 29.
9. The Báb, quoted by Bahá'u'lláh, in the *Kitáb-i-Badí'*, and also in English in *Epistle to the Son of the Wolf*, p. 171.
10. *ibid.*, pp. 154–5.
11. *ibid.*, p. 153.
12. *ibid.*, p. 155.
13. *ibid.*, p. 153.
14. *ibid.*, p. 159.
15. Nabíl-i-A'ẓam, *The Dawn-Breakers*, p. 139 (Brit.), pp. 191–2 (U.S.).
16. Quoted by Muḥammad-'Alí Faizi, *Khánidán-i-Afnán*, pp. 169–70.
17. *ibid.*, p. 161 ff.
18. *ibid.*, pp. 165–6.

CHAPTER 18: *Súriy-i-Ghuṣn*

1. Bahá'u'lláh, quoted by Shoghi Effendi, 'The Dispensation of Bahá'u'lláh', *The World Order of Bahá'u'lláh*, p. 135.
2. *ibid.*
3. Shoghi Effendi, *God Passes By*, p. 241.
4. 'Abdu'l-Bahá, quoted by Shoghi Effendi, 'The Dispensation of Bahá'u'lláh', op. cit., p. 133.
5. *ibid.*, p. 138.
6. *ibid.*, pp. 131–2.
7. *ibid.*, p. 134.

CHAPTER 19: BAHÁ'U'LLÁH'S DEPARTURE FROM ADRIANOPLE

1. Quoted by Shoghi Effendi, *God Passes By*, p. 186.
2. Bahá'u'lláh, *Epistle to the Son of the Wolf*, pp. 68–9.
3. Shaykh Káẓim-i-Samandar, *Táríkh-i-Samandar*, p. 199.

4. *ibid.*, p. 268.
5. Bahá'u'lláh, *Má'idiy-i-Ásamání*, vol. IV, p. 173.
6. Bahá'u'lláh, *Iqtidárát*, p. 225.
7. 'Abdu'l-Bahá, *Má'idiy-i-Ásamání*, vol. II, p. 12.
8. Quoted by Muḥammad-'Alíy-i-Faizí, *Ḥaḍrat-i-Bahá'u'lláh*, pp. 195–6.
9. Quoted by Shoghi Effendi, *God Passes By*, p. 180.
10. Ḥusayn-i-Áshchí, unpublished memoirs.
11. Shoghi Effendi, *God Passes By*, pp. 180–82.
12. Shaykh Káẓim-i-Samandar, *Táríkh-i-Samandar*, pp. 222–3.
13. Quoted by Fáḍil-i-Mázindarání, *Asráru'l-Áthár*, vol. I, p. 131.
14. Bahá'u'lláh, quoted by Shoghi Effendi, *The Promised Day Is Come*, p. 62.
15. Bahá'u'lláh, quoted by Shoghi Effendi, *God Passes By*, pp. 179–80.
16. *ibid.*, p. 180.
17. Bahá'u'lláh, quoted by Shoghi Effendi, *The Promised Day Is Come*, p. 75.
18. Bahá'u'lláh, quoted by Shoghi Effendi, 'The Dispensation of Bahá'u'lláh', *The World Order of Bahá'u'lláh*, pp. 105–6.
19. *Qur'án*, lv. 29. Quoted by Bahá'u'lláh, *Kitáb-i-Íqán*, p. 43 (Brit.), p. 67 (U.S.).
20. Bahá'u'lláh, *Gleanings from the Writings of Bahá'u'lláh*, section xvi.
21. Shoghi Effendi, *The Promised Day is Come*, pp. 14–15, 16, 121.

APPENDIX II: A VISIT TO ADRIANOPLE BY MARTHA L. ROOT

1. Martha Root, excerpts from an article in *The Bahá'í World*, vol. V, p. 581.

APPENDIX III: ḤÁJÍ MÍRZÁ ḤAYDAR-'ALÍ OF IṢFAHÁN

1. Ḥájí Mírzá Ḥaydar-'Alí, *Bihjatu'ṣ-Ṣudúr*, p. 105.
2. *ibid.*, p. 110.
3. *ibid.*, p. 111.
4. *ibid.*, p. 112.
5. *ibid.*, p. 114.
6. *ibid.*, p. 147.
7. *ibid.*, pp. 147–8.
8. *ibid.*, pp. 148–9.

INDEX

Part I of this index consists of the titles of Tablets and Writings of Bahá'u'lláh described or mentioned by the author, including a few which were revealed before 1863 or after 1868. Part II contains all other entries. Titles of Tablets and books are italicized. Footnotes are indicated by the abbreviation n. after the page number; if the name or subject occurs both in the text and in a note, this is indicated by 'p. — and n.'.

I. TABLETS AND WRITINGS OF BAHÁ'U'LLÁH

II. GENERAL INDEX

Covenant-breakers, 118, 138–9, 179, 236–8, 267, 272–3, 289–90, 374, 375
Creation, 185; world of, 184

'Day of God', 16–17, 30, 32, 116, 183, 249
Dervish, *see* Ṣúfí
Detachment, 23, 26–7, 34–43 *passim*, 128, 214–16, 232, 264, 280–2 (and wealth), 316
Divines, *see* Clergy

Egypt, 202, Appendix III *passim*

Faith: steadfastness in, 46, 127–8, 259; dissimulation of, 111 and n.; tests of, ch. 12; power of, 126–8, 255–9; and intellect, 216, 217–19, 220; acquiring of, 216–21
Fáṭimih-Bagum, sister of Áqá Muḥammad-'Alí of Gázur, 105–6
Fu'ád Pá<u>sh</u>á, Turkish Foreign Minister, 312, 398

Gallipoli, 408, 410, 412
God: the Unknowable, 17, 26, 145; the Merciful, 138–9, 375; bounties of, 35, 82; and Man, 35–6; essence and attributes, 39–40, 184–5; progressive revelation of, 126; and atheists, 313–14; forgiveness of, 401; fear of, 94–6; wrath of, 375; also, 81; *see* Cause of, Day of, Kingdom of, Manifestations of, Word of, Man
Gordon, General, British Governor of the Sudan, 446–7

Ḥabíb-i-Marág<u>h</u>i'í, Mírzá, 65
Ḥabíb Mu'ayyad, Dr., 45
Ḥádí, Mírzá, of Iṣfahán, 202–4
Hádíy-i-Qazvíní, Mírzá (Letter of the Living), 144–5; Tablet to, 144
Hádíy-i-<u>Sh</u>írází, Áqá Mírzá, 298
Haifa, 411
Hand(s) of the Cause, 402
Ḥasan, Mírzá (King of the Martyrs), 203 and n., 205, 334
Ḥasan-i-Bajistání, Mullá (Letter of the Living), 145
Ḥasan-i-Ṣafá, Ḥájí Mírzá, 56–8, 398
Ḥasan-i-Zunúzí, <u>Sh</u>ay<u>kh</u>, 212 and n., 333
Ḥasan <u>Kh</u>án-i-<u>Kh</u>ú'í, Mírzá, Persian Consul in Egypt, 332, 440
Há<u>sh</u>im <u>Kh</u>án, 33–4
Ḥaydar-'Alí, Ḥájí Mírzá, 68–73, 77 194–202, 332, 340, 370, 438–50; quoted, 7–10, 11–12, 42–3, 52–3; 68–73, 116–17
'Him Whom God shall make manifest', 84, 85, 114, 116, 146, 152, 161, 182, 237, 371, 376, 377–81
History of the Martyrs of Yazd, 46–51, 358
Holy Spirit, Most Great Spirit, 124
House of Justice, 122, 272; Universal, 122 n., 265, 269
Houses of the Báb and Bahá'u'lláh, pilgrimages to, 240
Ḥusayn, Mírzá (Beloved of the Martyrs), 204 and n., 205, 334
Ḥusayn-i-Á<u>sh</u><u>ch</u>í, 169, 404
Ḥusayn-i-Bu<u>sh</u>rú'í, Mullá (First Letter of the Living), 15, 129, 146, 203, 211, 255–6, 386, 388
Ḥusayn-i-Ká<u>sh</u>ání, Áqá Siyyid, 59
Ḥusayn-i-Naráqí, Áqá, 59
Ḥusayn <u>Kh</u>án, Ḥájí Mírzá, Persian Ambassador in Constantinople (Mu<u>sh</u>íru'd-Dawlih), 1, 55–9, 278, 320–1, 325–8, 332, 370, 398–401

Imám(s), 75, 182, 287; *see* Islám
Ímán, Ḥájí, 224, 225
Írán, *see* Persia
'Iráq, 66, 67, 138, 258, 274, 303, 336
Iṣfahán, 340
'I<u>sh</u>qábád, 107, 226
Islám: misconceptions about, 21–3; decline of and Ṣúfism, 27; and Bábí Faith, 352; also, 107, 288; *see* Imám(s)
Ismá'íl, Siyyid, of Zavárih, 112, 415
'Izzat Áqá, house of, 291, 427, 433, 436

Revelation of Bahá'u'lláh: *Cont'd* 192–3, 304; Bahá'u'lláh's apologia for, 370; His description of, 143–4, 239; brings tests, 214; consequences of rejection, 309–11; and break-up of society, 417–21
Riḍá Big, house of, 162, 164, 171, 181, 210, 291, 427, 436
Riḍáy-i-Qannád, Áqá, of Shíráz, 403, 404

Sacrifice, 96
Ṣádiq-i-Khurásání, Mullá, 110, 293 n., 388
Sa'íd Khán, Mírzá (former Foreign Minister of Persia), 131–4
Salmán, Shaykh, 67, 168, 208, 263, 283, 384, 400
Sámsún, port of, 6
Shamsí Big, house of, 2, 3, 58
Shaykhís, 202
Shíráz, 240
Shoghi Effendi, Guardian of the Bahá'í Faith, 237 n., 238, 298
Ṣidq-'Alí, Darvísh, 164–5, 188, 329, 330, 402, 409
Sincerity, 7, 128
Ṣiráṭ ('road'), 74 and n., 345
Síyáh-Chál, prison of, 356
Star-fall of 1866, 270–2, 422–6
Spiritual worlds, *see* Worlds of God
Sudan, 332, Appendix III *passim*
Suffering (and tribulation), 46
Ṣúfís, 24–8, 57, 108, 109, 211, 296, 433 n.
Sulaymáníyyih, 25
Sulṭán Salím, mosque of, in Adrianople, 62, 63, 293, 294, 428, 437

Ṭabarsí, Shaykh, fort of, 129, 146, 180, 210–11, 246, 256
Ṭáhirih (Letter of the Living), 71, 171–8, 180, 204

Teaching the Bahá'í Faith, 91–106, 238; with wisdom, 97–8
Ṭihrán, 174–6 *passim*, 219
Transmutation of elements, 268
Turkish Government: 326; attitude to Bahá'u'lláh, 1, 55, 325; allowance from, 57, 327

Umm-i-Ashraf (mother of Ashraf); *see* Ashraf, Siyyid, of Zanján; 223–30 *passim*
Umm-i-'Aṭṭár, Tablet to, 127
Universal language, 3–4

Vaḥíd (Siyyid Yaḥyáy-i-Dárábí), 47, 175, 180, 211–12, 256–8
Vísí Pásh̲á, house of, 3

Word of God, 287; creative power, 121–3, 192–3
World Order, New, of Bahá'u'lláh, 41, 88
Worlds of God, 144, 285
Writings of Bahá'u'lláh: aspects of style, 19, 29; transcription and dissemination of, 200, 269, 279, 283, 373; some destroyed, 269; also, 218

Yaḥyá, Mírzá (Ṣubḥ-i-Azal), half-brother of Bahá'u'lláh, 39, 66–75 *passim*, 181–2, 242 n., 247, 262–3, 268, 284, 298, 326, 402; opposition to Bahá'u'lláh, 1, 152–5, ch. 14; attempts on Bahá'u'lláh's life, 152–5, 158–61; separation from Bahá'u'lláh, 161–70
Ya'qúb, Siyyid, 343–5
Yazd, 99–102, 256, 272, 358

Zanján, upheaval of, 222, 224, 226
Zaynu'l-'Ábidín (Zaynu'l-Muqarrabín), Mullá, 69, 335–6
Zoroastrians, 103, 104 n.